DENVER, BOULDER & COLORADO SPRINGS

MINDY SINK

National Forest
Bailey
Mt Silverheels
4,213ft
Alma
Fairplay
Pike National Forest
Cheesman Lake
Castle Rock
Parker
Water Line
Antero Reservoir
Spinney Mountain Reservoir
Lake George
Woodland Park
Elevenmile Canyon Reservoir
Manitou Springs
Colorado Springs
Pikes Peak
4,303ft
Cripple Creek
Fountain
San Isabel National Forest
Salida
Cañon City
285
9
24
67
85
25
86
83
21
94
115
50
69
70
0
15 mi
15 km
© AVALON TRAVEL

DENVER, BOULDER AND COLORADO SPRINGS

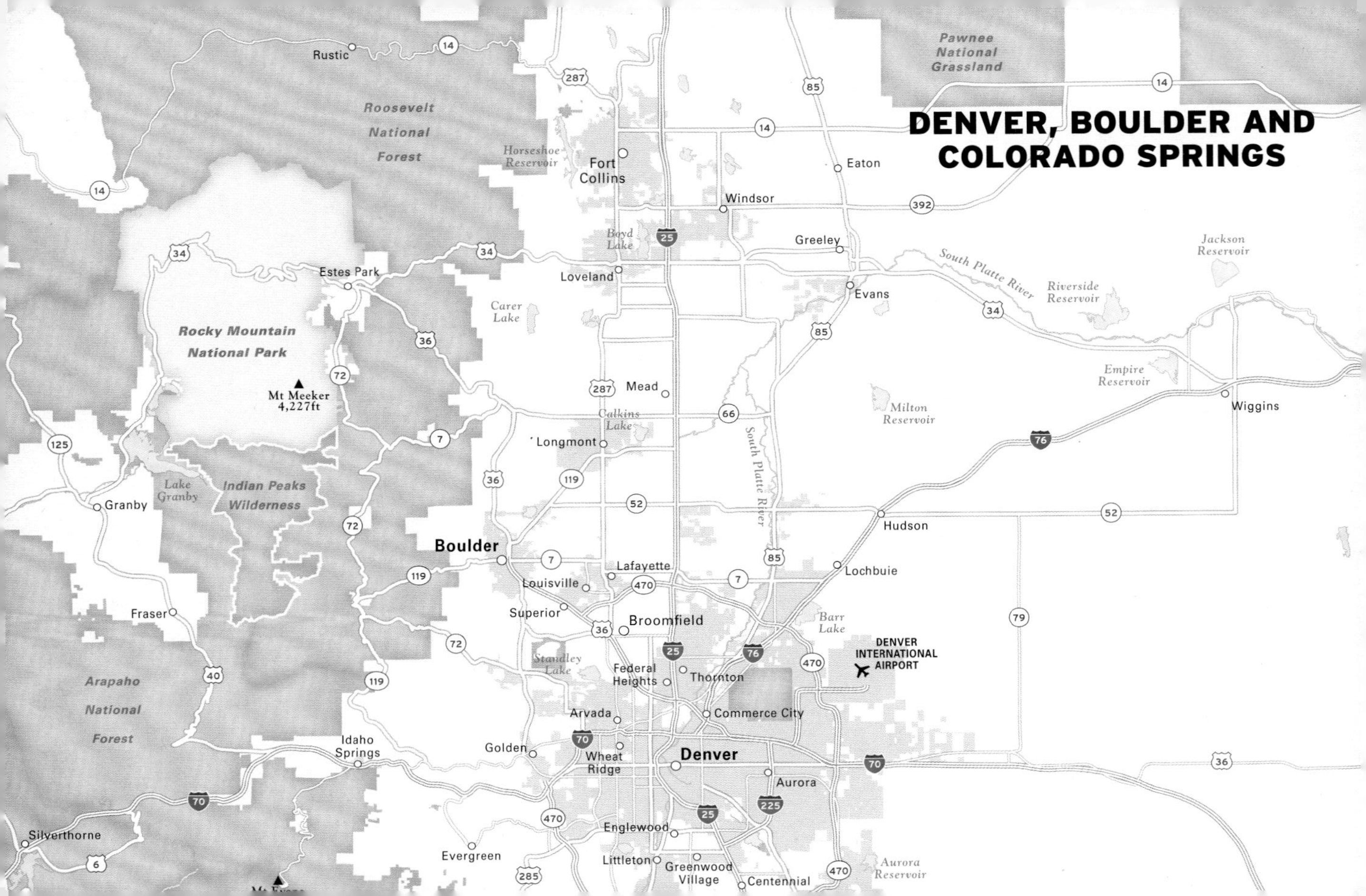

Contents

DISCOVER

Denver, Boulder & Colorado Springs

Colorado's Front Range cities straddle the land between the foothills east of the Rockies and the Great Plains that stretch out to the horizon. While Denver, Colorado Springs, Boulder, and Fort Collins share some similarities, each has its own personality, natural appeal, and distinct history that sets it apart.

Denver is the Mile-High City—5,280 feet above sea level with a 140-mile vista of the Rocky Mountains to the west. Recreation is a way of life here, but this diverse city also includes neighborhoods rich in ethnic and local foods, cutting-edge architecture, historic sites, packed bars and nightclubs, and an abundance of open space. Key attractions include the Denver Art Museum and the Red Rocks Amphitheatre.

Just west of Denver, the city of Boulder sits nestled up to the foothills. Home to the University of Colorado, the town offers a plethora of outdoor opportunities—visitors can hike or rock climb the Flatirons, or meander around on two wheels. Though Boulder is gaining recognition as a start-up hub for tech companies, it continues to offer classic college-town appeal with sophisticated dining and nightlife.

North of Boulder, is another college town with different roots to the past.

Clockwise from top left: Seven Falls waterfall in Colorado Springs; canoeing near Pikes Peak; hikers near Boulder's Flatirons; "Welcome to Golden"; the History Colorado Center; cherry trees along Cherry Creek.

Fort Collins's historic downtown is fueled in part by a robust craft brewing scene. Bike paths wind alongside the Cache La Poudre River as it runs through town, and cyclists can glimpse river rafters who've just hit the rapids upstream.

South of Denver, Colorado Springs was founded as a resort town and there is still a touch of luxury here. Today it's known as home to a few notable military installations—Fort Carson, NORAD, the U.S. Air Force Academy—but the city also offers boutique shopping, world-class art, film festivals, and luxurious resorts.

On a visit to the Front Range, historic towns, distinctive architecture, mountain peaks, and funky college towns are all within easy reach.

Clockwise from top left: the Crawford Hotel at Union Station in Denver; peach tulips along Boulder's Pearl Street Mall; bear at Cheyenne Mountain Zoo in Colorado Springs; deer near Garden of the Gods.

BOTTLES

Planning Your Time

Where To Go

Denver

Denver is home to the country's 10th-largest **downtown**. Neighborhoods such as **LoDo** (short for Lower Downtown) and the **Golden Triangle** are home to major sights like **Union Station** and the **Denver Art Museum.** Adjacent to the Golden Triangle is **Capitol Hill,** one of Denver's oldest neighborhoods and filled with historic homes and mansions. Known for being **gay- and lesbian-friendly,** this neighborhood offers quick access to **City Park** and is home to some of the city's **best music venues.**

Just south of the downtown core, you'll find a distinctive **arts district** in the Lincoln Park neighborhood and **hip galleries** and **eclectic shops** in **SoBo** (the South Broadway corridor).

North of downtown, **Contemporary Art Denver, Centennial Gardens,** and **Commons Park** anchor the **Platte River Valley** area. West of the Platte River, the **Highlands** neighborhood has exploded with growth and is where you'll find the city's most talked-about **restaurants** and **bars.**

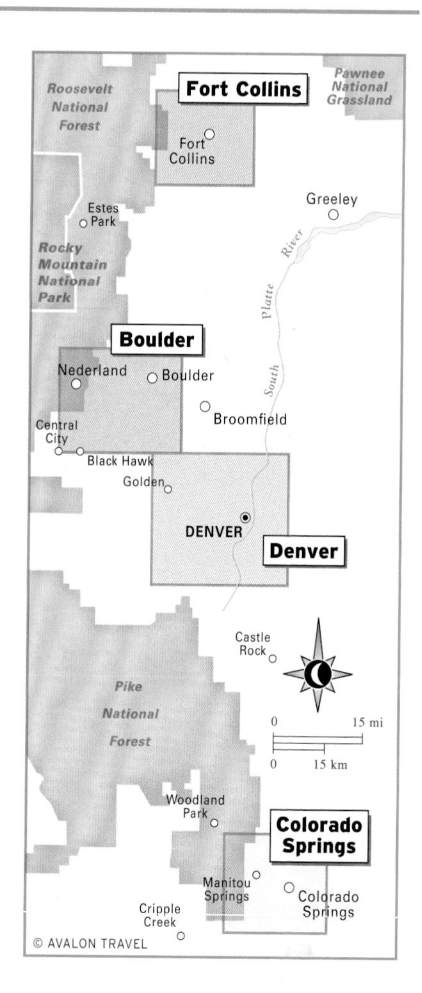

Boulder

Just 30 miles northwest of Denver, Boulder is a small yet scenic college town with easy access to **outdoor recreation**. Wander through the **Boulder County Farmers Market** in summer, ride a bike along Boulder Creek and into the foothills, and hike in **Chautauqua Park.** For more urban adventures, take in an outdoor movie or enjoy an amazing meal at one of the city's many impressive **regional-fare restaurants.**

Fort Collins

Fort Collins is a quiet college town about 60 miles north of Denver. Its charming **Old Town** invites visitors to enjoy a relaxing stroll among the shops and historic buildings. Plan a day of sampling **craft beer** at some of the city's many breweries, and maybe **ride bikes** from one to the

the Denver Art Museum at dusk

next to really feel like a local. The **Great Stupa of Dharmakaya** offers a scenic excursion an hour west.

Colorado Springs

Though Colorado's second-largest city, Colorado Springs isn't as well-known as Denver or Boulder. Situated one hour south of Denver, the city maintains a large military presence and offers a variety of sights and activities. **Colorado College** provides an energy and diversity of events that fly under the radar. Be sure to stop by **Ivywild** for a drink or a meal near downtown. Families will love a stay at **The Broadmoor** and a trip to the **Cheyenne Mountain Zoo.** Outdoors enthusiasts can scale **Pikes Peak** or wander the **Garden of the Gods.** And couples can embrace the historic charm of **Manitou Springs.**

When to Go

When most folks think of Colorado, they think of snow and skiing. But locals know that there is more to see and do in the warmer seasons. Denver is a draw for tourists year-round, but is generally more crowded in the **summer.** This is high season, when there are music festivals and blockbuster theater and art shows, and driving into the foothills and mountains is easier. Hotel rates tend to be at their peak.

Spring is the shoulder season. Flowers are in bloom at the lower elevations in Denver, Boulder, Colorado Springs, and Fort Collins, even though it's still snowing in the mountains. There is a reverse migration of sorts as people who live in the mountains come to the lower elevations for that taste of spring. When spring fever hits, the bicycles come out to replace snowshoes and skis for a little outdoor fun.

The Flatirons are dusted with snow above Boulder.

Fall is a lovely time to visit, especially in the foothills as the trees change from green to gold and light up the hillsides. Boulder, Colorado Springs, and Fort Collins often see these fall colors sooner than Denver does.

The low season in the Front Range cities is **winter,** when hotels and attractions offer many discounts as locals and tourists alike flock to the ski slopes in the Rockies. Those who don't want (or cannot get up) to the ski slopes find ways to snowshoe, cross-country ski, sled, and even snowboard at city parks to make the most of the season.

No matter what time of year you come here, you might here a local remark, "If you don't like the weather, just wait five minutes." In a single day you might need to wear a T-shirt and shorts, a fleece coat and pants, and a sun hat or a wool cap.

The Best of Denver, Boulder, and Colorado Springs

Spend the week exploring Colorado's Front Range. Following are some suggestions for where to go and what to do in each city.

Denver

DAY 1

Fly into **Denver International Airport** and check into the **Crawford Hotel** at **Union Station.** If it's summer and you've got little kids in tow, they can cool off in the splash fountain on the plaza. Do a little shopping at **Tattered Cover Book Store** and **5 Green Boxes,** then enjoy a meal at **Mercantile** or one of the station's many on-site restaurants. If it's baseball season, walk roughly two blocks north from Union Station and see if there are some cheap "rockpile" seats for the Colorado Rockies game at **Coors Field.** If the Rockies aren't in town, you can take in some greenery at the **Denver Botanic Gardens.**

At night, make reservations for dinner at **The Kitchen,** or opt for relaxing pub fare at one of Denver's fine craft breweries, such as **Wynkoop Brewing Company.**

It's hard to resist those mountains, but stick to sightseeing in the city while you acclimate to the altitude (it *is* 5,280 feet above sea level).

DAY 2

Take the free shuttle bus down to the **16th Street Mall,** then walk across Civic Center Park to visit the **Denver Art Museum.** After exploring the wealth of exhibits on offer, stop at **Palette's Restaurant;** the museum's restaurant serves a tasty lunch (there's often a special menu

Artist Lonnie Hanzon's "Evolution of the Ball" greets visitors as they enter Coors Field.

Little Man Ice Cream in Denver

the Boulder County Farmer's Market

themed to the current exhibit). If it's a Tuesday or Thursday in summer, stop for lunch at **Civic Center Eats** instead, where the city's best food trucks park. About a block away is the **History Colorado Center,** where you can learn about the entire state in an interactive way—do a ski jump, visit a "mine shaft," and more. For a more budget-friendly option, head for the **Denver Public Library,** which has an art gallery and free kids' activities, and stop to see the **Big Blue Bear.**

In the late afternoon or early evening, walk west on 16th Street over the **Millennium Bridge** for a view of the mountains at sunset. Stop for dinner at **Zengo,** at the foot of the bridge, or continue through Commons Park and over the South Platte River into the Highlands neighborhood. Dine at **Root Down** or just enjoy a drink at **Williams & Graham.** If the line isn't too long, top off the night with a scoop from **Little Man Ice Cream.**

Boulder

DAY 3

After breakfast at **Snooze,** you're off to Boulder for a little taste of the mountains. (You can drive to Boulder in a half hour, or take the bus from Union Station to reach downtown Boulder in an hour.) Plan your trip for a Saturday in summer or early fall to be there in time for the **Boulder County Farmers Market.** Eat lunch at one of the market vendors or stop for tea at the **Dushanbe Teahouse** by Boulder Creek.

Chautauqua Park is the starting point for a **hike** in the foothills, a meal, or a concert in the historic auditorium. Bonus: Kids that don't make it far on the hike will love the playground. In the evening, enjoy a top-notch dinner at **Frasca,** though families might be happier at **The Kitchen** or **Pizzeria Locale.**

If not visiting Boulder as a day trip from Denver, check in at the **Hotel Boulderado** downtown. Summer visitors should try to score a room or rent a cabin at Chautauqua Park for easy access to all its amenities.

DAY 4

Get up early to wait in line for chicory coffee and beignets at **Lucile's Creole Café,** just a block away from the Hotel Boulderado. Afterward, stroll two blocks south for some

Welcome to Beertown

Sample Denver's beer culture.

Denver is to beer what Napa is to wine. Forget about monikers like "Queen City of the Plains" and "Mile-High City"; nowadays Denver is being called "Suds City" and "The Napa Valley of Beer."

There are at least 23 brewpubs and microbreweries in Denver. Colorado's governor, John Hickenlooper, was one of the founders of the **Wynkoop Brewing Company** (page 57), reportedly one of the largest brewpubs in the world.

For serious beer lovers, October is the time to visit. The celebration begins with **Denver Beer Fest** which kicks off the week ahead of the three-day **Great American Beer Festival** (page 73). This is the Olympics of beer, where thousands of brews are sampled and gold, silver, and bronze medals are awarded among an ever-growing array of beer styles.

Any time of year, there are brewery tours where visitors can see how vast quantities of their favorite ales and lagers are made; then they can sample a few. In Denver, there are tours at **Wynkoop Brewing Company, Breckenridge Brewery,** and **Great Divide Brewing Company** (page 56). Beyond Denver, there are tours in Golden at the **MillerCoors Brewery** (page 134). Whether you're just curious to find out if beer goes as well with cheese as wine does (**Great Divide Brewing Company,** page 56), or if you want a classic beer at a Colorado Rockies baseball game (**Blue Moon Brewing Company,** page 57), you will find it here.

This love of ale is not limited to Denver; Boulder and Fort Collins are helping turn this region into the "Denver Beer Triangle." Fort Collins is home to craft breweries such as the **New Belgium Brewery, Fort Collins Brewery,** and **Odell Brewing Company** (page 199), as well as industry giant Anheuser-Busch. With competition comes creative ideas to get you in the brewery door—tours, tastings, pairings, movies, and bike tours are just some of the ways you might sip a cold one.

Boulder is getting into the act with local brewers such as **Avery Brewing, Walnut Brewery,** and **Mountain Sun** (page 147).

For those in Colorado Springs and thirsty for beer, check out **Phantom Canyon Brewing Company** or **Bristol Brewing Company** (page 227).

window-shopping at the **Pearl Street Mall.** A short drive south, the **University of Colorado** campus includes museums, a planetarium, art exhibits, and—if you're visiting June-August—the **Colorado Shakespeare Festival.** Or head 30 minutes west to experience the counterculture vibe in **Nederland;** if it's winter (specifically March), your visit might coincide with the town's annual **Frozen Dead Guy Days.**

At night, head back to the hotel for drinks at **The Corner Bar** or **License No. 1** before dining on-site at **Spruce Farm & Fish.**

Fort Collins

DAY 5

Begin your day by feasting on a hearty breakfast at **The Buff.** Today, we leave Boulder to explore Fort Collins and the best way to get there is by car. Once in Fort Collins though, you can leave the car parked and explore by foot or bicycle.

In town, rent a bicycle from the **Fort Collins Bike Library** and take the **Spring Creek Trail** to explore the town from alongside Spring Creek. **Old Town** is a sight in itself with plenty of shops—including candy and toy shops for the little ones—to wander through. Bike over to the **Fort Collins Museum of Art** to view the public art outside, or lock up the bike to go inside and check out a current exhibit.

Brewery tours and tastings are all the rage here, and you can ride a bike or walk from one to another. Tours at the popular **New Belgium Brewing** (11:30am-4:30pm Tues.-Sat., reservations recommended, free) run every half hour and include storytelling, souvenirs, and sipping samples.

If you couldn't get reservations at **The Kitchen** location in Denver, fortunately there's another one in Fort Collins. At night, take in a show at **Avogado's Number** before bedding down at the **Armstrong Hotel.**

Colorado Springs

DAY 6

You'll want a car for today's two-hour drive south to Colorado Springs. Enjoy the scenic

The Garden of the Gods

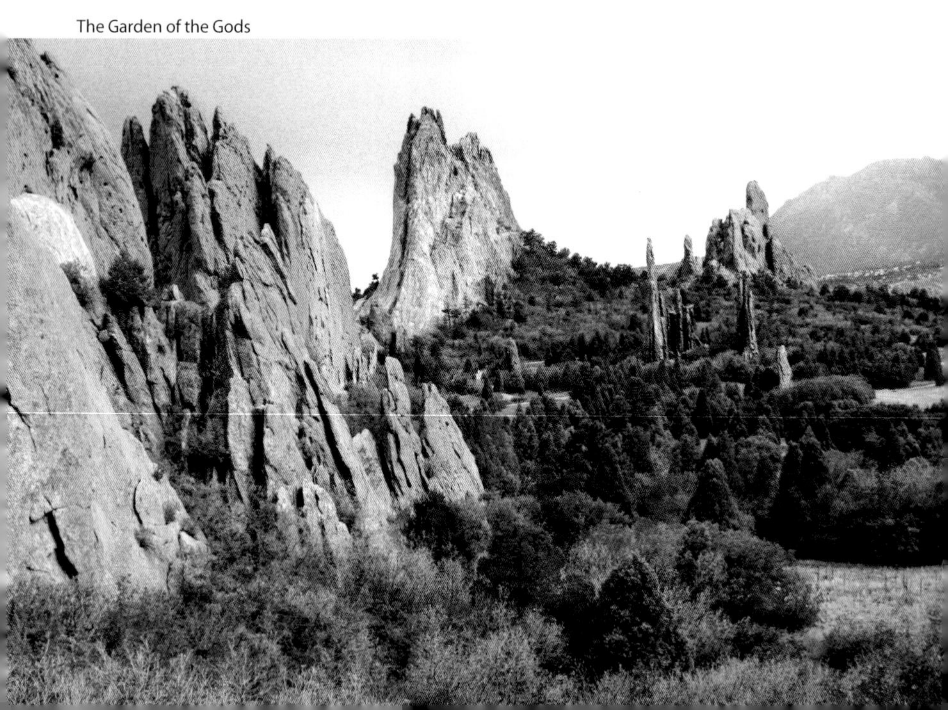

The Broadmoor in Colorado Springs

route and turn off for **Garden of the Gods** to wind through the jutting red rocks. Once in Colorado Springs, one-of-a-kind museums such as the **ProRodeo Hall of Fame & Museum of the American Cowboy,** the **World Figure Skating Museum,** and the **Peterson Air & Space Museum** offer options to fill the afternoon.

Aim to stay at **The Broadmoor,** where you can dine at some of the region's best restaurants, pamper yourself with spa treatments, golf, swim, or tour a world-class Western art collection. If this one-stop resort is booked, opt instead to stay downtown at **The Mining Exchange,** where you can walk to the **Colorado Springs Fine Arts Center** for some culture. If you're not staying at The Broadmoor, enjoy a casual dinner at one of the **Ivywild** establishments.

DAY 7

The resort town of **Manitou Springs,** at the foot of Pikes Peak, beckons just a short drive away and a visit here is truly charming. Walk along the creek and sample the **mineral springwater** that is piped through at different fountains scattered around town. In summer, 14,110-foot **Pikes Peak** is within easy reach thanks to the popular **Pikes Peak Cog Railway** that clicks up the mountain. It's breathtaking at the top in more ways than one. Seeing so much of Colorado from this great height is the perfect way to sign off on your Front Range excursion.

Marijuana Tourism

Mile High? Yep, we've heard all the jokes by now. The 2014 legalization of marijuana now means that you can legally buy and privately smoke recreational and medical marijuana in Colorado. It's become a huge draw for tourists, and entrepreneurs have found myriad ways to profit, with yoga, painting, 420-friendly lodgings, smoking accessories, and private clubs catering to smokers.

Coloradans age 21 and older may purchase up to one ounce; out-of-state visitors are limited to one-quarter ounce. Public smoking of marijuana is illegal. Instead, visit one of the private clubs and other locations that permit—even encourage—smoking cannabis on the premises.

Denver

Denver is the epicenter of marijuana tourism, with the largest number of cannabis dispensaries.

- **3D Cannabis Center** (4305 Brighton Blvd., 303/297-1657, www.visit3d.com)
- **Euflora Cannabis Dispensary** (401 16th St., 303/534-6255, www.eufloracolorado.com)
- **Natural Remedies** (1620 Market St., Ste. 5W, 303/953-0884, www.lodosdispensary.com)
- **Pure Marijuana Dispensary** (1133 Bannock St., 303/534-7873, www.puremmj.com)

The following accommodations are designated 420-friendly.

- **Bud and Breakfast At The Adagio** (1430 Race St., Denver, 303/370-6911, www.budandbfast.com)
- **Capitol Hill Mansion Bed And Breakfast Inn** (1207 Pennsylvania St., 800/839-9329, www.capitolhillmansion.com)
- **Lumber Baron Inn & Gardens** (2555 W. 37th Ave., 303/477-8205, http://lumberbaron.com)

The following companies specialize in cannabis tours:

- **420 Airport Pickup** (720/369-6292, www.420friendlyairportpickup.com) is a private shuttle company with airport pick-up, stops at a retail marijuana shop, and hotel drop-off.
- **Colorado Cannabis Tours** (303/420-8687, www.coloradocannabistours.com) offers a marijuana-friendly party bus that stops at several Denver dispensaries.
- **Elevated Rental** (303/872-0710, www.elevatedrental.com) rents vaporizers, bongs, dabbing rigs, and other paraphernalia.
- **High Urban Hikes** (630/699-5071, www.huhdenver.com) offers tours of Denver with an emphasis on marijuana-related esoterica.
- **My 420 Tours** (855/694-2086, www.my420tours.com) offers weekly tours dispensaries, grow facilities, and glass galleries.
- **Sunset Luxury Limos** (303/426-9668, www.sunsetlimo.com) rents vaporizer-friendly stretch limousines, Hummers, and party buses.

Boulder

Cannabis dispensaries in Boulder include:

- **The Farm** (2801 Iris Ave., 303/440-1323, http://thefarmco.com)
- **Native Roots Boulder** (1146 Pearl St., 720/726-5126, www.nativerootsboulder.com)
- **Terrapin Care Station** (1795 Folsom St., 303/954-8402, ext. 2, www.terrapincarestation.com)

There are no designated "420 marijuana-friendly" hotels in Boulder yet, but there are

3D Cannabis Center was the first to sell recreational marijuana in 2014.

private residences (such as those found on AirBnB) available for those who want a place to partake.

Fort Collins

Cannabis dispensaries in Fort Collins include:

- **Choice Organics** (813 Smithfield Dr., Unit B, 970/472-6337, www.choiceorganicsinc.com)
- **Flower Power Botanicals** (1310 Duff Dr., 970/672-8165, www.flowerpowerbotanicals.com)
- **Organic Alternatives** (346 E. Mountain Ave., 970/482-7100, www.organicalternatives.com)

The following accommodations are designated 420-friendly:

- **The Shangri-la Inn at Gaia's Farm and Gardens** (4328 W. County Road 54G, Laporte, 970/817-2186, www.gaiascsa.com)
- **Stoney River Lodge** (80 Idlewild Ln., Loveland, 970/663-5532, www.stoneyriverlodgecolorado.com)

Colorado Springs

Colorado Springs still prohibits marijuana sales, so you must buy before you get there or make the short drive to Manitou Springs.

- **Maggie's Farm** (141 Manitou Ave., Manitou Springs, 719/685-1655, www.maggiesfarmmarijuana.com)

Cannabis entrepreneurs created social clubs inside the city for people to smoke the cannabis they bought outside of the county.

- **420 Speakeasy** (1532 N. Circle Dr., 719/471-3398)
- **Lazy Lion** (2502 E. Bijou St., 719/634-8337, www.thelazylion420.com)
- **Speak Easy Vape Lounge** (2508 E. Bijou St., 719/445-9083, www.speakeasycannabisclub.com)
- **Studio A64** (332 E. Colorado Ave., 719/930-9846, www.studioa64.com)

The following accommodation is 420-friendly:

- **Boulder Crescent Inn and Hostel** (312 N. Cascade Ave., 303/912-3538, www.bouldercrescenthostel.com)

Get Outside

whitewater river rafting

No trip is complete without time spent basking in the Colorado sun. Fear not: Athletic skill is not required, but you must be mindful of the elevation and your body's ability to acclimate to heights thousands of feet above sea level.

Best Hiking

- **Red Rocks Amphitheatre** (Morrison, page 47)
- **White Ranch Open Space Park** (Golden, page 135)
- **Chautauqua** (Boulder, page 160)
- **Flagstaff Mountain** (Boulder, page 160)
- **Lory State Park** (Fort Collins, page 195)
- **Garden of the Gods** (Colorado Springs, page 221)
- **Manitou Incline** (Manitou Springs, page 234)

Best Biking

- **Cherry Creek Bike Path** (Denver, page 93)
- **Boulder Creek Bike Path** (Boulder, page 158)
- **Spring Creek Trail** (Fort Collins, page 191)
- **Pikes Peak** via Challenge Unlimited (Colorado Springs, page 220)
- **Garden of the Gods** (Colorado Springs, page 220)

Best Rock Climbing

- **Boulder Flatirons** (Boulder, page 161)
- **Boulder Canyon** (Boulder, page 161)
- **Garden of the Gods** via Front Range Climbing Company (Colorado Springs, page 222)
- **Lory State Park** (Fort Collins, page 194)

Best Outdoor Tours and Events

- Ride a hot-air balloon with **Adventure Balloon Sports** (Boulder, page 158)
- Climb a 14er via the **Pikes Peak Cog Railway** (Manitou Springs, page 232)
- Bike the **Tour de Fat** (Fort Collins, page 188)

Denver

Look for ★ to find recommended sights, activities, dining, and lodging.

Highlights

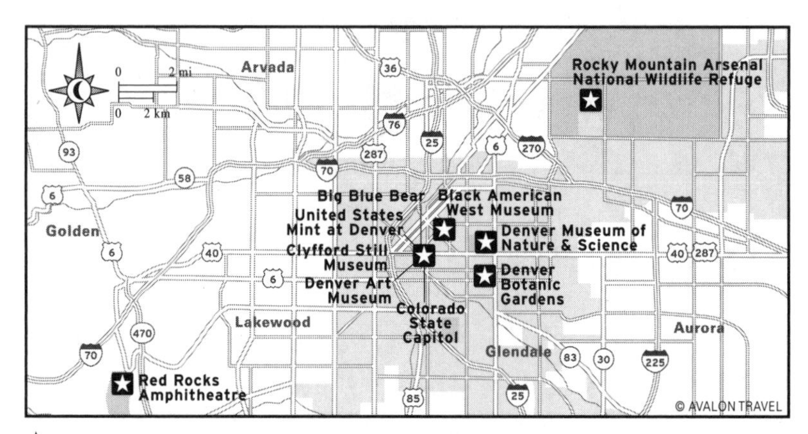

★ **Big Blue Bear:** At 40 feet tall, this is Denver's most recognizable piece of public art (page 26).

★ **Black American West Museum:** Discover the rarely heard stories of pioneering African Americans throughout the West, with a special emphasis on those who lived in Colorado (page 26).

★ **United States Mint at Denver:** Free tours provide a chance to see coins being made and a peek inside the elaborate interior of the original historic building (page 27).

★ **Clyfford Still Museum:** This cool museum devoted to a single artist enables curators to create fresh new exhibits from its namesake's lifetime of work (page 30).

★ **Denver Art Museum:** This building—a work of art in itself—houses regional and international artworks (page 31).

★ **Colorado State Capitol:** The gold-domed capitol not only features gold mined from Colorado, but much of the building was created from marble, onyx, and granite quarried here as well (page 40).

★ **Denver Botanic Gardens:** Enjoy some outdoor time among the beautiful plants, relaxing amid nooks for peaceful contemplation and meandering along extensive pathways through the gardens (page 41).

★ **Denver Museum of Nature and Science:** Come for blockbuster shows, a planetarium, an IMAX theater, and interactive displays, plus a stunning view of the city's skyline framed by snowcapped peaks (page 41).

★ **Rocky Mountain Arsenal National Wildlife Refuge:** Hike the trails to see more than 300 animal and bird species, including bison, eagles, and deer (page 47).

★ **Red Rocks Amphitheatre:** The natural beauty of the red rocks and the view of the expansive plains to the east combine to make this a quintessential Denver stop for a concert (page 47).

Denver is a sophisticated city exploding with everything hip and desirable: outdoor recreation, locavore dining, and a variety of culture and sports for intellectual stimulation and entertainment.

Denver's location at 5,280 feet above sea level is an attraction in itself, with sights such as Coors Field and City Park marking mile-high spots. Touring the city's sights could mean riding a bicycle past the white-water rapids on the South Platte River in Confluence Park, or meandering through the bronzed statues of Civic Center Park on the way to the Denver Art Museum's striking new addition. Or hop onto the city's light rail and quickly zip from the Museum of Contemporary Art Denver to the Black American West Museum. No matter how you get from Point A to Point B, it's always an adventure to explore the city's rich past or discover its latest additions.

In the past, Denver was the city that people seemed to come to for business or pass through as they continued on to the mountains. Today, this former "cow town" offers museums, a zoo, parks, gardens, shops, and restaurants, and the largest airport in Colorado.

PLANNING YOUR TIME

Plan to spend **two days** in Denver. Downtown Denver is your best bet for a home base, with transportation available to and from the airport and public transportation, rental bikes, and bike paths within easy walking distance. Once downtown—or even in a surrounding neighborhood like Capitol Hill—you can see much of what Denver has to offer without driving a car. It's only when you go to the foothills that you'll need a car, and even then you might be able to ride a bike or hire a tour guide.

Devote one day to exploring the city. Start with the Denver Art Museum and take in the Denver Botanic Gardens, which has a pavilion with waterfalls, walkways, and tropical and subtropical plants that can be enjoyed year-round. (In summer, opt for an early start to the day in order to avoid crowds, lines, and potential midday heat.) Add time for a little shopping in the LoDo neighborhood before

Previous: kayakers at Confluence Park; Denver Skyline from City Park. **Above:** 16th Street Mall.

dining out. Make reservations at Denver's iteration of The Kitchen, or explore craft brews and pub fare at Wynkoop. The next day, plan a quick trip into the nearby foothills and take a long bike ride or an early-morning hike.

Many of Denver's sights are family-friendly, with rooms and activities devoted to kiddos: Make art at the Denver Art Museum, cruise along the stroller-size walkways at the Denver Botanic Gardens, or dig for "bones" at the Denver Museum of Nature and Science. Downtown hotels with pools—such as the Four Seasons—will appeal to the kids in summer and will put you within walking distance (or a short drive) of theaters, museums, gardens, and more.

ORIENTATION

In the **LoDo** neighborhood is **Union Station,** a historic train station revitalized into a modern transportation hub, a stylish hotel, a dining and nightlife destination, and an urban hotspot. You can go to a baseball game at **Coors Field,** dine out, or shop—it's all here. The **Denver Art Museum** anchors the **Golden Triangle** neighborhood, with other museums and galleries to be explored. Just outside of downtown is a distinctive arts district along Santa Fe Drive in the **Lincoln Park** neighborhood.

Leaving downtown, you'll find the hip galleries, diverse restaurants, eclectic shops, and dynamic dance clubs and bars that have brought vibrancy to the South Broadway corridor, popularly known as **SoBo.** If you're into handmade culture, indie rock, and vintage, don't miss the core blocks that make this neighborhood so popular.

Heading west from the heart of downtown, you cross from LoDo through the **Platte River Valley,** which has exploded as an urban neighborhood and destination. Major sights, such as the **Museum of Contemporary Art Denver, Centennial Gardens, and Commons Park,** are all found in this area. Platte Street is home to a few restaurants and shops worth visiting as you make your way west.

The **Highlands** neighborhood is a short walk over the South Platte River and, in recent years, it has exploded with growth. Here you'll find restaurants and bars such as **Williams & Graham** and **Root Down;** the local ice cream shop, **Little Man Ice Cream,** is famous here. Lodgings are minimal in this part of town, but it's worth the walk from downtown. You can loop a visit to this area in with a **Denver Broncos** game at **Sports Authority Field at Mile High.**

Instead of going west, you could easily walk from downtown to one of Denver's oldest neighborhoods—Capitol Hill or Curtis Park and Five Points. **Capitol Hill** is densely packed and always lively. The neighborhood is home to some of the city's best music venues along Colfax Avenue, including the **Bluebird Theater** and **Ogden Theatre.** Expansive **City Park** is large enough to be home to the **Denver Zoo** and the **Denver Museum of Nature and Science,** plus many lakes, a golf course, and the Mile High Loop jogging path. **Five Points** and **Curtis Park** are north of downtown.

Sights

DOWNTOWN

American Museum of Western Art

Directly across the street from the Brown Palace Hotel is the historic Navarre Building, built in 1880, which has served as a school, hotel, brothel (which may have once included a tunnel to bring "clients" over from the Brown), and a dining and jazz club. In 1997, it was bought by the Anschutz Corporation and refurbished for its private offices and to become the **American Museum of Western Art** (1727 Tremont St., 303/293-2000, www.anschutzcollection.org, tours 10am and 1:30pm Mon. and Wed., $10 adults, $7 seniors and students) from the corporation's private collection. This is serious art that has been previously on loan for exhibits around the world, so viewing is limited to the two-hour tours twice a week, with no children under

Downtown

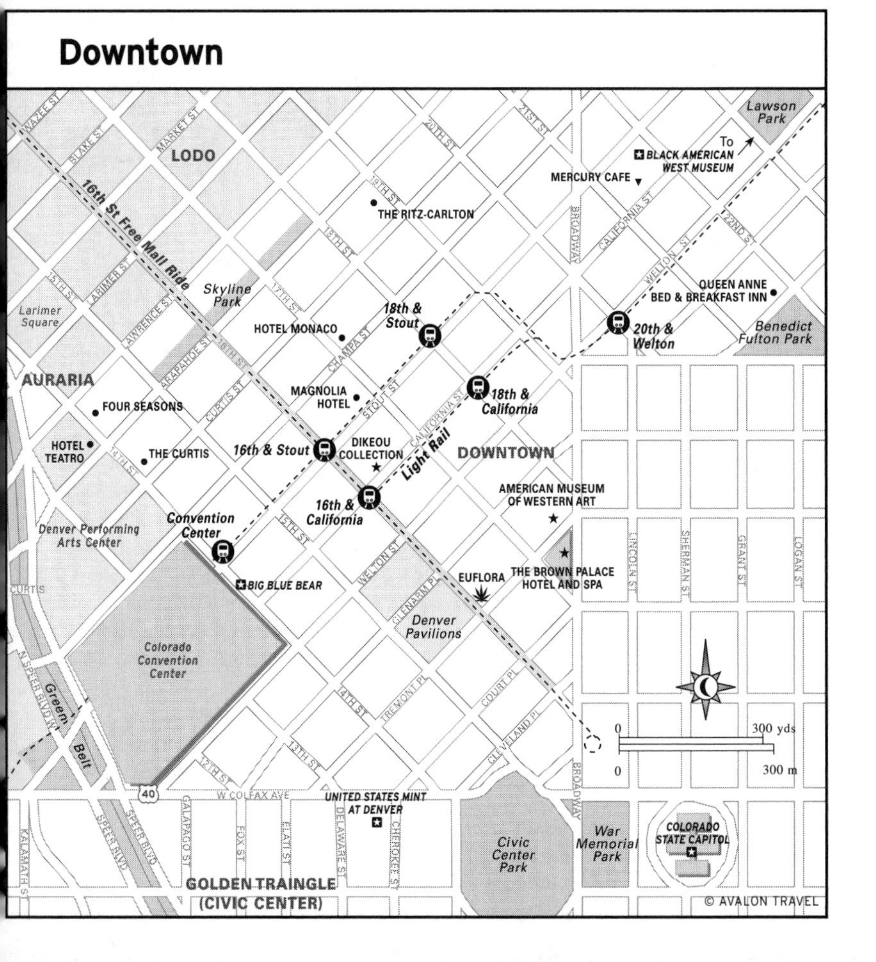

age eight permitted; children under 16 must be accompanied by an adult. Artists in the collection of 400 paintings on display include Georgia O'Keeffe, Albert Bierstadt, Thomas Moran, Ernest Blumenschein, Frederic Remington, and many more.

★ Big Blue Bear

Part whimsy, part serious artwork, with much left to personal interpretation, the 40-foot-tall **Big Blue Bear** (700 14th St., 303/228-8000, http://denverconvention.com) peering into the windows of the Colorado Convention Center has become the most popular and recognizable piece funded by the city's public art program. First installed in 2005, the sculpture is officially titled *I See What You Mean,* and was designed and created by Denver artist and art professor Lawrence Argent. It is constructed from polymer concrete and a steel frame, covered in a bright blue that is evocative of the bluish hue of the nearby Rocky Mountains.

the Big Blue Bear

But like any bear you might meet in the mountains, you can't get too close. At times, the bear has been loved too much and is occasionally roped off to keep visitors at a safe distance.

★ Black American West Museum

A tiny house contains the **Black American West Museum** (3091 California St., 720/242-7428, www.blackamericanwestmuseum.com, 10am-2pm Fri.-Sat., $8 adults, $6 children, $7 seniors), which shares the little-known history of the West's African Americans, particularly those who made a life in Denver and Colorado. The building itself is the former home of Justina L. Ford, the first female, African American licensed doctor in Colorado. The house—now in the National Register of Historic Places—was saved from demolition and moved from its original location before being restored.

The museum's curator rattles off astonishing facts about African Americans in the West. For example, a third of all cowboys were black, and the only two stained glass portraits of African Americans hanging in a U.S. state capitol are at the Colorado State Capitol. And local businessman Barney Ford (a former slave) opposed statehood for the territory because black men did not have the right to vote. The top floor of the museum has displays of Buffalo Soldier uniforms and rodeo memorabilia from the likes of Nat Love, aka "Deadwood Dick," who was reputed to be the greatest black cowboy, and Bill Pickett, a rodeo cowboy who was the first black honoree in the National Cowboy Hall of Fame.

The museum also owns a portion of Dearfield, Colorado, a ghost town northeast of Denver that was formerly a black township.

Brown Palace Hotel

Unquestionably the city's most famous hotel, the **Brown Palace Hotel** (321 17th St., 303/297-3111, www.brownpalace.com, tours 3pm Wed. and Sat., $10, free for hotel guests, reservations required) offers enough history and architectural beauty to be visited even by those not staying the night. Ohio businessman Henry Brown came to Colorado in 1860 and bought a few acres of land, including the triangular plot where the three-sided hotel opened in 1892. Working with architect Frank Edbrooke, who also worked on the design of the state capitol, Brown opted for a grand, Italian Renaissance style with a Tiffany stained glass atrium that rises eight floors in the center of the building.

To this day, the hotel relies on its own artesian well, located beneath the building, for water. With so many famous guests over the years—from presidents to rock stars—the hotel took to naming some rooms after them. Now ordinary folks can spend a night in the Beatles or Eisenhower Suites.

In a long-held tradition, each January the hotel puts the National Western Stock Show's prize-winning steer on full display in the lobby, where anyone can be photographed with the bovine. Year-round, visitors can simply take in the ambience by dining in one of the hotel's three restaurants, going on a 45-60-minute tour with the hotel's historian, or sipping a **traditional English tea** (noon-4pm daily, reservations highly recommended) in the atrium.

the Black American West Museum

Dikeou Collection

The **Dikeou Collection** (1615 California St., Ste. 515, 303/623-3001, www.dikeoucollection.org, 11am-5pm Wed.-Fri., free) is an art treasure unknown to even most Denverites, but it should not be missed by anyone with a curiosity about contemporary art. This is the private art collection of Devon Dikeou, an artist who divides her time between Denver and New York, where she also publishes *Zing Magazine.* Not far from the architecturally famous museum buildings in downtown, the Dikeou Collection is housed on the fifth floor of a historic office building (just a few doors down from the Jamba Juice on the corner of the 16th Street Mall), with giant pink inflatable bunnies by artist Momoyo Torimitsu greeting visitors in the first of many rooms.

★ United States Mint at Denver

Perhaps inspired by the rebellious spirit of the West—or just naked entrepreneurial ambition—the **United States Mint at Denver** (320 W. Colfax Ave., 303/405-4761, www.usmint.gov, tours 8am-2pm Mon.-Thurs., free, reservations required) was originally founded as a private bank in the 1860s by an attorney who had the bright idea to mint coins from the gold and silver being mined in the mountains to the west. The mint was eventually sold to the government, and laws were made to prohibit private money-making. Today there are only four mints in the country, and the United States Mint at Denver is the only one with guided tours.

In 1906 the government opened the mint in this building, which is now in the National Register of Historic Places. An example of elaborate Italian Renaissance architecture, the mint appears to be two stories tall but is actually five. Starting in 1935, several additions have been made to the building to accommodate increased coin production; making billions of coins each year, the mint now occupies an entire city block.

Tours begin at the entrance to one of the building's more modern additions. Security at the mint is tighter than at any airport, and visitors cannot bring in anything larger than a wallet.

Before the official tour begins, you can peruse *Money, Trade and Treasure,* a lobby display of primitive money and the evolution of currency. A tour guide and an armed security guard take groups into the coin production part of the plant, where you might see coins before they are pressed or as they are being sorted. It's not until the very end of the tour that you get to see the original marble hallways and unique Tiffany chandeliers of the 1906 building. Most fascinating about the tour are the facts—particularly the actual costs of making money and what materials are used to make coins. A visit here could be a last chance to see pennies being made; no one knows how much longer pennies will be produced given their low value and high cost to make.

The United States Mint at Denver can boast of never having been robbed, thanks in part to its "machine-gun nest," or "sentry box," that was always manned until the 1960s. That relic is on display (now staffed by a mannequin), and current security measures are top secret.

To get a few of your own state's quarters or other collectible coins, stop in at the gift shop located just outside of the mint. Even the change from each purchase is given in locally minted coins.

GOLDEN TRIANGLE, LINCOLN PARK, AND SOBO

Byers-Evans House Museum

A visit to the **Byers-Evans House Museum** (1310 Bannock St., 303/620-4933, www.historycolorado.org, House Gallery 10am-4pm Mon.-Sat., House Museum tours 10:30am, 11:30am, 12:30pm, 1:30pm, and 2:30pm, $6 adults, $5 seniors and students, $4 children age 6-12, free for children under 6) is an opportunity to learn about Denver and Colorado history through the stories of two prominent families who once lived in this Italianate-style house. Visitors can see exactly how an upper-middle-class family lived in the early 1900s, as the house contains all original furnishings, including the family's Haviland china and Baccarat crystal, 1760 Queen Anne highboy, and original artwork.

The house was built for William N. Byers in

the Brown Palace Hotel

Golden Triangle, Lincoln Park, and SoBo

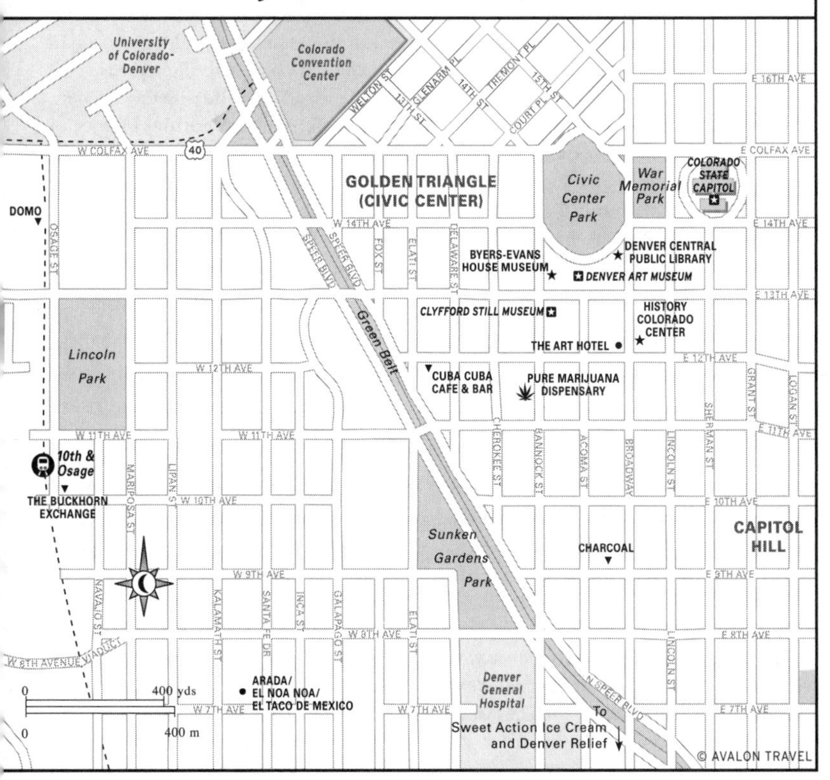

1883. Mr. Byers was a prominent Denver citizen who printed the *Rocky Mountain News*, the city's first newspaper. After six years, he sold the house to William Evans, the son of the state's second territorial governor, John Evans. (Today there are mountain peaks named after both Byers and the elder Evans because of their significant contributions to the state, and the younger Evans made his own mark on the city and state as head of the Denver Tramway Company.) The daughters of William Evans lived in the home with few modern modifications until 1981, even as the neighborhood around them slowly fell away and changed. The house was added on to five times as the family grew over the years, and has since been lovingly restored to the 1912-1924 period; today it's worth visiting to see a well-furnished example of WWI-era style.

The house museum can only be seen on a guided tour. Each tour lasts about 45 minutes.

Civic Center Park

Listed in the National Register of Historic Places, **Civic Center Park** (101 W. 14th Ave. Pkwy., 720/913-1311, www.denvergov.org, 5am-11pm daily) is today the reflection of years of input from various mayors, architects, and landscape architects. In 1904, Mayor Robert Speer was inspired by the City Beautiful movement and began to consult with planners and designers on the project, but citizens rejected his request for funding for the park and, by 1912, Speer was out of office. The next mayor also hired experts to tinker with the park design, and when Speer was reelected in 1917, bits of each plan were incorporated with the new architect's design. The park was officially opened in 1919 and various statues and memorials have been added since.

Reflecting its name, Civic Center Park is flanked by government buildings, including the historic **City and County Building** (1437 Bannock St., 720/865-7840, www.denvergov.org)—home of Denver's mayoral offices—to the west, and the **Colorado State Capitol** (200 E. Colfax Ave., 303/866-2604, www.colorado.gov) to the east. The **Greek Theater** (720/913-0700 for events and permitting) is the most distinctive structure within the park. It hosted public concerts as far back as 1920, and in modern times is often the staging area for a variety of cultural and political events. Two bronze sculptures in the middle of the park represent the West, portraying a cowboy and a Native American; Alexander Phimister Proctor created *Bronco Buster* in 1920 and *On the War Trail* in 1922.

The park extends east across Broadway where the 45-foot-tall **Colorado Veterans Memorial** was dedicated in 1990. The memorial is made of Colorado red sandstone.

The entire neighborhood around Civic Center Park has undergone tremendous growth in recent years, leading to more interest in its use and future design plans. In the spring and summer, the flowerbeds in the center of the park are filled with vivid blooms. The Greek Theater and **Voorhies Memorial** (on the north or Colfax Ave. side of the park), which features murals by the artist Allen True on the ceiling, provide welcome shade on hot days. The park is used for a variety of free public events year-round, including a Cinco de Mayo celebration and the Martin Luther King Jr. Day Parade.

★ Clyfford Still Museum

As someone who feels that Abstract Expressionism is, well, abstract, I have to say that my first visit to the **Clyfford Still Museum** (1250 Bannock St., 720/354-4880, www.clyffordstillmuseum.org, 10am-5pm Sat.-Thurs., 10am-8pm Fri., $10 adults, $6 students and seniors, $3 children age 6-17, free for children under 5) brought me a long way toward appreciating if not the entire genre, then certainly this giant of the field. Clyfford Still is considered one of America's most influential modern artists, and yet, like me, you might not have heard of him. Still's

the Clyfford Still Museum

peers became almost household names—Jackson Pollock, Willem de Kooning, and Mark Rothko, among them. At some point in his career, Still severed ties with commercial art galleries, and after his death in 1980 the Clyfford Still Estate was sealed off from public and scholarly view. In his will, Still stipulated that his entire estate be given to an American city that would be willing to establish a permanent museum dedicated solely to his work. In 2004, Denver Mayor John Hickenlooper was able to secure the collection with the promise of a museum.

Practically under the eaves of the Denver Art Museum, the Clyfford Still Museum opened in late 2011. The architecture of this building is nearly as interesting as the 2,400 drawings, paintings, and prints of the artist. Designed by Brad Cloepfil of Allied Works Architecture, the interior includes a unique, waffle-like concrete ceiling that lets in natural light, which makes the paintings look slightly different at various times of the day or year. Note that the second floor consists of nine distinct galleries, each with different ceiling heights to emphasize different elements of the collection. At two points in the galleries, visitors can step onto planted patios for a breath of fresh air.

The exhibits here will regularly change, as only a fraction of Still's massive body of work can be displayed at one time. With the collection's proximity to the Denver Art Museum, it is possible to cram in a lot of viewing in one day, but it is recommended to set aside half a day to thoroughly experience the work of this American artist.

★ Denver Art Museum

The Frederic C. Hamilton Building that houses portions of the **Denver Art Museum** (100 W. 14th Ave. Pkwy., 720/865-5000, www.denverartmuseum.org, 10am-5pm Tues.-Thurs., 10am-8pm Fri., 10am-5pm Sat.-Sun., $10-13 adults, $8-10 seniors and students, free for children under 18) has become an attraction in itself. Designed by architect Daniel Libeskind, the 146,000-square-foot building is all sharp angles and severe points—intended as an interpretation of rock crystals and of the jagged peaks of the Rocky Mountains. The building has received its fair share of criticism, being largely panned by national art critics and with visitors complaining of vertigo inside and questions about whether the art is enhanced or hampered by the architecture. Nonetheless, it's created a lot of exciting energy in the neighborhood and the city.

The Hamilton Building is connected to the original Denver Art Museum building, a seven-story "castle" that has been home to the museum since 1971 and was also once controversial for its design. Now called the North Building, it was designed by Italian architect Gio Ponti.

Once inside either of the museum's buildings, visitors will discover more art and activities than can be seen in one day. The museum's **Institute for Western American Art** includes works by well-known masters, including Charles Deas's *Long Jakes, The Rocky Mountain Man,* as well as the work of local contemporary artists. Like much of the museum, the Western American art rooms include interactive areas, especially for children. In this room, visitors can make their own postcards using ink stamps with iconic Western images and colored pencils.

Other collections at the museum include African art, American Indian art, Oceanic art, and a Modern and Contemporary collections room with thousands of pieces by artists including Andy Warhol, Man Ray, and many others. The permanent collections are not all exhibited at one time, but on a rotation, though some public art pieces, such as the Mark di Suvero sculpture *Lao-Tzu*, are always on display outdoors.

The parking garage for the museum is directly across the plaza from the Hamilton Building. The Museum Residences, also designed by Mr. Libeskind, are above the garage. The glass "walls" of these private homes are meant to complement the titanium-skinned museum that they face.

Public Art Tours

The City of Denver has an ordinance requiring that 1 percent of any $1 million capital improvement project be spent on the acquisition of public art. As a result, the city has a considerable public art collection to show off that includes works from international artists as well as those who hail from Colorado. The work of Dale Chihuly, Herbert Bayer, Barbara Jo Revelle, Vance Kirkland, and many more artists is exhibited both outside and inside public buildings, including Coors Field, the Denver Center for Performing Arts, and the Denver Art Museum.

Even if your visit to Denver is so short that you never leave the airport, there is a large collection of public art on display there as well—much of it permanent, but with some temporary exhibits, too. Even the little windmills along the train tunnels are a public art installation. My personal favorite is Gary Sweeney's *America, Why I Love Her,* just off the main terminal. Sweeney's wall-size map of the United States is an homage to bizarre tourist sites around the country.

Pick up a **self-guided walking tour** (720/865-4307, www.denvergov.org) of the city's public art and find out when guided tours of indoor public art are scheduled.

Denver Central Public Library

Denverites love their libraries; statistics show that the city has the highest number of library cardholders per capita in the country. But the **Denver Central Public Library** (10 W. 14th Ave. Pkwy., 720/865-1111, www.denverlibrary.org, 10am-8pm Mon.-Tues., 10am-6pm Wed.-Fri., 9am-5pm Sat., 1pm-5pm Sun.) is no ordinary library—it holds not just books, but also a large art collection, photograph archives, and genealogy data.

The Central Library was designed by well-known architect Michael Graves and opened in 1995 with 47 *miles* of books. Each section is roomy and huge windows bring in the natural light. Visit the fifth floor's Western Art Gallery and Gates Western Reading Room to see the library's Western art collection. Only a fraction of the library's 400 framed pieces (including works by Albert Bierstadt, Frederic Remington, and Thomas Moran) and thousands of sculptures, etchings, lithographs, and other artifacts dating back to the mid-1800s can be on display at one time. While taking a peek at the art that is hung in an entryway hallway and set out between the stacks, you're bound to see people quietly conducting research, as this is also the Western History/Genealogy Department; it boasts a massive collection of digital photographs related to the history of the American West and Colorado.

If you still have time, the library's seventh floor has not just administrative offices, but also long hallways bedecked with a bit more Western art. The Vida Ellison Gallery hosts exhibits of artwork made by local artists (including library staff), and the gallery provides a nice view of Civic Center Park and downtown.

The library also hosts themed film series, guest lectures, book clubs, concerts, knitting and cooking classes, and more events throughout the year. Pick up the *Fresh City Life* magazine at any library for the current month's schedule.

History Colorado Center

It's been called "the first great history museum of the 21st century" by Smithsonian Affiliations Director Harold Closter, and the **History Colorado Center** (1200 Broadway, 303/866-3682, www.historycoloradocenter.org, 10am-5pm daily, $12 adults, $10 seniors and students, $8 children age 6-12, free for children under 5) is still adding permanent exhibits as well as rotating temporary exhibits. The 200,000-square-foot building was designed by Tryba Architects of Denver and has opened in stages since 2012. The approach to history here is to feature high-tech, hands-on learning about the people and the environment that shaped the Centennial State. The experience begins with H. G. Wells-inspired "time machines" in the four-story atrium, where the mobile devices can be pushed around a terrazzo floor map of the state to learn about everything from the preservation of Mesa Verde to the tomato wars. While still in the atrium, look up to see a two-story media presentation. This six-minute video gives a taste of the historic places, first peoples, and traditions in Colorado. Step from this futuristic display into the past, where parts of the town of Keota, Colorado—inspiration for James Michener's novel *Centennial*—are re-created and others have been salvaged. Inside this former agricultural town on the Eastern Plains, kids can gather eggs, slide in the barn, and "meet" town residents. Then it's time to head upstairs for a virtual ski jump, a mine tour, and a step inside an old fort in the *Destination Colorado* exhibit, where eight stories about the state are told.

A sometimes humorous exhibit is *Denver A-Z;* on the more serious side is an exhibit about how the harsh, dry environment shaped life in Colorado. **Café Rendezvous** (303/447-8679, www.historycoloradocenter.org, 8am-4pm Mon.-Fri., 10am-4pm Sat.-Sun.) and the **History Colorado Museum Store** (10am-5pm daily) are on the first floor.

LODO AND PLATTE RIVER VALLEY

Larimer Square (Larimer St. btw. 14th and 15th Sts., 303/534-2367, www.larimersquare.com) is not really a square, but a preserved city block—the historic buildings along each side are now used for offices, restaurants, and shops. The history of this place goes back to the city's earliest days, when the area was inundated with people who wanted to strike it rich from gold found in the nearby creek. General William H. Larimer Jr. arrived in 1858 and built a cabin on what is now Larimer Square. The city quickly grew and by the 1880s, there were 25 buildings on Larimer Street, including a bank, a drugstore, and a bookstore.

Over time, saloons and bars prospered here and this block became known as Denver's "skid row." In the 1960s, officials were ready to start anew, but preservationists gathered support to save the block from the wrecking ball. With its 1870s and 1880s buildings fully restored, the block was listed in the National Register of Historic Places. Now it's the heart of LoDo and draws people year-round.

Auraria Campus

The **Auraria Campus** (900 Auraria Pkwy., 303/556-3291, www.ahec.edu) on the outlying rim of LoDo is Colorado's largest educational campus, with about 38,000 students, and is home to three separate institutions: the Community College of Denver, the Metropolitan State College of Denver, and the University of Colorado at Denver. One addition to this commuter campus is the teaching hotel—a Springhill Suites that will be mostly operated by students as part of the hospitality program. As the campus was once a town of its own before merging with Denver in the 1860s, there are several historic sights worth visiting here.

The Ninth Street Historic Park is the oldest restored block in the city and includes 13 Victorian homes (now administrative offices) and a turn-of-the-20th-century grocery store (now a bagel and coffee shop). It's free to stroll along the block and read the small signs in front of each home, which tell a bit about the architecture and the people who originally lived there.

Not far from the historic park is the relocated and restored **Golda Meir House,** one-time home of the former Israeli prime minister. When she was a girl, Meir left her parents' home in Milwaukee to live with her sister and brother-in-law in Denver in their tiny duplex. She went to high school in the city and worked in the family laundry business. In literature describing Meir's time in Denver, she is quoted as saying, "It was in Denver that my real education began." One side of the duplex contains artifacts from Meir's life, while the other side is used for small conferences. Tours are available (303/556-3292).

The city's oldest church structure is now

LoDo and Platte River Valley

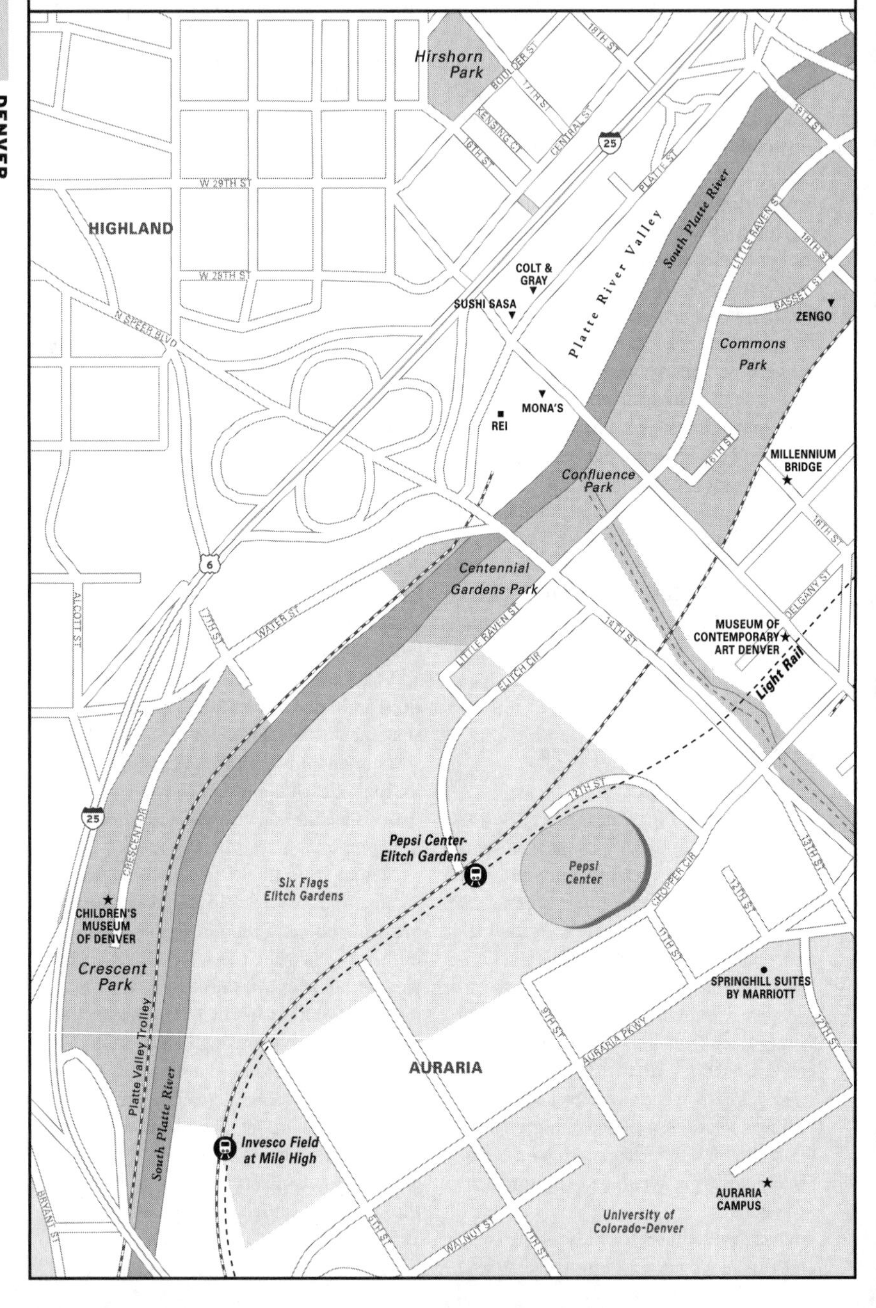

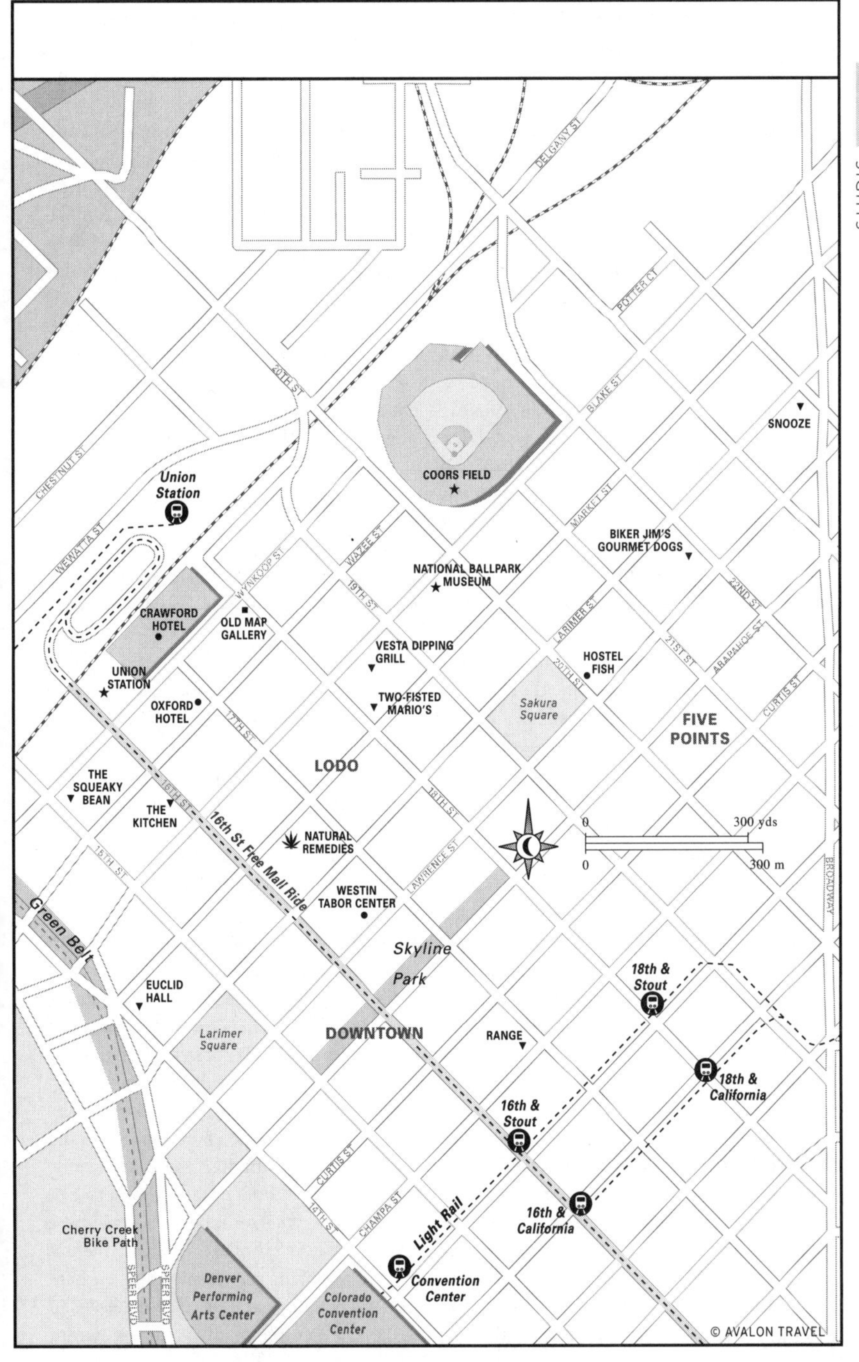
DELGANY ST
POTTER CT
20TH ST
BLAKE ST
SNOOZE
CHESTNUT ST
Union Station
COORS FIELD
MARKET ST
WEWATTA ST
WAZEE ST
BIKER JIM'S GOURMET DOGS
WYNKOOP ST
NATIONAL BALLPARK MUSEUM
19TH ST
22ND ST
CRAWFORD HOTEL
OLD MAP GALLERY
LARIMER ST
VESTA DIPPING GRILL
21ST ST
ARAPAHOE ST
HOSTEL FISH
UNION STATION
20TH ST
CURTIS ST
OXFORD HOTEL
TWO-FISTED MARIO'S
Sakura Square
17TH ST
FIVE POINTS
LODO
THE SQUEAKY BEAN
18TH ST
16TH ST
THE KITCHEN
16th St Free Mall Ride
0
300 yds
NATURAL REMEDIES
15TH ST
LAWRENCE ST
0
300 m
BROADWAY
WESTIN TABOR CENTER
Green Belt
Skyline Park
18th & Stout
EUCLID HALL
DOWNTOWN
RANGE
Larimer Square
18th & California
16th & Stout
CURTIS ST
14TH ST
CHAMPA ST
16th & California
Light Rail
Cherry Creek Bike Path
Convention Center
SPEER BLVD
SPEER BLVD
Denver Performing Arts Center
Colorado Convention Center
© AVALON TRAVEL

the **Emmanuel Gallery** (303/556-8337, www.emmanuelgallery.org, hours vary depending on exhibit), serving as an art gallery for the campus. The little stone chapel was built in 1876 for Episcopalians, then was converted into a Jewish synagogue in 1903; it eventually became an artist's studio, a purpose it served until 1973. The gallery displays artwork by faculty and students in changing exhibits.

Still an active Catholic parish, **St. Elizabeth's Church** (also called St. Elizabeth of Hungary, 1060 St. Francis Way, 303/534-4014, http://stelizabethdenver.org) was founded by German immigrants in 1878. When the congregation grew too large for the original church, the building was torn down and the current one constructed in 1898. The monastery was added in the 1930s. To learn more about the sometimes bizarre history of the church—a murdered priest, panhandling nuns—go to www.archden.org/noel.

St. Cajetan's (1190 9th St., 303/556-2755, www.ahec.edu), a Spanish colonial church, was built in 1925 for the Latino community. The parish relocated in 1973 and the church is now used for campus functions. Call ahead to schedule guided tours of these historic buildings (720/556-3291).

The most distinctive building on campus is the **Tivoli Student Union** (900 Auraria Pkwy., 303/556-6330, www.tivoli.org), which started out in 1866 as one of Denver's earliest breweries. The building had subsequent additions and uses, and today includes a multiplex movie theater where some screenings of the annual **Denver International Film Festival** are held. There are no tours offered of the Tivoli building; it is open to the public as a student union and holds various eateries and campus offices.

Centennial Gardens Park

In 2009, stewardship of this garden was transferred from the Denver Botanic Gardens to the city, and the city has since made it open only by permit for special events—though I have occasionally still found it open on random weekends, so I recommend taking a chance and stopping by to see if the gates are open. The gardens can still easily be viewed when the gates are closed, even if you can't walk through them.

Centennial Gardens Park (1101 Little Raven St., 720/913-1311, www.denvergov.org/parks, by permit only) is a lovely little example of the transformation of the entire South Platte Valley from urban wasteland to dynamic neighborhood. People jogging, bicycling, or sauntering along the paths parallel to the South Platte River can detour into the gardens (when open) and view dozens of carefully pruned topiary trees, smell the lavender plants, listen to the fountains trickling, or watch birds flit from trees to birdbaths.

Centennial Gardens Park is a formal garden, inspired by the gardens of Versailles in France. In the 1990s, former Denver mayor Wellington Webb and his wife, Wilma, visited Versailles and were inspired to create a formal public garden in Denver. What makes this small garden unique is the use of only native plant species and drought-tolerant plants in the neatly patterned five-acre space. There is always a spot of brilliant color among the tidy green hedges; in the spring, yellow, purple, and white crocuses push up through native buffalo grass just before miniature irises and daffodils appear around deciduous trees and rows of junipers. A small pavilion with benches provides shade on warm days.

Children's Museum of Denver

Whether you are traveling with a small child or are just tired of having the kids make a mess in your own house, the **Children's Museum of Denver** (2121 Children's Museum Dr., 303/433-7444, www.mychildsmuseum.org, 9am-4pm Mon.-Tues., 9am-7:30pm Wed., 9am-4pm Thurs.-Fri., 10am-5pm Sat.-Sun., $10 ages 2-59, $8 children age 1, $8 seniors, free for children under 1) is a good place to explore. The museum offers several "playscapes" for a variety of ages—such as the "assembly plant" for ages four to eight, where kids use real tools and recycled materials to build whatever they want, or the "Center for the Young Child" for newborns to four-year-olds, where creepers can practice on carpeted slopes and toddlers can play house in a tree. The simplest play areas are the best here: a painting room, a small puppet theater, a mirrored wall to dress up and dance in front of, a real fire engine to "drive," and the outdoor playground near the bike path and South Platte River.

Every day of the week there is a story time at the museum, and the first Tuesday of each month the museum is open late with free admission. The museum also hosts temporary exhibits and shows such as the Blue Man Group. They also offer additional games and events for Easter, Halloween, and other holidays. Eat Street Café has grown-up and kid food with little tables and chairs for sitting inside. There are also picnic tables outside near the playground. The least crowded time to visit the museum is right when it opens or mid-afternoon.

At the time of this writing, the museum was expanding both indoors and outdoors with a larger art studio, a climbing area with a 3.5-story structure, zip-lining, a teaching kitchen, and more.

Commons Park

The broad and winding waters of the South Platte River have attracted dreamers since the earliest days of the city. In the late 1800s, this land was used for a castle and an amusement park, among other delights. As years passed, this broad expanse of land that sits roughly between LoDo's Union Station to the east and the South Platte River to the west was lost to the ravages of time and nature, and the river started being used as a dumping ground for old cars, refrigerators, and other debris. A severe flood along the river in 1965, in which lives, homes, and businesses were lost, led to long-needed changes all along the South Platte: a dam was built upstream and the water was no longer used as an illegal garbage dump. Still, it took decades for new dreams to take shape and remake the land into a recreation area once again.

The **Commons Park** (15th and Little Raven Sts., 720/913-1311, www.denvergov.org, 5am-11pm daily) people visit today was years in the making. In 2001 the city unveiled the ambitious 20-acre park along the east side of the South Platte River. One portion of the park was designed to re-create how it would have looked before the settlers arrived, complete with native grasses, trees, and sand. Atop a man-made hill—popular for sledding in the winter and, in warmer weather, flying kites—there is a sunken black granite east-west directional sculpture that can't be seen from below. There are views of the Rocky Mountains and the city's skyline from the hilltop. One side of the park follows a street and looks up at condominiums and apartments, while the other drops down to foot- and bike paths along the river. Bridges on either side of Commons Park lead to shopping and dining districts in historic neighborhoods. On any given day, depending on the season, you will see fitness classes, sports contests, skiers, sledders, and dog walkers or dogs in obedience classes. Public art inside the park is user-friendly—it can all be walked in, sat on, and touched.

Coors Field

Even in the off-season, there's a chance to tour **Coors Field** (2001 Blake St., 303/762-5437, http://colorado.rockies.mlb.com, tours 10am, noon, and 2pm on nongame days and 10am and noon on evening game days Mon.-Sat Apr.-Sept.; noon and 2pm Mon., Wed., Fri., and Sat. Oct.-Mar; $10 adults, $7 children, $8 seniors), home of the Colorado Rockies baseball team, and see parts of the field that are off-limits during games. The ballpark has been a major part of the redevelopment of LoDo from neglected warehouse district to hip urban neighborhood with expensive condominiums and dozens of bars and restaurants.

Since opening in 1995, Coors Field has been noted for its modern yet classic architecture. The 75-minute tours at Coors Field include the field, the upper deck where a row of purple seats marks 5,280 feet above sea level, the guest clubhouse, and suites. The upper seats have a great view of the Central Platte Valley and the Rocky Mountains.

After the tour, you can walk around the stadium and check out some of the public art on display. To the north is Erick C. Johnson's *Bottom of the Ninth,* which shows a neon baseball figure sliding into home plate, and to the south is Lonnie Hanzon's *The Evolution of the Ball,* which is like an arched gateway to the stadium.

There is a large gift and souvenir shop on the Blake Street side of Coors Field, where just about anything in the team's purple and black can be found—blankets, hats, jackets, T-shirts, and more.

Millennium Bridge

Upon its 2003 opening, the **Millennium Bridge** (16th St. at Chestnut St.) became an instant landmark in Denver and an important part of the redevelopment of the Central Platte Valley. The 16th Street Mall used to end at Wynkoop Street, where railroad tracks emanating from behind Union Station dominated the landscape. Now 16th Street has extended beyond its old boundary in LoDo, and the Millennium Bridge brings people up and over the railroad tracks into the Platte Valley, the bustling Riverfront Park development area, and Commons Park. Up out of the flat prairie floor rises a 200-foot white mast held in place on a wide deck by multiple steel cables. The bridge has stairs on either side as well as elevators, and is the most scenic walk from downtown to parks and the South Platte River. Additional bridges on the other side of Commons Park lead to restaurants and shops on Platte Street and then to the eastern edge of the Highlands neighborhood, which has a growing number of popular restaurants.

With its dramatic backdrop of the city's skyline and its distinctive architecture, the bridge has become a favorite spot for fashion shoots, selfies, and family portraits. In 2007, the inaugural Riverfront Fashion Series was held at the base of the bridge. As coal trains rattle below night and day, there are typically tourists and art students taking in the view from the bridge and trying to get a good shot of the mast.

Museum of Contemporary Art Denver

Not quite as talked about as the Denver Art Museum, but still an important aspect of the culture here, is the **Museum of Contemporary Art Denver** (1485 Delgany St., 303/298-7554, www.mcadenver.org, noon-7pm Tues.-Thurs., noon-9pm Fri., 10am-5pm Sat.-Sun., $8 adults, $5 after 5pm, free for children 18 and under), also with a building designed by an internationally known architect. Note that this is the rare cultural institution where admission fees have *decreased* in recent years, including free admission for anyone 18 and under. Free!

The museum had humble beginnings in 1996 in a former fish market at downtown's Sakura Square block. Incredible success clashed with space limitations and the museum had to relocate. After hiring London-based architect David Adjaye, the museum reopened in late 2007 in a black glass box of a building perched on the corner of 15th Street. At first glance, the minimalist, modern building can seem as challenging as contemporary art itself—and the hidden front door adds to this perplexity—but inside it is full of welcome surprises where couples can meet for a cultural date and families can interact and be artistic.

The museum was designed as an environmentally sustainable building and strives to reduce its carbon footprint—from offering locally grown food and drinks in the café to encouraging volunteers and staff to commute to work in an eco-friendly manner. Atop the building is the **MCA Café** (noon-7pm Tues.-Thurs., noon-9pm Fri., 10am-5pm Sat.-Sun.), which includes an outdoor bar. There is also a rooftop garden, which itself is a piece of artwork, designed by Colorado landscape architect Karla Dakin. Ceramic sculptures inside the café were made by Kim Dickey, a Colorado artist.

Children and families will find a small library with a selection of art books and the "Idea Box," where small tables and art supplies invite kids of all ages to get creative. Or, for a more laid-back experience, simply lounge in a room full of beanbag chairs.

Exhibit space in the museum was designed as individual galleries so that video installations, photography, paintings, and other media are all displayed at once but separately. Past exhibitions have featured artists Jeff Starr, Chris Ofili, and many other internationally recognized artists. The exhibits here are often interactive for all ages, such as sculptures to walk through, light and sound that continuously change, or live carrier pigeons that can be brought home temporarily. The MCA's bimonthly "Mixed Taste" summer lecture series, which pairs two unrelated topics and experts, has outgrown the museum and been moved to a new location in the Highlands neighborhood. If your idea of a fun night out includes an intellectual discussion on who knows what, this event is for you. Topics are not limited to art: You might find yourself listening to a scientist, an author, or a professor of film studies.

National Ballpark Museum

Enhance your ballpark experience by visiting the **National Ballpark Museum** (1940 Blake St., 303/974-5835, www.ballparkmuseum.com, noon-5:30pm Tues.-Fri., 11am-5:30pm Sat., $5) before you see the game. This is an impressive private collection that goes beyond the Colorado Rockies. Did you know there was a Denver baseball team before the Rockies? Come see what the team was called and when it played. Bits and pieces of other stadiums are part of the collection—bricks, light fixtures, pieces of bats, a telephone, uniforms, and lots more.

Union Station

Union Station (1701 Wynkoop St., 303/592-6712, http://unionstationindenver.com) is the perfect representation of how far Denver has come in a relatively short time. The regal historic building has been renovated into a hotel, transportation hub, nightlife hotspot, and urban playground for all. Yet the old charm of the train station remains with the high-backed wooden benches and soaring high ceilings setting the stage for a weekend of fun in the city.

Outside on the plaza of the station there is a splash park with intermittent fountains shooting up sprays of water for kids (and grown-ups) to run through or soak themselves in during the summer. Diners on the various restaurant patios can enjoy the squeals of joy as kids cool off and dare each other to run through. In the winter, people come here to take holiday card photos next to the enormous and impeccably decorated Christmas tree.

It's almost easy to forget that this is still a working station where you can walk in and buy tickets from the Amtrak window and catch a train to Chicago or Los Angeles. In addition, you can walk out the back door and down some steps into a shiny new bus station where regional buses regularly take people to Boulder and other cities in the greater metro area. On the other side of the bus terminal is the light rail station, with trains that take passengers west to Golden, south to the suburbs, and elsewhere throughout the metro area.

CAPITOL HILL AND CITY PARK

Cathedral Basilica of the Immaculate Conception

The **Cathedral Basilica of the Immaculate Conception** (1530 Logan St., 303/831-7010, www.denvercathedral.org, 6am-6pm daily), situated on a slight hill with its twin, 210-foot bell tower spires poking into the sky above, looks as if it reaches up into the heavens. This Catholic church has both captivating history and architecture.

J. J. Brown, husband of Molly Brown, joined with a few investors to buy the land for the cathedral and, in 1902, ground was broken to start the new building. The French Gothic structure is made from limestone and granite, while Italian marble was used for the altar, communion rail, statuary, and bishop's chair. The stunning interior features a 68-foot vaulted ceiling and 75 German-made stained glass windows—more than any other Catholic church in the country. In 1912, lightning struck one of the church's spires and toppled 25 feet off the top of the bell tower. Repairs were made before the church's dedication later that year. In 1993, Pope John Paul II read mass here during World Youth Day.

This grand church is located on the corner of busy Colfax Avenue and Logan Street, just a stone's throw from the state capitol. There is a small garden with statues and benches on the north side of the building.

There are three masses held daily at the cathedral, and six on weekends.

City Park

The city's largest park (at 370 acres and a mile long) is **City Park** (3300 E. 17th Ave., 303/331-4113, www.denvergov.org, 5am-11pm daily), located east of downtown. Denver's answer to New York's Central Park, City Park offers pretty much anything you could ask for in a park, sometimes in multiples: lakes, playgrounds, athletic fields, historic statues and fountains, running and cycling paths, a golf course, the **Denver Zoo,** and the **Denver Museum of Nature and Science.**

When the park was laid out in 1882, there was no surrounding neighborhood and downtown trolleys took people to this large patch of green. But it didn't take long for the city to grow around the park and beyond. The best time to visit is in summer, when paddleboats are rented by the hour on Ferril Lake and free jazz concerts are held in the park's historic pavilion.

The park is easily traversed by paved roads—some more like paths—but take note that from May through September the roads are closed on Sundays. The park includes the Mile High Loop, a contour that is 5,280 feet above sea level, and a multiuse path that goes right by the Denver Museum of Nature and Science. Walk around during spring and enjoy a lilac garden, blooming trees, rows of tulips, and more greenery.

★ Colorado State Capitol

A visit to the **Colorado State Capitol** (200 Colfax Ave., 303/866-2604, https://www.colorado.gov, 7:30am-5pm Mon.-Fri., tours 10am-3pm, free) is a history lesson in the making, especially when the legislature is in session (Jan.-May) and the governor and lawmakers are hard at work. Quiet visitors can watch the legislators in action from just outside their respective chambers during sessions.

The story of the capitol building began in 1868, when Henry C. Brown, who also had the Brown Palace built a few blocks away, donated the land to the state of Colorado. Brown later tried to take it back, even going so far as to return grazing animals to the site because he was not pleased with construction delays. After a court battle, the state was able to keep the land. Two architects and 22 years later, the capitol was completed.

Tours (reservations recommended) of the building highlight the use of native materials: marble, granite, sandstone, onyx, and gold. The original gold leaf used on the dome was a gift from Colorado miners. When standing on the first floor of the capitol, look 150 feet up to the rotunda ceiling. High up inside the rotunda is the stained glass "Hall of Fame" that features portraits of 16 people who made remarkable contributions to the state. There are other stained glass portraits seen on the tour as well. Before ascending the 77 marble steps of the Grand Staircase, you'll learn about the Water Murals; added in 1940, these murals are an artistic interpretation of the story of one of the state's most precious resources.

The true highlight of touring the capitol is the view from the dome's observation gallery. Like the hike up the 99 steps to the dome's interior, the views of the city and the mountains to the west from the dome are breathtaking. About halfway to the dome there is a small museum, Mr. Brown's Attic, in honor of Henry C. Brown's donation of the land. The museum includes a pop art replica of the capitol made from old soup cans by local engineering students.

On the west-side steps of the capitol, you'll find the mile-high markers that indicate the point at which the city reaches 5,280 feet above sea level. This is a popular spot for tourist photos.

★ Denver Botanic Gardens

The **Denver Botanic Gardens** (1005 York St., 720/865-3500, www.botanicgardens.org, 9am-9pm daily May-Sept., 9am-5pm daily Sept.-Apr., $12.50 adults, $9.50 seniors, $9 students, $9 children age 3-15, free for children under 3) was designed with all types of weather in mind, making it enjoyable year-round regardless of snow or blazing sun. The 23-acre gardens sit at the back side of Cheesman Park and are on the outer edge of the Capitol Hill neighborhood. Each summer has brought a new sculpture show with accompanying artist-led tours and events at the gardens. Perhaps their biggest success was a show by glass artist Dale Chihuly in 2014; visitors can still see a colorful sculpture given to the gardens by the artist. Other recent shows have been big draws to the gardens too.

When the gardens' original site in City Park was repeatedly damaged by people who came to steal plants, the city and local gardening enthusiasts agreed to transform an old cemetery into the new gardens. The 1960s addition of the Boettcher Memorial Tropical Conservatory, which houses tropical plants in a steamy hot dome, made the gardens more than a summer attraction. While in recent years there has been a design emphasis and financial investment on making at least a portion of the gardens friendly to special events (such as weddings), the original mission to highlight thriving native plants remains obvious. The Rock Alpine Garden, Water-Smart Garden, and Dryland Mesa in particular are a reminder of the arid climate of the region, and they show off what grows so well with so little water. Also check out the "green" roof of the gift shop as a progressive idea for environmental design. New in 2014 was the Science Pyramid, where visitors can learn more about the science of the plants here.

Throughout the gardens, there are shaded benches and tables and chairs set up for enjoying a picnic—there is a small snack bar within the gardens—or taking a relaxing, pleasantly scented rest.

In 2011, the Mordecai Children's Garden was opened atop the new parking garage across the street from the main gardens. With its own gift shop at the entrance, the garden includes various water features, bridges, caves, and, of course, plants.

During the summer, the Denver Botanic Gardens host a summer concert series with big-name bands, and tickets can be hard to come by. Membership to the gardens has many advantages, including discounts on those concert tickets and members-only hours when the gardens have the ambience of a lovely backyard party.

★ Denver Museum of Nature and Science

It is difficult to imagine the humble beginnings of the **Denver Museum of Nature and Science** (2001 Colorado Blvd., 303/322-7009, www.dmns.org, 9am-5pm daily, $14.95 adults, $9.95 children age 3-18, $11.95 seniors) as an oversized collection of treasured fauna specimens in the log cabin home of naturalist Edwin Carter. Today, features such as the Gates Planetarium, the Phipps IMAX Theater, and the Morgridge Family Exploration Center (which added another 126,000 square feet and five levels of exhibit and activity space in 2014) combine to make the museum a top-notch destination.

In 1908, the original Colorado Museum of Natural History opened in a stately building on a hilltop on the eastern side of City Park. The building has been expanded considerably since then, and the variety and type of exhibits have increased. Some of the museum's oldest displays are of animals prepared by taxidermists and staged in large naturalistic settings behind glass windows—it's like a really quiet, clean zoo. Kids enjoy running

Capitol Hill and City Park

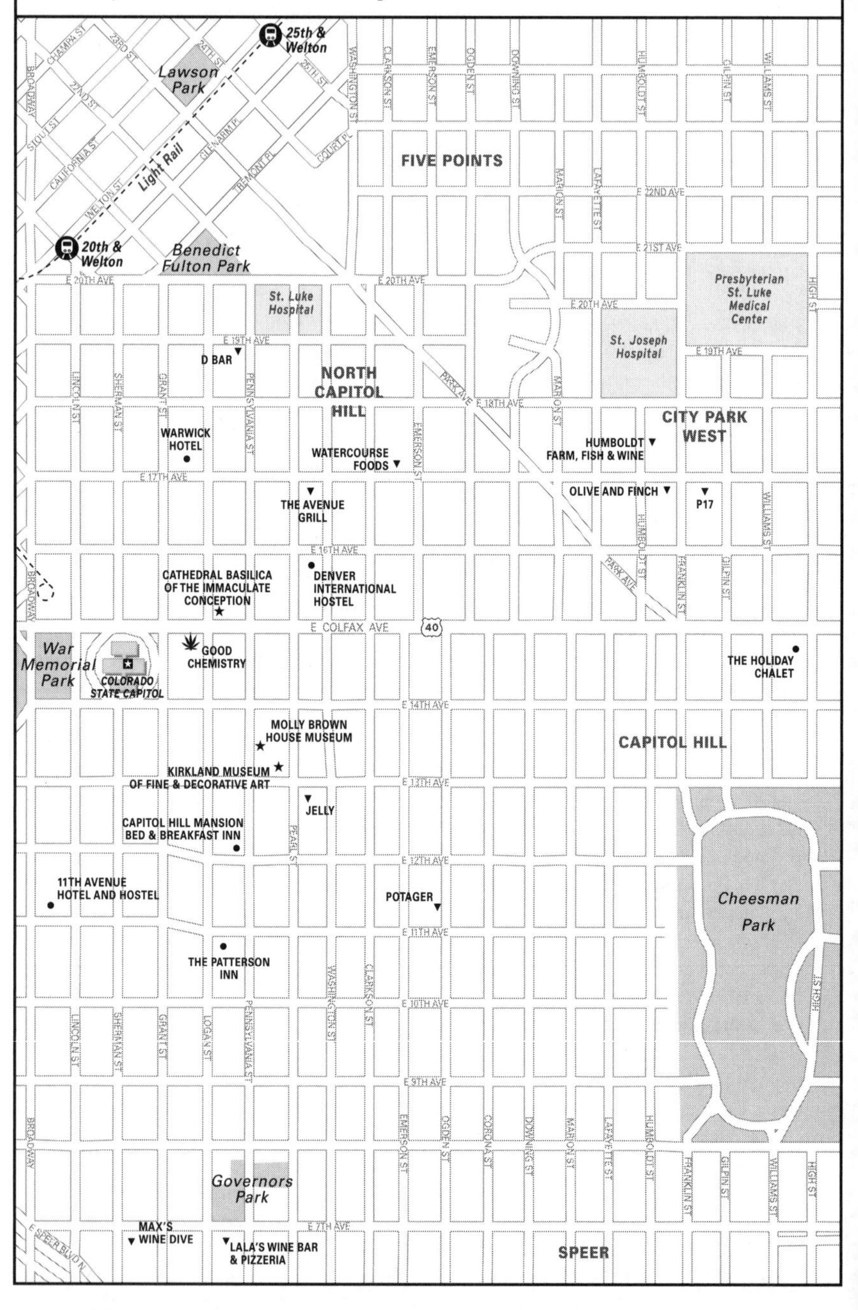

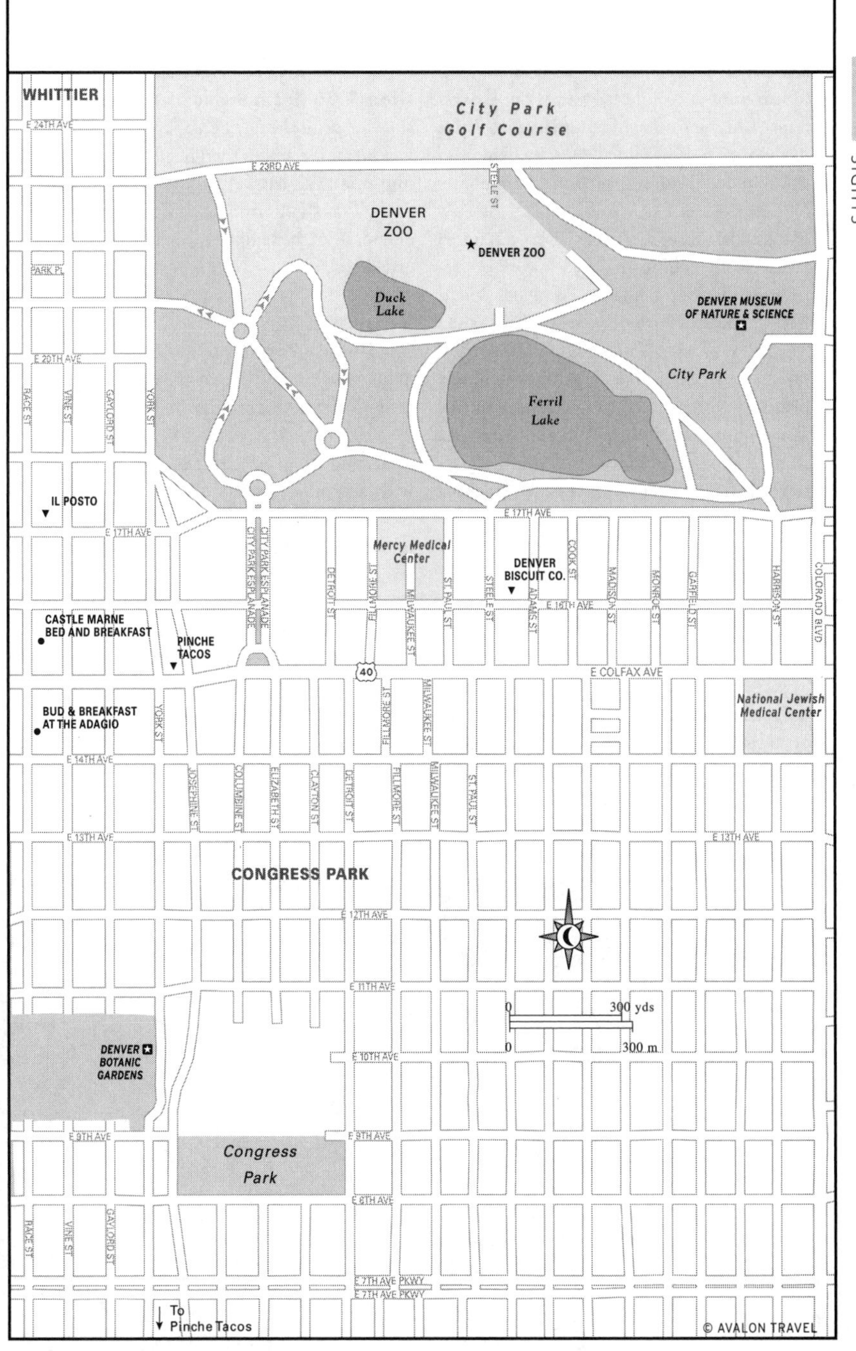
WHITTIER
City Park Golf Course
DENVER ZOO
DENVER ZOO
Duck Lake
DENVER MUSEUM OF NATURE & SCIENCE
City Park
Ferril Lake
IL POSTO
Mercy Medical Center
DENVER BISCUIT CO.
CASTLE MARNE BED AND BREAKFAST
PINCHE TACOS
E COLFAX AVE
National Jewish Medical Center
BUD & BREAKFAST AT THE ADAGIO
CONGRESS PARK
300 yds
300 m
DENVER BOTANIC GARDENS
Congress Park
To Pinche Tacos
© AVALON TRAVEL

through these wide halls and pushing the buttons to hear the sounds of cougars, buffalo, and other wildlife. Head to the third level to learn about Colorado's variety of ecosystems (and the plants and animals that thrive in them). The *Prehistoric Journey* exhibit in the Explore Colorado section offers plenty of huge dinosaur skeletons, and it's the only place in the museum where visitors can watch the typically behind-the-scenes work of preparing fossils for display. A family favorite is *Expedition Health* where people of all ages can learn about their own health by riding bikes, taking walks, breathing, and other seemingly ordinary things. Each gadget has a fun way to measure one's ability. While the museum is one hands-on activity after another, particularly for children, a variety of educational programs are also offered off-site.

With its perch on the hill over City Park, the museum also offers two places to catch the best view of the city—the Leprino Family Atrium and the Anschutz Family Sky Terrace, both on the building's west side.

Note that admission to the museum does not include tickets to special traveling exhibits or to the IMAX or Gates Planetarium shows (several daily). The museum can be especially crowded during morning school field trips; lines at the ticket windows are often much shorter in the afternoon.

The **T-Rex Café** (11am-2pm daily) and **Grab & Go** (10am-4pm daily) make it possible to spend the day here with the family as you break for lunch, then head back into the museum. The **Museum Shop** (10am-5pm daily) is a wonderful place to get a souvenir, and many of the temporary exhibits also have gift shops.

Denver Zoo

The **Denver Zoo** (2300 Steele St., 303/376-4800, www.denverzoo.org, 9am-5pm daily Mar. 1-Nov. 1, 10am-4pm daily Nov. 2-Feb. 29, $17 adults, $12 seniors, $12 children age 3-11, children under 3 free) is insanely popular with tourists and residents alike. Like many modern-day zoos, the Denver Zoo is trying to make its animal habitats look and feel more natural and its residents look less like caged wild animals. One example of this is the $50 million **Toyota Elephant Passage**, which takes up 10 acres and is not only home to elephants, but also rhinos, tapirs, leopards, birds, and reptiles. The **Giraffe Encounter** (10am, 12:30pm, or 2:30pm daily) allows visitors to feed these towering creatures a healthy snack.

There are 29 primates found in the

the Denver Botanic Gardens

Free Admission Days

the Denver Museum of Nature and Science

In Denver, taxation equals free admission on specified days at many of the city's most popular sights. During a downturn in the economy in the 1980s, the state legislature eliminated funding for several of the city's main attractions, including the Denver Art Museum and the Denver Botanic Gardens. New admission fees did not provide enough financial support for these institutions, so a small sales and use tax of 0.1 percent (or $0.01 on every $10 purchase) was implemented in the surrounding seven-county area. The small tax adds up to millions, and that money is then distributed to scientific and cultural institutions throughout these seven counties. It's enough that the institutions can now afford to offer limited periods of free admission.

While the city's five largest facilities—the **Denver Center for the Performing Arts, Denver Art Museum, Denver Zoo, Denver Botanic Gardens,** and the **Denver Museum of Nature and Science** get the lion's share of the $40 million in funds annually, much smaller theaters, art museums, and nature and science centers receive funding as well. Studies have shown that these millions invested in the city's cultural facilities equal billions spent in Denver in return.

The number of free days per year varies from one place to the next, but they are generally scattered so that not every institution has a free day on the same date. And free days are not a secret—show up early because each of these places fills up quickly, and it's first-come, first-served where seating is limited at the Ricketson Theatre and Stage Theatre in the Denver Center for the Performing Arts. Free days differ each calendar year. Go to www.scfd.org or pick up a bookmark listing the year's free days at any of the five major facilities.

seven-acre **Primate Panorama,** and **Predator Ridge** offers 14 different animal species from Africa, including lions and hyenas. The **African Kraal** and **Lorikeet Adventure** are interactive animal exhibits where visitors can pet goats or feed the birds.

In addition to the 4,000 animals packed into this 80-acre space within City Park, the zoo is pulling in crowds with features beyond its residents and habitats. A huge annual draw during the holidays is **ZooLights,** when nearly half the zoo is illuminated with sparkling and colorful lights. Zoo-goers are treated to a glimpse of whatever nocturnal animals are out, as well as the sounds of choirs singing, a Kwanzaa performance, live ice-sculpture carving, and fire dancers.

The best time to visit the zoo is generally

mid-afternoon, after school groups have come and gone. In winter, plan for time inside the hot and humid **Tropical Discovery**, where there are fish, turtles, snakes, bats, and Komodo dragons.

For a relaxing break from animal viewing, take a nostalgic ride on the zoo's **Endangered Species Carousel** ($2) Children and adults can choose from 48 hand-carved zoo animals or chariots. Look for the mother polar bear and two bear cubs, which were made especially for the zoo in honor of its most famous animal residents, Klondike and Snow, two infant cubs that were hand-fed and raised by zoo staff and have since moved to another zoo.

Kirkland Museum of Fine & Decorative Art

The **Kirkland Museum of Fine & Decorative Art** (1311 Pearl St., 303/832-8576, www.kirklandmuseum.org, 11am-5pm Tues.-Sun. $8 adults, $6 seniors and students) is one of Denver's cultural gems. This space began as artist Vance Kirkland's studio, and it has been preserved as if the man himself might reenter and hang from his special harness to begin another dot painting. The museum was established after his death and took over the building next door to open in 2002. In 2003, the collection of over 3,000 examples of arts and crafts, art nouveau, pop art, art deco, and more could be seen on the first and basement floors of the museum. In addition to the modernist decorative works that date from 1880 to 1980, Mr. Kirkland's impressive body of work and rotating exhibits of Colorado artists are on display. Children under 13 are not allowed (teens aged 13-17 must be accompanied by an adult).

Note that there are plans to relocate this museum to the Golden Triangle neighborhood by 2017.

Molly Brown House Museum

For being one of Denver's better-known residents, Molly Brown's fascinating life story sure isn't very well known. "The Unsinkable Molly Brown" is of course best known for surviving the 1912 sinking of the *Titanic*, but the tale of how she made it off the ship while valiantly trying to help others is just the tip of the iceberg.

In 1886, at age 19, Molly married 31-year-old miner J. J. Brown—*before* he struck it rich. After the Browns became wealthy from a gold mine, they moved to Denver in 1894 and eventually bought the Pennsylvania Street house that is now the museum. The Browns' renovations on the house are still evident today. Even during Molly Brown's lifetime, the house was rented out and eventually became a run-down boardinghouse. By the 1970s, it was barely saved from demolition and then painstakingly restored to its Victorian period of glamour.

The **Molly Brown House Museum** (1340 Pennsylvania St., 303/832-4092, www.mollybrown.org, 10am-3:30pm Tues.-Sat., noon-3:30 pm Sun., guided tours 10am-4pm Tues.-Fri., 10am-3:30pm Sat., noon-3:30pm Sun. in summer, $8 adults, $7 seniors, $5 children age 6-12, children under age 6 free) can only be viewed during guided tours, which are 30 minutes long and given on the hour and half hour. Visitors sign up for tours in the carriage house out back, which is also the museum's large gift shop, filled with books and movies about Molly Brown and other Victorian-era items. On the tours, visitors are led through the first floor, where rooms have been decorated to match photographs from when the Browns lived in the house. The tour then goes up to the second floor and back through the kitchen before ending on the home's back porch. Save time to watch a short movie about Molly Brown (included in the cost of the tour) and view artifacts on display on the porch.

Throughout her life, Molly Brown worked as a progressive social activist and was a tireless fundraiser and philanthropist. As visitors learn on the guided tours, the details of her full life are more than could be squeezed into a Broadway musical or Hollywood movie.

Tours do not include the home's third floor, but there are formal teas held there regularly. Check the website for details on annual teas such as the Harvest Tide Full Tea in the fall and the Mother's Day Full Tea in May. Note that you get a more comprehensive tour that includes interesting history about Molly Brown's life that isn't included on the tea and tour.

GREATER DENVER

★ Rocky Mountain Arsenal National Wildlife Refuge

It's an odd combination—nerve gas, natural beauty, and tourists—but somehow it works, and less than 15 miles from downtown, the **Rocky Mountain Arsenal National Wildlife Refuge** (Havana St. and E. 56th Ave., Commerce City, 303/289-0930, www.fws.gov/rockymountainarsenal, visitors center 9am-4pm Wed.-Sun., refuge 6am-6pm daily, tour times vary monthly, free) has become one of Denver's gems.

It's easy to spend the better part of a day at this oasis on a guided bus tour or walking through the miles of trails that traverse woodlands, wetlands, and prairie. Every season there is a chance to see some of the 300-plus species that call this place home, and it's become a destination for bird-watchers. Summer is the best time to see burrowing owls and Swainson's hawks, while fall brings an opportunity to see deer with their full antler racks. In winter, the bald eagles are more visible, and in spring, the migratory songbirds and pelicans fly in. At any time of the year, you might spy coyotes, raptors, prairie dogs, and a variety of waterfowl. Over 20 bison (which were brought from Montana in 2007) live at the refuge and can be easily seen on most tours.

As the name suggests, this was not always a wildlife refuge. In the 1940s, the U.S. Army took possession of family farms to create a 27-square-mile chemical weapons facility, Rocky Mountain Arsenal. Mustard gas and napalm were manufactured here before the site was used to make agricultural pesticides. While the center of the arsenal has been described as one of the most polluted square miles on Earth, the buffer zone has been attracting wildlife for decades; a 1989 *New York Times* headline about the Rocky Mountain Arsenal reads, "Nature Sows Life Where Man Brewed Death." In the 1990s, the 15,000-acre area was fenced in to protect wildlife and work began to turn the arsenal into a refuge. Optimists talk of how nature has triumphed here, while skeptics point out soil contamination concerns.

The arsenal is closed sporadically for months at a time for ongoing clean-up efforts and federal holidays.

★ Red Rocks Amphitheatre

Given its worldwide reputation as a premier outdoor concert venue, **Red Rocks Amphitheatre** (18300 W. Alameda Pkwy., Morrison, 303/697-4939, www.redrocksonline.com, 8am-7pm daily May-Sept., 9am-4pm daily Oct.-Apr.) hardly needs any introduction. The Beatles, U2, the Grateful Dead, and many more big names in music have played here over the years, even immortalizing the shows in concert movies. Red Rocks has a summer concert lineup that includes some annual events, such as Reggae on the Rocks and 1964: The Beatles Tribute Band, as well as whoever is touring that year, such as James Taylor or Florence & The Machine. Plan to come early on concert days to be able to park and walk around a bit.

Red Rocks is known for its phenomenal open-air acoustics and live concerts, but the scenery can be enjoyed here anytime, even without music. This nearly upright ring of red sandstone cliffs to the west of Denver is surprisingly close to the city and offers more than just great concerts. Depending on the weather, visitors can either choose a hiking trail around the red rocks, where wildlife such as deer can be seen wandering about, or check out the visitors center at the top of the amphitheater to see photos of previous concerts. This is also a popular place for mountain biking and cycling. On days when there are no shows scheduled, visitors are allowed to roam the amphitheater for free. There is no climbing allowed on the rocks anywhere in the park, however, as they can be slippery and fragile.

Greater Denver

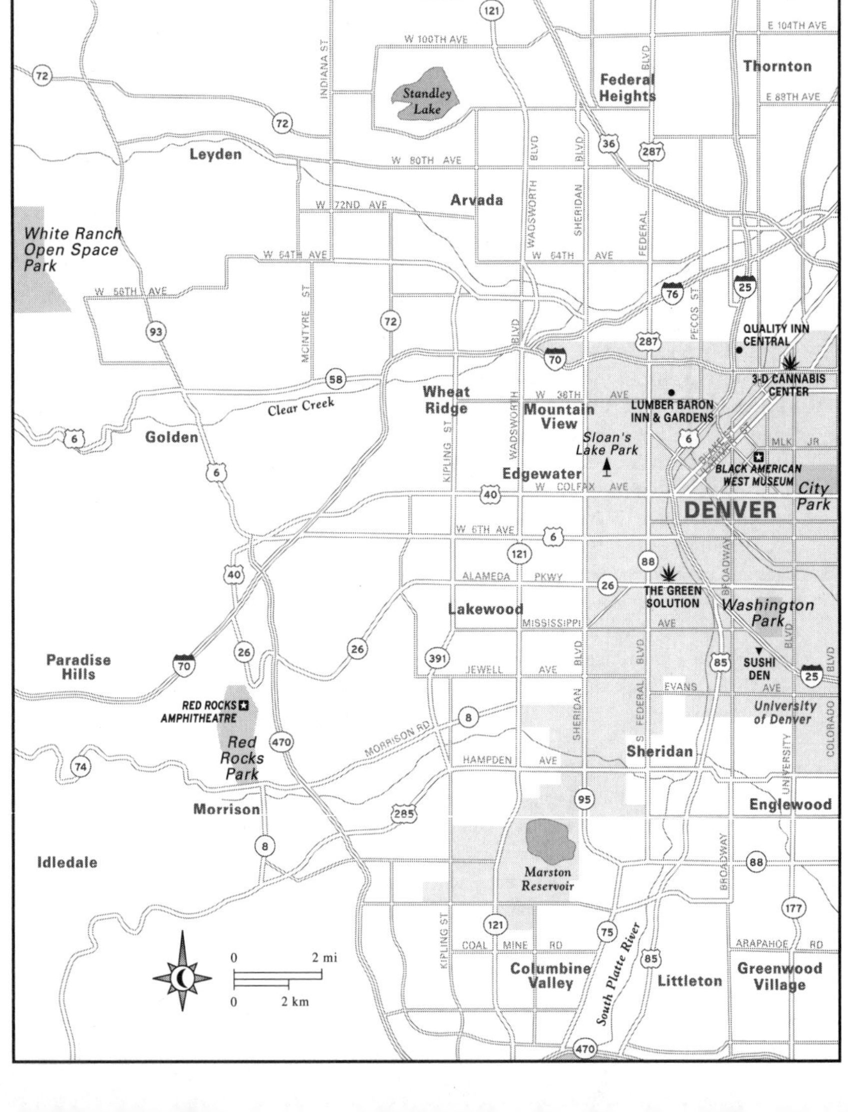

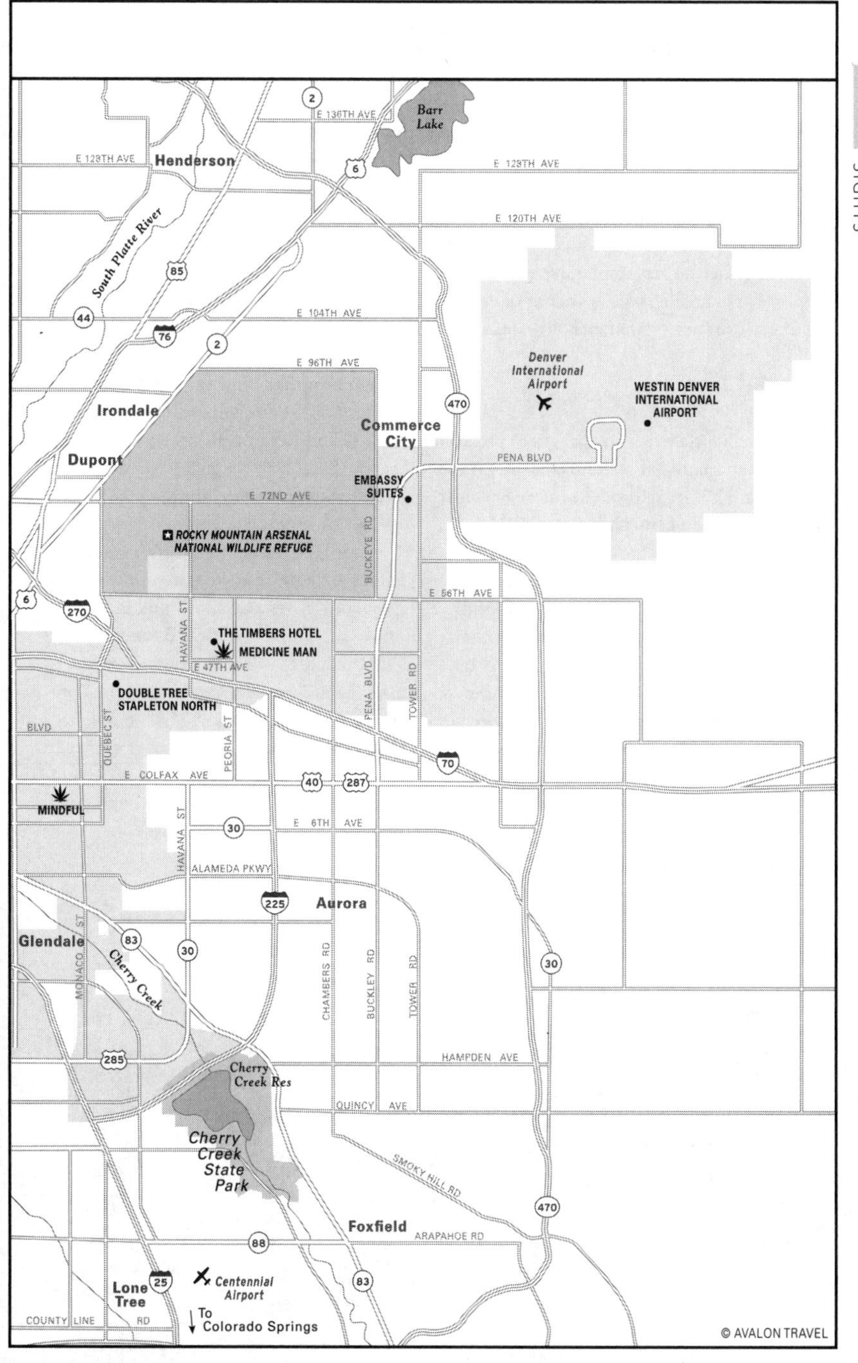

Barr Lake
E 136TH AVE
E 128TH AVE
Henderson
E 128TH AVE
E 120TH AVE
South Platte River
E 104TH AVE
E 96TH AVE
Denver International Airport
WESTIN DENVER INTERNATIONAL AIRPORT
Irondale
Commerce City
Dupont
PENA BLVD
EMBASSY SUITES
E 72ND AVE
ROCKY MOUNTAIN ARSENAL NATIONAL WILDLIFE REFUGE
BUCKEYE RD
E 56TH AVE
HAVANA ST
THE TIMBERS HOTEL
MEDICINE MAN
E 47TH AVE
DOUBLE TREE STAPLETON NORTH
PENA BLVD
TOWER RD
BLVD
QUEBEC ST
PEORIA ST
E COLFAX AVE
MINDFUL
E 6TH AVE
HAVANA ST
ALAMEDA PKWY
Aurora
Glendale
MONACO ST
Cherry Creek
CHAMBERS RD
BUCKLEY RD
TOWER RD
HAMPDEN AVE
Cherry Creek Res
QUINCY AVE
Cherry Creek State Park
SMOKY HILL RD
Foxfield
ARAPAHOE RD
Centennial Airport
Lone Tree
COUNTY LINE RD
To Colorado Springs

Entertainment and Events

NIGHTLIFE

Given that a saloon was reportedly Denver's first building, the city has long had a rich nightlife to offer and the options just keep growing. Whether it's for music, drinks, or dancing, Denver has impressive credentials. Most bars and clubs close at 2am or earlier, but you can find a few after-hours spots too.

Downtown

BARS

Since a 2006 state law was passed to prohibit smoking in bars and restaurants, about the only place it is legal to smoke inside is a cigar bar, such as the **Churchill Bar** (321 17th St., 303/297-3111, www.brownpalace.com, 11am-11pm daily) in the Brown Palace Hotel. The Churchill Bar has the feel of an old gentlemen's club, with large brown leather chairs in a quiet room tucked away from the bustle of the hotel lobby and other restaurants. They offer a selection of 60 cigars, as well as scotches, bourbons, and cocktails.

The Curtis Hotel is hooked on themes, and that includes the decor and everything else at its **Corner Office Restaurant and Martini Bar** (1401 Curtis St., 303/825-6500, www.thecornerofficedenver.com, 6am-close daily). The design is unabashedly 1970s, for better and worse, and beyond that, it's about the nine-to-five life. Every clock in the Corner Office is set to 5pm—time to leave the office for a drink. And some of the specialty cocktails and martinis carry on the concept with names like "Working Stiff" and "The Secretary." The bottom line is that the Corner Office is best for a drink after a night at the theater. If you're in the mood for something sweet, make sure to try the surprising desserts, such as the wispy cotton candy and the "psychedelic boat trip." Closing hours vary depending on how busy the restaurant is.

One of Denver phenom Frank Bonanno's handful of adored eateries, **Green Russell** (1422 Larimer St., 303/893-6505, www.greenrussell.com, 5pm-10:45pm Sun.-Mon., 5pm-11:45pm Tues.-Thurs., 5pm-12:45am Fri.-Sat.) is actually known more for its bar scene. To get here, you'll walk down a stairway in mid-Larimer Square to enter what looks like a

Red Rocks Amphitheatre

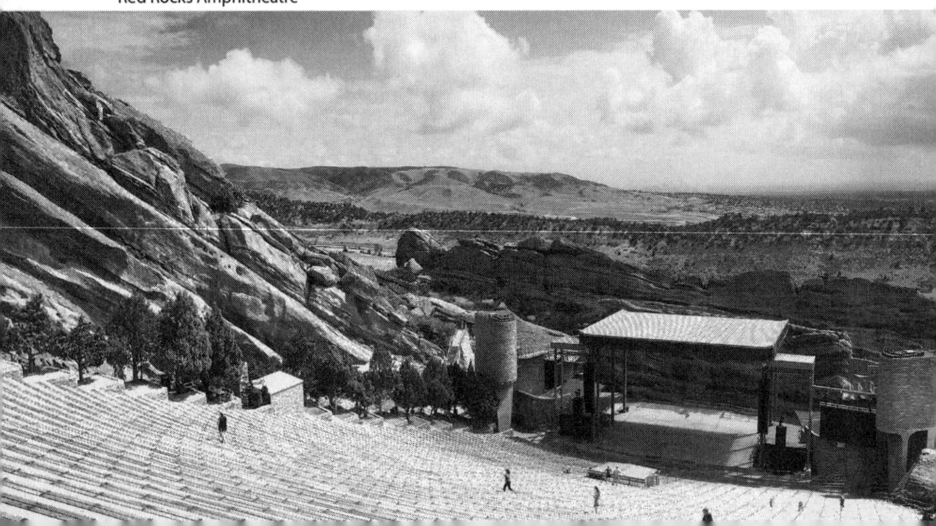

bakery. (It is. Wednesday's Pie is another gem by the same owner.) Upon being greeted by the host, it all clicks—this is a speakeasy. Lucky for you, there's no password other than trust in your bartender, who may feel free to concoct you something not on the menu. That's half the fun, although the listed cocktails are great, too.

On the edge of what has become known as the River North Arts District (or RiNo) is **The Matchbox** (2625 Larimer St., 720/437-9100, www.matchboxdenver.com, 4pm-2am Mon.-Fri., noon-2am Sat.-Sun.). The name was inspired in part by a fire that gutted the building in 2009. Now it's been reborn, with an open-air beer garden and bocce ball court out back, and a narrow but large interior with exposed brick that reveals a mural of historic signs. This is a place for drinking, not eating, but local food trucks make a stop on special nights.

BREWPUBS

No Denver neighborhood is complete without a craft brewery, and RiNo has **Our Mutual Friend Brewing Company** (2810 Larimer St., 720/722-2810, www.omftbeer.com, 4pm-10pm Tues.-Thurs., 2pm-midnight Fri.-Sat., 2pm-10pm Sun.). Stop in on Tuesday for "Keep the Glass" night (it's literal). In summer, step outside on the patio and sit on the bench while sipping your ale. There's no kitchen, but there is usually a food truck parked outside.

LIVE MUSIC

Jazz at Jack's (500 16th St., Ste. 320, 303/433-1000, www.jazzatjacks.com, 5pm-1am daily) is partly owned by local jazz band Dotsero, which performs at the club every Saturday night. On Tuesday, it's funk night; there is no cover for Sunday happy hour; and the rest of the week is filled in by a selection of well-known jazz artists on tour, such as Steve Cole, Dave Grusin, and many more. And you never know who might drop in and play with the band. To find Jack's, look for the neon saxophone in the Denver Pavilions on the 16th Street Mall. The name comes from the first location, which was on Platte Street in the old Jack's Carpet Warehouse building; this new spot is a big improvement over that cramped and hot room. Here there is ample seating and even a year-round patio.

Local music legend Lannie Garrett has found her groove with **Lannie's Clocktower Cabaret** (1601 Arapahoe St., 303/293-0075, http://lannies.com, 7pm-close) in the basement of the landmark D & F Clocktower on the 16th Street Mall. This purple, red, and gold room hosts a wide range of entertainers, including drag queens, burlesque performers, nationally known bands, and singers like Erica Brown in a variety of shows like Lannie's own long-running country-western spoof, "The Patsy DeCline Show." Every Tuesday night is open mike night, where anyone can come and show off their vaudeville talents.

A popular stop for indie bands, the **Larimer Lounge** (2721 Larimer St., 303/291-1007, www.larimerlounge.com, 4pm-2am Mon.-Fri., 6pm-2am Sat., call for Sun. hours) is a good blend of hip and gritty. The space is intimate, which can also mean pretty loud. Bands usually don't go on until about 9pm or later. Past shows here have included Thurston Moore, ManCub, So-Gnar, and many others.

If you like your live music up close and personal, almost as if you are getting a private concert in your basement, then welcome to **Meadowlark** (2701 Larimer St., 303/293-0251, www.meadowlarkbar.com, 4pm-2am Mon.-Fri., 6pm-2am Sat.-Sun.), a basement space of cellar proportions, but with stylish ambience. *Westword* has dubbed Meadowlark Denver's "best place to learn to be a rockstar," among other accolades. In summer an outdoor patio and performance space makes the bar twice as appealing (and twice the size). Rocker wannabes should be there for Open Stage Night on Tuesdays.

The **Mercury Cafe** (2199 California St., 303/294-9281, www.mercurycafe.com, 5:30pm-1am Tues.-Sun.) has a little something for everyone, depending on the night of the week. Their all-ages shows range from blues and swing to tango and acoustic, and dancing classes are offered as well. The entertainment doesn't stop with these specialty bands though—there's also "open stage" Wednesday for magicians, comics, and musicians, and poetry readings on Friday. The Mercury revels in its reputation as a "hippie" hangout for bohemian types, but anyone who enjoys dancing and live music will feel at home. Service can be spotty, so allow extra time for a night out here. No credit cards are accepted, but there is an ATM on-site.

If you're looking for a night on the town, consider **Nocturne Jazz & Supper Club** (1330 27th St., 303/295-3333, www.nocturne-jazz.com, 6pm-1am Mon.-Thurs., 6pm-1:45am Fri.-Sat.), located in the heart of Denver's up-and-coming RiNo district. You'll enter through an unassuming warehouse door between Larimer and Walnut and then find yourself in a renovated space that recalls old Hollywood glamour. Move beyond the velvet curtains, order a Manhattan at the bar, and find your seat while the musicians warm up. Stay for a bite and a drink, or plan ahead to enjoy a "Renditions" dinner—special five- to eight-course meals created to pair with the sounds of visiting jazz musicians. Come early to find parking, or plan to call a cab.

From the owners of Root Down and Linger, **Ophelia's Electric Soap Box** (1215 20th St., 303/993-8023, www.opheliasdenver.com, 4pm-close Tues.-Fri., 10am-2:30pm Sat.-Sun.) offers something especially unique in Denver—a "gastro-brothel." That's right: The Airedale building (which dates back to 1889) has been home to peep shows, an adult bookstore, and even a brothel. Now the space has been transformed into a modern restaurant (5pm-close Tues.-Sun.), bar, and live music venue, keeping hold of the swanky, retro vibe and artistic details that harken back to its more sinful days. Try the mussels, arepas, or a Greek lamb gyro salad as you check out naughty art on the wall or in a viewfinder. Catch live music most Thursdays, Fridays, and Saturdays (often with a $15 cover).

The historic **Roxy Theatre** (2549 Welton St., 720/429-9782, www.theroxydenver.com, 5:30pm-1am Tues.-Sun.) in the Five Points neighborhood has owners intent on making it a hip place once again. The 500-seat theater was once a movie house, and it has changed hands over the years in its life as a music venue. Although there is an emphasis on hip-hop music, there is a wider variety than that on the calendar. The history of the theater is explored down the street at the Blair-Caldwell African American Research Library.

Golden Triangle, Lincoln Park, and SoBo

BARS

I often hear people say that Denver would be perfect if it only had a beach. Good news! **Adrift** (218 S. Broadway, 303/778-8454, www.adriftbar.com, 5pm-close Mon.-Thurs., 2pm-close Fri.-Sat.) is Denver's tiki bar, with Polynesian island decor (puffer fish lanterns, for one thing), cocktails, staff attire, and menu. The drink names alone are worth a visit—there are the Zombie, Paralysis, and Painkiller, in addition to daiquiris and mai tais. The patios are perfect for playing beach "staycation" in the summer.

Wine on tap? That's kind of the idea at **The Living Room** (1055 Broadway, 303/339-6636, www.coclubs.com, 4pm-11pm Tues.-Thurs., 4pm-2am Fri.-Sat.), a wine bar on the fringe of the Golden Triangle neighborhood. An Enomatic machine allows you to sample up to two dozen wines by the ounce by simply pushing a button. The concept is similar to a copy machine: buy a $10 card, then each sample gets deducted from the total. They also have beer and small plates so you can lounge about in the booths. Check their calendar for various music and film nights.

Sputnik (3 S. Broadway, 720/570-4503, www.sputnikdenver.com, 10:30am-2am Mon.-Fri., 10am-2am Sat.-Sun.) is the satellite bar right next door to the concert venue Hi-Dive. Sputnik features DJs six nights a week, playing everything from 1960s garage rock to punk to the latest releases by bands that have played or will play at Hi-Dive. The bar also has a rather wild bingo night on Mondays. In addition to a menu of eclectic comfort food, Sputnik has a full espresso and liquor bar. The music and clientele match the Hi-Dive for the most part—loud, young, a bit grunge, and up for a very late night.

BREWPUBS

Pint's Pub (221 W. 13th Ave., 303/534-7543, www.pintspub.com, 11am-midnight Mon.-Sat., 11am-8pm Sun.) is a traditional British pub that screams that fact from the curbside with cheery, red, old-fashioned telephone booths and the flag of England flying (or emblazoned) on the sign. Just down the street from the Denver Art Museum and Byers-Evans House Museum, Pint's is a welcoming place to stop in for a pint and fish-and-chips for lunch or dinner. The pub is known for its cask-conditioned ales and single-malt whiskeys.

You know a neighborhood has reached a tipping point from up-and-coming to found when it gets its own brewery. Now the Santa Fe Arts District has the **Renegade Brewing Company** (925 W. 9th Ave., 720/401-4089, http://renegadebrewing.com, 2pm-10pm Mon.-Thurs., 1pm-11pm Fri., noon-10pm Sat., noon-9pm Sun.)—craft beer among the arts and crafts of the area. Renegade partners with local food truck vendors, so if you're hungry as well as thirsty, check the website to find out which truck is there on each day of the week.

With so much craft beer competition, a start-up has to stand out and **Former Future Brewing Company** (1290 S. Broadway, 303/441-4253, www.embracegoodtaste.com, 4pm-10pm Tues.-Thurs., 2pm-11pm Fri.-Sat., 2pm-8pm Sun.) does so with kooky flavors like Salted Caramel Porter or silly names like Gadabout. The decor is just as clever as the brews: tables made from reclaimed wood and a bar top made from repurposed airplane wings. They serve snacks here, or you can order from Maria's Empanadas next door.

Niche breweries are a thing now, and **TRVE Brewing Company** (227 Broadway #101, 303/351-1021, www.trvebrewing.com, 4pm-11pm Tues.-Thurs., 2pm-midnight Fri.-Sat., 2pm-10pm Sun.) is a heavy metal brewery, so get ready for some headbanging tunes to set the tone for your tasting. After finding the somewhat hidden entrance, the dark decor may be off-putting to some, but the bartenders are friendly and the beer is good.

You have to mean to end up at **Strange Craft Beer** (1330 Zuni St., 720/985-2337, www.strangecraft.com, 3pm-8pm Mon.-Thurs., noon-9pm Fri.-Sat., 1pm-6pm Sun.) as it's not quite in a pedestrian-friendly zone near much else of interest. However, it's worth the stop to see what they mean by "strange." Cherry, grapefruit, and watermelon are some of the highlights in the brews here. In summer, you can play horseshoes in their patio area and enjoy the evening outside.

LOUNGES

The **Funky Buddha Lounge** (776 Lincoln St., 303/832-5075, www.coclubs.com, 5pm-close Tues.-Sun.) has one of the best rooftop bars and lounges in Denver, with views of the Rocky Mountains and the city lights. The semi-enclosed space has limited heat, so it can be enjoyed even on chilly nights. Inside the narrow space, with leather booths on one side of the room and barstools on the other, the Funky Buddha can quickly become packed and loud. DJs play hip-hop and house music as the young, good-looking regulars mingle.

For something a bit more laid-back than the many dance clubs and live music venues along Broadway, step into **Milk** (1037 Broadway, 303/832-8628, www.coclubs.com, 9pm-2am Wed.-Sat.). Downstairs from Bar Standard, the pillow-festooned seating invites patrons to sit and sip while listening to DJs play everything from goth to 1980s to industrial music. Milk-white booths with sheer curtains allow a bit more privacy than the main room. The club attracts a young and trendy crowd.

GAY AND LESBIAN VENUES

Denver's antismoking laws led a staple of the gay and lesbian nightclub scene to significantly improve. The **Compound** (145

Broadway, 303/722-7977, www.compound-denver.com, 7am-2am daily) made Denver's antismoking laws work in their favor by adding a smoking patio out behind the building; they also expanded the dance floor as part of a $600,000 renovation. During the day, the club is a friendly bar; after 6pm on Wednesdays through Sundays, it is a wild dance party for mostly gay men and lesbian women (though not exclusively), with DJs playing the latest music. Compound's bartenders are also known for their generous pours on all drinks.

DANCE CLUBS

What sets **Bar Standard** (1037 Broadway, 303/832-8628, www.coclubs.com, 9pm-2am Fri.-Sat.) apart from many Denver clubs is its retro art deco decor and ambience. The music is Afropop, indie-electric, house, and "nujazz," with different themes and guest DJs each night, as well as burlesque dancers. While the music and dancing are great at Bar Standard, comfy booths and a reasonable volume make this a place for chatting with friends and hanging out for the evening. This is a 21-and-over club.

The name of this Denver nightclub is literal: **The Church** (1160 Lincoln St., 303/832-2383, www.coclubs.com, Thurs.-Sun. 9pm-2am, no cover) is a beautiful historic church that has been transformed into a nightclub that highlights the original architecture with colorful lights illuminating the Gothic windows and immense ceilings. The Church has three dance floors, each with different reverberating dance music, along with several bars scattered throughout three floors and a sushi bar. The Church is a bit of a singles scene for young urban professionals, but fun for anyone in the mood to dance.

This local institution for salsa dancing has a loyal fan base because it offers dependable music from both DJs and live salsa bands rocking the house. You don't have to be a pro—**La Rumba** (99 W. 9th Ave., 303/572-8006, www.larumbam-denver.com, 9pm-2am Thurs.-Sat.) is for rookie salsa dancers as well as the experts. It's all about sensuous dancing to beautiful and fun music.

LIVE MUSIC

Consistently chosen as a Denver favorite for jazz in local surveys and by music magazines, **Dazzle Restaurant and Lounge** (930 Lincoln St., 303/839-5100, www.dazzlejazz.com, 4pm-2am Mon.-Thurs. and Sat., 11am-2am Fri., 9:30am-2am Sun.) offers live music nightly from local, national, and international musicians. Dazzle has two rooms, the Dazzle Showroom and the Dizzy Room, each featuring a different band or event every night of the week. The lineup changes daily here—one night might be a mix of Latin jazz, the next night a CD release party, followed by torch singers—and each act is locally or nationally recognized. There are jazz brunches on Sundays, a Friday Lunch Club, and happy hour and dinner are nightly.

Since 2004, **Hi-Dive** (7 S. Broadway, 720/570-4500, www.hi-dive.com, 8pm or 9pm to 2am) has been one of Denver's best punk and indie rock dive bars to see bands like the Thermals, Why?, the Ya-Ya's, and many more nationally known and local acts. The venue holds fewer than 300 people, so it gets packed quickly for the really popular shows. Hi-Dive offers both 16-and-over and 21-and-over shows about five nights a week. The club is connected to Sputnik, where they serve food and drinks.

Rockabilly and honky-tonk music dominate weekends at the **Skylark Lounge** (140 S. Broadway, 303/722-7844, www.skylark-lounge.com, 4pm-2am Mon.-Fri., 2pm-2am Sat.-Sun.). The Skylark has been around since 1943, but it was relocated to the current location in the 1990s. Still, the Skylark has a 1950s vibe with a yellow-and-black-tiled dance floor, a jukebox, and pool tables. Downstairs is where bands play on weekends, and the occasional Thursday night as well; upstairs is a bit quieter for conversation and games like shuffleboard and pinball. This is a 21-and-over club.

Along the bar and restaurant strip of South

Broadway that has grown significantly in recent years, **3 Kings Tavern** (60 S. Broadway, 303/777-7352, www.3kingstavern.com, 5pm-2am daily) stands out with its mix of live country, rock, blues, and punk rock on weekends and DJs on weeknights. Before the shows start or for a diversion from the music, 3 Kings also has several pool tables, pinball, and video games. This is a 21-and-over club.

LoDo and Platte River Valley

BARS

Denver's only champagne bar offers a small-plates menu to complement the selection of bubbly. Located in historic Larimer Square next to Rioja, **Corridor 44** (1433 Larimer St., 303/893-0044, www.corridor44.com, 4pm-2am daily) is cleverly named after the 44-foot-long hallway that links the bustling front bar to the more intimate dining room in the rear. The small plates range from oyster shooters to mini-sandwiches and salads to a caviar tasting plate. Champagnes are available by the glass or full or half bottle.

Step back in time to the 1930s in the pink-hued, art deco **Cruise Room** (1600 17th St., 303/825-1107, www.theoxfordhotel.com, 4:30pm-11:45pm Sun.-Thurs., 4:30pm-12:45am Fri.-Sat.), on the first floor of the historic Oxford Hotel in LoDo. It's hard to get up and leave the Cruise Room once you've settled into one of their cushy booths and ordered a few of their fabulous martinis from the excellent bartenders. The Cruise Room, which opened the day after Prohibition ended in 1933, is modeled after a cruise ship lounge on the *Queen Mary*. The bar is great for a romantic date night or just a casual night out for drinks with friends.

When I first heard of **Fluff Bar** (1516 Wazee St., 720/295-3583, http://fluffbar.com, 11am-11pm Tues.-Thurs., 11am-2am Fri.-Sat., noon-7pm Sun.), I could not imagine gaily drinking while allowing someone to cut my hair. I've since been set straight; people primarily come here to have their hair styled more than cut (though cuts and colors are also on the menu). And it's not just about fluffing up one's hair—you can also get a shave (gentlemen), brows contoured, and makeup done, all while sipping on a "Spam-tini," a "Fluff-arita," or simply a glass of champagne.

In the heart of LoDo, **Freshcraft** (1530 Blake St., 303/758-9608, www.freshcraft.com, 11am-midnight Mon.-Thurs., 11am-2am Fri.-Sat., 11am-midnight Sun.) serves upscale comfort food in a buzzing urban bar setting. Guests socialize over food, beer, and spirits during a quick lunch, relaxing dinner, happy hour (3pm-7pm daily), or late-night snack. Fresh quality ingredients take center stage in craveable items like the Whiskey Barbecue Chicken and the Turkey Pretzel Baja. With 20 taps and 100 bottled options, there's a beer for everyone. Not into beer? The signature cocktails are no slouch, either.

In the mix with LoDo's mega sports bars and brewpubs, all walking distance from Coors Field, is **Herb's Hideout** (2057 Larimer St., 303/299-9555, www.herbsbar.com, 7pm-2am Mon.-Thurs., 5pm-2am Fri.-Sat., 3pm-2am Sun., $5 Fri.-Sat. after 10pm), a classic drinking bar. The result of location and history is an intriguing mix of committed barflies and hipsters either lost or looking for something off the beaten track. There is live jazz and blues music at Herb's every night of the week. Reasonable prices, decent barbecue, and friendly bartenders keep people coming back for more. The sign outside reads "Herb's," but locals know it as Herb's Hideout.

My Brother's Bar (2376 15th St., 303/455-9991, 11am-2am Mon.-Sat.) is best known for being a one-time hangout of writer Jack Kerouac's Denver buddy, Neal Cassady, a well-known barfly. It is one of Denver's oldest bars, and not much seems to change here year after year. The patio out back is a great place to spend a summer evening drinking a cold beer before or after a football or baseball game nearby. The main menu item here is the hamburgers, but also try the vegetarian Nina (a cheese sandwich named after a former waitress). Brother's does not have any kind of sign out front, but you can't miss it: It's right on the corner of Platte and 15th Streets, and there is always classical music playing on its outdoor speakers.

Games and drinking go together like salt and pepper, yet **The 1Up** (1925 Blake St., 303/779-6444, www.the-1up.com, 3pm-2am Mon.-Thurs., 11am-2am Fri.-Sat. Oct.-Mar.; 11am-2am daily Apr.-Sept.) is a fairly unique concept for Denver: Classic arcade games such as Pac-Man, Donkey Kong, Tron, and lots more line the walls, and there are also pinball machines, Skee-Ball, and Giant Jenga to play while drinking beer or cocktails. To complete the time-machine feel, hit the jukebox for some classic tunes.

BREWPUBS

Beer lovers are not just limited to Denver; many towns throughout Colorado have spawned terrific brewpubs of their own. **Breckenridge Brewery** (2220 Blake St., 303/297-3644, www.breckbrew.com, 11am-midnight Sun.-Thurs., 11am-1am Fri.-Sat.) became a staple of its namesake town before adding another location near the ballpark in LoDo. This immense space offers basic pub food and handcrafted ales. It is a favorite on Colorado Rockies game days, and there are numerous TVs showing sports at any time of year.

The **Celtic Tavern** (1801-1805 Blake St., 303/308-1795, www.celtictavern.com, 11am-midnight Mon.-Fri., 5pm-2am Sat., 5pm-midnight Sun.) is that rare Irish pub that does not serve Guinness. Instead, the bartenders pour Murphy's Irish Stout, which is brewed in Ireland, and a long list of other beers brewed nowhere near Ireland. The tavern also has an impressive selection of single-malt scotch and whiskeys. The scene here is a mix of regulars who enjoy the leather easy chairs and volumes of books, and LoDo barhoppers.

Part of what seems like the Celtic Tavern compound is **Delaney's Bar** (1801-1805 Blake St., 303/308-1795, www.theceltictavern.com, 11am-midnight Mon.-Fri., 5pm-2am Sat., 5pm-midnight Sun.), a cigar bar with an ambience separate from the Celtic. There is dark wood, exposed brick, and, in private rooms, comfy upholstered chairs in which to spend time leisurely smoking, drinking, or perhaps browsing through a book while enjoying the fireplace. This claims to be "the only place in North America" where you can smoke a cigar *and* go bowling. It's a full-service bar with a full menu, plus a selection of whiskeys and other drinks.

The **Denver Beer Company** (1695 Platte St., 303/433-2739, http://denverbeerco.com, 3pm-11pm Mon.-Thurs., noon-midnight Fri.-Sat., noon-9pm Sun.) has a bit of the essence of some guys coming up with new brews in their garage—just like the founders once did. The beers here change seasonally, and this constant reinvention has led to some award-winning brews. As a result, this is the place to try something new, not necessarily tried and true.

Beer aficionados are repeat customers at the **Falling Rock Tap House** (1919 Blake St., 303/293-8338, www.fallingrocktaphouse.com, 11am-2am daily), one block from Coors Field. There are about 70 local, national, and international beers on tap to sample here, as well as some bottled brews. This bar is the favorite hangout during the annual Great American Beer Festival in October. There are billiard tables and dartboards for fun and games. While this is a friendly bar, it's not really a place for the family to come after a game.

At the **Great Divide Brewing Company** (2201 Arapahoe St., 303/296-9460, www.greatdivide.com, 2pm-8pm Sun.-Tues., 2pm-10pm Wed.-Sat.), beer is celebrated, not just consumed. Choose between seasonal, year-round, or barrel-aged brews. Plan to come for a beer-and-cheese pairing night, a "Hop Disciples" night to discuss "all things beer related," or take a tour of the place. Don't forget to shop! They have clothing and bottle openers adorned with the company logo, and, of course, beer to go.

Looking for a bar atmosphere downtown? **Mile High Spirits** (2201 Lawrence St., 303/296-2226, www.drinkmilehighspirits.com, 3pm-midnight Mon.-Wed., 3pm-2am Thurs.-Fri., 11am-2am Sat.-Sun.)—a distillery and bar combined—is worth a shot. With a giant outdoor patio, distillery tours, and award-winning spirits to its name, Mile High Spirits offers something more than the typical bar experience. Try the Punching Mule—a Moscow mule in a can.

In the midst of the swanky nightclubs and lounges of LoDo is a comfy pub with the feel of a neighborhood bar. The barstools are the best seats in the house at the **Pourhouse Pub** (1435 Market St., 303/623-7687, www.pourhousepubdenver.com, 2pm-2am Mon.-Fri., noon-2am Sat.-Sun.), but also check out the heated roof deck, a great spot year-round. The music at Pourhouse does not drown out conversations, and the bartenders are friendly and fun to talk to. While not a typical sports bar, Pourhouse does have TVs tuned to sports channels.

Coors didn't just put their name on the Colorado Rockies' home field, they also set up a brewery and restaurant at Coors Field. **Sandlot Brewery** (2161 Blake St., 303/298-1587)—or Blue Moon Brewery at Sandlot, as it is also called—features the Coors Brewing Company's Blue Moon label and other award-winning beers. The atmosphere at Sandlot is family-friendly, with a kids' menu, too. The brewery is only open on Colorado Rockies game days and a ticket is required for access.

Denver's first brewpub remains one of the city's favorites. At the corner of 18th and Wynkoop Streets, the **Wynkoop Brewing Company** (1634 18th St., 303/297-2700, www.wynkoop.com, 11am-2am daily) was one of the pioneer businesses in transforming the LoDo neighborhood. One of the cofounders of the Wynkoop is John Hickenlooper, Colorado's governor. The brewery offers free tours (Sat.) to watch its signature line of beers be made on-site. On the first floor of this historic mercantile building is the main bar and restaurant with a traditional pub menu and patio seating. The second floor has a bar, 22 pool tables, and a few dart lanes.

Just a couple of blocks from Coors Field, the cavernous **Breckenridge Colorado Craft** (2220 Blake St., 303/297-3644, www.breckbrew.com, 11am-10pm Mon.-Fri., 11am-11pm Sat.-Sun., $10-20) can hold most of the baseball crowd on a warm summer night. With five Colorado locations under various names, Breckenridge Brewery offers beers that are unique to each location or the season, such as Ball Park Brown and 2220 Red at this Denver location, or the Summerbright Ale served only during summer months. Avalanche Ale is their most popular brew year-round. The menu is typical brewpub fare,

the Denver Beer Company

but look for items mixed with the brew itself, such as the Southwestern green chile made with Avalanche Ale.

LOUNGES

With Tim Burton-esque decor in dimly lit reds, blacks, and purples, **Mario's Double Daughter's Salotto** (1632 Market St., 303/623-3505, www.doubledaughters.com, 5pm-2am daily) is typically described as LoDo's only "goth" bar. Named after fictitious conjoined twins, the Double Daughter's Salotto embraces all things freakish, with drinks named "Six-Toed Kitten" and "Rabid Monkey." There is always a DJ playing the best hip-hop and electronica music, and excellent pizza is available from Two-Fisted Mario's Pizzeria next door. The crowd is a mix of young and old, tattooed and buttoned-up, and it can be hard to snag one of their curvy red booths on a busy weekend night.

The **Ninth Door** (1808 Blake St., 303/292-2229, www.theninthdoor.com, 4:30pm-close Mon.-Fri., 5pm-close Sat.-Sun.) brings some unique ideas to Denver's bar and restaurant scene: The emphasis here is on Spain and South America in decor, food, and wine. The wine list—with sparkling wines, whites, and reds all from Spain, Argentina, Chile, and Portugal—changes seasonally. The menu includes true Spanish tapas and paella, which can be served at the community table made from old Spanish doors. The name is a reference to a bar favored by expatriate writers in a Spanish town. On Tuesday nights there is live flamenco guitar music and on weekends there is a DJ.

GAY AND LESBIAN VENUES

In the 1980s, **Tracks** (3500 Walnut St., 303/863-7326, www.tracksdenver.com, 9pm-2am Thurs.-Sat., 8pm-2am Sun., women only 9pm-2am first Fri. of the month, $5-7) was Denver's premier gay and lesbian nightclub, where a mixed crowd mingled for sweaty, fun-filled nights on the dance floor. But when the land was sold in 2001 to make way for new development along the old railroad tracks, the club was shuttered. In June 2005, Tracks reopened in a new location and resumed its status as one of the city's best dance clubs for all. On Thursday night, the club is open to those 18 and over, and on Saturday nights, it is 21 and up only.

DANCE CLUBS

Denver's world-class nightclub is **Beta** (1909 Blake St., 303/383-1909, www.betanightclub.

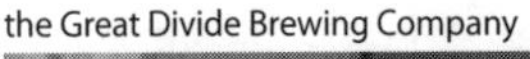
the Great Divide Brewing Company

com, hours vary Thurs.-Sat.), which has been recognized by *DJ Mag* and *Rolling Stone* as one of the top nightclubs in the country. Both local and internationally known DJs have played here, including Steve Bug, Modeselektor, Danny Tenaglia, Wyatt Earp, and DJ Foxx. Within Beta is the **Beatport Lounge**, a separate club with its own Funktion One sound system (the main floor has one, too). The patio area is more of a lush summer garden with abundant flowers and grass. But the grass isn't the only thing green at Beta: The club was designed with environmental awareness and features acoustic panels made from recycled blue jeans.

Chloe Discotheque (1445 Market St., 720/383-8447, www.lotusclubs.com/chloe, 8pm-2am Wed.-Sat.) is three things: a restaurant, a garden patio, and a disco. Come for drinks, enjoy some dinner, and then end the night dancing. The vibe here is designed to attract celebrities, scenesters, and others who "dress to impress" on a night out. (In other words, leave your sports-bar look and attitude at home.) Chloe has a reputation for special event nights, such as a sexy Halloween weekend.

If you are in LoDo and not in the mood for the typical dance club, try the **Cowboy Lounge** (1941 Market St., 303/226-1570, www.tavernhg.com/cowboy_lounge, 8pm-2am Thurs.-Sat., $5, free Thurs.) for some country-and-western tunes and traditional dancing on the spacious dance floor. On Thursdays, ladies get in free and enjoy drink specials. A large patio out front with tables and chairs is perfect for smokers and those needing to cool off after dancing. Private parties here can pull out all the Western stops, with two-step and line dancing lessons, a mechanical bull, a shoot-out game, and lots of other clichés that make the night memorable.

LIVE MUSIC

Once on the edge of downtown in a seedy locale, **El Chapultepec** (1962 Market St., 303/295-9126, http://thepeclodo.com, 11am-1am daily, music starts at 9pm nightly, $2 cover Fri.-Sat.) hasn't bothered to change its appearance since the neighborhood has developed a thriving nightlife scene near Coors Field. That gritty, dive-bar quality is part of the appeal, though. Note this is a cash-only bar—no credit cards. Stop in for a cold beer and a burrito at the bar anytime, or come by later to hear local jazz musicians and even some jazz greats play nightly. Opened in 1951, El Chapultepec has hosted Tony Bennett, Frank Sinatra, and even the Rolling Stones.

Awarded "Best Sound System" in 2015 by *Westword* magazine, the **Summit Music Hall** (1902 Blake St., 303/487-0111, www.thesummitmusichall.com, box office 11am-5pm Mon.-Fri. on show night) is a 12,500-square-foot space for punk, metal, hip-hop, and industrial music shows. When the former dance club isn't filled up with concertgoers for these big acts, the venue can shrink to host local bands still building an audience. Many of the shows here are all ages, but some are for 18 and over only. You never know who might be playing here—The Charlie Daniels Band? Check. Collective Soul? Check. Suicide Girls Blackheart Burlesque? Them too. All shows are general admission.

Capitol Hill and City Park

BARS

Don's Club Tavern (723 E. 6th Ave., 303/831-0218, www.donsclubtavern.com, 2pm-2am Mon.-Fri., 11am-2am Sat.-Sun.) has been around since 1947, and nobody wants it to change. It is routinely named the city's best dive bar for its simple qualities: a few pool tables, worn-out booths, threadbare carpet, and beer and cocktails without pretension.

The hundreds of tequilas to choose from at **Mezcal** (3230 E. Colfax Ave., 303/322-5219, www.mezcalcolorado.com, 3pm-1am daily, 10am-2pm Sat.-Sun. brunch) make it the place to come for margaritas or shots. The place is done up in a Mexican movie madness theme, with posters of bodacious Latinas on the walls and Mexican church candles flickering. Across the street from the Bluebird Theater, Mezcal attracts concertgoers as well as neighborhood locals. Check their calendar for the annual taco-eating contest and for live music nights. Note that there is both an early *and* late happy hour here. Parking can be very limited on nearby side streets and along Colfax Avenue.

Think back to a time when drinking was not almost universally accepted and celebrated, but unlawful and unacceptable—a time of prohibition. At **Prohibition** (504 E. Colfax Ave., 303/832-4840, www.prohibition-denver.com, 4pm-2am Mon.-Tues., 11am-2am Wed.-Fri., 11am-2am Sat., 10am-2am Sun.) in the Capitol Hill neighborhood, prohibition seems kind of stylish, with an ancient bar anchoring the refurbished space that includes banquettes and tables with framed, vintage newspaper headlines about the real time of Prohibition. Some cocktails of the era are even served in tin cups. The food is a mix of burgers, salads, pot pie, and bar snacks. In this still-rough patch of Colfax Avenue, Prohibition is aiming for a more upscale and trendy crowd.

This neighborhood dive has a rich history in the neighborhood. Before it was **Vesper** (233 E. 7th Ave., 720/328-0314, www.vesperdenver.com, 4pm-close Mon.-Fri., 2pm-close Sat.-Sun.), it drew locals to its watering hole for years. Now this Frank Bonanno gem—sandwiched between the acclaimed chef's Bones and Mizuna—serves up surprisingly great Greek-style pub food alongside cocktails on tap. Sit at the bar, in a booth, or at one of the low tables, and share a trio of hummus dips with your pals. If you're really hungry, order a Colorado shaved lamb gyro. And for the full experience, sip a house vesper cocktail, based on James Bond's signature martini.

This narrow bar with dark red lighting is a decent place to start an evening or grab a drink while waiting for a table at a nearby restaurant. The only drawback to **The Thin Man** (2015 E. 17th Ave., 303/320-7814, www.thinmantavern.com, 3pm-2am daily) is its success as the anti-LoDo place to be—it can be challenging to find a barstool or table in the packed bar, especially on a weekend, and it's also very loud. But the terrific bartenders and tasty appetizers keep regulars happily squeezed in.

BREWPUBS

Like football? A lot? For lovers of world football (according to this bar's website, there are more than six billion such fans), **The Three Lions** (2239 E. Colfax Ave., 303/997-6886, www.threelionsdenver.com, 11am-2am Mon.-Fri., 9am-2am Sat.-Sun.) is a place to watch, cheer, and drink. The fare here is American-style pub food, with chicken wings on the menu alongside fish and chips; wash it down with local or European ales. The theme here is to embrace the British way of things in as many ways as possible.

GAY AND LESBIAN VENUES

Before there was *Brokeback Mountain*, there were many gay cowboys and cowgirls looking for a dance partner, even in the wilds of Denver. **Charlie's** (900 E. Colfax Ave., 303/839-8890, www.charliesdenver.com, 11am-2am daily) in Capitol Hill is the city's gay and lesbian country-and-western dance club. There are free dance lessons, and for those not into the country scene, a separate dance floor with a DJ playing house and disco music creates a different vibe. Charlie's is the home of the Colorado Gay Rodeo Association.

LIVE MUSIC

The **Bluebird Theater** (3317 E. Colfax Ave., 303/377-1666, www.bluebirdtheater.net) was originally built in 1913 and used as a movie house. After many incarnations and a bit of neglect, it was turned into one of Denver's most popular concert venues in 1994. All shows at the Bluebird are 16 and over, though anyone under 21 is restricted to the balcony during a concert while alcohol is served on another level. There is a wide range of acts that play at the Bluebird—from Shelby Lynne to Oasis to Slim Cessna's Auto Club to less well-known groups still getting their start.

This hole-in-the-wall is a great little place

to stop in for a cold beer, with no worries about style or who's who. Live music at the **Lion's Lair** (2022 E. Colfax Ave., 303/320-9200, 3pm-2am Mon.-Fri., 2pm-2am Sat.-Sun.) can be extremely loud, with the band right in the center of the small room. The bands tend to be punk and hard rock, and sometimes alt-rock. Drinks are always reasonably priced, and seating at the bar is the best in the house.

HIGHLANDS

BARS

Not willing to settle for having one of Denver's best French restaurants, if not *the* best, Patrick DuPays opened **À Côté** (2245 W. 30th Ave., 303/477-1111, www.zcuisineonline.com, 5pm-10pm Tues., 5pm-midnight Wed.-Sat.), a Parisian wine bar, two doors down from Z Cuisine. Just like the restaurant, the bar was an instant success. Both places have the feel of a true bistro—small, warm, personable, simple, and fresh—and feature art and fixtures made by local artisans (don't miss the chandeliers by Tracey Barnes). The bar also offers the same French fare found at Z.

At the place where the Highlands neighborhood begins on 15th Street is **Forest Room 5** (2532 15th St., 303/433-7001, www.forestroom5.com, 4:30pm-2am Mon.-Sat.), where patio seats offer a view of the city lights. With flickering candles and large windows in the front room, Forest Room 5 is a hip little neighborhood bar that offers more than a few drinks and tapas. Forest Room 5's back room features dance music and is perfect for private parties.

Past the busy sushi chefs working near the entrance of Sushi Hai and past diners seated on black leather banquettes, stairs lead to the **Hai Bar** (3600 W. 32nd Ave., Ste. D, 720/855-0888, www.sushihai.com, 8pm-1am Wed.-Sun.), a cool underground room with exposed rock walls and mellow lighting. Named in reference to its home, the Highlands (Hai-lands, get it?), the Hai Bar is an inviting place for late-night sushi and specialty martinis and sake. Kick back and watch some TV or a pool game from the cushy lounge seating. The sushi bar serves until midnight and happy hour begins at 10pm.

Tennyson Street is being revitalized, and that means new businesses are bringing spark to the neighborhood's commercial strip. **Local 46** (94586 Tennyson St., 720/524-3792, www.local46bar.com, 3pm-2am Mon.-Thurs., 2pm-2am Fri., noon-2am Sat.-Sun.) opened in 2012 in a building that has been a beauty salon, a convenience store, and, more recently, the Music Bar (until rent shot up with the revitalization underway). Check the entertainment page of Local 46's website to find out if it's karaoke night, game night, a battle of the bands, open mike, or some other live music playing.

While **Lola** (1575 Boulder St., 720/570-8686, www.loladenver.com, 5pm-close daily, 10am-2pm Sun. brunch) is a Mexican restaurant, what it's really known for is its bar and, specifically, its tequila selection. Judging by the almost daily overflow crowds on the outdoor patio, people come here to drink together. It's happy hour at Lola all night on Mondays, from 4pm to 6pm Tuesdays through Fridays, and 2:30pm-5pm on Saturdays and Sundays. There is also live music on Sunday.

Patsy's Inn Italian Restaurant (3651 Navajo St., 303/477-8910, www.patsysinn.com, 11am-9pm Mon.-Thurs., 11am-10pm Fri., 5pm-9:30pm Sat., 4pm-8pm Sun.) is a throwback to the neighborhood's days as an Italian immigrant enclave. The bar and restaurant were opened in 1921, and not much has changed at Patsy's in that time, from menu to decor (the murals of the old country are charming). But the block has changed to include a handful of art galleries, making Patsy's the perfect place to have a drink and discuss art before or after cruising the latest gallery openings. The drinks and good food are very reasonably priced.

It's a bar! It's an art gallery! It's a recording studio! It's **Tennyson's Tap** (4335 W. 38th Ave., 303/455-4269, www.tennysonstap.com, 6pm-2am Mon.-Fri., 11am-2am Sat.- Sun.), where what's on tap is Colorado

Highlands

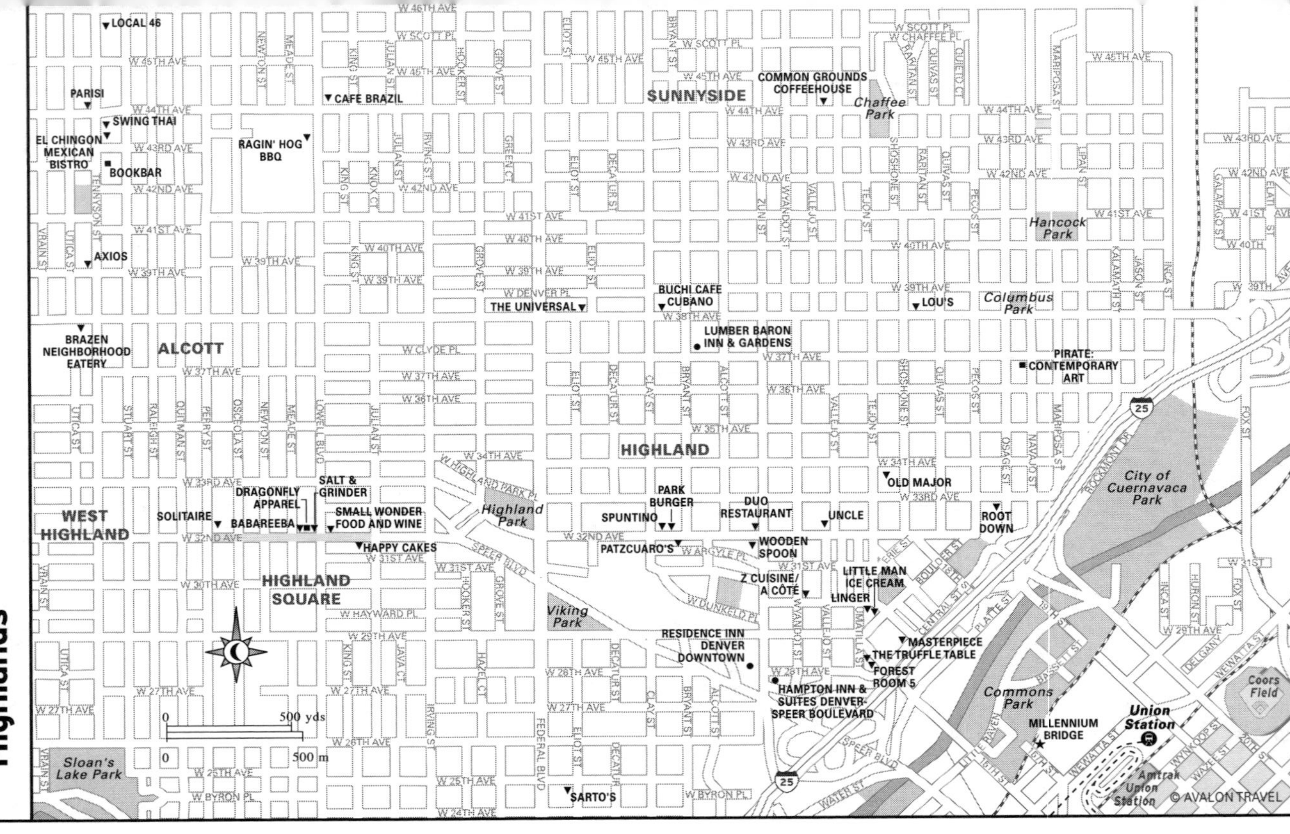
LOCAL 46
PARISI
SWING THAI
EL CHINGON MEXICAN BISTRO
BOOKBAR
AXIOS
BRAZEN NEIGHBORHOOD EATERY
WEST HIGHLAND
ALCOTT
RAGIN' HOG BBQ
CAFE BRAZIL
SOLITAIRE
BABAREEBA
DRAGONFLY APPAREL
SALT & GRINDER
SMALL WONDER FOOD AND WINE
HAPPY CAKES
HIGHLAND SQUARE
Sloan's Lake Park
Highland Park
Viking Park
THE UNIVERSAL
SUNNYSIDE
SARTO'S
SPUNTINO
PATZCUARO'S
PARK BURGER
HIGHLAND
BUCHI CAFE CUBANO
LUMBER BARON INN & GARDENS
RESIDENCE INN DENVER DOWNTOWN
DUO RESTAURANT
WOODEN SPOON
Z CUISINE/ A COTE
COMMON GROUNDS COFFEEHOUSE
HAMPTON INN & SUITES DENVER-SPEER BOULEVARD
UNCLE
LITTLE MAN ICE CREAM
LINGER
Chaffee Park
FOREST ROOM 5
THE TRUFFLE TABLE
MASTERPIECE
OLD MAJOR
LOU'S
ROOT DOWN
Columbus Park
Commons Park
MILLENNIUM BRIDGE
PIRATE: CONTEMPORARY ART
Hancock Park
City of Cuernavaca Park
Union Station
Amtrak Union Station
Coors Field
500 yds
500 m
© AVALON TRAVEL

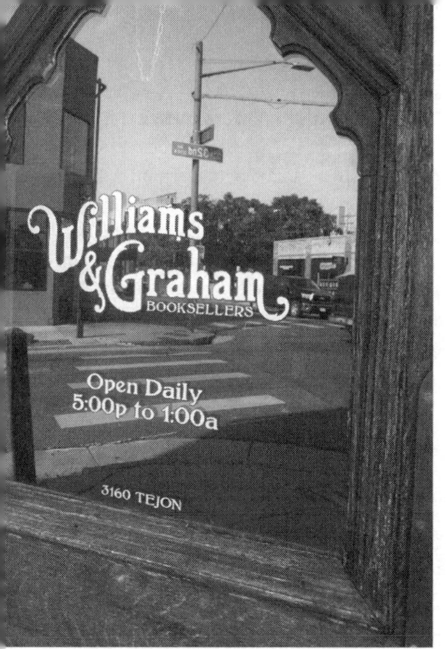

Behind this misleading door is a nationally recognized speakeasy.

spirits and brews. Patrons can come in and drink Stranahan's Colorado Whiskey, Zebra Vodka, and Left Hand Milk Stout or some other Colorado-made beer, all while listening to local musicians who specialize in jazz, blues, funk, and rock. There is also a comedy night.

People have not been this excited about a speakeasy since there were, well, speakeasies. Praised by *Esquire* and named the best cocktail bar in America at the Spirited Awards in 2015, **Williams & Graham** (3160 Tejon St., 303/997-8886, www.williamsandgraham.com, 5pm-1am daily) was quickly welcomed by Highlands locals for its unique faux-bookstore entrance, which cleverly hides the bar behind a velvet curtain. Staff members are dressed for the era in 1920s garb, but it's not costumey. The extensive liquor selection and tasty small plates have led this bar to the top of many lists. Reservations are recommended.

Down what used to be a working alley is the art deco **Zio Romolo's Alley Bar** (2400 W. 32nd Ave., 303/477-0395, www.pasquinis.com, 4pm-midnight Mon.-Thurs., 4pm-2am Fri., 11am-2am Sat., 11am-midnight Sun.). The bar includes an "exterior" wall with the original Coca-Cola sign painted on it. The 1950s-style neon signs and pressed-tin ceiling make Zio Romolo's a place to see as well as stop for a drink. Located in the evolving LoHi section of Highlands, Zio's is a friendly place for both locals and tourists.

BREWPUBS

Amato's Ale House (2501 16th St., 303/433-9734, http://alehousedenver.com, 11am-midnight Sun.-Thurs., 11am-1am Fri.-Sat., $11-24), one of the Breckenridge Brewery restaurants, serves more than 42 craft beers on tap that change daily. Amato's has developed a steady stream of regulars since opening in 2010, with a menu of salads, burgers, and generous appetizers that can fill you up before the entrée arrives. Parking is a challenge here, so take advantage of the restaurant's location next to the 16th Street pedestrian and bicycle bridge and walk or ride over from downtown.

Cherry Creek and Washington Park

WINE BARS

Not necessarily for oenophiles, but for regular people who might want to learn more about wine or sample wines not typically available by the glass, **Village Cork** (1300 S. Pearl St., 303/282-8399, www.villagecork.com, 11am-2pm and 4pm-10:30pm Mon.-Thurs., 4pm-midnight Fri., 5pm-midnight Sat., 10:30am-2:30pm Sun.) is a neat little Washington Park nook for a romantic date. Not far from the Louisiana-Pearl Street light rail stop, this can be the ideal after-dinner spot for a sweet treat and a glass of wine. Try the three sample wines for $10 before committing to a glass or bottle.

Need a break after a day of shopping in Cherry Creek? We've got just the thing. **Vinue Wine Bar** (2817 E. 3rd Ave., 720/287-1156, www.denverwinebar.net, 4pm-10pm Sun.-Thurs., 4pm-midnight Wed.-Sat.) lets you have wine your way with its unique self-serve program. Sample from the 68 different wines from around the globe in tastings of 1.5-, 3-, and 6-ounce pours. Or, order a traditional glass of wine or cocktail from the bar to pair with a selection of eclectic gourmet small plates. Vinue has a lounge-like ambience—and there's even a wine and painting parlor in a tiny space upstairs—making this wine bar a nice destination for group outings or a fun date night.

THE ARTS

If you fly into Denver International Airport, you'll immediately catch a glimpse of the Denver arts scene—many permanent exhibits by local artists are on view in the main terminal. Once downtown, you will begin to notice even more public art on display in the most unexpected spaces.

Known for sunshine, outdoor activities, and a touch of the Old West, Denver has also drawn notice for its role as a regional arts powerhouse. Beyond the established Denver Art Museum and Museum of Contemporary Art Denver, Denver museums are diverse, boasting eclectic art collections such as the Kirkland Museum of Fine & Decorative Art and the Forney Museum of Transportation, which holds the world's largest steam locomotive. In the summer the city hosts the Biennial of the Americas, with an international roster of the art world's who's who. There are museums here dedicated to single artists, whose work you may not see anywhere else in the world. A healthy art gallery scene means that artists can have actual careers here, patrons can get to know local artists, and visitors can spend their time seeing art that is only on display here—whether that's a cleverly curated traveling exhibit of Cartier jewels exclusive to the Denver Art Museum or student art at the Metropolitan State University's Center for Visual Art. This is no up-and-coming art scene—it has arrived and it's thriving.

Downtown

THEATER

The **Ellie Caulkins Opera House** (14th and Curtis Sts., 303/357-2787, www.denvercenter.org, box office Mon.-Sat. 10am-6pm) has been called the jewel in the crown of the Denver Performing Arts Complex (DPAC). The 1908 grand theater, formerly called the Auditorium Theatre, was completely renovated and can seat 2,268 for opera or other musical performances. Both the Opera Colorado and the Colorado Ballet perform at the "Ellie," as it is called locally. The theater is included on tours of the DPAC when performance schedules allow. Visit http://operacolorado.org for information on upcoming shows, buy tickets at the administrative offices at 695 South Colorado Boulevard, or call 303/778-1500 or 303/468-2030.

Within the Denver Performing Arts Complex is the 210-seat **Garner Galleria Theatre** (14th and Champa Sts., 303/893-4000, www.denvercenter.org, box office Mon.-Sat. 10am-6pm), which hosts cabaret-style shows. The Galleria was home to Denver's longest-running musical, *I Love You, You're Perfect, Now Change,* and continues to fill the house with *Defending the Caveman.* Shows typically run about four to six months at the Galleria, and if you're just passing through or spontaneously going out on the town, it's the best place at the complex to get a last-minute ticket any time of year. There is a bar in the theater, so drinks are served during the show, too.

The **Helen Bonfils Theatre Complex** (1101 13th St., 303/893-4000 or 303/893-4100, www.denvercenter.org, box office Mon.-Sat. 10am-6pm) is part of the larger, city-owned Denver Performing Arts Complex (DPAC) at 13th and Arapahoe Streets. There are four separate theaters in the Bonfils complex—the Stage, with 770 seats; the Space, a theater-in-the-round with over 400 seats; the Ricketson Theatre, with 250 seats; and the Jones Theatre, with just 200 seats. It's in one of these theaters that patrons are likely to see an original production by the Denver Center Theatre Company. The DPAC is the second-largest performing arts center in the United States, with 10 venues connected by an 80-foot-tall glass canopy. **Tours** (303/893-4100 or 303/446-4829) of the complex and various theater spaces are offered every week.

The **Temple Hoyne Buell Theatre** (1101 13th St., 303/893-4000, www.denvercenter.org, box office Mon.-Sat. 10am-6pm) at the Denver Performing Arts Complex has 2,830 seats and is typically the venue for big traveling Broadway shows and the crowds they draw. The theater is acoustically designed for musicals, but also hosts dramatic plays and comedies. The city-owned and -run Buell is a former sports arena that was gutted and renovated to become the theater it is today. It is the second-highest-grossing theater in North America with fewer than 5,000 seats.

DANCE

Led by its namesake founder, artistic director, and choreographer, the **Cleo Parker Robinson Dance** (119 Park Ave. W., 303/295-1759, ext. 13, www.cleoparkerdance.org) is known for its cross-cultural programs with African American traditions. The company is based in Five Points at the historic Shorter A.M.E. Church, but it performs at other locations in the city and around the world. This is also home to a dance school and various dance classes for children and adults. Like the performances, classes offered include a huge variety of styles, from ballet to tap to West African dance.

COMEDY

For anyone who has ever played Mad Libs, the **Bovine Metropolis Theatre** (1527 Champa St., 303/758-4722, www.bovinemetropolis.com, $8-16) takes it a step further with their regular "On the Spot" night, during which audience members make suggestions to the cast and a moderator for songs, games, and scenes that will basically create the show. Shows remain on the schedule for weeks to months, with titles like "Improv Hootenanny," "But Wait! There's More!," and other silly names. But that doesn't mean it's the same thing each week, since the nature of improv is to make it up as you go along. Because the Bovine does not serve alcohol, most shows are all ages, but be sure to double-check all of the details on the website for the most current rules, as there can be adult-only ribald humor late into the night.

CONCERT VENUES

Located in the Denver Performing Arts Complex, **Boettcher Concert Hall** (1000 14th St., 303/623-7876, www.coloradosymphony.org) is the home of the **Colorado Symphony Orchestra.** When it was built in 1978, Boettcher was the first symphony hall-in-the-round in the United States. About 80 percent of the hall's 2,634 seats are within 65 feet of the stage. There are no true vertical or horizontal surfaces in Boettcher, so that the sound is evenly dispersed.

Right off the 16th Street Mall in downtown is the historic **Paramount Theatre** (1621 Glenarm Pl., 303/825-4904, www.paramountdenver.com), a relatively small 1,870-seat venue. Listed in the National Register of Historic Places, the Paramount was originally a movie theater in the 1930s and still has original art deco touches. The original Wurlitzer organ that was installed to accompany silent movies is still played; it and a sister organ at Radio City Music Hall are among the last remaining such organs in the country. The Paramount has a somewhat sporadic schedule and hosts a wide variety of entertainment, including comedy, ballet, and music.

CINEMA

UA Denver Pavilions 15 (500 16th St., Ste. 10, 303/454-9086, www.denverpavilions.com), on the top level of the 16th Street Mall, is a multiplex theater that shows all the latest blockbuster movies several times each day. There are 15 screens to choose from, in rooms of various sizes and seating capacities. The lobby itself is an entertainment zone, with video games and snacks galore at the immense concession stand. You can't beat the variety of showtimes here, including weekday matinees.

Golden Triangle, Lincoln Park, and SoBo

MUSEO DE LAS AMERICAS

In the heart of the Santa Fe Arts District is the **Museo de las Americas** (861 Santa Fe Dr., 303/571-4401, www.museo.org, noon-5pm Tues.-Sat., $5 adults, $4 seniors, free for children under 13), the first museum in the Rocky Mountain states devoted to the art, history, and culture of Latin America. The mission of the Museo de las Americas is to share the diverse art and culture of Latin America, from ancient to contemporary. While its changing exhibits and artists makes it seem more like a gallery than a museum, it offers art education and community programs in conjunction with each exhibition. Artists whose work is on display give talks about their art on special nights during the exhibit. There are also hands-on workshops and customized art tours for children.

Every third Friday of the month is Spanish Happy Hour, when people can come to have a drink and a snack and view the art, all while speaking Spanish.

Opened in 1994, the Museo de las Americas has helped this evolving neighborhood become a draw for new art galleries and other businesses. Be sure to visit the unique gift shop before leaving.

GALLERIES

The Metropolitan State College's **Center for Visual Art** (965 Santa Fe Dr., 303/294-5207, www.msudenver.edu/cva, 11am-6pm Tues.-Fri., noon-5pm Sat.) is a reminder that downtown Denver is home to a large college campus. (Metro State is on the Auraria Campus, which can be seen from Larimer Square.) The off-campus facility fits right in with the high-end galleries along Santa Fe Drive, with its expansive exhibit space and crisp white walls. This nonprofit is not just a place for students; it also hosts unique contemporary art exhibits, such as an exhibition of prints and objects by Christo and Jeanne-Claude and a group show of female Vietnamese artists. The center is open until 8pm on the first and third Fridays during exhibitions.

The **gallery 910Arts** (910 Santa Fe Dr., 303/815-1779, www.910arts.com, 11am-5pm Thurs.-Sat.) is part of an artist colony along Santa Fe Drive where the green-built and colorfully painted building provides live/work space, artist studios, a coffeehouse, and a small courtyard garden. The gallery showcases visual as well as performing arts, often by 910 studio artists. A mission of 910Arts is to foster discussion about art, so, in conjunction with exhibits, there are gallery talks scheduled each month. The gallery is open until 9pm on the first and third Fridays.

Previously the Illiterate Gallery, the **Gildar Gallery** (82 S. Broadway, 303/993-4474, www.gildargallery.com, noon-6pm Wed.-Sat.) opened in 2012 and maintains the same commitment to local artists just getting their start in the art world. This is the place to spot young new talent in Denver, and there is no telling what's next at this contemporary art hot spot. Make a night of it on a First Friday and include Gildar on your route as you check out the restaurants, shops, and other galleries of SoBo.

What was previously The Space Gallery is now **Point Gallery** (765 Santa Fe Dr., 720/254-0467 or 303/596-2309, www.pointgallerydenver.com, 11am-5pm Tues.-Thurs., 11am-6pm Fri.-Sat.), with the same rooms for displaying art but a different take on curating what is shown. With enormous colorful canvases by local artists such as Susan M. Gibbons, David Menard, and Kim Gentile against the plain white walls, this looks like a movie set for an art gallery. Make it a stop during a First Friday Art Walk.

In addition to the large interior exhibit space at the **Space Gallery** (400 Santa Fe Dr., 720/904-1088, www.spacegallery.com, 11am-5pm Wed.-Fri., 10am-3pm Sat.), there is also an outdoor sculpture garden and second-floor mezzanine gallery that overlooks the main floor. *Westword* art critic Michael Paglia described the new building as so perfect that "The interior has just the right amount of drama to attract events—in fact, you could say that it's just about the best place in town to hold a pot-friendly same-sex wedding—or even a liquor-friendly regular one."

Given the loft-style space of **Walker Fine Art** (300 W. 11th Ave., 303/355-8955, www.walkerfineart.com, 11am-5pm Tues.-Sat., 6pm-8pm First Fridays), local artists such as Roland Bernier, Robert Delaney, and Munson Hunt are given ample room to display their two-dimensional and three-dimensional sculptures and large canvas works. The gallery is on the ground floor of a modern condominium building in the Golden Triangle, just four blocks from the Denver Art Museum. Even if you miss an opening or First Friday Art Walk, there is always an exhibit of new work in the rear of the gallery.

Among the handful of art galleries in the Golden Triangle, within walking distance of the Denver Art Museum, the **William Havu Gallery** (1040 Cherokee St., 303/893-2360, www.williamhavugallery.com, 10am-6pm Tues.-Fri., 11am-5pm Sat., 6pm-9pm First Fridays) stands out as one of the best for contemporary art. Havu represents a significant number of well-known Denver artists, many of whom choose to paint or photograph or sculpt the city and surrounding landscape. Artists include Tracy Felix, Homare Ikeda, and Stephen Dinsmore.

THEATER

The third-oldest Chicano theater in the country was started in the 1970s as a student group for those interested in the Chicano civil rights movement. Today, the **Su Teatro Cultural and Performing Arts Center** (721 Santa Fe Dr., 303/296-0219, www.suteatro.org) remains a community-based Chicano/Latino cultural arts center where visual and performing arts can be seen as well as learned in workshops.

The **Buntport Theater** (717 Lipan St., 720/946-1388, www.buntport.com) started many years ago when a group of college students moved to Denver and started their own theater company—just like that! They are hilarious and talented. They do theater for all ages on the second Saturday of each month and performances at the Denver Art Museum in addition to their seasonal calendar of shows here.

DANCE

The **Colorado Ballet** (1075 Santa Fe Dr., 303/837-8888, www.coloradoballet.org) moved into a new home in 2014. The Armstrong Center for Dance will continue to be home to its dance school, while performances remain downtown. Colorado Ballet has the dependable annual performance of *The Nutcracker* during the holidays that reliably draws sold-out crowds. Otherwise, each season is a surprise, with a small handful of other dances running for limited engagements. The company performs at the Ellie Caulkins Opera House, as well as doing onetime performances at other venues, such as the Arvada Center. Some students at the Academy of Colorado Ballet become principal dancers who perform regularly with this company. There are no box office services at the Colorado Ballet headquarters at 1278 Lincoln Street. Tickets can be purchased two hours before each performance at the Ellie Caulkins box office (14th and Curtis Sts., 303/837-8888 ext. 2, www.coloradoballet.org).

To say **Wonderbound** (1075 Park Ave. West, 303/292-4700, www.wonderbound.com) is innovative doesn't quite capture the creativity behind this unique dance company. Wonderbound has put on shows that include a local mentalist magician and scents by a local essential oils lab. Housed in a former post office garage, this very urban space allows for some degree of interaction between dancers and audience members during performances. Whether it's a rock ballet or a customized take on a fairy tale, this is one dance you won't forget.

CINEMA

The theater itself is worth a visit at the unique art deco-style **Mayan Theatre** (110 Broadway, 303/744-6799, www.landmark-theatres.com/denver/mayan-theatre), which has three screens—one large theater on the main level, and two smaller theaters upstairs. When the glorious building was saved from the wrecking ball in the 1980s, there wasn't much of a scene on this strip of Broadway. Now this neighborhood has its own trendy moniker, SoBo (as in South Broadway), and there are many wonderful restaurants, bars, and shops within walking distance of this neighborhood hot spot. Fans of foreign and independent cinema love the Mayan.

the Mayan Theatre

LoDo and Platte River Valley

GALLERIES

The emphasis at **David Cook Fine Art** (1637 Wazee St., 303/623-8181, www.davidcook-fineart.com, 10:30am-6pm Tues.-Sat.) is on American regional art, including Native American pieces such as drums, jewelry, sculptures, fetishes, and other items. Certainly the West and Southwest are well represented here, but artifacts from tribes all over can be found here, too. Gustave Baumann, Vance Kirkland, George Biddle, and dozens of other familiar and lesser-known artists' work is for sale at David Cook. The gallery is located around the corner from the historic Oxford Hotel in LoDo.

The only problem with the exhibits at the **Robischon Gallery** (1740 Wazee St., 303/298-7788, www.robischongallery.com, 11am-6pm Tues.-Fri., noon-5pm Sat.) in LoDo is that they do not stay up long enough. Jim Robischon and his wife, Jennifer Doran, select such exquisite artists that it is tempting to visit more than once. The gallery hosts about seven shows per year with a variety of mediums—photography, painting, prints, and installations. Well-known artists whose work has been shown here include Richard Serra, Robert Motherwell, and Judy Pfaff, to name just a few. Other artists whose work has been displayed here include Colorado's Jack Balas, Wes Hempel, Jae Ko, and Manuel Neri, and group shows of contemporary Chinese art.

While names of the hottest contemporary Russian artists may not be on the lips of most people, some of the best can be found right in Denver at the Sloane Gallery. The **Sloane Gallery of Art** (1777 Larimer St. #102b, 303/595-4230, www.sloanegalleryofart.com, noon-7pm Tues.-Sat.) has been in business since 1981 and represents artists whose work is found in major museum collections around the world. These include Russian-born and Russian American artists, as well as some from former republics of the Soviet Union. The subject matter in the paintings on display and for sale at Sloane tends to range from darkly humorous to starkly political.

COMEDY

Roseanne Barr is perhaps more famous than this club where she got her start, but **Comedy Works** (1226 15th St., 303/595-3637, www.comedyworks.com, $12-45) is still the best-known comedy place in town, often with lines out the door. Comedy Works is where you are likely to see big-name comedians—the ones who have made it to TV, like Wanda Sykes and George Lopez. On Tuesday night, it's a chance to try out or catch up-and-coming jokesters on New Talent Night. The seating can be a bit cramped in this basement space, and there is a two-drink minimum. Parking can be found at the Larimer Square Parking Garage on Market Street or at metered spots on the street. Note that there are two locations for Comedy Works, and its online calendar lists both locations. Shows are 18 and over and 21 and over.

Sometimes the funniest comedy teams aren't found in a comedy club. Denver's own **The Grawlix** (www.grawlixcomedy.com) performs at places like the **Bug Theatre** (3654 Navajo St., 303/477-9984, www.bugtheatre.org) when in town.

Families can enjoy ***Rodents of Unusual Size*** (985 Santa Fe Dr., 720/394-3833, www.coloradoimprov.com). Think you're funny? Then sign up for one of the improv classes here.

CONCERT VENUES

Home to two of Denver's major league sports teams—the Colorado Avalanche hockey team and the Denver Nuggets basketball team—the **Pepsi Center** (1000 Chopper Cir., 303/405-1100, www.pepsicenter.com) is also a concert venue for big-name acts like Madonna, Bruce Springsteen, Coldplay, and Celine Dion. When Red Rocks Amphitheatre is closed for the season, the Pepsi Center is the place for big concerts.

CINEMA

The **Lowenstein Theatre Complex** (2510 E. Colfax Ave., 303/595-3456, www.denverfilm.org) has become a miniature cultural hub on East Colfax Avenue, with the Tattered Cover Book Store in the historic theater building and the Denver Film Society setting up in the addition next door. The Denver Film Center/Colfax has become the new home to the annual Denver Film Festival, which has screenings at other locations around town, too. There are three main screens, plus a café seating area in the lobby.

Capitol Hill's art house movie theater has two screens devoted to independent and foreign-language films. The **Esquire** (590 Downing St., 303/352-1992, www.landmarktheatres.com), the Mayan, and the Chez Artiste theaters are all operated by the Landmark Theatres Company, which runs historic movie houses throughout the country. This is the kind of theater where you can get herbal tea with your popcorn. There is a small parking lot adjacent to the theater, but otherwise, on-street parking in this residential neighborhood can be tricky.

For thrilling, really-big-screen movie adventures, go to the **IMAX Theater at the Denver Museum of Nature and Science** (2001 Colorado Blvd., 303/322-7009, www.dmns.org, $8-10). Perhaps it's just the nature of IMAX films, or the fact that the theater is part of the museum, but the movies shown at this IMAX seem to always have a connection to the museum's theme. Viewers can visually explore coral reefs, beavers building dams, or humans scaling mountain peaks. Admission to the museum and planetarium are not included in IMAX ticket prices.

Capitol Hill and City Park

CONCERT VENUES

The **Fillmore Auditorium** (1510 Clarkson St., 303/837-1482, www.fillmoreauditorium.org) is a wonderfully refurbished former ice rink that hosts national touring acts such as Erykah Badu, Widespread Panic, George Clinton, and Rufus Wainwright. Located on the corner of Clarkson Street and Colfax Avenue in Capitol Hill, the Fillmore is walking distance from downtown. With a seating capacity of about 3,000, the Fillmore is the ideal space for audiences slightly smaller than those hosted at larger venues like Red Rocks Amphitheatre.

One of Denver's premier concert venues for small to midsize shows is the **Ogden Theatre** (935 E. Colfax Ave., 303/830-2525, www.ogdentheatre.com). The Ogden is on the National Register of Historic Places, and ornate detail and interesting architectural touches can be seen throughout the building. With a capacity of about 1,200 people, the theater hosts smaller shows than the Fillmore down the street. The Smashing Pumpkins, the Hives, Jimmy Cliff, and the Goo Goo Dolls have all played at the Ogden.

Highlands

GALLERIES

Pirate: A Contemporary Art Oasis (3659 Navajo St., 303/458-6058, www.piratearton-line.org, 6pm-10pm Fri., noon-5pm Sat.-Sun.) has given many fledgling Denver artists their start, and this contemporary artists cooperative has changed little since it began. Only recently did the Pirate lose a bit of the old grittiness that was part of its charm, getting a makeover with big windows and a neon sign out front. Longtime members Phil Bender and Louis Recchia have gone on to have their work collected by the Denver Art Museum, and alumni include other well-known artists such as Dale Chisman. This little corner is an art hot spot in the Highlands.

The corner of 37th and Navajo Streets is a little arts colony of mostly visual arts galleries, as well as the **Bug Theatre** (3654 Navajo St., 303/477-9984, www.bugtheatre.org), where emerging filmmakers are showcased and original or little-seen plays are produced. The Bug started out in 1912 as a nickelodeon theater and went through many other uses before it fell into neglect; it was rescued by local artists who renovated it and found it easy to fill with popular productions like the annual *Santaland Diaries* or amateur night with *Freak Train*. It's always an affordable night out at The Bug.

THEATER

An old-fashioned puppet theater has been enhanced by Zook's, a coffee-and-treats shop, and a courtyard with a fountain. The **Denver Puppet Theater** (3156 W. 38th Ave., 303/458-6446, www.denverpuppettheater.com, 10am Wed.-Fri., 1pm Sat. in summer; 10am Thurs.-Fri., 1pm Sat.-Sun. in winter, closed Sept., $7) offers marionette shows based on classic children's stories, such as "Little Red Riding Hood," "Aesop's Fables," "Jack and the Beanstalk," and more. The shows are geared for ages three and up, and children are expected to sit quietly during showtime. Before and after shows, kids can make a souvenir puppet ticket and play with puppets, and their parents can buy a variety of puppets to bring home.

FESTIVALS AND EVENTS

The arts are routinely celebrated throughout Denver. There are monthly First Friday events when galleries around the city open their doors for a casual evening of browsing and cocktails, the city boasts a full Arts Week in the fall, and the Cherry Creek Arts Festival is one of the city's biggest annual events.

Spring

One of the largest **Cinco de Mayo** (Civic Center Park, 100 W. 14th Ave. Pkwy., 303/534-8342, www.cincodemayodenver.com) celebrations in the United States is held in Denver every spring in a two-day event. It's a chance to eat Mexican food and enjoy Mexican music while learning more about the culture. There is a parade, live music, dancing, and a green chile cook-off. The organized festival takes place at Civic Center Park, but the Highlands neighborhood, where there is a significant Latin American population, is also a hot spot for the weekend of or near May 5 every year. This often translates to streets clogged with cruisers waving Mexican and American flags.

The **Denver March Powwow** is Denver's largest powwow and one of the largest in the nation. Held for three days every March at the Coliseum (4600 Humboldt St., 303/934-8045, www.denvermarchpowwow.org, 10am-10pm daily), this gathering of Native American tribes focuses on dance performances in elaborate costumes to the beat of live drums. To watch any of the dances—men's or women's, fancy or traditional—is to learn about a particular tribe, region, or history. There are also a lot of vendors selling Native American jewelry, food, artwork, and fetishes. Different activities and performances take place daily.

From its beginnings as a small neighborhood fair in the 1980s, the **Highlands Square Street Fair** (32nd Ave. and Lowell St., www.highlands-square.com, free) has exploded into one of the bigger annual festivals, with several blocks around Highlands Square closed off for a full day in mid-June. There is live music on three stages, more than 100 vendors set up on the blacktop, and parking lots filled with kids' games and activities. The quality of the festival depends a lot on the weather—it can be scorching hot in mid-June, cold and rainy, or just right. It's best to arrive early before 32nd Avenue becomes too crowded to walk through.

While the **Spring Bear Powwow** (Regis University, 3333 Regis Blvd., www.springbearpowwow.org) at the Regis University Field House has a traditional grand entry performance, drumming, and dancing, it is a no-contest event. This one-day community gathering, with free admission to all, is typically held in mid-May. Native American foods and crafts are sold, and dancers and drummers are invited to perform. The Regis campus is located just north of the Highlands neighborhood.

It's not like events in Chicago or Boston, but Denver's **St. Patrick's Day Parade** (starts at 27th and Blake Sts., www.denverstpatricksdayparade.com) is huge and very popular. The parade winds its way through a portion of LoDo—where, conveniently, there are many brewpubs and bars—with a variety of things Irish or not, like bagpipers and beauty queens riding in convertibles and little dogs doing tricks. The weather can sometimes be downright wintry in March, but people still dye their hair green to match their outfits and come out for a day of celebration. The parade is held on the weekend closest to March 17 on any given year.

What makes the **Tesoro Foundation's Indian Market and Powwow** (The Fort Restaurant, 19192 Hwy. 8, Morrison, 303/839-1671, www.tesoroculturalcenter.org) worth the drive up to Morrison is the location. The market is held on the outdoor patios of The Fort Restaurant, where artisans display their wares in individual tents and booths. The powwow takes place in an open field behind the restaurant. The setting, combined with the sounds of Native American drumming and chanting, transports visitors to another time and place to truly absorb the unique experience that is a celebration of the West, Southwest, and Native American cultures. This is usually a two-day event in mid-May, with performances scheduled at different times each day.

Summer

Just beyond the bars and nightclubs of LoDo is a relatively small high-rise building and shopping complex, Sakura Square. This quiet, serene city block stands out with its little bonsai garden and Japanese public art on display. While one can go to the Asian food market or restaurants at the square year-round, the best time to come is during the **Cherry Blossom Festival** (Sakura Square, between Lawrence, Larimer, 19th, and 20th Sts., www.cherryblossomdenver.org) in June, to celebrate Japanese American culture and hear traditional music, watch dancers, tour the temple, and sample authentic Japanese food.

Every Fourth of July weekend, the streets of the **Cherry Creek North** (btwn. 1st and 3rd Aves., and Clayton and Steele Sts., 303/355-2787, www.cherryarts.org) shopping district are barricaded for three days to host a huge outdoor celebration of the arts. The emphasis is on the artwork to be sure, but there is also live music and a whole street devoted to culinary creations. Wander the various booths until something catches your eye, then duck inside the tent, where you might find yourself having a one-on-one chat with one of the artists. The free festival includes local artists as well as those who have come from around the world to participate.

Sunday evenings in the summer (June-early Aug.) are the perfect times to mellow out with some live jazz music and a few thousand fellow citizens in **City Park** (3300 E. 17th Ave., 303/744-1004, www.cityparkjazz.org). There are 10 concerts in all, featuring local jazz musicians playing in the bandstand near Ferril Lake or closer to the Denver Museum of Nature and Science in the Meadows. The concerts are free; blankets and chairs are not provided, but some food is available for sale on-site. Parking is limited, so biking or walking to the weekly concerts is encouraged. Concerts are held rain or shine.

Just before the heat of summer settles in, Larimer Square transforms its blacktop into a sort of piazza for one weekend in June. At the **Denver Chalk Art Festival** (Larimer Square, Larimer St. between 14th and 15th Sts., 303/685-8143, www.larimerarts.com) amateur and professional artists use chalk to make beautiful and detailed murals on the city street. Those not drawing can watch the process while enjoying Italian foods, such as gelato and pizza, and step into the wine-tasting tent to sample Italian wines. There's even a special spot for kids to practice their chalk expertise. By Sunday night, all of the art is washed away and Larimer Square returns to normal.

A lot has changed in Five Points over the years as the community has been gentrified. Much of its intriguing past—soul food restaurants, jazz clubs—is on display in the galleries of the Blair-Caldwell African American Research Library. The two-day **Juneteenth** (24th-28th and Welton Sts., 720/276-3693, www.juneteenthmusicfestival.org) festival, which celebrates the end of slavery in the United States, includes a parade, live music, and food. The festival takes place in June every year, but the exact date of the event changes annually.

Boat racing meets cultural recognition and celebration at the annual **Dragon Boat Festival** (Sloan's Lake Park, corner of Stuart St. and 23rd Ave., 303/722-6852, www.cdbf.org). This has become the largest Pan-Asian festival in the region, with crowds of about 100,000 gathered to learn more about Asian American and Pacific Islander communities. The main draw at this two-day event in July is the boat racing across the lake—and the competition gets more fierce every year, as racers learn from the previous year and more types of races are offered. "Explore Asia" is

the Denver Chalk Art Festival in Larimer Square

one aspect of the festival where local ethnic groups—Hmong, Filipino, Mongolian, and others—can demonstrate cultural traditions. Admission to the festival is free; it's best to consider the shuttle service options for getting there.

The Gay, Lesbian, Bisexual, and Transgender Community Center of Colorado hosts the annual **Pridefest** (Civic Center Park, 100 W. 14th Ave. Pkwy., www.glbtcolorado.org) each June. The two-day event includes a parade (in a sign of how far this community has come, it is now called the Coors Light Pridefest Parade) that starts in Capitol Hill's Cheesman Park and is the highlight of the festival, with outrageous floats and costumes. At Civic Center Park there is a dance stage and booths with everything from food to crafts to health-awareness information. There is always a huge turnout for the festival, so plan accordingly when it comes to parking. This has become the third-largest pride festival in the country.

Labor Day weekend in Denver is a chance to sample various Colorado culinary specialties and gourmet favorites in a three-day eating extravaganza called **A Taste of Colorado** (Civic Center Park, 100 W. 14th Ave. Pkwy., 303/295-6330, www.atasteofcolorado.com). Chefs do demonstrations, and attendees can enjoy a full meal or just snack throughout the day at every little booth. Over the years, the food has become just one part of the festival; there's also live music, arts and crafts, and other special exhibits. At this time of year, be on the lookout for fresh melons and peaches, though any kind of barbecue seems to always be the favorite. Parking can be a problem, so be prepared to walk off whatever you eat on the way back to the car.

For four days in July the SoBo business district is taken over by the **Underground Music Showcase** (720/570-4500, www.theums.org), with hundreds of bands performing in different venues. This is a chance to discover new favorite bands, check out live music venues, stroll along South Broadway, and just have a lot of fun. Diehards plan ahead when deciding which bands they want to see, while others just wing it and look forward to the surprises.

Fall

Denver Arts Week (www.denver.org/denver-arts-week) is a way for the entire city to celebrate its culture, super-sized for one week each year. The week usually starts off on a Friday, with free admission to all museums, which have extended hours and shuttle service between each facility. Art galleries host the First Friday Art Walk, and there are special artistic activities for kids at the Denver Zoo and Denver Botanic Gardens. The week also overlaps with the Denver International Film Festival, and it's not just about visual art, but also performance art and more.

Yes, the stars do come out to walk the red carpet at the annual **Denver International Film Festival** (303/595-3456, www.denverfilm.org), with famous directors and actors in attendance and giving special talks. The big gala nights are typically held at the Denver Performing Arts Complex, with the majority of films shown at the Sie FilmCenter. Be sure to check the schedule for any local filmmakers who might be showcasing their latest work. It's wise to buy tickets in advance instead of at the door, as shows can sell out fast.

Thirsty? Check out the three-day **Great American Beer Festival** (Colorado Convention Center, 700 14th St., 303/477-0816, www.greatamericanbeerfestival.com), where a ticket to just a single day of the event is a pass to try as many one-ounce samples of over 2,200 beers as possible in one evening. It might sound like a bad frat-party idea, but this is a truly serious beer competition held every October. It's basically the Beer Olympics, and the brewers and tasters mean business. Though the festival is only three days, there is a whole week of related activities around town. The festival, which takes place at the Colorado Convention Center, is now featured in the book *1,000 Places to See Before You Die.*

Before the winter weather creeps in and while fall colors are on display, runners take to the streets over one weekend in September for the **Rock 'n' Roll Denver Marathon** (starts at the Colorado State Capitol, 200 Colfax Ave., www.runrocknroll.com/Denver). The event includes a half marathon and a marathon. This Boston Marathon qualifier race begins and ends at the Colorado State Capitol, and is a sightseeing tour of many of Denver's best sights, including Larimer Square, Coors Field, and City Park.

Learn about and experience the rugged life in this part of the world before it was Colorado at the **1830s Rendezvous and Spanish Colonial Art Market** (The Fort Restaurant, 19192 Hwy. 8, Morrison, 303/839-1671, www.tesoroculturalcenter.org), where mountain men and women posted in historically accurate camps and trading posts are ready to answer questions about "their" life. It's not so much "cowboys and Indians" as it is frontiersmen and Native Americans, with Spanish heritage to boot. During the two-day annual event in late September, sit inside tepees, chat with fur trappers, and check out Spanish Colonial artwork.

Winter

When the gardens are sleeping for the winter and most of the color is evergreen shrubs, brown dirt, or brilliant-white fresh snowfall, the annual holiday **Blossoms of Light** (1005 York St., 720/865-3585, www.botanicgardens.org) is a welcome burst of color. For about six weeks through December and part of January, the Denver Botanic Gardens puts up over one million lights (with energy-efficient bulbs), draped across evergreen trees or shaped into luminescent flowers. On select nights there are carolers or other special events. The exact dates, times, and costs vary each year.

Beginning with one festive night every year, downtown streets and buildings are brightly lit with thousands of colorful holiday lights. Downtown Denver's **Grand Illumination** (Union Station, 16th Street Mall, and Larimer Square, 303/534-6161, www.downtowndenver.com) kicks off at Union Station in LoDo, where carolers sing and officials count down to the flip of the switch, when a large tree made of strings of lights and the building itself suddenly glow. The 16th Street Mall (where energy-efficient LED lights are used), Larimer Square, and the

cattle drive during the annual National Western Stock Show Parade

Denver City and County Building all turn on their yellow, red, green, and blue lights as huge crowds gather to watch and take part in the festivities.

Denver becomes a cow town each January when the **National Western Stock Show** (National Western Complex, 4655 Humboldt St., 303/297-1166, www.nationalwestern.com, $2-14) is held over three weeks. One major highlight is the cattle drive right through the middle of downtown, in which longhorn steers are guided up 17th Street from Union Station to the Brown Palace. The event schedule at the complex is packed with 4-H competitions, horse shows, bull riding, and other rodeo shows, as well as an array of special performances like the popular Mexican Rodeo Extravaganza and Martin Luther King Jr. African American Heritage Rodeo. Overall attendance at the stock show in 2011 was over 644,000 during the 16-day event.

Usually, the Denver Zoo is a quiet place at night as most of the animals slumber, but during the holiday **Zoo Lights** (2300 Steele St., 303/376-4800, www.denverzoo.org, 5:30pm-9pm daily, $8 adults, $4 children, free for children under 2, $6 seniors) it becomes a festive gathering place for people and animals, with lights blazing through about half of the zoo. It's more than just lights shaped like zoo animals and sparkling trees, though—there are ice sculptures made on-site, a Kwanzaa celebration, dances, and carolers. It's a busy time as families enjoy being outside in the crisp winter air and take the chance to see the zoo at a different time of day.

Cannabis Dispensaries

Sprouting up in many retail places around town are cannabis dispensaries. Included are a few of the better establishments for buying marijuana in Denver.

DOWNTOWN

The only marijuana outlet on the 16th Street Mall, **Euflora** (401 16th St., 303/534-6255, www.eufloracolorado.com, 10am-6:45pm daily) boasts a visitor-friendly atmosphere to match its prime location. The modern and spacious 6,000-square-foot basement-level shop features slick display tables decked out with aroma jars and tablet computers so customers can see, smell, and learn about each strain before making their purchase. No wonder the owner refers to the store as an "Apple Store of weed." While some visitors grumble about the quality of the herb available, consider Euflora akin to one of the many souvenir shops that line the pedestrian mall: While you might not find one-of-a-kind treasures among its product lines, it's a great way to get a taste of everything the state has to offer.

GOLDEN TRIANGLE, LINCOLN PARK, AND SOBO

Tucked away in a hip stretch of Broadway in the southern part of town, **Denver Relief** (1 Broadway, Ste. A150, 303/420-6337, www.denverrelief.com, 8am-6:45pm daily) is the kind of joint where the cool kids hang out. A longtime Denver dispensary run by major local players—one cofounder is the chairman of the National Cannabis Industry Association, another also runs a Denver pizza chain and launched an ongoing series of marijuana-friendly stand-up comedy shows—this is the sort of place that's trying to set national standards through how it operates. That includes its stellar product selection, which features signature house strains like "Dopium" and "Bio Jesus," complete with individual colorful logos, like merit badges for weed.

Just south of the Denver Art Museum, **Pure Marijuana Dispensary** (1133 Bannock St., 303/534-7873, www.puremmj.com, 9:30am-7pm daily) is known as a great all-around marijuana shop. It has an airy, friendly

420-Friendly

Of course Denver would offer marijuana-friendly yoga classes. Every Friday evening and Sunday morning, **Twisted Sister Yoga** (3835 Elm St., Capitol Hill and City Park, 303/523-5891, www.twistedsister.yoga) offers sessions designed to heighten the effects of cannabis consumed before class (no on-site consumption allowed). Trust us, your "Oms" will have never sounded so profound.

Sure, you've had a massage, but have you ever had a *marijuana* massage? That's the promise of **Primal Therapeutics** (719/429-7651, www.cannabismassagecolorado.com), which comes to your home or hotel room and offers deep-tissue rubs, sports massages, full-body scrubs, and other therapies featuring cannabis-infused lotions. While the psychoactive components of marijuana can't be absorbed through the skin, rubdowns like this are still quite the trip.

Puff, Pass & Paint (2087 S. Grant St., www.puffpassandpaint.com, $50) is an inspired way to cash in on Denver's culture and cannabis. Bring your own cannabis to this marijuana-friendly art class, where you'll be artistically inspired by the two hours of formal instruction, not to mention all the joints your fellow classmates are passing around. If Van Gogh had options like this, he might have skipped his whole "Blue Period."

location, true "weed nerds" behind the counter, and the sort of product selection that gets online reviewers raving. Thanks to the fact that Pure boasts its own extracts operation, Colorado Cannabis Company, it's also a great place to sample marijuana concentrates, oil cartridges for vape pens, and topical lotions.

LODO AND PLATTE RIVER VALLEY

Occupying the fifth floor of a historic brick building, **Natural Remedies** (1620 Market Ste. 5W, 303/953-0884, www.lodosdispensary.com, 9am-7pm daily) is the place to go for recreational marijuana in Lower Downtown. This place is known for its welcoming atmosphere and strong selection of strains—good thing, since you're going to need it after the long hike up the stairs!

CAPITOL HILL AND CITY PARK

Good Chemistry (330 E. Colfax Ave., Denver, 720/524-4657, www.goodchem.org, 11am-6:45pm daily), a nondescript shop on busy Colfax just around the corner from the state capitol, is easy to miss—blink and you'll overlook the lowercase "g" that marks the store above its front window—but those in the know seek it out for some of the best-quality cannabis around. Drawing rave reviews for its killer strains and dense quality buds, Good Chemistry more than lives up to its name.

GREATER DENVER

3D Cannabis Center (4305 Brighton Blvd., 303/297-1657, www.visit3d.com, 8am-7pm daily) originally stood for "Denver Discreet Dispensary," but these days the marijuana shop just off I-70 in north Denver has shed its modest roots, proudly celebrating the fact that on January 1, 2014, the operation was the first in the state—or anywhere else in the world, for that matter—to complete a legal recreational marijuana sale. The shop's historical significance isn't the only reason 3D is a good option for first-timers; the waiting area features a viewing corridor with windows into an adjoining growing facility, so shoppers can see exactly where their product is coming from. Consider it as immersive a marijuana experience as you can get without donning 3-D glasses.

With 12 locations and counting in the Denver metro area and beyond, **The Green Solution** (2601 West Alameda Ave., 303/990-9723, www.tgscolorado.com, 8am-6:45pm daily) is a prime example of the consolidation that's taking place throughout the state's cannabis industry, with large operations snapping up and rebranding mom-and-pops that struggled to navigate Colorado's complicated regulations and pricey licensing fees, not to mention a lack of banking options available to marijuana businesses. Still, once you walk into the Green Solution's main Denver location on West Alameda and check out its clean, professional atmosphere, you'll be asking yourself if being the McDonald's of marijuana is really such a bad thing.

Proudly calling itself the largest marijuana dispensary in Denver, **Medicine Man** (4750 Nome St., 303/373-0752, www.medicinemandenver.com, 8am-7pm daily) is a family-run operation in an industrial part of north Denver that tends to draw attention; the store was the focus of international media coverage when Colorado first legalized retail marijuana, and for a while there was talk of a reality show based on its owners. Thankfully, there's substance behind the hype: Expertly trained budtenders are on hand to carefully guide you through the store's dizzying array of strains and marijuana-infused products, making sure you take home just the right medicine.

A good option on the east side of town, **Mindful** (5926 E. Colfax Ave., 303/573-6337, www.bemindful.today, 10am-7pm daily) resembles a boutique coffee shop with its white-and-gray interior and steel and natural wood accents. While you can't get fair-trade beans here, you can score a wide variety of handcrafted, locally grown strains. And if you feel like doing a little gambling with your cannabis consumption, you can check out "1859," Mindful's operation in Black Hawk, located in an old-timey storefront just down the street from the mountain casinos.

While Denver offers marijuana shops aplenty, you'll be out of luck if you're looking to score in the later evening; per city rules, all dispensaries have to close by 7pm. After that, your best option is to head over to neighboring municipalities with more lenient regulations over operating hours, such as Edgewater, a small community just east of the city that supports a cottage industry of late-night pot shops right on its border with Denver. Of these, **Native Roots** (5610 W. 20th Ave., Edgewater, 720/476-4856, www.nativeroots303.com, 9am-midnight daily) is the most tourist-friendly; part of a statewide chain, the shop exudes professionalism, even late at night.

CANNABIS TOURS

Talk about a unique service: **420 Airport Pickup** (720/369-6292, www.420friendlyairportpickup.com, $75) is a private shuttle company that will pick you up at the airport, drive you to a retail marijuana shop, then drop you off at your hotel. Sure, the price tag is a bit more than your standard airport pickup, but what a way to start your trip.

Colorado Cannabis Tours (303/420-8687, www.coloradocannabistours.com, noon-4:20pm Sat., $99) offers a marijuana-friendly party bus that takes riders on an odyssey featuring stops at several Denver dispensaries, a live glass blowing demonstration, a tour of a 40,000-square-foot indoor marijuana grow, and a lunch break at Cheba Hut Toasted Subs (yes, the restaurant's name is a cannabis reference). It's a trip you won't soon forget—or rather, depending on how many samples you try, maybe you will.

Want top-of-the-line equipment to use for your cannabis purchases, but don't want to shell out big bucks for something you'll use just for a few days? **Elevated Rental** (303/872-0710, www.elevatedrental.com) lets travelers rent vaporizers, bongs, dabbing rigs, and other paraphernalia for the duration of their trip. If only trying out toys was this simple when you were a kid.

This isn't your granddaddy's walking tour. **High Urban Hikes** (630/699-5071, www.huhdenver.com, $49-55), also known as HUH Denver, offers colorful three-hour tours of Denver's sites, culture, and history, with an emphasis on marijuana-related esoterica. While you're not allowed to consume cannabis during the tour, "High-kers" are encouraged to partake ahead of time—and even if you don't, with names like the "Toxic Schizophrenia Twilight Tour," these are events that leave everyone feeling like they've gone on a trip in more ways than one.

There's a reason **My 420 Tours** (855/694-2086, www.my420tours.com, $129) has garnered international media attention. The tourism company offers several tours each week of dispensaries, grow facilities, and glass galleries; customized cannabis tours for bachelor parties and other events; and even all-inclusive marijuana vacation packages. Not only that, but the company also hosts marijuana cooking classes every Sunday morning—and yes, you get to sample the treats.

While Denver doesn't allow people to consume marijuana in establishments like bars, clubs, and theaters, doing so in party buses is A-OK. **Sunset Luxury Limos** (303/426-9668, www.sunsetlimo.com, $310-600) offers stretch limousines, Hummers, and spacious party buses that are all vaporizer-friendly, perfect for a magical mystery tour of your own creation.

Shopping

Shopping in Denver can be an all-day outing that includes a leisurely lunch and plenty of easy strolling. Whether you are looking for antiques, Western attire, a sexy dress, or the perfect shoes, there are a number of stores to check out. Heading out to do a little shopping is one of the best ways to experience Denver like a local.

Denver certainly has large malls with all the familiar stores, such as Cherry Creek Mall and the Denver Pavilions on the 16th Street Mall, but sprinkled around Denver's best neighborhoods are some appealing shopping districts, including tony Cherry Creek North, hip Highlands Square, and funky South Broadway. Each of these neighborhoods has a mixture of cafés and shops so people can wander from store to store browsing the goods, then grab a bite to eat and, once fortified, go back to spending.

In each neighborhood, the shops tend to represent the character of the area. On South Broadway near Ellsworth, it's about being original at the Fancy Tiger, where up-and-coming designers sell their latest creations, or find a mix of vintage and new duds at Decade. In Cherry Creek North, you can find beautiful clothes at Max, Garbarini, or Lawrence Covell that allow you to dress to impress. The best cowboy boots, shirts, and other Western-style clothing and accessories are mostly found in LoDo at Rockmount Ranch Wear and at Cry Baby Ranch in Larimer Square. The Highlands has a mix of shops, with stunning flowers at the Perfect Petal; toys, gear, and clothes for the wee ones at Real Baby; and accessories to accent an outfit in any season at Kismet. Even the museums in Golden Triangle, Capitol Hill, and along Santa Fe Drive offer great shopping opportunities in their gift shops.

DOWNTOWN

Right in the heart of downtown, **Denver Pavilions** (500 16th St., 303/260-6000, www.denverpavilions.com, 10am-9pm Mon.-Sat., 11am-6pm Sun.) is an open-air mall with all of the usual stores and restaurants, including a Banana Republic, The Gap, Barnes & Noble, Hard Rock Café, and Corner Bakery Café. On the third level is a United Artists movie theater and a Lucky Strike Lanes, as well as Jazz at Jack's. The Pavilions hosts weekly farmers markets, live music, and an annual arts festival.

Arts and Crafts

Sure, you'll end up paying three times what you would if you just bought a mug or a plate already painted, but it's so fun to personalize one! **Ceramics in the City** (1912 Pearl St., 303/200-0461, www.ceramicsinthecity.com, 11am-9pm Mon.-Sat., noon-6pm Sun.) in the Uptown neighborhood is so popular that sometimes you have to make reservations to get a table. (No, there is no alcohol or food served here.) Adults and children come to make keepsakes and special gifts. The staff is friendly and patient with people of all ages and ability levels. Plan ahead—it can take several days before your piece gets fired and is available for pickup.

Clothing and Accessories

Heloise (300 University Blvd., 303/997-5261, www.heloisechildrensboutique.com, 10am-6pm Mon.-Sat.) is such a proper boutique that it almost feels as if children might not be allowed inside. Each hanger is perfectly spaced, the stack of cardigans is neatly folded on a precious table, and it's all just so achingly sweet. Yes, it's more spendy here than say, Gap Kids, but then again, your child is unlikely to match other kids by wearing a brand that is less well known. Maybe your little girl needs something in velvet or faux fur? It's here.

Gift and Home

When I first heard about this shop, I could not figure out where it was because I did not believe it was in a mall. A store all about the local in a place all about the franchise? The **I Heart Denver Store** (500 16th St., 303/720-9069, www.iheartdenverstore.com, 10am-9pm Mon.-Sat., 11am-6pm Sun.) is almost like an art gallery that celebrates the city, with locally made and designed crafts and clothes. The goal is to support creative entrepreneurs through sales at the store. Even for window shoppers and browsers, it's an impressive selection of what's made in Denver. Oh heck, just drop in to see cute little Denver, the shop mascot and the owner's corgi. He's so charming that a few of the items in the shop capture his image—you can buy a needlefelt little Denver, wear him in a pin, or mail a postcard with his photo.

GOLDEN TRIANGLE, LINCOLN PARK, AND SOBO

Hipster alert! **SoBo** (along S. Broadway from Ellsworth to Bayaud Aves.) is short for South Broadway, part of what was once Denver's own Miracle Mile of commerce. While the neighborhood has had some ups and downs in its history, things are on the upswing with a new energy and thriving businesses of all kinds that attract a mostly young and hip crowd. **Fancy Tiger** is both a fabric shop and retail store for local designers—like a slice of Etsy. Somewhere between vintage shops and places

the Denver Pavilions shopping center

like **True Love Shoes** and **Starlet,** you can truly dress yourself like a rock star when shopping SoBo.

Arts and Crafts

Sewing one's own clothes is fashionable again, and it doesn't get any more hip than **Fancy Tiger Crafts** (959 Broadway, 303/733-3855, www.fancytiger.com, 10am-7pm Mon. and Wed.-Sat., 10am-9pm Tues., 11am-6pm Sun.), where adults and children can take classes to learn about knitting, sewing, felting, fashion design, and a lot more creative stuff. The raw materials for sale here include organic cotton fabrics by the yard, and organic yarn made from hemp, llama, and cotton. After picking a pattern and a cute printed fabric, head across the street to Fancy Tiger Clothing to buy clothes made by Fancy Tiger students and alums, as well as more mainstream designers.

the I Heart Denver Store downtown

Clothing and Accessories

One of Denver's oldest vintage apparel stores, **Boss Unlimited** (10 S. Broadway, 303/871-0373, www.bossvintage.com, 11am-6pm Mon.-Sat., noon-5pm Sun.) could dress the entire family with clothes for Mom, Dad, and the kids. Boss is pretty much a traditional vintage store, with racks stuffed with clothes from every decade, some more costumey than others. There are also shoes, handbags, and the store's own line, Daredevil, with a rockabilly theme on screen-printed T-shirts and jackets.

Wander past the retro home decor items, tempting toiletries, adorable baby gifts, and the fat store cat at **Decade** (56 S. Broadway, 303/733-2288, 11am-6pm Mon.-Sat., noon-5pm Sun.) to find a women's boutique. This is a mix of new and used clothing, with lacy to modern styles in jeans, T-shirts, skirts, and lingerie. There is a small section for men, but Decade is really all about femininity. Locally made jewelry is also for sale at the front counter. Decade is the perfect place to find a little something girly to wear out for a casual evening—and not at an astronomical price.

The sign out front simply reads "SEWN" in large, colorful letters, and with the designer and seamstress working in sight—**Jil Cappuccio** (18 S. Broadway, 303/832-1493, www.jilcappuccio.com, 11am-6pm Mon.-Sat., 11am-5pm Sun.) has been known to work on her latest designs right in the shop—SEWN sells one-of-a-kind items. Cappuccio's dresses and pajamas are all roomy and colorful pieces, with a few little ones for children, and she makes men's shirts, too. The shop also carries items from other local designers, including very lovely knitwear by Pearl. Customers will find more local designers of everything from soap to pillows.

What's better than shoes? Affordable shoes, of course! The whole idea at **True Love Shoes** (42 Broadway, 303/860-8783, www.trueloveshoes.com, 11am-7pm daily) is for women to find a fabulous new pair of shoes, and still be able to afford a second pair. Colorful, sparkly, feminine, flats, wedges, heels, and on it goes with a selection of stylish shoes for women in every season. And what makes this shoe store even more unusual is that all of its products are vegan.

Gift and Home

It's always so tempting to flop into one of the overstuffed sofas or chairs at **Djuna** (9899 N. Broadway, 303/355-3522, www.djuna.com, 10am-5pm Mon.-Sat.) and just hang out, taking in the richly hued variety of rugs, mirrors, pillows, throws, and other furnishings artfully crammed together in the store. Many of the beds and other furniture are custom-made for Djuna. On the one hand, Djuna is a store for people with large homes to decorate right down to the last detail; on the other hand, there are some wonderful linens and fabrics that appeal to smaller budgets and spaces.

Hazel & Dewey (70 S. Broadway, 303/777-1500, http://hazel-dewey.com, 11am-7pm Mon.-Fri., 11am-6pm Sat., 11am-5pm Sun.) has a yummy variety of kitchenwares that are artfully arranged in this clean space. It has been voted Denver's Best Kitchen Store by *Westword* magazine. This is the place for Helvetica-character cookie cutters, cast-iron teakettles, and other perfect housewarming or hostess gifts.

Part art gallery, part jewelry and curio shop, the **Native American Trading Company** (213 W. 13th Ave., 303/534-0771, www.nativeamericantradingco.com, 10am-5pm Wed.-Fri., 11am-4pm Sat., 5pm-9pm First Fridays) is a place to find unique Southwestern and Native American wares. Only one block from the Denver Art Museum and across the street from the Byers-Evans House, the store is in a 1906 mission-style townhome. It's easy to walk into the Trading Company for a quick visit, and end up staying an hour or more looking at artwork and listening to the owners' stories of their relationships with the various artists and artisans whom they represent.

Health and Beauty

Artemisia & Rue (70 Broadway, 303/484-8982, www.artemisiaandrue.com, 11am-6pm Tues.-Sat., noon-6pm Sun.-Mon.) is a place for herbal healing, as well as a scented showroom of herbs, elixirs, and tinctures. There is a separate clinic for herbal and massage healing, with a focus on women's reproductive health, as well as a naturopathic doctor and certified master herbalist on staff. Check the online schedule for free classes featuring beneficial herbs and how to use them. Once a year during Mother's Day, the shop also sells fresh garden plants.

LODO AND PLATTE RIVER VALLEY

When it comes to shopping in **LoDo** (bounded by Wynkoop St. to the west, 14th Ave. to the south, Lawrence St. to the east, and 20th St. to the north), Larimer Square is the indisputable center of the universe, with restaurants and shops tightly packed into this historic block. These are mostly locally owned boutiques with distinctly Denver style, such as **Cry Baby Ranch.** Beyond Larimer Square, the shops are more random and include anything from **Patagonia** to the historic **Rockmount Ranch Wear.** Check the calendar to see if any of your favorite authors will be speaking and signing books at the **Tattered Cover Book Store** in this neighborhood, too.

Clothing and Accessories

Two guys brought their NYC fashion experience to Denver to open **Armitage & McMillan** (1550 Platte St., 303/284-6222, www.armitageandmcmillan.com, 11am-7pm Mon.-Sat., noon-6pm Sun.), a shop catering to stylish young men who like to get their whole outfit—pants, shirts, shoes—all in one place. Brands sold here aren't found at the mall: Unis New York, Save Khaki, The Brooklyn Circus, and Epperson Mountaineering, to name just a few.

Looking for something new, but don't want to spend more than $50? Go straight to **Common Era** (1543 Platte St., 303/433-4633, www.mycommonera.com, 11am-7pm Mon.-Sat., 11am-5pm Sun.), where there are racks of colorful simple-but-sexy dresses, tops, and tees to choose from at very reasonable prices. The styles are so versatile here that they can appeal to both a teenage girl and her mother. Don't be scared off if you happen by in October, when the store gets a bit over-the-top for Halloween, with crazy platform shoes, wigs, and other themed attire—by Thanksgiving they are back to normal.

Cry Baby Ranch (1421 Larimer St., 303/623-3979, www.crybabyranch.com, 10am-7pm Mon.-Fri., 10am-6pm Sat., noon-5pm Sun.) is an unusual hybrid of kitschy Western everything with a dash of bohemian style in the form of cute kids' clothes and women's shirts. The specialty here is the West—Western shirts; cowboy boots for men, women, kids, and even babies; home decor; jewelry; and a whole lot of other stuff that no one ever knows they need until they see it here. Look for Annie Oakley action figures, Boss Lady toiletries, state of Colorado pillows, and books galore for grown-ups and kids.

Mostly full of teen to thirtysomething males, **Emage** (1620 Platte St., 720/855-8297, www.emagenetwork.com, 11am-9pm Mon.-Sat., noon-6pm Sun.) is located just a couple of blocks from the Denver Skatepark with the purpose of outfitting anyone who likes to skateboard and snowboard. It also sells skateboards, snowboards, and all the parts and accessories needed for either sport. Emage has a good selection of shoes for the complete look, with Adidas, Nike, and Vans.

In the heart of LoDo, between Coors Field and the Pepsi Center, is the aptly named **Players** (91501 Wazee St., 303/752-9377, www.playersclothing.com, 10am-6pm Mon.-Fri., 10am-5:30pm Sat.) clothing store for men. The clientele here is not made up of sports fanatics, but men who live and work in the neighborhood and favor the "business casual" look. It's not quite "casual Friday," but more spiffy, with cashmere sweaters and brushed-cotton shirts. Look for familiar lines such as Cole Haan shoes, Tommy Bahama, Hiltl, and Remy.

There was a time when a man got fitted for a shirt and there was no small, medium, large in a rainbow of colors. Now that concept has returned, with made-in-the-U.S.A. shirts for men that are custom fitted by appointment only. The secret is out about **Ratio** (2559 16th St., 720/515-4348, www.ratioclothing.com, appointments available 10am-6pm Mon.-Fri., 10am-4pm Sat.)—they've appeared on CNN and in *Men's Journal.*

Rockmount Ranch Wear (91626 Wazee St., 303/629-7777, www.rockmount.com,

Rockmount Ranch Wear

8am-6pm Mon.-Fri., 10am-6pm Sat., 11am-4pm Sun.) is famous for a lot of things: the founder and owner, affectionately called "Papa Jack," who worked daily at the store until he died in 2008 at 107 years old; the original snap-front cowboy shirts; the celebrities and rock stars who have bought many of Rockmount's ornate Western shirts; and the legacy of being in business in the same historic building since 1946. This is part office, part store, part museum. Don't think you can pull off a Western shirt? No problem, as one of Denver's best souvenirs is a Rockmount T-shirt featuring a bucking bronco rider in men's, women's, and children's sizes and styles.

Sous le Lit (1550 Platte St., 303/455-1622, www.souslelit.com, 11am-7pm Mon.-Sat., noon-5pm Sun.) fills a small shop space with shoes, hats, dresses, jeans, tops, and jewelry. Even though Sous le Lit started with just shoes and accessories, the business has since grown the offerings for customers without physically expanding its space. The service here is always friendly and not overbearing.

Joining the made-in-the-U.S.A. garment movement in Denver is **Sully & Co.** (2443 Eliot St., 720/398-8064, www.sullyandco.com, 11am-6pm Tues.-Sat., noon-5pm Sun.), a menswear boutique. Guys, this is where we ladies want you to shop for yourselves. While not household names—yet—you might be familiar with Baldwin Denim, Dapper Classics, Schott, and others. Still an up-and-coming pocket of the greater Highlands neighborhood over here in Jefferson Park, Sully & Co. is worth the stop for a snappy new look.

Gift and Home

The **Old Map Gallery** (1550 Wynkoop St., 303/296-7725, www.oldmapgallery.com, 10am-5pm Mon.-Sat.) caters to serious map collectors and experts, and for the rest of us, it's a fascinating peek into the world of cartography and a place to find a unique piece of artwork or a gift for someone obsessed with a specific place. Along with antique maps featuring countries, oceans, celestial bodies, and food and wine, there are very affordable current maps for sale.

Outdoor Gear and Apparel

On the ground floor of the historic Studebaker building, and only two blocks from Larimer Square, is a **Patagonia** (1431 15th St., 303/446-9500, www.patagonia.com, 10am-7pm Mon.-Sat., 11am-5pm Sun.) store that offers men's, women's, and children's clothing, and just a small amount of gear. The children's section includes a Lego table and other toys, and there is a small—one chair—reading area for grown-ups to pass the time. Patagonia seems to generally inspire brand devotion in its customers, and this store is certainly a destination for those types. The parking around here is not easy.

This is the **REI Denver** (1416 Platte St., 303/756-3100, www.rei.com, 10am-9pm Mon.-Fri., 10am-7pm Sat., 10am-6pm Sun.) flagship store and it definitely stands out from other locations. REI occupies a historic tramway building right along the South Platte River. The enormous space has a 37-foot climbing pinnacle and there are multiple levels selling clothing, gear, shoes, and outdoor equipment. There is also a small bookstore and a huge map selection. Up on the children's level, parents can let kids romp in the indoor playground near the sale merchandise. Equipment rental is also available here.

Outdoor-gear bargain hunters head to the **Wilderness Exchange Unlimited** (2401 15th St., 303/964-0708, www.wildernessx.com, 11am-8pm Mon.-Fri., 10am-7pm Sat., 10am-6pm Sun.), about one block from the REI flagship store near Confluence Park. The store has a small but regularly refreshed inventory of men's and women's clothing, tents, sleeping bags, and shoes, which are all appropriate to the current season. The Wilderness Exchange buys and trades used outdoor gear at this location, and merchandise includes those used items as well as manufacturer's overstock, discontinued items, and slightly damaged items.

Specialty Foods

It's a genius idea: packaging spices in an appealing and original way. The spices and blends at **Savory Spice** (1537 Platte St., 720/283-2232, www.savoryspiceshop.com, 10am-6pm Mon.-Fri., 10am-5pm Sat., 11am-4pm Sun.) are cleverly named after local geographical highlights, such as rivers, canyons, 14,000-foot peaks, and even neighborhoods. Of course, there are also familiar herbs and spices, such as cinnamon, ginger, paprika, and so much more, but within each of these, there are myriad choices: origin, organic or not, whole or ground. It's hard to resist this shop when the spice scents waft out the door for half a block or so. Now a successful franchise business in at least seven different states, it all started here in this cute little shop.

CAPITOL HILL AND CITY PARK

Books and Music

Capitol Hill Books (300 E. Colfax Ave., 303/837-0700, www.capitolhillbooks.com, 10am-6pm Mon.-Sat., 11am-5pm Sun.) is a simple, old-fashioned bookstore with that musty smell and overflowing bookshelves stuffed with a wide variety of books. Though there are a few rare and antique books for sale here, this is a general bookstore with various paperbacks and hardbacks available. Located on the block just behind the Colorado State Capitol, Capitol Hill Books is easy walking distance from anywhere in downtown or Capitol Hill. This is a mellow place to spend a few hours just browsing the stacks.

Denver's beloved independent bookstore has three large locations: LoDo, Colfax Avenue, and the suburb of Littleton. The layout of this **Tattered Cover Book Store** (2526 E. Colfax Ave., 303/322-7727, www.tatteredcover.com, 9am-9pm Mon.-Sat., 10am-6pm Sun.), within the historic Lowenstein Theater on Colfax Avenue, is unique—with bookshelves where theater seats used to be—and takes some getting used to. Each store has thousands of books and periodicals, as well as a coffee shop and event space for book readings and signings. Check the Tattered Cover website or get on the mailing list to stay up-to-date on visiting authors, book signings, and more. The LoDo location can be found at 1628 16th Street at Wynkoop Street (303/436-1070), and the Littleton store is in the Aspen Grove center at 7301 S. Santa Fe Dr. (303/470-7050).

Hands down, **Twist & Shout** (2508 E. Colfax Ave., 303/722-1943, www.twistandshout.com, 10am-9pm Mon.-Sat., 10am-6pm Sun.) is Denver's favorite independent music store. The store has joined the Tattered Cover Book Store at the Lowenstein Theater complex on Colfax Avenue, and it's better than ever. Shoppers can hang out and comfortably listen to tunes before purchasing, and the sales staff is always helpful and knowledgeable, or can find someone who knows even more. There are frequently free live music performances at the store, so check the website often to see if your favorite band is playing.

For anyone who still has a record player and not enough music to play on it, **Wax Trax** (638 E. 13th Ave., 303/831-7246, www.waxtraxrecords.com, 10am-7pm Mon.-Thurs., 10am-8pm Fri.-Sat., 11am-6pm Sun.) is the place to go for rare 45s and LPs. That's right, records—as in vinyl. The stock is not completely vintage; the shop carries CDs and DVDs to round out more recent decades of music. This is the original Wax Trax—started by the owners of the more famous Chicago store and then bought and basically preserved by new owners way back in the 1970s.

Clothing and Accessories

It seems there is a **Buffalo Exchange** in every town now, or at least in every town with a college or university in it. This Capitol Hill store (230 E. 13th Ave., 303/866-0165, www.buffaloexchange.com, 11am-8pm Mon.-Sat., noon-6pm Sun.) is dependable; its skillful buyers, with good to wild taste, regularly buy new used items that make thrift shopping fun. While many of the clothes and shoes here are vintage and evoke a bygone era of fashion, some are recently used items from the mall, available here at a discount. There is a larger store in SoBo (51 Broadway, 303/866-0165).

Talulah Jones (1122 E. 17th Ave., 303/832-1230, www.talulahonline.com, 10am-6pm Mon.-Fri., 10am-5pm Sat., 11am-4pm Sun.) is a little shop of girly and kids' treasures. The well-stocked inventory of stationery, soaps, jewelry, handbags, scarves, toys, books, and children's clothing takes some patient digging through to find that just-right item. The largest area of the two-room store is devoted to kids, with a few things set out for playing with as moms burrow through a basket of musical instruments or wiggle toys. While there are many small, independent labels here, there are also more recognizable items, such as the Calico Critters line of toys.

Health and Beauty

Woodhouse Day Spa (9941 E. 17th Ave., 303/813-8488, www.denver.woodhousespas.com, 9am-7pm Mon.-Wed., 9am-8pm Thurs.-Sun.) is a favorite for spa treatments, according to several local surveys and word of mouth. Nothing has been overlooked at Woodhouse, including attention to male clients, for whom there is a menu of services ranging from massage to facials. A day at the spa would take over six hours to enjoy with various manicures, pedicures, and "refreshers." The location in a stunning old home along 17th Avenue is ideal for people who are staying downtown and don't want to travel too far to a spa.

HIGHLANDS

The heart of the greater Highlands neighborhood is **Highlands Square** (stretching from Julian St. to Meade St. along 32nd Ave.). Just like Larimer Square in LoDo, there is no actual square here, but rather a cluster of businesses spread over a few blocks. What makes this an appealing place to shop is the range of goods—gifts for expecting parents or their little ones at Real Baby, women's apparel at Dragonfly with shoes at Strut next door, and accessories at Kismet, right across the street. Book lovers can unwind at Westside Books, and the Perfect Petal has flowers and an assortment of gifts perfect for housewarmings.

Books

It's hard to decide if this should be under bars or bookstores—because it's both. You can just stop by for a small plate and a glass of wine or run in for a gift or plan to have your book club meet here and do both. You're doing good on so many levels when you patronize **BookBar**

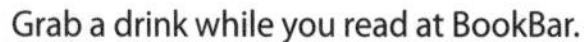

Grab a drink while you read at BookBar.

(4280 Tennyson St., 3720/433-2227, www.bookbardenver.com, 10am-10pm Mon.-Sat., 10am-8pm Sun): supporting literacy, supporting an independent business, supporting local food and beverage makers. It's win, win, win! Be sure to check out their new backyard and patio.

Children's Clothing

Founded and owned by parents in the Highlands neighborhood, **Real Baby** (4315 Tennyson St, 303/477-2229, www.realbabyinc.com, 10am-7pm Mon.-Sat., 11am-5pm Sun.) is the real deal when looking for everything from hip and casual maternity clothes to baby clothes and toddler furniture, toys, and books. A Thomas the Tank Engine table set up in the book and toy area makes it easy for parents to keep shopping while junior is busy playing nearby. Don't rush through here; there are books for grown-ups about babies and kids, CDs for the whole family to enjoy, and body care products for moms and babes, all tucked into cubby shelves lining the wall.

Clothing and Accessories

At **Babareeba Then & Now** (3629 W. 32nd Ave., 303/458-5712, 11:30am-5:30pm Sun.-Wed., 10:30am-7pm Thurs.-Sat.), Highlands Square's only vintage shop, the notion is of "recycled" clothes, not used. True vintage women's clothing is seamlessly blended with newer styles, making the 1960s and the 2000s a perfect match. The owner seems to prefer dresses and casual wear to business attire when she is buying (or recycling) clothes to sell in the shop. In addition to apparel, there are shoes, handbags, and all kinds of accessories.

The most casual of the local men's boutiques, **Berkeley Supply** (3615 W. 32nd Ave., 303/433-6331, 11am-6pm Tues.-Sat., noon-5pm Sun.) is geared toward the man who likes a sturdy pair of jeans or casual pants and a hip T-shirt; the emphasis is on American-made products. Brands here include Filson, Stitch, Red Wing, and Rogue Territory.

When women need a new outfit or top with jeans for a girls' night out or a date with someone special, **Dragonfly** (3615 W. 32nd Ave., 303/433-6331, 10:30am-6:30pm Mon.-Sat., 11am-5pm Sun.) should be a first stop. Everything from small designers to larger, established brands are carried here. Check out Tart Collections, Velvet, Harper Clothing, SOLD Design Lab, Ella Moss, Trina Turk, and lots more. Head next door to Strut to complete the look with a new pair of shoes.

Here is cute and affordable women's clothing. The concept at this boutique is to keep prices under $50 as much as possible. The emphasis at **Inspyre Boutique** (2021 W. 32nd Ave., 303/718-2645, www.inspyreboutique.com, 11am-8pm Mon.-Sat., 11am-6pm Sun.) is on women, and the window displays of sexy and colorful dresses make it appear as if the boutique is just for the fairer sex, but gentlemen are welcome and might find jeans or a hip T-shirt. These are not household brand names, but when you find that perfect summer dress or sexy top, who cares? It's always better to wear something more original, anyway.

Looking for that perfect colorful scarf, a stylish summer hat (or winter one), or just some unique jewelry? **Kismet** (3640 W. 32nd Ave., 303/477-3378, www.kismetaccesories.com, 10:30am-6:30pm Tues.-Sat., 11am-5pm Sun.-Mon.) is my personal fave for these items, but they also have sweet little dresses, tops, handbags, belts, and shoes. In the heart of Highlands Square, Kismet is a must-do part of the shopping experience in the neighborhood. The store has two other locations in the greater metro area; check the website for details.

Crammed with colorful accessories, from hats to necklaces to sunglasses and purses, **Starlet** (3450 W. 32nd Ave., 303/433-7827, www.shopstarlet.com, 11am-6pm Mon.-Sat., 11am-5pm Sun.) is an accessory shop for all tastes. There is a second location, which is equally tiny, in the SoBo neighborhood at 26 Broadway. Starlet is a terrific place to find that last-minute hostess gift for a girlfriend who is so hard to shop for. There is more than a hint of vintage in the items at Starlet, which makes them even more special.

Looking for that shoe that you can't find anywhere else in Denver? **Strut** (3611 W. 32nd Ave., 303/477-3361, www.strutdenver.com, 11am-4pm Sun.-Mon., 10am-6pm Tues.-Sat.) probably has it. Miss Sixty, Butter, Ted Baker, and a dozen more shoe brands can be found at Strut, with styles ranging from elegant sandals and flats to knockout heels. Strut is a handbag and accessories store to boot—find Rebecca Norman hoops, Foxy Originals matching necklaces and earrings, and other jeweled surprises. The knowledgeable sales staff can help find a great-looking but still comfortable pair of women's shoes.

Gift and Home

Considered one of Denver's top floral shops, the **Perfect Petal** (3600 W. 32nd Ave., 303/480-0966, www.theperfectpetal.com, 9am-8pm Mon.-Sat., 11am-5pm Sun.) is also a charming boutique in the heart of Highlands Square. It's really one of those very girly shops with cute stationery, antique jewelry, cookbooks, candles, and other sweet-smelling and -looking goods. The flowers are up some steps in the rear of the store and can be bought by the stem or made into creative and unusual arrangements.

Wild Yarns (1227 21st St., 303/433-3762, www.wildyarns.com, noon-3pm Tues., 11am-6pm Wed.-Sat., noon-3pm Sun.) has a friendly, helpful staff and regular classes for beginning to more advanced knitters. For those of us novice knitters, the idea of "local" yarn is as foreign as purling, but the name Wild Yarns is actually a clue to the fact that this shop specializes in Western-produced yarns. Sign up to learn how to knit a purse, socks, blankets, and much more.

Specialty Foods

The selection at **St. Killian's Cheese Shop** (3211 Lowell Blvd., 303/477-0374, www.st-killianscheeseshop.com, 1pm-6pm Mon., 11am-7pm Wed.-Sat., noon-5pm Sun.) keeps growing, though the shop has remained the same size. Choosing cheese can be as daunting as finding the right wine—it requires a bit of knowledge and expertise. The owners of St. Killian's are happy to let customers sample the cheese, and they explain the flavors and origins of each oh-so-patiently. It's the perfect place to pick up a picnic lunch with salamis and cheese, along with bread from the **Denver Bread Company** down the street (3200 Irving St., 303/455-7194, http://thedenverbreadcompany.com, 10am-6pm Sun.-Fri., 9am-5pm Sat.). Pick up a bottle of wine next door at **Mondo Vino** (3601 W. 32nd Ave., 303/458-3858, www.mondovino.net, 10:30am-10pm Mon.-Thurs., 10:30am-11pm Fri.-Sat., noon-8pm Sun.), and it's a meal.

WASHINGTON PARK AND CHERRY CREEK

Cherry Creek is also a shopping district, not just an actual creek winding through Denver. Here you'll find a large and appealing mall adjacent to Cherry Creek North, a neighborhood of boutiques, cafés, and galleries. Many of these boutiques cater to an elite clientele, but don't let it deter you—there are always bargains to be found.

The greater Washington Park neighborhood offers mini shopping districts with South Gaylord Street walking distance from the park and South Pearl Street south of the park by car or a short walk from a light rail stop.

Books and Music

For those in search of first editions and rare books, the **Hermitage Bookshop** (290 Fillmore St., 303/388-6811, www.hermitagebooks.com, 10am-5:30pm Mon.-Fri., 10am-5pm Sat.) is the best place to go in search of everything from military history to children's books to Western Americana. Just below the sidewalk-level storefronts of Cherry Creek North, the Hermitage is designed for comfortable study of its many texts, with sofas, leather chairs, and coffee tables set up between the bookshelves. It's best to settle in and leisurely browse the inventory of 35,000 titles.

Children's Clothing

From infants to eight-year-olds, **Nest** (2808 E. 6th Ave., 720/287-1372, www.nestdenver.com, 10am-6pm Mon.-Sat., noon-4pm Sun.) can dress your boy or girl fashionably without breaking the bank. Every time I am in this shop, the racks are full to bursting with the latest collections from Tea, Petit Bateau, Splendid, Ella Moss, and Mimi & Magee—and that's just the clothes. There is also a small selection of infant and toddler shoes, hair accessories, and toys for the little ones. A second location in Larimer Square (1408 Larimer St., Ste. 102, 303/534-1974) has less inventory and only goes up to five-year-olds, but still carries the same brands.

Clothing and Accessories

In a first for Goodwill Industries of Denver, **Deja Blue** (9303 University Blvd., 303/996-5668, www.goodwilldenver.org/dejablue, 10am-6pm Mon.-Sat., 11am-6pm Sun.) is a boutique that features only gently used high-end fashions and accessories. Your wallet and your conscience will like shopping here. The store opened in March 2012, and it is not a donation site, but the proceeds from sales here go to Goodwill programs. Deja Blue also features repurposed fixtures and displays.

Eccentricity (290 Fillmore St., 303/388-8877, www.eccentricity.com, 10:30am-5:30pm Mon.-Fri., 10:30am-5pm Sat.) is the kind of shop someone might walk right by, were it not for that great, eye-catching jacket or sweater hanging in the window that is simply irresistible. This is one of the shops where, at first glance, it seems there isn't a lot in stock, but the genius is that Eccentricity has carefully selected the cream of the crop. With Lucchese cowboy boots and colorful sweaters and shawls, this is the place to piece together that urban Southwestern look.

Many years ago, Terri Garbarini started a small shoe store, which has since expanded to a one-stop shop for women's fashion. While there are still very fine shoes to be found at this store, there are also heaps of sexy women's fashions to choose from. **Garbarini** (3003 E. 3rd Ave., Ste. D, 303/333-8686, www.garbarinishop.com, 10am-6pm Mon.-Sat., noon-5pm Sun.) stays on the cutting edge of the latest styles, and the store is always crammed full of options—from flirty Nicole Miller dresses to sexy Rebecca Beeson T-shirts. The sales staff is knowledgeable, helpful, and honest when it comes to helping you put together an outfit or find that perfect-fitting pair of jeans.

What started as a custom leather goods shop in nearby Boulder in the 1960s has evolved into one of the country's best shops for a sophisticated and discriminating clientele. While **Lawrence Covell** (225 Steele St., 303/320-1023, www.lawrencecovell.com, 10am-6pm Mon.-Sat.) sells both men's and women's clothing, this is the place for men who can afford to shop in style but aren't sure what that style is. Personal shopping and wardrobe consultation are available, with the owners as experts to help the most fashion-challenged. What man doesn't look his best in a Kiton suit and necktie or a Jil Sander shirt?

No appointment is necessary for a personal bra fitting at **Le Soutien** (9246 Milwaukee St., 303/377-0515, www.lesoutien.com, 10am-6pm Mon.-Fri., 10am-5pm Sat.), where customers can select from only the best lingerie lines—Chantelle, Simone Perele, and Cosabella, to name a few. Just like all fashion, lingerie has seasons, so there are new choices in spring and fall in different colors and styles. Le Soutien also has swimwear, which needs to fit all those same areas just as perfectly, if not better.

Long considered a high-water mark of women's fashion in Denver, **Max** (264 Detroit St., 303/321-4949, www.maxfashion.com, 10am-6pm Mon.-Sat., noon-5pm Sun.) is the store to visit for the woman who needs an extra-special dress, skirt, or outfit. At any one of Max's stores, a customer may be helped by the owner himself, Max Martinez. Max and his staff know women, and how to dress them properly in the best styles. Look for Stella McCartney, Chloé, Prada, Thakoon, Versace, and many other fabulous designers. Finances pinched? Head down to the lower level for the Max outlet store, with lower prices on the same hot designers. Hours differ for the outlet store, so call ahead.

Finding a good bra-fitting expert like those at **SOL** (Cherry Creek North, 248 Detroit St., 303/394-1060, www.sollingerie.com, 10am-6pm Mon.-Sat.)—which is short for "Store of Lingerie"—is just as important as finding a good hairdresser. Once a woman has been properly fitted for a bra, there's no going back to guessing sizes on her own. Sexy, lacy, comfortable, and practical are all found at SOL in the form of thongs, panties, bras, camisoles, and pajamas, including slinky sleepwear and loungewear from SOL's own line.

Men's casual sportswear lines are found at **Trout's American Sportswear** (1077 S. Gaylord St., 303/733-3983, www.trouts.net, 10am-6pm Mon.-Fri., 10am-5:30pm Sat., 11am-4pm Sun.) among the shops and restaurants on Old South Gaylord Street in the Washington Park neighborhood. Men who like Cole Haan footwear and the colorful prints and simple khakis of designers like Tommy Bahama and Bills Khakis will enjoy outfitting themselves at Trout's. Imagine a well-dressed man on a long vacation—that's the idea for Trout's clientele.

Gift and Home

The **Artisan Center** (2757 E. 3rd Ave., 303/333-1201, www.artisancenterdenver.com, 10am-5:30pm Mon.-Sat., noon-5pm Sun.) is a can't-miss store for people who like precious gifty items or are looking for the perfect present. Outside the store there are colorful wind chimes or garden items, and inside it's a plethora of trinkets. There are baby clothes, soaps, candles, jewelry, dishes, scarves, rugs, cards, and little bowls of even tinier things, like matchbox shrines. It seems like there is never a season when this store is not busy with customers carefully selecting just the right treasure—and they've been doing it since 1977. The Artisan Center also offers free and lovely gift wrapping.

Really two stores, **5 Green Boxes'** locations are one block apart and have slightly different concepts. The original, what is called the "Little Store" (1596 S. Pearl St., 303/777-2331, www.5greenboxes.com, 10am-6pm Mon.-Sat., noon-5pm Sun.), is chock-full of knickknacks that include pretty little shoes, colorful scarves, jewelry, and more. The "Big Store" (1705 South Pearl St., 303/282-5481) offers home decor items, including its own line of upholstered chairs (very shabby chic) and footstools. Need a wool three-tiered wedding cake? This is the place. They also have a location in Union Station.

At first glance, **HW Home** (199 Clayton Ln., 303/394-9222, www.hwhome.com, 10am-6pm Mon.-Thurs., 10am-7pm Fri.-Sat., 11am-5pm Sun.) appears to be an upscale chain furniture store, but in fact, it is a locally owned shop with three locations in Colorado. What makes this store fabulous is its ability to put it all together so it looks meant to be, and maybe even like you did it yourself. It's not straight from a catalog cookie-cutter style, and emphasizes top-notch designs for living rooms, bedrooms, and dining rooms.

Beyond eco-friendly and green shopping is recycled, or **Revampt** (2601 E. 3rd Ave., 720/536-5644, www.revamptgoods.com, 10am-6:30pm Mon.-Sat.)—goods that have found a second life as some useful home furnishing or decor. Skateboards are now earrings, cabins are now trunks, bike rims and sprockets are now side tables, silverware has become napkin rings, barrels are turned into one-of-a-kind chairs, and the list of seemingly improbably transformations goes on.

Even with the rise in postage rates and increasing use of email, there is still room in the world for old-fashioned stationery. At **The Stationery Company** (2818 E. 6th Ave., 303/388-1133, www.stationerycompany.com, 10am-6pm Mon.-Fri., 10am-5pm Sat.), the owner and her excellent staff are there to help pick out wedding and birth announcement cards, or just let customers browse the shelves of greeting cards, boxes of stationery, and other odds and ends, such as baby blankets and books, wrapping paper, toiletries, and clocks.

Health and Beauty

Just a block or so away from the busy sidewalks of the Cherry Creek North shopping district is the calm oasis of fabulous skin care at **Edit Euro Spa** (159 Adams St., 303/377-1617, www.editeurospa.com, 9am-5:30pm Mon.-Sat). In a two-story Victorian house, rooms have been transformed into miniature day spas where the city's best facials and waxing are done. One look at the owner's gorgeous skin and anyone will be sold on the services and products at Edit. To combat Colorado's dry climate and harsh sunshine, be sure to check out the hydrating treatments and skin care line.

Open-Air Markets

The **Cherry Creek Fresh Market** (N. Cherry Creek Dr. at University Blvd., 303/442-1837, www.coloradofreshmarkets.com, 8am-1pm Sat. May-Oct., 9am-1pm Wed. June-Sept.) is very popular on Saturday mornings in summer, when fresh produce and flowers are available weekly from farms around the state. It's a chance to meet the people growing your food and hear their stories of farm life. Check out the website to see what's in season and expected soon at the market. Colorado specialties include apples, peaches, and Rocky Ford melons.

Smaller than the Cherry Creek Fresh Market, the **Old South Pearl Street Farmers Market** (S. Pearl St. between E. Florida and Iowa Aves., www.oldsouthpearlstreet.com, 9am-1pm Sun. June-Oct.) is utterly charming. The market is set right on the blocked-off street, which is lined with restaurants open for breakfast and brunch, and shops set to open shortly. Because this tends to be a quieter event, it's easy to chat with the farmers and learn more about where the produce is grown and maybe even how to best prepare it.

Toys

As much for adults as kids, the **Wizard's Chest** (230 Fillmore St., 303/321-4304, www.wizardschest.com, 10am-7pm Mon.-Fri., 10am-5:30pm Sat.-Sun.) is a year-round toy store, but it is *the* place to go for Halloween costumes every fall. With its faux castle storefront, the Wizard's Chest practically screams playful to passersby. The name is also a clue to the many magic tricks available here—cards, prankster items, kits, and DVDs. Ask any of the helpful sales staff to point you in the direction of the toy you seek, whether it be stuffed animals or dolls, novelty items, action figures, science experiments, or those wacky costumes.

Shopping Centers and Districts

Cherry Creek Mall (3000 E. 1st Ave., 303/388-3900, www.shopcherrycreek.com, 10am-9pm Mon.-Sat., 11am-6pm Sun.) is the counterpoint to Cherry Creek North, drawing lots of shoppers to its anchor stores like Nordstrom, Saks, Neiman Marcus, and Macy's. The other 160-plus stores include Tiffany & Co., Burberry, and Calvin Klein. There is a movie theater on the second level, and the restaurants inside the mall tend to be fast food, with pizza, ice cream, and cookies. The most popular place in the mall is a free play area with giant foam pieces of breakfast food for babies and young children to climb on. At Christmastime, the lines for Santa Claus are some of the longest in the city. Outside of the mall are additional stores and restaurants generally considered part of the mall, such as **Elway's Restaurant** (2500 E. 1st Ave., 303/399-5353, www.elways.com). Parking at the mall is free and shaded.

Cherry Creek North (bounded by 1st Ave. to Adams St. to the north, 3rd Ave. to the west, and Josephine St. to the south) has long had a reputation for being a shopping district for the well-to-do, and it does not disappoint in this regard. Located across from the Cherry Creek Mall, the Cherry Creek North shopping district is known for the locally owned shops that have been here for decades. As boutiques have become vogue again in contrast to malls, national stores have begun to rent space in Cherry Creek North rather than in the mall and some have the appearance of being one of the local shops. Around every corner is another shop for every occasion—menswear, womenswear, gifts, art, and more.

Sports and Recreation

Recreation is part of everything Denverites do. Rather than inhibit activity, the thinner air at 5,280 feet above sea level encourages it, since the body is working that much harder and burning calories much more efficiently. Plus, it's easy to get motivated when there are more sunny days here than in Miami, Florida. Nearby parks in the foothills mean that city dwellers can get their mountain fix by driving 30 minutes or less to a trailhead for a day hike amid forests and wildflowers.

DOWNTOWN

Biking

You can rent a bike to ride around Denver at your convenience. **Denver B-cycle** (2737 Larimer St., 303/825-3325, http://denver.bcycle.com) provides red bicycles from dozens of docking stations around the city. There is a fee to check out the bikes and, like a taxicab, there are rates being added on as long as you keep the bike checked out after the first 30 minutes. This was the first large-scale municipal bike-sharing system in the United States, and it has now spread to many other cities. Fun features of each bike include a front basket and a hidden computer system that can track the distance ridden, the calories burned, and the carbon offset from riding instead of driving.

Health Clubs

The **Denver Athletic Club** (1325 Glenarm Pl., 303/534-1211, www.denverathleticclub.cc) is as much a social club as a place to work out, and it is also home to the Denver Petroleum Club, which was established in 1948 for members of the oil and gas industries to schmooze. Founded in 1884, the Denver Athletic Club is one of the oldest private clubs in the country. It is walking distance from the Colorado

B-cycle is Denver's bike sharing program.

Convention Center and many hotels. Situated in a landmark historic building, the interior of the club is completely modern with a swimming pool, racquetball and squash courts, volleyball and basketball courts, exercise studios, and a bowling alley. The 125,000-square-foot club has the latest fitness equipment and is open 24 hours a day, 365 days a year.

The **YMCA** (25 E. 16th Ave., 303/861-8300, www.denverymca.org) just off the end of the 16th Street Mall is a nice, affordable place to work out for people who live and/or work downtown. The only downside is that there is no pool at this location, though a membership at this YMCA location is valid at other locations in the city with pools. At the downtown location, there are treadmills, indoor cycling, weight machines, and fitness classes. There is a chance to relax in the sauna or steam room, or with a massage.

Ice-Skating

Sponsored by Southwest Airlines, the Southwest Rink at **Skyline Park** (1701 Arapahoe St., www.downtowndenver.org, mid-Nov.-mid.-Feb., free, $2 skate rentals) has become an annual holiday tradition for many Denver families (including mine!). Skating downtown from about Thanksgiving through Valentine's Day is a great way to enjoy seeing the city all dressed up for the season. The rink is located at the base of the D&F tower, where there is a small outdoor pizza restaurant and bar. Families, couples, experts, and novices all come out to slip, slide, and glide around the small rink during winter.

GOLDEN TRIANGLE, LINCOLN PARK, AND SOBO

Biking

Bikes need regular maintenance just like automobiles. Schedule a tune-up at the **Bicycle Doctor** (9860 Broadway, 303/831-7228, www.bicycledr.com, 10am-7pm Mon.-Fri., 10am-5pm Sat.) and get the wheels aligned and the tires checked, along with other advice on fixing up your bike. The shop also sells lots of cycling gear and rents quality bicycles. Unlike the city's popular bike rental program, here there is a large selection of bikes to rent with a friendly staffer to offer advice and tips on where to go and the best routes for bikes.

LODO AND PLATTE RIVER VALLEY

Inside the **REI flagship store** (1416 Platte St., 303/756-3100, www.rei.com, 10am-9pm Mon.-Fri., 10am-7pm Sat., 10am-6pm Sun.) at Confluence Park is a small counter adjacent to the bookstore called the **Outdoor Recreation Information Center** (ORIC, www.oriconline.org). Have a question about where to go and explore? This is the place to go for free advice, maps, and brochures. ORIC is partnered with a long list of official organizations, including the U.S. Forest Service, Colorado Division of Wildlife, Colorado State Parks, and more. There are also maps and books for sale.

Parks

The point where Cherry Creek merges with the South Platte River is the approximate spot where gold was discovered by prospectors in 1858, leading to the founding of Denver. The confluence is now a mecca for outdoor enthusiasts. Rushing water carries kayakers through chutes and under bridges, while cyclists and runners whir past on riverside paths and families relax on the grassy knolls and sandy beaches throughout **Confluence Park** (15th St. between Platte and Little Raven Sts., 720/913-1311, www.denvergov.org, 5am-11pm daily). A large deck on the side of the REI store in the enormous former Denver Tramway Building invites people to sit and rest from all the activity or contemplate their next move while having a bite to eat.

Don't miss the historical signs posted along pedestrian paths in the park that tell the tragic story of the Native Americans who first called this spot home. Nearby Little Raven Street is named in honor of the Arapaho chief who struggled to coexist with white settlers.

At the time of this writing, there was

construction on Confluence Park, though many bike paths remain open. Trails were being upgraded for wheelchair accessibility.

Biking

The **Cherry Creek Bike Path** (Confluence Park to University Blvd.) is one of the most popular off-street recreation paths in the city. There is a concrete path along either side of Cherry Creek, with one side designated for wheels and the other for pedestrians. Starting at Confluence Park, the creek and paths run below the street level of busy Speer Boulevard all the way to the Cherry Creek shopping district, where Speer Boulevard intersects with University Boulevard. There are ramps at intervals on the paths to climb up to street level and see the nearby sights. Down below the streets, it's a world away from traffic and urban life, with greenery and the sounds of the water to listen to instead. It's 4.4 miles from Cherry Creek to University Boulevard, but the trail continues on to the Cherry Creek Reservoir (another nine miles from University Blvd.).

The bike paths along the **Platte River Greenway** (Confluence Park to Bear Creek Trail) are truly appealing, with lots of cottonwood trees and other greenery along the way. Leaving from Confluence Park in either direction, there are some stretches through industrial sites that are less attractive. Heading south from the park, the concrete path goes out to the nearby suburbs and affords views of the Front Range at different intervals. To go all the way to Bear Creek Trail is an easy ride of 8.6 miles.

The Cherry Creek Bike Path and Platte River Greenway are the main activity paths within the city, but each extends beyond the county lines with offshoots to many other popular paths for bicycling, running, and other sports.

Climbing

The **REI Denver Flagship Pinnacle** (1416 Platte St., 303/756-3100, www.rei.com, 10am-4pm Sat., $10 non-members, free for members' first climb, $5 all additional climbs) is a 47-foot imitation of the actual sandstone climbing rocks west of town. The pinnacle is a 6,400-square-foot surface of hand-sculpted formations, including hand- and footholds instead of bolts. REI offers classes for beginners, women, kids, and more with a schedule that changes monthly. (Classes are for REI members, but it's easy to join.) While most of the people who scale this monolith are serious about climbing, it's become a favorite snapshot spot with people paying to climb just high enough for that "Look at me!" moment.

Kayaking

The South Platte River through **Confluence Park** (15th St. between Platte and Little Raven Sts., www.denvergov.org) has been slightly manipulated to create an exciting white-water park with Class II-III rapids, depending on the flow. From behind REI to just below 20th Street, there are 13 drops in 1.5 miles of river. Don't be shy about your kayaking skills here, though, because bridges hover right over the chutes, making this as popular a spot to watch boaters as it is to boat. Also be careful with those rollovers, as the water quality is highly questionable.

Whether you're looking for advice and gear to head up to the white water of the mountains, or just interested in a quick lesson steps away on the South Platte River, **Confluence Kayaks** (2373 15th St., 303/433-3676, www.confluencekayaks.com, 10am-9pm Mon.-Thurs., 10am-7pm Fri., 10am-6pm Sat., noon-5pm Sun.) is the place to go. If you are in Commons Park or Confluence Park during the warm months, chances are you will spot a few kayakers either in the chutes or dripping wet as they walk back to Confluence Kayaks to return their rented boat. Pool and lake lessons are taught at other locations, and private instruction is also available.

Sledding

Depending on your perspective, Denver has been either blessed or cursed with some blizzards in recent years. Sure, the roads were a nightmare of icy potholes, but it made for great urban sledding conditions and a chance for residents to sample what's within walking distance of their homes. One of the more popular sled slides is in **Commons Park** (15th and Little Raven Sts., 720/913-1311, www.denvergov.org, 5am-11pm daily), where different sides of the hill provide a variety of speeds and chutes for all ages. For those who aren't close enough to walk and don't want to drive on winter roads, Commons Park is just a short walk from the light rail station behind Union Station.

Skateboarding

One of the largest free public skateparks in the country is the **Denver Skatepark** (2205 19th St., www.denverskatepark.com, 5am-11pm daily, free), on the northern edge of Commons Park just off the South Platte River. Its three acres (or 50,000 square feet) of concrete are meant to mimic an urban skate environment. The park includes a half-pipe, a 10-foot-deep "dog bowl," handrails, and a lot more features. Though helmets and pads are always recommended, they are not required by law at the skatepark. Check out the website to see photos of the park and find links to other skateparks around the state.

Spectator Sports

Even amid a recent run of losing seasons, the **Colorado Rockies** (Coors Field, 2001 Blake St., 303/762-5437, http://colorado.rockies.mlb.com) continue to attract committed fans to home games at Coors Field. The team played its first game in 1993 at the original Mile High Stadium (now Sports Authority Field at Mile High, previously Invesco at Mile High, and rebuilt) to such huge success that architects working on the new Coors Field expanded the seating capacity to over 50,000 for the 1995 opening game. The "rockpile" cheap seats and attractive stadium keep the fans donning the purple-and-black team colors, even when the Rockies aren't winning a lot of games. An on-site playground and the Buckaroo snack bar make the baseball field popular with families. There are 75-minute tours of Coors Field offered throughout the year. Call ahead to join a tour that goes down into the clubhouses and up to the "mile high" seats.

Certainly a number of big-name basketball players have been on the **Denver Nuggets** (Pepsi Center, 1000 Chopper Cir., 303/405-1100, www.nba.com/nuggets) team over the years, but that hasn't translated into titles. A championship win still eludes the Nuggets despite regular playoff appearances. The Nuggets' home games are almost more entertaining during breaks in the game itself, with performances by the cheerleaders and various contests. This National Basketball Association team plays at the Pepsi Center in LoDo.

The **Denver Broncos** (Sports Authority Field at Mile High, 1701 Bryant St., 720/258-3333, www.denverbroncos.com) continue to have a serious fan base year after year. Once the team's Super Bowl-winning quarterback, John Elway is now executive vice president of the team and Peyton Manning is working hard to bring the team back to its full glory. This is a football kind of town, and Broncos fans will brave the coldest weather to cheer on their team.

After relocating from Canada, the **Colorado Avalanche** (Pepsi Center, 1000 Chopper Cir., 303/405-7646, http://avalanche.nhl.com) was the team to beat in the National Hockey League. The 1996 and 2001 Stanley Cup dream team has changed as players have retired, but a recent influx of young talent has again made the Avalanche a team that is exciting to watch. And some former star players, such as Joe Sakic, have become team executives to help oversee this next generation. The Avalanche plays home games at the Pepsi Center in LoDo.

CAPITOL HILL AND CITY PARK

Boating and Fishing

At 25 acres, **Ferril Lake** (City Park, 3300 E. 17th Ave., www.denvergov.org/parks, 5am-11pm daily) is the largest lake in City Park. It allows fishing in a fairly serene setting, considering that it is in the middle of the city and walking distance from downtown. Ferril Lake has yellow perch, sunfish, and carp stocked in the fall, and rainbow trout stocked in the spring. Only rented novelty paddleboats are allowed in Ferril Lake, and fishing is only permitted from piers or platforms.

While 6th Avenue may seem a long way from a perfect fly-fishing spot, Denver is just a couple hours' drive from some great rivers ideal for hooking a big one. **Trout's Fly Fishing** (1303 E. 6th Ave., 877/464-0034, www.troutsflyfishing.com, 10am-7pm Mon.-Wed., 10am-8pm Thurs.-Fri., 9am-6pm Sat., 10am-5pm Sun.) not only sells gear and flies, but also teaches the necessary skills in its outfitting and education center. Visit the store or the website to find out about fishing events in the area and to get local fishing reports, along with a list of the best places in Colorado to fish.

Golf

The location of the 18-hole regulation **City Park Golf Course** (2500 York St., 303/295-2096, www.denvergov.org/denvergolf) is pretty great, given its proximity to downtown and views of the skyline and mountain peaks beyond. Tree-lined fairways can make the course a little challenging. There is also a pro shop, a driving range, and the pleasant Bogey's on the Park restaurant at the golf course. The golf course is part of City Park, but a road separates it from the main park and attractions, such as the Denver Zoo and the Denver Museum of Nature and Science.

Parks

Where the Capitol Hill neighborhood blends into the Congress Park neighborhood is **Cheesman Park** (Franklin and 8th Sts., 720/913-1311, www.denvergov.org, 5:30am-11pm daily), which abuts the Denver Botanic Gardens' south end. The large Parthenon-like pavilion in Cheesman Park is popular for wedding pictures, with a stunning view of the Rocky Mountains serving as a backdrop. Many high-rise apartment buildings overlook the park, an oasis of green in the densely packed neighborhood. There is a large playground and a gravel running path in Cheesman. Due to the sizable gay and lesbian population in Capitol Hill, Cheesman is known as an LGBT hangout and is the place where the annual Pridefest parade begins.

HIGHLANDS

Parks

Though the greater Highlands

Denver's Cheesman Park

neighborhood has numerous small parks and is also close to downtown parks (such as Commons Park), the gem in this part of town is **Sloan's Lake Park** (Sheridan Blvd. and W. 26th Ave., www.denvergov.org, 5am-11pm daily). The park is primarily the lake itself, which is encircled by a mile-or-so-long running and biking path. There are two playgrounds, tennis and basketball courts, and athletic fields. Boating, water-skiing, and fishing are all permitted on the lake. It rarely feels crowded at Sloan's Lake, except during the very popular **Dragon Boat Festival** each summer.

WASHINGTON PARK AND CHERRY CREEK

Parks

With two lakes, tennis courts, jogging and bicycle paths, playgrounds, a soccer field, a recreation center, flower gardens, and more within its 165 acres, **Washington Park** (S. Downing St. and E. Louisiana Ave., 303/698-4962, www.denvergov.org, 5am-11pm daily) is one of the city's most popular parks. People are drawn to this neighborhood for the historic bungalows that surround the park as much as for the active lifestyle of the park. Poet and journalist Eugene Field lived in Denver for two years in the late 1800s and is remembered in Washington Park with a statue titled *Wynken, Blynken and Nod* after his most well-known poem. Rent a boat or go fishing in the summer to get a different perspective from the water in this park. Views of the mountains can be had from various spots in the park, too.

Smith Lake is one of three lakes at Washington Park that offer many recreational options, including fishing. The 19-acre Smith Lake is stocked with carp, catfish, largemouth bass, and rainbow trout. Smith Lake also allows sailboats, canoes, kayaks, and rowboats, and it has a fishing pier. Willow trees provide a bit of shade on hot days, and a boathouse at the lake can be rented out for private parties. **Grasmere Lake** is also 19 acres with a similar selection of fish to catch, but the difference is that this lake is a little less busy than Smith, which has the boathouse on one side. **Lily Pond** is a mere one acre and is designated for children under 16 to practice their fishing skills.

Tennis

Located just beyond the shops and mall of Cherry Creek is **Gates Tennis Center** (3300 E. Bayaud Ave., 303/355-4461, www.

A couple sits by Smith Lake in Washington Park.

gatestenniscenter.info, 7am-10pm daily, $5-8), a 20-court outdoor tennis center. There is an indoor pro shop and lounge. The center is open in the winter, but it's hit-or-miss based on current weather conditions. There are private lessons, group programs, adult mixers, and peewee classes all taught by professionals.

Accommodations

There have been some exciting additions to lodging options in Denver recently. Those flying in and out of Denver International Airport may be delighted to discover that there is now a Westin hotel there. In the city, the new kid in town is also the old guard: the Crawford Hotel at the historic Union Station. Most of Denver's accommodations are within walking distance of recommended sights, shops, restaurants, bars, nightclubs, and recreation areas. Not only are many of these wonderful places to stay, they are also home to some of the city's top-notch restaurants and bars.

Budget travelers will have the toughest time finding a decent, affordable room that is very close to the action of the city's sports venues, bars, restaurants, and nightclubs. Options include hostels and a couple of hotels that overlook downtown from the eastern edge of the Highlands neighborhood. Bed-and-breakfasts in the Capitol Hill neighborhood give visitors the best chance to experience life like a local in an area of historic homes and a few apartment buildings. Capitol Hill is also close enough to downtown to walk. East of the city center, there is a strip of hotels along Quebec Street. While this is not walking distance from downtown, there are parks and restaurants nearby.

Some Denver hotels condone cannabis consumption, but don't openly advertise. For links to these and marijuana-friendly rental properties, visit **Colorado Pot Guide** (www.coloradopotguide.com) or **Visit Denver** (Convention and Visitors Bureau, www.denver.org/hotels).

The rates listed are based on double occupancy in the high season (summer).

DOWNTOWN

$150-250

Formerly the Comfort Inn, the **Holiday Inn Express Denver Downtown** (401 17th St., 888/465-4329, www.ihg.com, $150-299) has been freshly renovated. Here you can enjoy some of the amenities of staying at the Brown Palace while lodging at this more affordable hotel just across the street. The two hotels are connected by a skybridge, which allows easy access to the Brown's restaurants, shops, and spa. Guests here can also order room service from the Brown. The Holiday Inn Express is just one block from the 16th Street Mall and its shops and restaurants, and it's an easy walk from the Colorado Convention Center. While rooms here are budget-sized, they are designed to maximize views of downtown (with little glimpses of mountains between skyscrapers when you face west) with windows letting in the natural light. There is a fee for parking.

The **Courtyard by Marriott Denver Downtown** (934 16th St., 303/571-1114, www.marriott.com, $189-399) is right on the 16th Street Mall and just down the street from the Denver Performing Arts Complex. This Marriott hotel has 177 rooms and a nice restaurant, the Rialto Café, which has patio seating on the mall itself. Being near the Colorado Convention Center, the hotel is ready for business travelers, too, with desks and free high-speed Internet access. This is a pet-free and smoke-free hotel. Parking is tricky at the Courtyard, which offers $20-per-day valet parking. The hotel will also recommend nearby parking lots of varying rates.

The **Crowne Plaza Denver Downtown Hotel** (1450 Glenarm Pl., 303/573-1450 or

877/227-6963, www.hoteldenver.net, $220-440) has a key location within walking distance of the Colorado Convention Center, the Denver Art Museum, the 16th Street Mall, and many restaurants and shops. In addition to the 332 guest rooms and 32 suites, there is a rooftop swimming pool and expanded fitness center.

Guests need a sense of humor and playfulness to truly enjoy **The Curtis** (1405 Curtis St., 303/571-0300, http://thecurtis.com, $159-1,000) and its whimsical touches. The hotel is located across the street from the Denver Center for the Performing Arts and one block from the Colorado Convention Center, so it caters to a spectrum of theater types and business travelers, with an emphasis on youthful attitude. The common areas are themed, from Austin Powers to Elvis (whose voices can also be ordered for wake-up calls), but the 326 rooms are simple and contemporary with modern amenities. An entire floor of rooms is dedicated to travelers with pets.

The 14-story **Denver Marriott Residence Inn City Center** (1725 Champa St., 303/296-3444 or 800/331-3131, www.marriott.com, $169-439) features 229 studio and one-bedroom guest suites that include full kitchens, with separate living areas in the one-bedroom suites. There is both wired and wireless Internet access throughout the hotel, in rooms as well as in the lobby and business center. After a hectic day of meetings, head up to the eighth floor and enjoy the rooftop hot tub for a relaxing soak amid the city lights.

The **Embassy Suites Denver-Downtown/Convention Center** (1420 Stout St., 303/592-1000, http://embassysuites1.hilton.com, $329-400) is taking full advantage of its across-the-street proximity to the Colorado Convention Center. There are 400 rooms, plus meeting and banquet space. And the best part: daily, complimentary, cooked-to-order breakfast and a nightly Manager's Reception in the atrium. But it's not exclusive to business travelers—this hotel boasts family-friendly amenities that include a children's menu, cribs, and playpens.

At Hampton/Homewood Downtown Denver, **Hampton Inn & Suites** (550 15th St., 303/623-5900, www.hamptoninndenver.com, $249-399) and the **Homewood Suites by Hilton** (303/534-7800) form Denver's first "combo hotel." Inside this single 13-story building there are two distinctly different hotels—two lobbies, two front desks, unique decor for each, different kitchens for each, and 302 rooms to choose from in total. The name says it all—it's about proximity for convention-goers here. Amenities include an indoor pool, a gym, complimentary high-speed Internet access, and complimentary breakfast.

The **Hotel Monaco** (1717 Champa St., 303/296-1717 or 800/990-1303, www.monacodenver.com, $199-499) has a playful Western design that welcomes guests. In addition to 189 guest rooms, there is a 24-hour fitness room available to guests, an Aveda Spa and Salon, and Panzano, a restaurant featuring Italian fare. The hotel is so pet-friendly that guests can request a goldfish swimming in its own bowl be brought to their room for company during their stay, or bring their dog with them and schedule Fido for a "pawdicure."

The 13-story **Magnolia Hotel** (818 17th St., 303/607-9000, www.magnoliahotels.com, $249-449) is in a luxuriously remodeled 1906 bank building with 246 guest rooms and suites. With its proximity to the convention center and the city's business district, the Magnolia caters to guests who appreciate high-speed Internet access and a conference room. Harry's Bar and the billiards room offer places to wind down before calling it a night.

With nearly half of their 600-plus rooms designed for business travelers, the **Marriott City Center** (1701 California St., 303/297-1300, www.marriott.com, $179-450) definitely has a niche clientele. It is a three-block walk from the convention center and has more than 25,000 square feet of meeting space, along with a full-service business center. The hotel also attracts leisure travelers, and has laundry and babysitting services available for families. The Marriott City Center has a fitness center and pool, but spa services are at other nearby locations.

Between the skyscrapers of downtown and the historic homes of the Five Points neighborhood is one of the most charming blocks in Denver, home to the ★ **Queen Anne Bed and Breakfast Inn** (2147 Tremont Pl., 303/296-6666, www.queenannebnb.com, $155-230). The inn is made up of two separate late-1800s Victorian houses, connected by a large backyard and patio area. Typically, bed-and-breakfasts are not the preferred lodging of business travelers, but because the Queen Anne is so close to downtown (as well as many restaurants and sights), it attracts business travelers as well as tourists on a romantic getaway.

After a $70 million renovation, the former Adam's Mark Hotel was transformed into the **Sheraton Denver Downtown Hotel** (1550 Court Pl., 303/893-3333 or 800/325-3535, www.sheratondenverdowntown.com, $182-432), which anchors the east end of the 16th Street Mall. A portion of the 1,231 rooms and 82 suites are in an I. M. Pei-designed building. Features include an outdoor heated pool, a fitness center, and a selection of sexy and comfortable restaurants on the ground floor with windows to watch the world go by along the mall.

Over $250

Since first opening its doors in 1892, one hotel has been a symbol of lodging elegance and luxury in Denver. So it's not that the ★ **Brown Palace Hotel and Spa** (321 17th St., 303/297-3111, www.brownpalace.com, $269-1,700) needed to be improved, but that's exactly what happened with a $10.5 million renovation that has given 200 rooms a contemporary look that still respects the classic Victorian bones of the hotel. The triangular building has a beautiful, eight-story stained glass atrium where visitors can enjoy cocktails or English tea service while listening to live piano music. The 230 rooms range from standard rooms to suites and remodeled presidential suites (so named for the many presidents who stayed in them, such as Eisenhower, Roosevelt, and Reagan). The Brown is just a short walk from the Colorado State Capitol, the Denver Art Museum, and many other sights. Or stay in and enjoy the hotel's spa and salon, award-winning restaurants, and cigar bar. **Ship Tavern** (11am-11pm daily, $26-48) has an Old World pub atmosphere and an extensive menu of burgers, prime rib, Rocky Mountain trout, seafood, pasta, and salads, as well as live music (8:30pm Wed.-Sat.). The atmosphere at the **Palace Arms** (5:30pm-9pm Tues.-Sat., $40-55) is one of opulence, and it has long been considered one of Denver's very best restaurants.

The Brown Palace also capitalizes on having truly local amenities: sip a Palace Pale Ale made from the hotel's own artesian well water or sample some of the spa's Rooftop Honey Amenity Line of beauty products made from honey produced on the hotel's rooftop. The hotel has maintained a bee colony on the roof since 2010 (this is the only hotel in Denver, if not the United States, with its own beekeeper), and uses the honey in the daily afternoon tea service. Colorado residents can take advantage of discounted rates on summer weekends thanks to the "Local Love" program, when fabulous rooms can be had for about half price.

Not just one of Denver's finer hotels, the **Four Seasons Hotel Denver** (1111 14th St., 303/389-3000, www.fourseasons.com/Denver, $400-2,500) is also an important piece of the city's skyline, with a distinctive spike sitting atop 45 stories of residences and guest rooms. It hosts a unique combination of travelers and locals, which means that you might be swimming next to a Denverite in the third-story pool, or mixing it up with conventioneers in the hotel's spa. The **Edge Restaurant & Bar** (303/389-3343, www.edgerestaurantdenver.com, 6:30am-2:30pm and 5pm-10pm daily) just off the grand lobby feels elegant for dinner and casual for lunch. What you see is what you get here—the photos on the website accurately show the terrific views of downtown and the mountains, as well as the luxurious decor.

One of the larger downtown hotels is the **Grand Hyatt Denver** (1750 Welton St.,

303/295-1234, www.granddenver.hyatt.com, $399-499), with 512 rooms. Like other downtown hotels, the Grand Hyatt is walking distance to the Colorado Convention Center, the 16th Street Mall, and numerous sights, restaurants, and other attractions. The hotel's unique entrance is found in an alleyway between buildings. The valet parking fee is $37 daily, or there are other parking lots and garages nearby for self-parking. Guests can enjoy a game of tennis on the hotel's rooftop or swim in the indoor pool.

As Denver's boutique luxury hotel, the ★ **Hotel Teatro** (1100 14th St., 303/228-1100, www.hotelteatro.com, $299-519) never disappoints with its excellent service, comfortable rooms (with Frette linens), and award-winning restaurant. The hotel is named for its proximity to the Denver Center for the Performing Arts theater complex across the street, and the lobby is decorated with photographs and costumes of past productions. Amenities at the 110-room Teatro include complimentary transportation in a Cadillac Escalade anywhere in downtown, Godiva chocolates with turndown service, and many perks for pets.

Paired with the Colorado Convention Center, the **Hyatt Regency** (650 15th St., 303/436-1234, www.denverregency.hyatt.com, $189-650) was built to welcome business travelers to Denver. The 1,110 spacious rooms and suites afford mountain and city views, as does the hotel's Peaks Lounge on the 27th floor. Floor-to-ceiling windows in the hotel's restaurant Altitude, as well as in the Strata Bar, offer city views from a lower level. The state-of-the-art hotel features ergonomic chairs at workstations, high-speed wireless Internet access, individual climate control, and the low-tech option of being able to open the windows in guest rooms.

The historic Colorado National Bank building has been transformed into the **Renaissance Denver Downtown City Center** (918 17th St., 303/867-8100, www.rendendowntown.com, $419-599). Of course you're here to stay in one of the 221 guest rooms and suites, but what's special about this hotel is the atrium where white marble columns dominate the space and restored murals by renowned artist Allen Tupper True adorn the walls (other murals by True are found in the City and County Building, Civic Center Park, and the Colorado State Capitol). This lobby has ample seating, a bar, and a hip ambience for hanging out before you hit the town for the evening. The building's banking history is a bit of a theme in the decor with an old vault that serves as a meeting room. Dining options include *range*, open for breakfast, lunch, and dinner, and the Teller Bar, open for happy hour and dinner with a yummy selection of apps to go with your cocktails.

With the largest standard guest rooms in downtown, **The Ritz-Carlton** (1881 Curtis St., 303/312-3800, www.ritzcarlton.com, $589-3,500) is a plushy place to stay, either as an extravagant stopover after a week of skiing and snowboarding, or while on a business trip. The hotel's 202 rooms all have marble bathrooms with two sinks and separate oversized bathtubs for soaking, as well as 37-inch flat-screen TVs. Two years in a row, The Ritz-Carlton Denver received the AAA Five-Diamond Award—making it the first hotel in Denver to receive the prestigious designation. Guests dine at the award-winning Elway's, a popular steakhouse owned by NFL Hall of Fame quarterback John Elway.

GOLDEN TRIANGLE, LINCOLN PARK, AND SOBO

Over $250

After opening in the summer of 2015, the ★ **Art Hotel** (1201 Broadway, 303/572-8000, www.thearthotel.com, $309-419) immediately had its own niche thanks to its $100 million art collection on display. Located on the same block as the Hamilton wing of the Denver Art Museum, the hotel claims to be the "only hotel of its kind to showcase original works of this caliber." The in-house curator, Diane Vanderlip (former curator of the Denver Art Museum), selected contemporary art—Andy

Warhol, Claes Oldenburg, Ed Ruscha—for the hotel's two galleries and other spaces. Each floor of the hotel is "inspired" by a particular artist and their style is "translated" in the rooms on that floor. With 165 rooms, that's a lot of style. Dining and cocktail options include FIRE Terrace (4th fl.), with a view of the city's skyline, FIRE Lounge (next to the main restaurant) for intimate cocktails, and FIRE, which serves breakfast, lunch, and dinner. Get comfortable in the Living Room, where you can watch TV, sip an adult beverage, or just visit with friends. When selecting your room, think of what you want your window to frame: a museum view, a mountain view, or an urban view.

LODO AND PLATTE RIVER VALLEY

Under $150

I declare this Denver's most stylish hostel. The ★ **Hostel Fish** (1217 20th St., 303/954-0962, www.hostelfish.com, $45 shared bunkroom, $87.50 private room), which opened in 2015, is only a couple of blocks from Coors Field and many of the bars in LoDo. The historic building has a varied history: It was once home to a saloon, a brothel, and a peep show. Now the first story is where you'll find Ophelia's, a hip bar and music venue that also opened in 2015. On the second floor are the affordable accommodations, which include amenities like free use of iPads and a complimentary breakfast. The rooms are best described as "urban rustic" with wooden floors, stylish bathrooms... and a view of the parking lot below.

$150-250

Visitors to ★ **Springhill Suites Denver Downtown** (1190 Auraria Pkwy., 303/705-7300, www.springhillsuitesdenver.com, $189-369) can rest assured that the employees here will be graded on everything they do: This is one of only 10 college student-operated hotels in the country—and the only one in an urban setting. Springhill Suites is on the Metropolitan State University of Denver campus, and approximately 80 percent of the staff are students enrolled in the school's hospitality program. There are 150 guest rooms, meeting space, and more. Let's give them an A-plus for being Denver's first LEED Gold hotel, which means this building promotes clean, renewable energy. Hospitality students aren't the only ones to be represented here: All of the art you see here was made by students, faculty, and alumni of MSU.

For loyal Westin clients, the **Westin**

Next to the Denver Art Museum is the Art Hotel.

Tabor Center (1672 Lawrence St., 303/572-9100, www.westindenverdowntown.com, $120-400) will not disappoint, with its signature Heavenly Bed and Heavenly Bath, as well as some rooms with views of the Rocky Mountains. The hotel's location can't be beat: It is right off the 16th Street Mall, around the corner from Lannie's Clocktower Cabaret, and just a couple blocks from historic Larimer Square and several restaurants, shops, and nightclubs. The hotel provides maps compiled by *Runner's World* magazine that provide three- and five-mile jogging and walking routes from the hotel. With 430 rooms, this is one of Denver's larger hotels.

Over $250

The renovated historic ★ **Oxford Hotel** (1600 17th St., 303/628-5400, www.theoxfordhotel.com, $240-500) is no longer relying on guests who are interested in Victorian charm alone; it is also meeting the needs of busy executives. The hotel has its beginnings in 1891, when Union Station was a thriving transportation hub for the Rockies and all those train travelers needed a classy place to rest. The Oxford was designed by Frank Edbrooke, who also designed the Brown Palace Hotel. The 80 rooms are still appointed with lovely antiques, but now include high-speed Internet access and dual phone lines. Stop in the Cruise room for a cocktail and for a feel of what it was like back in the day. On the hotel's first floor is **McCormick's Fish House & Bar** (1659 Wazee St., 303/825-1107, www.mccormickandschmicks.com, 6:30am-10pm Sun.-Thurs., 6:30am-11pm Fri.-Sat., $15-50), with a budget-friendly happy hour ($3-6).

Ooh-la-la! When friends and family come to town, the ★ **Crawford Hotel** (1701 Wynkoop St., 720/460-3700, www.thecrawfordhotel.com, $289-649) is where I suggest they stay. The transformation of Denver's historic train station into a 112-room luxury hotel is fabulous and worth a visit even if you're not staying here. The area where people once whiled away their time waiting for trains is now the "Great Hall" with a flower shop, The Terminal Bar, a handful of shops and restaurants, tabletop shuffleboard, and plenty of comfortable seating. You might be surprised to look up from the Great Hall and see hotel rooms, but there is minimal noise and full privacy in these Pullman rooms (evocative of train sleeping cars). All the rooms and suites—and the hallways—have artwork by Colorado artists.

Among the **restaurants** here are

the Oxford Hotel in LoDo

Mercantile, Snooze, Stoic & Genuine, The Kitchen Next Door, and the Milkbox Ice Creamery (serving Little Man Ice Cream). **Bars** include the Cooper Lounge, with its unique view to the west, and the Terminal Bar; both have a selection of Colorado craft brews. **Shops** here include The Tattered Cover Book Store and 5 Green Boxes. Guests have access to the Oxford Hotel's spa a half block away.

This is the only hotel in Denver where you can arrive at the back door by train, or buy your train tickets for your next trip. The central location is ideal—mere blocks from Coors Field, the Museum of Contemporary Art Denver, Larimer Square, and the 16th Street Mall, from where a free bus will zip you a mile east to the Civic Center Park and more.

CAPITOL HILL AND CITY PARK

Under $150

It's a bargain at the **11th Avenue Hotel and Hostel** (1112 Broadway, 303/894-0529, www.11thavenuehotelandhostel.com, $23 dorm room, $45 private room with shared bath, $55 private room with private bath), which is just steps from the Denver Art Museum, History Center Colorado, Civic Center Park, the Colorado State Capitol, and many other local sights. All accommodations include use of the community room and free Wi-Fi.

The flip side of modern accommodations is found at **The Holiday Chalet** (1820 E. Colfax Ave., 303/437-8245, www.theholidaychalet.com, $120-210), but that's not a bad thing. This 1896 restored brownstone with 10 guest rooms has a homey style and feel, with lacy curtains, flowery bedspreads, and antiques throughout. When not busy whipping up a gourmet breakfast and running the chalet, the owner is also a fashion designer whose clothing and jewelry can be found in the She She Boutique. The Holiday Chalet is pet-friendly, and the owner's dog is there to greet guests.

You just can't beat the price and location of the **Denver International Hostel** (630 E. 16th St., 303/832-9996, www.denverinternationalhostel.com, $20). For a low nightly rate, you can share a dorm room with fellow travelers, have access to free Wi-Fi, walk to many restaurants, bars, and sights in the city and come and go as you please with a key. A common room and shared kitchen round out the amenities.

$150-250

Located on an unexpectedly peaceful street

Castle Marne is a bed-and-breakfast near downtown.

between the bars and restaurants of Colfax Avenue and 17th Street, **Castle Marne Bed and Breakfast Inn** (1572 Race St., 303/331-0621, www.castlemarne.com, $169-300) offers a unique stay in the middle of the city. The 1889 mansion has nine antique-filled rooms, and original woodwork and artifacts are on display in the parlor and dining room, where tea service is held daily. The presidential suite in the distinctive turret includes a solarium, fireplace, and private balcony.

Historically known as the Croke-Patterson-Campbell Mansion, **The Patterson Inn** (428 E. 11th Ave., 303/955-5142, www.pattersoninn.com, $241-347) has a reputation as a haunted house. Built in 1891 from sandstone blocks, this castle-like building has been used as offices and apartments over the years, and has now been converted into nine guest rooms that highlight many of the original features, such as the hand-carved oak stairway and stained glass windows. The rumors of ghosts began in the 1970s and surely will be part of the allure for some guests. Breakfast is included in the room rate.

While certainly not unique to Denver, the **Warwick Hotel**'s (91776 Grant St., 303/861-2000, www.warwickdenver.com, $189-389) outstanding reputation is upheld here. The 219 large rooms and suites include marble bathrooms and antique European furniture, with ample room for sitting on comfortable chairs and couches. Amenities include a fitness room with views of the city, a heated rooftop pool that is open year-round, and dining at the inviting Randolph's restaurant, with outdoor patio seating for warmer days and indoor tables near the hearth in winter.

HIGHLANDS

Under $150

There are limited lodging options within the Highlands neighborhood. Located on the eastern edge of Highlands and perched on a hill overlooking downtown, the **Hampton Inn & Suites** (2728 Zuni St., 303/455-4588, www.hamptoninn.com, $169-209) is a relative bargain compared to many of the hotels right in downtown. The 62 hotel rooms and public areas are pretty basic, with both smoking and nonsmoking options. Just off the top of an I-25 exit ramp, the hotel is convenient for road-weary travelers.

$150-250

The 189-room **Residence Inn Denver Downtown** (92777 Zuni St., 303/458-5318, www.marriott.com, $179-209) is situated on the eastern edge of the Highlands neighborhood, within walking distance of Sports Authority Field at Mile High, the Pepsi Center, and all downtown restaurants, shops, and parks. Hemmed in by a couple of busy streets and a gas station, the hotel's location is a bit odd, but the entire property is fenced in and in a world of its own.

CHERRY CREEK

$150-250

There is reasonably affordable lodging to be found in Cherry Creek North, within easy walking distance of the neighborhood's specialty shops and restaurants. The **Inn at Cherry Creek** (233 Clayton St., 303/377-8577, www.innatcherrycreek.com, $190-500) has 35 rooms plus two corporate residences available. The rooms and suites vary in size and amenities, and those with terraces are the most appealing. All rooms include free high-speed Internet access and LCD flat-screen TVs. Limited parking is offered to guests for an additional fee. The inn's restaurant, The Weber, serves breakfast, lunch, and dinner.

Over $250

After years as a drop-in destination neighborhood, Cherry Creek has made itself into a vacation destination with the addition of the 196-room **JW Marriott** (150 Clayton Ln., 303/316-2700, www.jwmarriottdenver.com, $249-509) on the rim of the Cherry Creek North shopping district. This luxury hotel includes suites with surprising views of the Rocky Mountains to the west. The hotel's **Second Home Kitchen + Bar** (303/253-3000, www.secondhomedenver.

com, 7am-2pm Sun.-Thurs., 7am-2pm and 5pm-10pm Fri.-Sat., $14-29) serves a fun pajama brunch on weekends. The perks extend to canine guests, with special pet-friendly services available.

CANNABIS-FRIENDLY

True to its name, **Bud and Breakfast at the Adagio** (1430 Race St., 303/370-6911, www.budandbfast.com, $179-399)—and its companion mountain operation in Silverthorne—is all about infusing the traditional bed-and-breakfast with a touch of marijuana. Check in to one of the property's six imaginatively decorated suites and get ready for "wake and bake" themed breakfasts, a 4:20 Happy Hour celebration every day, and cannabis-infused massage therapy treatments. Talk about high hospitality. Formerly a regular bed-and-breakfast, the Victorian-era house maintains the same room names with a classical music theme (e.g., "The Vivaldi").

Back in the day, when Molly Brown was in residence just a few blocks away, Capitol Hill was a neighborhood of stately mansions with views of the Rocky Mountains. While it's more crowded with apartments and office buildings now, inns like the ★ **Capitol Hill Mansion Bed and Breakfast Inn** (1207 Pennsylvania St., 800/839-9329, www.capitolhillmansion.com, $154-229) offer guests an opportunity to experience life in that bygone era, with a few modern touches. Meet your fellow guests over a gourmet breakfast each morning or during a two-hour beverage meet and greet with the innkeeper and others. The eight-room inn makes a point of welcoming families and gay and lesbian guests, as well as business travelers. Guests are free to smoke and vape on the balconies of rooms and in a designated area in the garden. Listen carefully and you might hear the ghosts of Colorado's mining barons giving their approval.

The Highlands neighborhood is brimming with exquisite turn-of-the-20th-century homes, but perhaps none more special than the 8,500-square-foot **Lumber Baron Inn & Gardens** (2555 W. 37th Ave., 303/477-8205, http://lumberbaron.com, $149-239). The inn is something of a special events center, hosting weddings and other events in the third-floor ballroom, as well as bed-and-breakfast guests. Each of the five well-appointed rooms has a whirlpool tub and free Wi-Fi. The inn is walking distance from some good restaurants, and is only a mile from the sights of downtown. A spacious garden with flowering trees and seating areas make it more inviting in the spring and summer. The large bed-and-breakfast has embraced fun and quirky activities, from murder-mystery parties to casino dinners, so it's fitting that this luxury inn has turned cannabis-friendly.

A popular budget hotel in north Denver, **Quality Inn Central Denver** (200 West 48th Ave., 303/296-4000, www.qualityinndenver.com, $119-149) is also the home of the 2015 High Times Cannabis Cup, and allows vaping in its rooms and marijuana smoking outside. Guests can even rent marijuana vaporizers from the front desk—all you have to do is provide the cannabis. Rooms go for less than $150 on a summer weekend.

GREATER DENVER

Under $150

When Denver International Airport (DIA) opened in the 1990s, the hotels across the road from the closed Stapleton Airport remained open. Eventually, new hotels began popping up closer to DIA, but today, Stapleton is an infill community; now the area is booming with malls and housing, and the old hotels are serving business travelers who don't want or need to go into downtown. Halfway between downtown and the airport, with complimentary shuttle service to DIA, the **Doubletree Stapleton North** (4040 Quebec St., 303/321-6666, www.denver.doubletree.com, $79-149) is a good bargain. Amenities include complimentary breakfast daily, an indoor pool, free Wi-Fi, and a fitness center.

$150-250

The **Embassy Suites** (7001 Yampa St., 303/574-3000, http://embassysuites1.hilton.

com, $150-300) is one of the closest hotels to Denver International Airport, just six miles away. The hotel has 174 two-room suites spread out on six floors surrounding a six-story atrium. There is free parking for guests and complimentary transportation to the airport. Amenities include a pool, a fitness center, and meeting rooms.

One of many hotels near Denver International Airport, **The Timbers Hotel** (4411 Peoria St., 303/373-1444 or 800/844-9404, www.thetimbersdenver.com, $99-129) sets itself apart with an inviting Western ambience, including antique Colorado maps and cowboy decor. Among the 127 rooms are executive and one-bedroom suites that include a full kitchen in a separate living area. The hotel offers free transportation to the airport, as well as complimentary transportation within a five-mile radius of the hotel. (Sorry, that doesn't quite reach downtown.) Guests also have access to the 24-hour business center and fitness center.

Pretty much since Denver International Airport opened, people have been asking why there isn't a hotel at the airport given its distance from the city. Well, it's here! The 14-story, 519-room ★ **Westin Denver International Airport** (8500 Peña Blvd., www.westindenverairport.com, 303/317-1800, $272-352) opened in 2015. The hotel mimics the airport's distinctive appearance, with glass walls in the shape of wings taking flight (though some have said it looks like a cruise ship or a moustache). Those walls offer nice views of the mountains to the west and triple-pane windows mean no outdoor noise (like say, a jet taking off) penetrates the rooms. Amenities include a conference center with ballrooms and boardrooms, a transit center, pool, fitness center, and restaurants.

Food

I don't know which is hotter—the restaurant scene or the real estate business in Denver. Trying to keep up with the incredible food scene in the Mile High City is like trying to hold Jell-O. Here is our best representation of the current dining options—alive with creativity, fresh ingredients, and some local celebrity chefs—plus the old favorites.

DOWNTOWN

Coffee and Tea

With coffee shops on almost every corner in downtown, does it really matter where you stop for a cup of joe? Yes! **Emily's Coffee** (1860 Lincoln St., 720/423-4797, www.emilyscoffee.com, 7am-1pm Mon.-Fri.) is part of the Emily Griffith Technical College (formerly Emily Griffith Opportunity School), where immigrants and refugees learn job skills. The shop also serves really good espresso. The pastries are baked by students in the school's baking program, and the coffee beans are locally roasted by Kaladi Brothers Coffee Company. Even the aprons worn here were made by women at the local African Community Center. Each cup of coffee bought here will have a community ripple effect.

Huckleberry Roasters (2500 Larimer St., 866/558-2201, www.huckleberryroasters.com, 7am-6pm Mon.-Fri., 8am-6pm Sat.-Sun.) is a tiny operation begun by two good friends passionate about coffee. Locals seek out friendly service and strong coffee—served in drip, pour-over, or aeropress form. Don't know what that means? Just ask a barista. Of course, shots of espresso and foamy cafe au laits (complete with latte art) are available too, as are biscuits, scones, and pie. The ambience is bright and airy, with a long coffee bar and petite tables good for couples and small groups.

Named for the thick, silky layer of umber-hued whipped foam—the hallmark of a well-crafted espresso—**Crema Coffee House** (2862 Larimer St., 720/284-9648, www.

cremacoffeehouse.net, 7am-5pm daily, $4-8) sees no shortage of bean connoisseurs. Even the website has espresso-tasting instructions. Did you know that so much of tasting espresso is in the nose? Order a shot, swirl it around, and give it a whiff as you check out this minimalist urban shop. If you're hungry, order a hearty breakfast burrito, quiche, and—if you want something really different—a Korean Reuben with duck pastrami, Sambal aioli, fresh kimchi slaw, and chèvre

Breakfast and Brunch

Ellyngton's (321 17th St., 303/297-3111, www.brownpalace.com, 7am-11am and 11:30am-2pm Mon.-Fri., 7am-11am Sat., 7am-10am Sun., $53.95/champagne brunch) is open for breakfast and lunch weekdays and attracts the city's power brokers, but what they are known for is their Dom Pérignon Sunday brunch buffet (10am-2pm, reservations recommended). Like the rest of the Brown Palace's restaurants, Ellyngton's is in an elegantly appointed room and the service is exceptional. The brunch includes waffles, an omelet station, salads, seafood (including fresh sushi), and a choice of champagnes. The brunch desserts are amazing, with crème brûlée as a standout.

Just off the beaten path downtown, the **Mercury Café** (2199 California St., 303/294-9258, www.mercurycafe.com, breakfast 9am-3pm Sat.-Sun., dinner 5:30pm-11pm Tues.-Sun., $7-16) is one of the city's most popular brunch hangouts. With an emphasis on organic and locally sourced ingredients, the menu offers a selection of hearty egg dishes, some with Colorado elk meat, as well as stuffed burritos—the "No More War Burrito" is a house favorite with green chile, polenta, and cheese. The café is also a nightclub with live music ranging from folk to swing bands and a variety of dance lessons offered, including tango, salsa, and belly dancing.

Visitors from the East Coast will find carb-y comfort in **Rosenberg's Bagels & Delicatessen** (725 E. 26th Ave., 720/440-9880, https://rosenbergsbagels.com, 6am-3pm Tues.-Sun., $1.25-11), owned by former Jersey resident Joshua Pollack. He's so dedicated to creating the perfect New York-style bagel that he figured out how to replicate NYC water in the Mile-High City, a key ingredient in his soft, chewy, oven-fresh bagels. Order yours with house-smoked and cured lox, a crisp salad, a cup of coffee—even a pastry! We recommend The Frenchie: a toasted cinnamon raisin bagel with scrambled egg, sausage, cheddar cheese, and maple syrup.

American

Attached to Green Russell is **Russell's Smokehouse** (1422 Larimer St., 303/893-6505, www.russellssmokehouse.com, 11am-10pm Mon.-Thurs., 11am-11pm Fri.-Sat., 5pm-10pm Sun., $12-25), a barbecue restaurant located beneath trendy Larimer Square. The creative craft cocktails and home-cooked goodness of smoked and barbecued meats draw those looking for something a little more rustic, but still encapsulated in an upscale space. Adorned in leather and wood, this place is cowboy-chic. Look up from your smoked pork shoulder with cheddar grits, okra, and corn bread, and notice the green ceiling and stained glass decor.

Work & Class (2500 Larimer St., 303/292-0700, www.workandclassdenver.com, 4pm-10pm Sun.-Thurs., 4pm-11pm Fri.-Sat., $6-28) is the brainchild of owner/chef Dana Rodriquez, who wanted an approachable, fun restaurant that offered affordable plates in a trendy atmosphere. Her dream came true, and it's housed in an intimate space—shipping containers form the walls—where the motto is "food for people who can eat." Visit for no-fuss Latin and American-style dishes that change seasonally but might include red chile-braised pork, coriander-roasted Colorado lamb, and blue corn empanadas. Work & Class is often full of people looking to relax and socialize after work—so it may get noisy. My advice? Order a drink and join the fun.

Asian

Chef Troy Guard is best known for his renowned TAG restaurant on Larimer Square, but **Bubu** (1423 Larimer St., Ste. 010, 303/996-2685, www.bubu-denver.com, 11am-5pm Mon.-Fri., $4-14)—his fast-casual, healthy Asian-fusion concept—also draws the lunchtime crowds. Pop in and choose a bowl of fresh, flavorful goodness, like the Hawaii Five-O bowl with hearts of palm, soybeans, crispy puffed rice, shiitake mushrooms, raw fennel, and soy onion dressing. Add rice, noodles, or salad, top it all off with your choice of protein, and you have yourself a quick and satisfying meal. A second location in Lowry offers increased seating, a full menu, cocktails, and even catering.

Contemporary

The Nickel (1100 14th St., 720/889-2128, www.thenickeldenver.com, 6:30am-2:30pm and 5pm-10pm Mon.-Thurs., 6:30am-2:30pm and 5pm-11pm Fri., 11am-3pm and 5pm-11pm Sat., 11am-3pm and 5pm-10pm Sun., $10-35) brings refined, chef-driven fare to downtown Denver's iconic Hotel Teatro. Make reservations here before or after a show at the Denver Center for Performing Arts, or make it your downtown dinner destination via light rail (or get discounted valet parking—ask your server for a voucher). Sip a Manhattan or try the Colorado lamb rack off the wood grill. Colorado's heritage is reflected in locally sourced ingredients, the custom furnishings, and industrial accents honoring the building's past as a tramway station—where customers would pay a nickel for a streetcar ride.

Delis

After spending the morning exploring downtown or River North (RiNo), you'll want a simple, delicious meal to fuel the rest of your day. At **Curtis Park Deli** (2532 Champa St., 303/308-5973, 10am-4pm Mon.-Sat., $5-10), you'll find fresh, handcrafted, and local items to build the perfect picnic or stock your own pantry, like farm eggs, yogurt, chocolate, tea, and fresh bread. You can order a sandwich to go or enjoy it there (note: there's no patio, and seating is limited). Try the Park with fried egg, prosciutto, white cheddar, and housemade butter, or the fish with smoked rainbow trout, housemade aioli, blue cheese, capers, and arugula.

Downtown Denver's 16th Street Mall has finally been blessed with a gourmet deli that offers the city's growing urban population a place to grab a quick meal to go, or a place to get artisan cheeses, fresh seafood, and other groceries. With hot soups, made-to-order hot or cold sandwiches, and a salad bar, **Cook's Fresh Market** (1600 Glenarm Pl., 303/893-2277, www.cooksfreshmarket.com, 9am-6pm Mon.-Fri., $8-10) is very popular during the busy lunch hour. There is seating available inside the market, with huge windows perfect for people-watching. Call in an order and have it delivered curbside, or buy some groceries during your lunch hour and Cook's will hold them until you're ready to go home.

Indian

If you happen to be in North Denver looking for a quick lunch or bright happy hour spot, give **Biju's Little Curry Shop** (1441 26th St., 303/292-3500, www.littlecurryshop.com, 11am-9pm Mon.-Sat., $5-10) a try. Owner Biju Thomas was born in southern India and grew up in Denver, lending a unique perspective to healthful, flavorful Indian curry. Build your bowl with beef, chicken, veggies, or Naadan—everything—and pay extra for the cashew and date biriyani. Sauces range from mild herbed yogurt sauce to hotter-than-heck Gunpowder sauce made with ghost pepper salt. The only downside about this place is parking, which can be hard to come by.

Italian

Panzano (909 17th St., 303/296-3525, www.panzano-denver.com, 6:30am-10am, 11am-2:30pm, 5pm-10pm Mon.-Thurs., 6:30am-10am, 11am-2:30pm, 5pm-11pm Fri., 8am-2:30pm, 5pm-11pm Sat., 8am-2:30pm, 4:30pm-9pm Sun., $25-32) has not only been called one of Denver's best restaurants, but one of the best in America, and it has won numerous awards. Located adjacent to the Hotel Monaco in downtown Denver, Panzano offers a taste of the northern Italian countryside. In addition to the fine food, diners are made aware of the sustainable practices behind the scenes so that they can make true the saying, "chi manga bene, vive bene (those who eat well, live well)." And if you think Italian food is synonymous with pasta, think again—chef Elise Wiggins has created gluten-free menus for both lunch and dinner.

You may have heard about restaurants built into shipping containers, but you won't believe it until you actually have a meal in one. **Cart-Driver** (2500 Larimer St., 303/292-3553, www.cart-driver.com, noon-midnight daily, $8-16) is one of Denver's first shipping container restaurants, serving wood-fired pizza, fresh oysters, prosecco on tap, and as much warm hospitality as you can fit into 640 square feet. The Italian inspiration is rooted in the Carrettiera, an Italian horse-drawn cart driver who delivers food to Italian villagers. Step up to the bar and order the namesake pizza with sausage, kale, mozz, and chile flakes. If it's nice, stretch your legs a bit on one of the two patios, and try the daily organic soft-serve gelato before you depart.

Latin American

Traditional Mexican food is delicious, but the masterminds behind **Los Chingones** (2461 Larimer St. #102, 303/295-0686, www.loschingonesmexican.com, 11:30am-10pm Mon.-Thurs., 11:30am-11pm Fri., 10am-11pm Sat., 10am-9pm Sun., $5-15) wanted to amp up the experience with adventurous proteins, sassy service, and plenty of excitement from brunch until late. Try the Mexican Sashimi with hibiscus and jalapeño, or the Colorado Empanadas with antelope, venison, elk, wild boar, and buffalo topped with crema and corn pico. Wash it down with a T&T—that's code for a tequila, lime, tang, and orange soda cocktail.

Dessert

Em's Ice Cream (951 16th St., 617/388-5349, www.emsicecream.com, 11:30am-8pm daily) brings mobile sweetness to Denver with its ice cream carts and truck, including one cart stationed on the 16th Street Mall between Curtis and Champa. Open May-October, this tiny shop (named after the owner's wife) is the only ice cream joint in Colorado that is certified organic—from the hand-churned, French anglaise-style cream to the handmade chocolate chips and caramel. Ingredients come from local farmers when possible, and a portion of each sale is donated to the Food Bank of the Rockies. Indulge in a cone or cup of Roasted Banana, Honey Lavender, or Chocolate Strawberry ice cream flavors, to name a few. Find them on Twitter for cart and truck locations: twitter.com/emsicecream.

GOLDEN TRIANGLE, LINCOLN PARK, AND SOBO

Coffee and Tea

This might be the ultimate work-from-home coffee shop for budding entrepreneurs. **Gather** (1062 Delaware St., 303/823-4172, http://gatherdenver.com, 8am-9pm Mon.-Fri.) is in the lobby of Galvanize, a digital start-up hub, so the energy here is a blend of creativity and pure ambition. It's a bonus that the coffee, tea, and food is really good. A Denver B-cycle docking station out front—and a location a half-block from the Cherry Creek bike path—means you can pedal over, open the laptop, order your coffee, and start building your business of the future.

American

Beatrice & Woodsley (38 S. Broadway, 303/777-3505, http://beatriceandwoodsley.com, 5pm-10pm Mon.-Wed., 5pm-11pm Thurs.-Fri., 10am-4pm and 5pm-11pm Sat., 10am-4pm and 5pm-10pm Sun., $9-33) emphasizes the woods in its decor. It is meant to be an indoor wilderness with an inspired use of wood throughout the restaurant. (This can make for unexpected bumps in the dining tables, but the bathroom area is really a hoot.) And the ever-changing menu is for the adventurous eater, with choices such as a chicken-fried duck burger, crawfish beignets, and Cornish hen, to name a few. A friend and I have plans to return soon for the brunch and share the grapefruit crisp and "monkey brains"—which are actually gooey cinnamon rolls. Weekend teas are by special appointment only.

Founded by one of frontiersman Buffalo Bill Cody's scouts, ★ **The Buckhorn Exchange** (1000 Osage St., 303/534-9505, www.buckhornexchange.com, 11am-2pm and 5:30pm-9pm Mon.-Thurs., 11am-2pm and 5pm-10pm Fri., 5pm-10pm Sat., 5pm-9pm Sun., $24-56) has been open for business since 1893, serving all variety of beef and game meats. Over time, the walls of the Buckhorn were filled with a menagerie of hundreds of taxidermied animals to reflect some of the menu selections, such as bison and elk. The kitschy decor of taxidermy trophies is done with a sense of humor—such as the "herd" of antelope heads near the front door. To round out the Old West feel, there is cowboy music in the upstairs lounge on weekends. With a light rail stop practically at the front door, the Buckhorn is more accessible from downtown than ever.

All that walking around the Denver Art Museum can make you hungry, and the in-house **Palette's** (100 W. 14th Ave. Pkwy., 303/534-1455, www.ktrg.net, 11am-3pm Tues.-Thurs., 11am-8pm Fri., 11am-3pm Sat.-Sun., $12-18) restaurant is the perfect place to recharge. Windows wrap around the dining room and offer a view of the museum's Hamilton Building and its outdoor sculptures. Billed as "contemporary cuisine," lunch and dinner are sophisticated takes on steak, lobster, salads, and sandwiches, with a menu for kids as well. Palette's is also a great place to bring the in-laws, with a little something for everyone on the menu and plenty of art to look at and discuss before or after a meal. During special exhibitions, plan your visit to include a meal here with a themed menu that matches the current exhibit.

Asian

Authentic Japanese peasant food is a rarity in Denver. Not far from the edge of downtown is ★ **Domo** (1365 Osage St., 303/595-3666, www.domorestaurant.com, 11am-2pm and 5pm-10pm daily, $17-25), a Japanese garden oasis of small ponds, burbling fountains, blossoming trees, and a unique menu of fresh seafood and "sea vegetables," along with a menu of artisan sake. On one side of the garden is a folk art museum that draws schoolchildren on field trips. Domo also has a tea menu for anyone who just wants to get away from the city and sip tea in this little garden. The restaurant's sushi presentations are works of art, and the goal is to give customers a very authentic experience (so forget about special orders or having soy sauce on your table to season your food).

Little sister to ChoLon on Denver's 16th Street Mall, **Cho77** (42 S. Broadway, 720/638-8179, www.cho77.com, 4pm-close Sun.-Thurs., 4pm-close Fri.-Sat., $8-27) is owner Lon Symensma's playful Asian street food eatery. The long and narrow dining room, which opened in 2015, is decorated in authentic Vietnamese, Thai, and Cambodian accents—like the bicycle cart above the entrance, and restroom sinks made out of real woks. Snack on vegetable samosas and a cup of teh tarik (Malaysian pulled tea), or linger over a bowl of Thai coconut curry. If you fancy an adult beverage, be sure to toast your neighbor with a hearty "Mot, Hai, Ba, Yo!"

Contemporary

After an environmental cleanup of this former gas and service station, **Bittersweet** (500 E. Alameda Ave., 303/942-0320, http://bittersweetdenver.com, 5pm-10pm Tues.-Sat., $11-42) has become one of Denver's hottest restaurants, garnering rave reviews from local and national press. The concept is a seasonally influenced menu of traditional foods with a modern twist. Think pork with rhubarb gastrique in the spring, for example. Given the word-of-mouth and terrific press, it's best to make reservations to dine here, as the small space can only accommodate so many diners on a busy night.

Denver diners now have a choice of Scandinavian-inspired restaurants. **Charcoal**'s (43 W. 9th Ave., 303/454-0000, www.charcoaldining.com, 11am-2pm and 5pm-close Mon.-Fri., 10am-2pm and 5pm-close Sat.-Sun., $11-30) menu spells out the country of origin when a dish differs enough from American fare. Try the Swedish pancakes or Swedish meatballs for brunch, or find out what mustard herring is for lunch or dinner. The menu does change depending on seasonal availability of ingredients.

Ethiopian

Arada (750 Santa Fe Dr., 303/329-3344, www.aradarestaurant.com, 11:30am-10pm Tues.-Sat., $10-30) offers diners classic Ethiopian food, with various spiced meats, vegetables, and sauces served on *injera,* a sourdough flatbread. Arada also offers Ethiopian coffee (along with a traditional coffee ceremony) and honey wine.

Latin American

Before stepping inside **Cuba Cuba Café & Bar** (1173 Delaware St., 303/605-2822, www.cubacubacafe.com, 5pm-10pm Mon.-Thurs., 5pm-10:30pm Fri.-Sat., $13-26), you get a sense of the colorful and playful Caribbean vibe. The restaurant occupies two little Victorian houses joined together and painted blue with yellow trim. It's mellow and even cozy inside, where the night gets off to a perfect start with a smooth mojito and a bowl of plantain chips while listening to some live music. The entrées at Cuba Cuba are traditional Cuban favorites done to perfection, such as a sandwich Cubano or *ropa vieja.* In the summer, the back patio is adorned with lanterns and it feels like an island vacation in the city.

Drawing repeat customers long before the bustling Santa Fe Arts District developed along this strip, **El Noa Noa** (722 Santa Fe Dr., 303/623-9968, http://denvermexicanrestaurants.net, 9am-10pm Mon.-Sat., 9am-9pm Sun., $10-15) has been serving icy margaritas and smothered burritos for decades. On weekends in the summer, a mariachi band plays music on the patio, where umbrella-sheltered tables make this the ideal place to nosh on reasonably priced chiles rellenos, fajitas, enchiladas, or tacos during the First Friday Art Walk. Although the patio is popular and fills up in nice weather, there is rarely a wait for a table inside. There is also live music on Thursday nights.

Next door to El Noa Noa is **El Taco de Mexico** (714 Santa Fe Dr., 303/623-3926, www.eltacodemexico.com, 7am-10pm Sun.-Thurs., 7am-11pm Fri.-Sat., $4-9), an almost roadside stand of a restaurant that takes cash only. The average customer at El Taco orders a traditional shredded beef taco and a *horchata* (cinnamon-flavored rice milk) for a quick, satisfying meal, but those in search of "authentic" Mexican food are thrilled to find tongue and brain on the menu as well.

Leña (24 Broadway St., 720/550-7267, www.lenadenver.com, 4pm-11pm Mon.-Thur., 4pm-midnight Fri., 10am-2pm and 4pm-midnight Sat., 10am-2pm and 4pm-11pm Sun., $7-30) is a fairly new addition to the South Broadway restaurant sector, bringing tasty tacos, wood-fired and smoked meats, and creative cocktails to the public. Enjoy a variety of Latin American-inspired fare. Try the spicy and sweet Tacos de Pescado with chile-spiced and seared sea bass, Cotija cheese, mango salsa, and housemade crème naranjilla sauce on scratch-made yellow corn tortillas.

Italian

Gozo (30 S. Broadway, 720/638-1462, www.gozodenver.com, 11am-close Tues.-Fri., 10am-close Sat.-Sun., $10-26) is a modern Mediterranean joint on a colorful strip of South Broadway and one of Denver's newest gathering places. Come for brunch, lunch, dinner, or drinks, and enjoy a bright and social space with exposed brick, trendy light fixtures, and great people watching. Try a variety of appetizers, pastas, or pizza, or splurge on a "grande" like three-day smoked short rib or 12-hour pork shoulder.

Dessert

Making the SoBo neighborhood just that much more hip is ★ **Sweet Action Ice Cream** (52 Broadway, 303/282-4645, www.sweetactionicecream.com, 1pm-10pm Sun.-Thurs., 1pm-11pm Fri.-Sat.), with its creative flavors, vegan options, and locally sourced ingredients. Try the molasses corn bread, Stranahan's whiskey brickle, or Thai iced tea—or better yet, try them in an enormous ice cream sandwich. The flavors change daily, so you might find something surprising as well as cool and refreshing.

LODO AND PLATTE RIVER VALLEY

Coffee and Tea

More than just another sandwich shop, **The House of Commons** (2401 15th St., 303/455-4832, www.houseofcommonstea.com, 10am-6pm daily, $8-11) will satisfy any Anglophile's need for a cup of freshly brewed, proper English tea in the afternoon. Much of the tea comes from Taylors of Harrogate in Yorkshire, England, and there is a selection of more than 30 flavors. There's also Devonshire cream, buttery scones, fresh lemon curd, and cucumber sandwiches on the menu. Brightly lit and with a couple of outdoor tables, The House of Commons is a cheery place to share a spot of tea with a friend.

Breakfast and Brunch

Mona's (2364 15th St., 303/455-4503, www.monasrestaurant.com, 7am-2pm Mon.-Fri., 7am-3pm Sat.-Sun., $6-12) is named after the Mona Lisa portrait painted on the exterior of the building by New York artist Stefano Castronovo in the '80s, when this space was an art gallery. The restaurant has an artistic flair that starts with the extra-large spoon that serves as a doorknob and the wall of curved chalkboards for diners to leave a quick review of their dining experience or to doodle on while they wait for their meal. On most weekends there is a long line out the door of this small establishment, where people happily wait for blueberry flapjacks, huevos rancheros, and sandwiches and salads.

It's no wonder that the pancakes at **Snooze** (2262 Larimer St., 303/297-0700, www.snoozeeatery.com, 6:30am-2:30pm Mon.-Fri., 7am-2:30pm Sat.-Sun., $8-13) have developed a loyal following: With options such as caramel glazes and shameless amounts of chocolate, they are somewhere between breakfast

Snooze is a very popular breakfast spot.

Union Station Dining Spots

The Denver Union Station revitalization completely transformed the city's iconic train station. The once dimly lit Great Hall now buzzes with business diners, stylish travelers, children and families, first dates, and late-night revelers. Grand dining options abound from morning until night. Following are some top picks:

- **Cooper Lounge** (1701 Wynkoop St., 720/460-3738, www.cooperlounge.com, 9am-11pm daily). The high-end cocktails will give you a taste of 1930s Hollywood glamour, a chance to rub elbows with local power brokers, and a sophisticated menu by local chef Lon Symensma.
- **Stoic & Genuine** (303/640-3474, www.stoicandgenuine.com, 11am-10pm Sun.-Thurs., 11am-11pm Fri.-Sat.). Owner/chef Jennifer Jasinski serves a creative selection of seafood-focused dishes and cocktails that includes signature granitas and house soda.
- **Mercantile** (720/460-3733, www.mercantiledenver.com, 7am-10pm Sun.-Thurs., 7am-11am Fri.-Sat.). This restaurant/marketplace offers everything from spices and cheeses to a full-service coffee bar with tasting flights.
- **Pigtrain Coffee** (720/460-3708, www.pigtraincoffee.com, 6am-11pm daily). Pick up local coffee from Denver's family-owned Novo coffee, with sensuous pastries and fresh-squeezed juice.
- **Snooze** (303/825-3536, www.snoozeeatery.com, 6:30am-2:30pm daily). One of Denver's most-loved breakfast diners dishes up creative pancake dishes amid sunny decor.
- **Next Door** (720/460-3730, www.thekitchen.com, 11am-close daily). From the owners of The Kitchen, this is a perfect spot for lunch or a relaxed dinner on the expansive patio.
- **Thirsty Lion Gastropub & Grill** (1605 Wynkoop St., 303/623-0316, www.thirstyliongastropub.com, 11am-midnight Mon.-Wed., 11am-1am Thurs.-Sat., 11am-11pm Sun.). This expansive restaurant serves plenty of shareable appetizers, draft beers, and sports on TV.
- **Protein Bar** (1755 16th St., 303/893-0898, www.theproteinbar.com, 7am-8pm Mon.-Fri., 10am-4pm Sat.). Denverites can find smoothies, bowls, and other healthful, protein-packed meals and snacks.
- **Acme Burger & Brat Corporation** (720/460-3706, www.acmeburgers.com, 11am-11pm daily). Perfect for handcrafted burgers and brats, artisan fries, and locally baked buns.
- **Milkbox Ice Creamery** (720/460-3707, www.milkboxicecream.com, 11am-11pm daily). This offshoot of the über-popular Little Man Ice Cream in Highlands has a new home here.

and dessert. There's even a pineapple upside-down pancake. The menu also features several savory egg dishes and sandwiches on the lunch side, though breakfast is served all day. The colorful and unique *Jetsons*-meets-*Happy Days* decor makes Snooze fun, too. Located near the ballpark in LoDo, Snooze is still in a slightly rough part of downtown. There are several Snooze locations around Denver and Colorado. No reservations are accepted, but you can come in early and put your name in to be texted when there is a table available. It is always busy so plan ahead.

American

Biker Jim's Gourmet Dogs (2148 Larimer St., 720/746-9355, www.bikerjimsdogs.com, 11am-10pm Sun.-Thurs., 11am-3am Fri.-Sat., $6.50-10) is the story of the quintessential American Dream, if that dream involves a jalapeño cheddar elk dog in a bun. Once a car repo man, Biker Jim fulfilled his dream of making gourmet hot dogs with exotic and unusual meats, like elk, Alaskan reindeer, rattlesnake, wild boar, pheasant, and duck. It's a place where a buffalo dog seems like the most normal item on the menu. The toppings are equally outrageous—as in, "harissa roasted cactus." Jim's dogs have been featured on shows like Anthony Bourdain's *No Reservations.* The restaurant includes a kids' menu and beer.

At the foot of the 16th Street pedestrian and bicycle bridge is one of Denver's best-reviewed restaurants. As cyclists whiz past the patio en route to the bike paths along the South Platte River one block away, waiters at **Colt & Gray** (1553 Platte St., 303/477-1447, www.coltandgray.com, 5pm-10pm Tues.-Thurs., 5pm-11pm Fri.-Sat., 5pm-9pm Sun., $18-95) are serving sophisticated dishes of pig trotters, sautéed sweetbreads, rabbit, and more. Named one of Denver's 25 best restaurants by *5280 Magazine,* Colt & Gray is a place for serious foodies.

The team from Rioja and Bistro Vendôme has branched out into comfort pub food with **Euclid Hall** (1317 14th St., 303/595-4255, http://euclidhall.com, 11:30am-2am Mon.-Fri., 2pm-2am Sat.-Sun.; kitchen open until midnight Sun.-Thurs. and until 1am Fri.-Sat., $12-16). For the overflow crowds from the nearby Auraria campus, Pepsi Center, and tourists visiting Larimer Square, there are cheese curds, chicken and waffles, and pad thai pig ears—and no, this is not your mom's comfort food! Also on the menu are "fresh hand-cranked sausages" and that Canadian favorite, poutine.

Almost as exciting as learning that there was a Trader Joe's coming to Colorado was finding out that the popular Boulder restaurant ★ **The Kitchen** (1530 16th St., 303/623-3127, www.thekitchen.com, 11am-9pm Sun.-Tues., 11am-10:30pm Wed.-Sat., $17-38) had opened a Denver location. In other words, there's a loyal fan base for this food. The menu is slightly different than the Boulder original, with a large selection of seafood. The ample starters can make for a fun sampling with friends (definitely order the goat gouda gougère) before selecting an entrée (you cannot go wrong with the Wisdom Farms chicken chargrilled). The sticky toffee pudding is so good that people seem to favor it over the *pot au chocolat.* **Community Hour** (3pm-6pm daily) is a chance to try the "nibbles" at discounted rates. If you're new in town, single, or just want to try a different dining experience, make a reservation for Community Night (Mon.), community-style dining with a prix fixe menu.

For a quick bite to go or a no-frills lunch, **The Market** (1445 Larimer St., 303/534-5140, 6am-10pm Sun.-Thurs., 6am-11pm Fri.-Sat., $9-10) is an old Denver favorite. In good weather, the outdoor café tables along the storefront and perched on the curb across the sidewalk are always occupied. The Auraria campus is a couple of blocks away, and The Market's clientele is a blend of students, businesspeople, and tourists. As Larimer Square has evolved into more of a tourist destination in the past 20 years, The Market has stayed the same. They offer hot and cold deli items, sandwiches, and ample-sized sweets all day long—their Spring Fling cake is a favorite.

Asian

Ask anyone if they have eaten at **ChoLon** (1555 Blake St., 303/353-5223, www.cholon.com/denver, 11am-2pm and 5pm-close daily, $10-15), a modern Asian bistro, and the answer is invariably, "Yes. I had the onion soup dumplings!" This explosion of flavor is just one example of the exciting tastes found at ChoLon, where the presentation is just as thrilling as the food itself. I don't even really like eggs, but I really wanted a dish with an "egg cloud" (kind of like French toast, it is a spicy custard-like egg mixture on toast points) and was also curious about "Chow Fun" (a noodle bowl with fresh, house-made tapioca rice noodles, shrimp, lobster, and black bean sauce) or a dish of short ribs. For those on a dining budget, come for the happy hour menu, with small plates at $5 each starting at 2pm on Saturdays.

It would be pretty hard to just stumble across **Sushi Sasa** (2401 15th St., 303/433-7272, www.sushisasa.com, 11:30am-2:30pm and 5pm-10:30pm Mon.-Thurs., 11:30am-2:30pm and 5pm-11:30pm Fri.-Sat.,

5pm-10:30pm Sun., $11-28) while out looking for a bite to eat. The acclaimed sushi restaurant's entrance is practically the back door of a large, historic building, just as the sidewalk ends before 15th Street heads over I-25. But inside, it is calm serenity, with bamboo and white decor and a perfectly balanced menu of Japanese dishes beyond just sushi. Noodle bowls, tempura, vegetarian plates, and a variety of salads with or without seafood—all are on offer alongside the extensive sushi list.

Contemporary

Located in the old saddlery building in LoDo, **The Squeaky Bean** (1500 Wynkoop St., 303/623-2665, http://thesqueakybean.net, 11am-2pm Tues.-Fri., 5pm-10pm Tues.-Thurs., 5pm-11pm Fri.-Sat., 10am-3pm Sat.-Sun., $11-35) has lots of natural light, tables that allow enough privacy (and noise levels) for people to hold a conversation, and quirky touches here and there. Diners can partake of the cheese cart that gets wheeled around the dining room and order by the ounce. There is an expansive cocktail, wine, and beer list. The menu, which changes seasonally, is a modern take on things like fried chicken (the skin comes in sheets).

Chef Troy Guard, owner of **TAG** (1441 Larimer St., 303/996-9985, http://tag-restaurant.com, 11:30am-2pm and 5pm-10pm Mon.-Thurs., 11:30am-2pm and 5pm-11pm Fri., 5pm-11pm Sat., 5pm-9pm Sun., $8-34), specializes in providing diners with something unexpected. Caramelized butterfish? How about Skuna Bay salmon with pickled watermelon *rind*? It would be easy to fill up on a variety of small plates here, but don't overlook the "principal" plates either. Plan ahead with the Omakase, which is a multicourse meal created by the chefs (24-hour advance notice strongly recommended), to get a full sense of all the menu has to offer.

There is more to food from Northern Europe than the meatballs from IKEA. The Scandinavian and American cuisine at **Trillium** (2134 Larimer St., 303/379-9759, www.trilliumdenver.com, 5pm-10pm Tues.-Thurs., 5pm-11pm Fri.-Sat., 5pm-9pm Sun., $12-32) offers expertly seasoned and presented cold-water fish and root vegetables. Small plates feature a roasted carrot pudding, toast "skagen," and sockeye salmon raaka, and turnips and radishes pop up in unexpected dishes. With huge front windows and 14-foot-high ceilings, the large space feels open and airy. The kitchen is "exhibition style," which allows diners to observe the chefs at work.

Named after a beautiful goddess, and designed with sensuous curves in the bar and large booths, **Vesta Dipping Grill** (1822 Blake St., 303/296-1970, www.vestagrill.com, 5pm-10pm Sun.-Thurs., 5pm-11pm Fri.-Sat., $18-36) is a sexy place, and great for a romantic date night. At Vesta, diners order an entrée accompanied by three sauces—the menu includes suggestions to complement each dish, but there are dozens to choose from and sample. The entrées themselves are almost as varied as the sauces, with steak, venison, tuna, duck, chicken, and vegetables. Portions are large, but much like eating fondue (with each bite dipped and flavored individually), it's fun to eat a lot or share family-style. Dipping sauces are also part of the desserts.

Just a few steps from the base of the Millennium Bridge and looking over Commons Park, **Zengo** (1610 Little Raven St., 720/904-0965, www.richardsandoval.com, 5pm-10pm Sun.-Thurs., 5pm-11pm Fri.-Sat., $9-49) is in a great location in the Platte River Valley neighborhood. With its large and vibrantly colored dining room, Zengo is fun with a group for family-style dining, or come alone to sit at the bar and enjoy a bowl of noodles. The Asian-Latin fusion works in just about every dish, such as wonton tacos or chipotle-miso soup. A personal favorite is the achiote-hoisin pork arepas for an appetizer.

It's easy to make yourself at home at range, where wood-fired entrées, hearty salads, and specialty beers and cocktails rule the New American West. That's how executive chef Paul Nagan describes ***range*** (918 17th St., 720/726-4800, www.rangedowntown.com, 6:30am-10pm daily, $10-30), which pays homage to the Rocky Mountain region's rugged cowboy culture. Enter through the recently renovated Renaissance Hotel so you can enjoy the awe-inspiring hotel lobby, complete with authentic murals by Colorado-born artist Allen Tupper True and heavy bank vault doors from the hotel's first life as the Colorado National Bank. Snack on the grilled jalapeño peppers, then order the Berkshire pork tenderloin, washed down with a house draft of Former Future Brewing Company's specialty cream ale.

French

Tucked in behind the shops of Larimer Square in the historic Sussex building is the charming **Bistro Vendôme** (1416 Larimer St., Ste. H, 303/825-3232, www.bistrovendome.com, 5pm-10pm Mon.-Thurs., 5pm-11pm Fri.-Sat., 5pm-9pm Sun., brunch 10am-2pm Sat.-Sun., $17-27), which has the feel of being off the beaten path in Paris or New York. Owned by the same women who started the restaurant Rioja across the street—chef-owner Jennifer Jasinski and manager-owner Beth Gruitch—Bistro Vendôme is one of Denver's most romantic date restaurants, with seating inside or outside on the small patio, and complimentary champagne for anyone celebrating a special event. Their weekend brunch features fresh croissants and crepes.

Italian

After moving to Colorado, Pam Proto craved the thin-crust Italian-style pizza of her childhood—in Connecticut. She opened her first pizzeria in Longmont, Colorado, and now has five locations of **Proto's Pizzeria Napoletana** (2401 15th St., 720/855-9400, www.protospizza.com, 11am-10pm daily, $6-24). A few months after starting her business, Proto visited Italy for the first time and was thrilled to discover that she was serving authentic Italian pizza in Colorado. At this Platte Street location, the colorful bar top made of broken tile pieces is the centerpiece of a tiny restaurant that fills up just about every night. Proto's does not have delivery, but does offer takeout. Friday nights are all about clam pizza, a surprisingly popular pie.

For an evening of sophisticated dining, visit **Rioja** (1433 Larimer St., 303/820-2282, www.riojadenver.com, 11:30am-2:30pm Wed.-Fri., 5pm-10pm Sun.-Thurs., 5pm-11pm Fri.-Sat., 10am-2:30pm Sat.-Sun., $12-32) in Larimer Square to try some delectable Mediterranean-inspired seasonal cuisine. The muted earth tones and copper-topped bar set off against exposed brick are reminiscent of the colors of the Spanish wine country, Rioja. The wine list, of course, features wine from the Rioja region. The dinner menu includes a memorable artichoke tortellini, unexpectedly light gnocchi, and hearty entrées, some made with handmade pastas. The bar menu has a few items under $5, and the pastas are available as appetizers. Rioja's patio is open when weather permits for lunch and dinner.

For lunch or a very late-night snack of lip-smacking good pizza by the slice or pie, try **Two-Fisted Mario's** (1626 Market St., 303/623-3523, www.twofistedmarios.com, 11am-2am Sun.-Wed., 11am-3am Thurs.-Sat., $3-20). The pizza shop and the bar next door, **Double Daughters Salotto** (1632 Market St., 303/623-3523, www.doubledaughters.com), are owned by the same people. This means that you can either hang out in the brightly colored Two-Fisted Mario's, where they play fairly loud music, or order some pizza while taking it easy at Double Daughters. During lunch hour, the bar ambience is less obvious, and kids really like the chaotic energy of this place as much as the pizza.

Latin American

On the southeast corner of Larimer Square, **Tamayo** (1400 Larimer St., 720/946-1433, www.richardsandoval.com, 11am-2pm and 5pm-10pm Mon.-Thurs., 11am-2pm and 5pm-11pm Fri., 10:30am-2:30pm and 5pm-11pm Sat., 10:30am-2:30pm and 5pm-10pm Sun., $13-29) has great views of the mountains from inside the main restaurant or, better yet, up on their rooftop deck. Tamayo is part of Richard Sandoval Restaurants, which has several different establishments in Denver, all with a similar theme of sophisticated Latin American food. The best way to experience Tamayo is from the rooftop, watching the sunset over the mountains.

CAPITOL HILL AND CITY PARK

Coffee and Tea

The theme at **St. Mark's** (2019 E. 17th Ave., 303/322-8384, www.stmarkscoffeehouse.com, 6:30am-midnight daily) is Venetian—from name to artwork—while the vibe is urban and original. St. Mark's offers Espresso Roma coffee from the San Francisco Bay Area and a selection of teas, tasty sandwiches, and too many yummy cookies, pastries, and desserts. An old garage door is yanked open on warm days, making the coffee shop feel even larger. With late hours and the Thin Man bar located right next door, St. Mark's can be a nice place to chill out before calling it a night.

Breakfast and Brunch

What makes biscuits so darn good is that they can be turned into a breakfast, lunch, or dessert with a few simple toppings. The **Denver Biscuit Company** (3237 E. Colfax Ave., 303/377-7900, www.denbisco.com, 8am-2pm Mon.-Fri., 8am-3pm Sat.-Sun., $3-11) has it covered with the basic biscuits and gravy (platter, no less!) and strawberry shortcake biscuits; then it goes to the next level with over-the-top biscuit sandwiches, a biscuit cinnamon roll, and the requisite Southern side dishes for mopping up a selection of jams, butters, and honey, or eggs and grits.

There are plenty of typical breakfast and lunch items on the menu at **Jelly** (600 E. 13th Ave., 303/831-6301, http://eatmorejelly.com, 7am-3pm daily, $7-10) that have nothing to do with the fruity spread. In fact, it only shows up on toast or biscuits or as the center of a doughnut. The cute decor, booths, and counter seats make Jelly feel like a retro diner with simple, tasty meals of pancake stacks, scrambles, hashes, and more.

Olive and Finch (1552 E. 17th Ave., 303/832-8663, www.oliveandfincheatery.com, 7am-10pm daily, $6-12.50) is a quaint and cozy café and bakery that brings all the joy and warmth of a countryside kitchen to the heart of Denver. This neighborhood spot serves freshly baked pastries, frothy cappuccino, vibrant juices, and a selection of sandwiches, salads, and soups every day. The space is intimate and fills quickly, but curbside pickup makes it easy to get what you need for a breakfast on the run or picnic lunch. In good weather, the patio is lovely—and dog-friendly! They have more than just breakfast, but they are known for this morning meal.

American

For years a staple of Uptown dining on 17th Avenue, **The Avenue Grill** (630 E. 17th Ave., 303/861-2820, www.avenuegrill.com, 11am-10pm Mon.-Thurs., 11am-11pm Fri., 10am-11pm Sat., 10am-10pm Sun., $10-36) has a solid reputation as a power-lunch spot for businesspeople, as well as a place for a casual family dinner—and it now brings in a brunch crowd on weekends. The menu here includes steak, but also has San Francisco, Asian, and Italian influences. The bar at The Avenue Grill is also a draw, with friendly bartenders mixing up what has been consistently voted "Best Martini" in local surveys.

After successfully creating sophisticated contemporary food with Vesta Dipping Grill, owners Josh and Jen Wolkon went retro and opened **Steuben's** (523 E. 17th Ave., 303/830-1001, www.steubens.com, 11am-11pm Mon.-Thurs., 11am-midnight Fri., 10am-midnight Sat., 10am-11pm Sun., $4-19) as an homage to 1950s style and food. The menu at Steuben's is all comfort food: mac 'n' cheese, fried cheese, fried chicken with mashed potatoes and gravy, root beer floats, cheeseburgers, and hot dogs. Booth seating inside adds to the nostalgic feel, and the patio on the side of the restaurant is modern and delightful. Easy curbside takeout is also available—and you might need it if you come for weekend brunch when lines stretch outside.

The Source of Good Eats

The Source houses restaurants, shops, and bars.

What is now referred to as RiNo (short for River North) used to be an industrial zone north of downtown. Today it's a hip area with art galleries, condos, and some of Denver's most talked-about restaurants. The main attraction is **The Source** (3350 Brighton Blvd., 720/443-1135, www.thesourcedenver.com). It opened in 2013 in an 1880s-era foundry building, and the gourmet marketplace became a trendy spot for food and beverages—from artisan breads to freshly butchered meats—as well as an industrial-chic date night destination. Following are more of the best places to stop when in RiNo.

- **Acorn** (720/542-3721, www.denveracorn.com, 11:30am-10pm Mon.-Sat., 5:30pm-10pm Sun. $10-30). The oak-fired oven and grill takes a leading role in the kitchen, producing seasonal and flavorful family-style plates and entrées under the eye of masterful chef/owner Steven Redzikowski.

- **Comida Cantina** (303/296-2747, www.eatcomida.com, 11am-10pm Mon.-Fri., 9am-10pm Sat.-Sun., $3-10). After starting his journey with a taco truck, owner Rayme Rossello opened this location to serve authentic Mexican street tacos from lunch until late night.

- **Crooked Stave Artisan Beer Project** (720/550-8860, www.crookedstave.com, noon-8pm Sun.-Mon., noon-11pm Tues.-Sat., $5-8). The Brettanomyces-focused beers served here bring all sorts of flavors to the palate, with beers like surette wood-aged farmhouse ale and pure guava and blackberry petite sour.

- **Boxcar Coffee** (303/527-1300, www.boxcarcoffeeroasters.com, 8am-4pm Sun.-Thurs., 8am-7pm Fri.-Sat., $2-6). Boxcar developed a high-altitude brewing system called the "Boilermakr" (steeping coffee in boiling water for the best flavor extraction). You can watch them do it here as they pour espressos and lattes from a bright and friendly counter.

- **RiNo Yacht Club** (720/485-5581, www.rinoyachtclub.com, 4:30pm-10pm Wed.-Sun.). This social lounge-like addition to the sprawling market space offers the opportunity for people watching from a comfy black leather perch.

- **Western Daughters** (303/477-6328, www.westerndaughters.com, 11am-7pm Wed.-Fri.)—a whole animal butchery—at 3326 Tejon Street. The meat here is sourced from within 250 miles of Denver, so it's some of the freshest, most local, and high-quality protein you can buy. Custom nose-to-tail carving is done on-site.

Asian

P17 (1600 E. 17th Ave., 303/399-0988, www.p17denver.com, 11am-10pm Mon.-Thurs., 11am-10pm Fri., 9am-3pm, 9am-9pm Sat.-Sun., $15-24) operates a globally inspired bistro, with classic Western fare inspired by Asian flavors. The menu changes seasonally, with small plates like duck confit tacos and lamb meatballs, and larger plates like shrimp and grits or the saignon crêpe with bean sprouts, sautéed mushrooms, and lemongrass chicken. Enjoy the wraparound patio seating on a sunny day; in cooler temps, cozy up to a bowl of P17 ramen or beef pho. Pair it with a drink from their selection of cocktails, wines, and house-infused spirits, and you'll be planning your next visit in no time.

Contemporary

Fruition (1313 E. 6th Ave., 303/831-1962, www.fruitionrestaurant.com, 5pm-10pm Mon.-Sat, 5pm-8pm Sun., $25-29) annually garners local and national awards for best chef, best farm-to-table cuisine, traveler's choice, and many more. Foodies can't stop raving about chef Alex Seidel's contemporary take on comfort food that emphasizes locally grown and seasonal ingredients. This small and cozy restaurant, where meals are paired with the perfect wine, is ideal for a special date night. In winter, there's fanciful chicken noodle soup; in summer, there are crisp, flavorful salads plus more extravagant entrées that include duck breast, pork belly, and pastas. Reservations are recommended.

Mizuna (225 E. 7th Ave., 303/832-4778, http://mizunadenver.com, 5pm-10pm Tues.-Thurs., 5pm-11pm Fri.-Sat., $28-45) is a must for anyone serious about food and gourmet dining. It's been voted Denver's number one restaurant by *Zagat,* and chef-owner Frank Bonanno has received nods from many other publications. Mizuna is known for delectable lobster mac 'n' cheese, as well as artfully presented ostrich loin and beef tenderloin. The seasonal menu is changed monthly, and the service is as impeccable as the food, with servers attending to every need but not aggressively so. Mizuna has published its own cookbook, available on the website. Reservations are strongly recommended.

★ **Potager** (1109 Ogden St., 303/832-5788, www.potagerrestaurant.com, 5:30pm-10pm Tues.-Sat., $10-29) was on the cutting edge of seasonal, locally grown ingredients long before those ideas became mainstream. Across the street from a launderette and a grocery store in the thick of the Capitol Hill neighborhood, Potager stands out as a simply elegant restaurant in the clatter of the city. There are tables out back, where the chef grows a few herbs and small vegetables, while inside crisp white tablecloths stand out against the pockmarked concrete walls. The menu changes frequently to keep up with what is seasonally available; some examples include spinach and nettle soup in spring, Colorado lamb and beef, fresh garden salads, and summer desserts with Colorado-grown peaches, rhubarb, and strawberries. No reservations are accepted; the best time to come is early or on a weeknight. There is limited free parking behind the restaurant.

A new addition to the hip Capitol Hill neighborhood, **Max's Wine Dive** (696 Sherman St., 303/593-2554, www.maxswinedive.com, 11am-11pm Mon., 4pm-11pm Tues.-Wed., 4pm-midnight Thurs.-Fri., 10am-midnight Sat., 10am-10pm Sun., $10-30) is the place to go for wine, a trendy bar atmosphere (which barely qualifies as a dive, in our opinion), and succulent fried chicken to boot. Try their small and large plates, brunch, and weekday happy hour. Don't miss the signature fried chicken, which is marinated in jalapeños and buttermilk and deep fried "slow and low," and served with savory mashed potatoes, briny collard greens, Texas toast, and house chipotle honey. The bartenders are knowledgeable and happy to let you sample any open bottle. Perk: The jukebox is free!

Although this former home to the long-standing Strings restaurant had big shoes to fill, **Humboldt Farm, Fish & Wine** (1700 Humboldt St., 303/813-1700, www.humboldtrestaurant.com, 11am-10pm Tues.-Thurs.,

11am-11pm Fri.-Sat., 11am-9pm Sun.-Mon., $10-25) represents how elegant, creative, and approachable Colorado cuisine can be. Executive chef Will Tuggle took the reins here, serving up savory dishes of lobster, beef, and pasta so full of bright colors and flavors that they're fit for presidents and rock stars (as evidenced by visits from Bill Clinton and U2's Bono). Oyster and moules-frites specials make the weekly menu at Humboldt even more delicious.

Diners

There are very few places open 24 hours in Denver, and **Pete's Kitchen** (1962 E. Colfax Ave., 303/321-3139, www.petesrestaurant.com, daily 24 hours, $5-25) has folks lined up out the door and waiting in any weather after the bars have closed and on weekends for breakfast. The food and ambience is classic diner with a Greek flair. Breakfast basics like eggs, pancakes, and hash browns are always available, as are gyros and souvlaki and burgers and burritos. Driving along East Colfax, look for the neon sign of a chubby chef flipping burgers.

The idea at **SAME Café** (2023 E. Colfax Ave., 720/530-6853, www.soallmayeat.org, 11am-2pm Mon.-Sat.) is simple: There are no prices, but the food is not free. Customers are expected to pay what they can, or what they feel their meal is worth, by dropping cash in a can by the door. The goal here is in the name: So All May Eat (SAME). And not eat just any food, but food made from fresh, organic ingredients. The menu changes daily, based on the availability of what's in season, but it generally includes soups, salads, pizzas, and a selection of desserts. If people cannot afford to pay anything for their meal, they are asked to do work at the restaurant as payment.

Italian

Discriminating diners quickly became regulars at **Il Posto** (2011 E. 17th Ave., 303/394-0100, www.ilpostodenver.com, 11am-2pm Mon.-Fri., 5pm-10pm Sun.-Thurs., 5pm-11pm Fri.-Sat., $17-35) shortly after it opened. The Italian food here is made in part with organic produce from Colorado farms and the menu changes daily. Guests appreciate that some of the servers have sommelier status and can offer wine pairings with any dish. Chef-owner Andrea Frizzi can be seen working in the open kitchen or out in the dining room greeting customers at their tables. Open a bit later than many Denver restaurants, Il Posto offers the chance for a late-night supper. Reservations are recommended.

Located in the heart of Capitol Hill, **Lala's Wine Bar + Pizzeria** (410 E. 7th Ave., 303/861-9463, www.lalaswinebar.com, 11am-midnight Mon.-Wed., 11am-2am Thurs.-Fri., 9am-2am Sat., 9am-midnight Sun., $6-17) is a modern gathering place with a youthful clientele and hip ambience. The approachable wine list is easy to decipher, making it a breeze to order something you'll enjoy without having to think too hard. The pizza is reliably yummy, and between happy hour, brunch, and Sunday Supper (four courses served family style, 3pm Sun., $12.95), you're bound to find something you like. Give yourself extra time, as parking can be tricky.

Latin American

One of the city's most popular food trucks has become a favorite restaurant, too, with street food on the menu. Order from ★ **Pinche Tacos** (1514 York St., 720/475-1337, http://tacostequilawhiskey.com, 3pm-10pm Mon., 11am-10pm Tues.-Sat., 11am-9pm Sun., $3-11) one taco at a time or like donuts—by the dozen—depending on your favorite. Just be sure to order *quesa a la plancha, rajas con crema y maiz,* and the *carnitas* as well. The restaurant also has a dizzying selection of tequilas. One tip: Because the word *pinche* translates to both something inoffensive (kitchen help) and something offensive (Shhh!), the name does not appear on the business at all... yet strangely remains plastered across the food truck seen in public parks. Come at off-times to avoid crowds and a long wait for a table or try their Highlands location.

Vegetarian

Denver's two best-known vegetarian restaurants have the same owner, but different names and menus. **City, O' City** (210 E. 13th Ave., 303/318-9844, www.cityocitydenver.com, 7am-2am daily, $6-25) is a pizza place, a coffee shop, a sandwich shop, and a bar all in one, where any eating and drinking needs throughout the day and into the night can be met. Its central location on the southern edge of the Capitol Hill neighborhood makes it walking distance from downtown and the Golden Triangle, and it attracts everyone from lawmakers to tattooed hipsters who call the neighborhood home.

Denver's premier vegetarian restaurant, ★ **WaterCourse Foods** (837 E. 17th Ave., 303/832-7313, www.watercoursefoods.com, 11am-10pm Mon.-Thurs., 8am-10pm Fri.-Sun., $10-14), has gone vegan. As of 2015, it also had new owners, but the menu will remain the same. The all-day menu at WaterCourse specializes in creative ways to eat tofu, salad, tempeh, pasta, and, of course, vegetables. Try the tamales for breakfast or dinner and design your own salad. There's also a wine and beer list, a variety of teas, and fresh smoothies.

When ★ **D Bar** (494 E. 19th Ave., 303/861-4710, www.dbardesserts.com, 11am-10pm Mon.-Thurs., 11am-midnight Fri., 10am-midnight Sat., 10am-10pm Sun., $11-20) first opened, people were drawn to the celebrity owner, Keeghan Gerhard from *Food Network Challenge.* Gerhard opened D Bar with his wife, Lisa Bailey, who is also a pastry chef. Now people come for the food first, whether it's the crazy-good desserts or the savory small(ish) plates. Reservations are recommended; just know that it's always worth the wait when the Southern Fried Belgian 2.0 (fried chicken and waffles) or Veggie-Licious arrives. Leave room for dessert because you do not want to miss the liquid-center chocolate cake (aka "Molten Cake Thingy Everybody Has...but simpler!").

HIGHLANDS

Coffee and Tea

Cuban coffee has its followers, and they come faithfully to **Buchi Café Cubano** (2651 W. 38th Ave., 303/458-1328, www.buchicafecubano.com, 8am-3pm Sun.-Wed., 8am-9pm Thurs.-Sat., $2-8) in the Sunnyside neighborhood of Highlands. Owner Emmet Barr is a native of Key West, Florida, where he grew up with traditional Cuban coffee shops almost within sight of Cuba itself. He's transplanted those tastes to the Mile-High City, and locals dine on tostone, empanadas, and panini-pressed sandwiches while sipping their *café con leche.*

An old favorite in a new location, **Common Grounds Coffeehouse** (2139 44th Ave., 720/502-2105, www.commongroundscoffehouse.com, 6:30am-9pm daily) is a neighborhood institution where people chat or sit quietly and read while sipping a cup of hot coffee. They offer pastries, sandwiches, and salads, as well as wine and beer. There is a second location in LoDo (1550 Wazee St., 303/296-9248); both locations have free Wi-Fi.

Novo Coffee (3617 W. 32nd Ave., 303/749-0100, www.novocoffee.com, 6:30am-8pm daily) has multiple cafes in Denver, and the newest one can be found on 32nd Avenue (opened in the spring of 2015). The family-owned business sources beans from all over the world, and roasts them in its local Denver roasting facility. Pop into the café for an espresso—and be prepared to share a table with the laptop brigade—or make a reservation at the roastery for an educational "cupping" session (coffee tasting).

Right along buzzing Tennyson Street is sweet little **Tenn. St. Coffee** (4418 Tennyson St., 303/455-0279, www.tennstcoffee.com, 6:30am-6pm Mon., 6:30am-9pm Tues.-Fri., 7am-9pm Sat., 7am-6pm Sun.). The shop is made up of two rooms—one with small tables where Dazbog coffee and quick bites are on offer (Bluepoint Bakery pastries, Udi's Deli sandwiches, fresh smoothies), the other with stacks of used books to browse or purchase while listening to the relaxing sounds of a local musician. When the weather is just right, grab a seat on the patio out front.

Breakfast and Brunch

Situated in Denver's Sunnyside neighborhood and open for breakfast, lunch, and weekend brunch, **The Universal** (2911 W. 38th Ave., 303/955-0815, http://theuniversaldenver.blogspot.com, 7am-2:30pm daily, $6.50-10) appeals to a wide audience. You'll find a menu full of classics like the two-egg standard and buttermilk pancakes, but look deeper for unique plates like pork green chile and grits, wild boar scramble with smoked gouda and sundried tomatoes, and the sweet and savory quinoa bowl with currants, maple syrup, and chèvre. Check the chalkboard for quiche and sammie specials and plan enough time to hang out and enjoy this sunny spot with friends and a steaming hot cup of coffee.

After being open for about two seconds, the ★ **Wooden Spoon Cafe & Bakery** (2418 W. 32nd Ave., 303/999-0327, www.woodenspoondenver.com, 7am-2pm Tues.-Fri., 8am-2pm Sat.-Sun., $7-11) became a neighborhood favorite for its scrumptious breakfast pastries (apple tarts, blueberry scones, croissants, and more) and hearty sandwiches. Located in a historic building amid a block filled with restaurants, the Wooden Spoon feels like a European shop. Or perhaps it's the strict rules on no screens—no laptops or phones allowed—that make it feel old-fashioned.

American

Chef Frank Bonanno, known in Denver for Mizuna and Luca D'Italia, has opened **Lou's Food Bar** (1851 W. 38th Ave., 303/458-0336, www.lousfoodbar.com, 11am-10pm Mon.-Thurs., 11am-11pm Fri., 10am-11pm Sat.-Sun., $6-17), serving "American food with a French twist." Though one does not typically think of Paris when gobbling up fried chicken and whipped potatoes, the housemade sausages don't seem out of line with a picnic lunch in the French countryside. The name in neon along busy 38th Avenue tells diners that this is a place to get a bite to eat, not plan a romantic night out.

Westerners love good barbecue. Luckily, there are several great places to find it in Denver. **Ragin' Hog BBQ** (4361 Lowell Blvd., 303/859-6003, www.raginhogbbq.com, noon-7pm Tues.-Sat., $13-25) offers pork, chicken, hot links, and ribs, all smoked daily and served with sides like collards, potato salad, and mac and cheese. Sauces are decided Southern (no Kansas City-style 'cue here), and meats are available by the pound for catered parties and backyard barbecues. This cash-only spot will close early if they sell out, so don't dally!

Craving a basic meal? Look no further than **Park Burger Highlands** (2643 W. 32nd Ave., 303/862-8461, http://parkburger.com, 11am-9pm Sun.-Thurs., 11am-10pm Fri.-Sat., $7-11) for a burger, hot dog, and fries. What makes Park Burger worth a stop is the fact that the burgers are not that basic. Along with never-frozen beef burgers, there is a turkey burger, veggie burger, and buffalo burger; turn one of those into a specialty burger with cheese, onions, egg, guacamole, and more. Then wash it all down with a milkshake, beer, wine, or cocktail.

After changing owners and undergoing extensive interior renovations, the former Coral Room became **Small Wonder Food and Wine** (3489 W. 32nd Ave., 303/433-2535, www.smallwonderfoodandwine.com, 11am-close Mon.-Fri., 9am-close Sat.-Sun., $13-27) in 2015. The new restaurant touts itself as a welcoming neighborhood spot, serving simple, fresh fare with an emphasis on local and organic ingredients. An order of duck pâté, a cheese platter (supplied by neighboring St. Killian's Cheese Shop), and a glass of wine makes for a pleasant snack or light dinner.

Asian

Come hungry but patient for the flavorful, savory ramen that **Uncle** (2215 W. 32nd Ave., 303/433-3263, www.uncleramen.com, 5pm-10pm Mon.-Sat., $3-16) is known for. A seat at the bar will afford a great view of the kitchen, where airy bao buns and rich pots of broth steam and bubble away. Start with an order of pork belly buns before diving into a hot bowl of the good stuff. Order the duck ramen with a soft egg over curly noodles and shoyu broth, or add an "umami bomb" of miso bacon jam or spicy seven pepper for even more yum factor. Uncle packs a crowd most evenings, so plan on a bit of a wait.

Contemporary

Brazen Denver (4450 W. 38th Ave. #130, 720/638-1242, www.brazendenver.com, 4:30pm-2am Mon.-Fri., 10am-2pm and 5pm-2am Sat., 10am-2pm and 5pm-10pm Sun., $5-27) boldly opens its doors to local and visiting diners, offering a warm, authentic dining experience in a rustic-chic space. Parking is a bit tricky, but once you're here you're seated in a friendly open kitchen (sit at the chef's counter if you can), guided through an enticing cocktail list, and encouraged to try small and large plates with seasonally inspired ingredients that aim to satisfy. Try the deviled eggs, braised meatballs, and roast chicken. Sitting outside? Stay after dark to enjoy a cocktail around the fire pit.

The owners at **Duo Restaurant** (2413 W. 32nd Ave., 303/477-4141, www.duorestaurants.com, 5pm-10pm Mon.-Sat., 5pm-9pm Sun., 10am-2pm Sat.-Sun., $19-28) are up front to greet diners, and the open kitchen offers a glimpse of the chefs hard at work on seasonal dishes for dinner or brunch. Duo is on the ground floor of a large historic building that has been renovated and filled with shops and restaurants. Pick a seat next to one of the large windows and watch the people stroll by, or sit at one of the tables along the exposed brick walls for a more intimate evening.

Linger (2030 W. 30th Ave., 303/993-3120, www.lingerdenver.com, 11:30am-2:30pm Tues.-Fri., 5:30pm-10pm Mon.-Thurs., 5:30pm-11pm Fri.-Sat., 10am-2:30pm Sat.-Sun., $7-33) found a way to turn a piece of the historic Olinger mortuary into a hot spot. Chef Justin Cucci created a menu of eclectic world tastes. Translation: Come here with a group of friends and order lots of small plates to sample dishes evocative of Asia, Africa, the Middle East, America, Europe, and Eurasia. The drink menu is nearly as extensive, with beers from as far as China, wines from Colorado and Austria, and cocktails with curious names like "Corpse Reviver." There is even a kids' menu (American-style with chicken tenders and mac 'n' cheese). Reservations are a must since there can be a line down the block *before* Linger even opens for dinner.

Playing off the theme of the building's former incarnation as a car repair garage, **Root Down** (1600 W. 33rd Ave., 303/993-4200, www.rootdowndenver.com, 5pm-10pm Mon.-Thurs., 5pm-11pm Fri.-Sat., 5pm-9pm Sun., 10am-2:30pm Sat.-Sun., $13-32) staffers don mechanic's shirts and some of the old signs (like one reading "Tires") remain. The theme of the food is global, inspired by local ingredients. Root Down strives to please the customer with options to make some entrées gluten-free or vegan, and a promise that a majority of the ingredients are organic. My fave is the veggie burger sliders with scrumptious sweet potato fries on the side. Try to get a seat on the patio that overlooks downtown on the east side of the restaurant.

There's so much to love about **The Truffle Table** (2556 15th St., 303/455-9463, www.truffletable.com, 4pm-10pm Tues.-Thurs. and Sun., 4pm-11pm Fri.-Sat., $7-27) in the LoHi area. The place is quiet enough to have lengthy conversations with your friends over dinner, and shared small plates make the meal part of the conversation as you dip into fondue and select meats and cheeses. Come on a Wednesday for all-you-can-eat raclette night.

Chef/owner Justin Brunson makes it a priority to serve the finest house-butchered meats and freshest seafood at **Old Major** (3316 Tejon St., 720/420-0622, www.oldmajordenver.com, 5pm-10pm daily, $5-30), a rustic yet urban space perfect for happy hour or a memorable dinner night. Start with an order of oysters, saucy mussels, or ham and biscuits.

All the entrées are hearty and satisfying, but the Nose to Tail plate—with Toulouse sausage, braised belly, smoked rib, crispy ears, peas, mushrooms, and baby potatoes—might be the dish that most exhibits what Old Major is all about. Intrigued? Come for happy hour (3pm-6pm Mon.-Fri.) on the patio.

Solitaire (3927 W. 32nd Ave., 303/477-4732, www.solitairerestaurant.com, 5pm-10pm Mon.-Sat., $10-25) opened in the former Highland Garden Café space and was totally transformed with a bold color scheme, outdoor fire pit, and renovated interior. Small plates are exciting if pricy, and revolve around seasonal and specialty ingredients like Colorado lamb and Pacific uni. When you see the crimson '38 GMC pick-up truck parked on the curb, you'll know you're in the right place.

Delis

Denver restaurant veterans and owners of **Masterpiece** (1575 Central St., 303/561-3345, www.masterpiecedeli.com, 8am-8pm Mon.-Fri., 9am-8pm Sat.-Sun., $6-13) Steve Allee and Justin Brunson have the skill to make some of the best sandwiches in Denver. Just steps from the pedestrian bridge that links 16th Street to the Lower Highlands (or Highlands) neighborhood, Masterpiece Delicatessen was an instant hit with locals who keep coming back. The simple salad and sandwich menu has some dynamite standouts, like the Cubano sandwich and the vegetarian sandwich with manchego cheese. Start the day here with a sandwich on a bagel and a cup of coffee. The indoor seating is limited, and outdoor seating is best in the late afternoon. The deli is good for takeout and delivery, too.

Try a hearty sandwich at **Salt & Grinder** (3609 W. 32nd Ave., 303/945-4200, www.saltandgrinder.com, 8am-8pm daily, $6-12), a closet-sized deli serving up hearty, locally made bread topped with burrata, salami, prosciutto, and even housemade egg salad. The breakfast sammies are a real delight, or stop in for a happy hour jarred cocktail or draft beer. Grab a table on the sidewalk patio for the best people-watching.

Greek

The Greek menu at **Axios Estiatorio** (3901 Tennyson St., 720/328-2225, http://axiosdenver.com, 11am-9pm Mon.-Thurs., 11am-10pm Fri., 10am-10pm Sat., 10am-9pm Sun., $8-24) is a welcome change in the neighborhood, with the restaurant's friendly service and affordable menu items. For lunch and dinner, stick to the Greek basics, which are

Root Down restaurant in the LoHi neighborhood

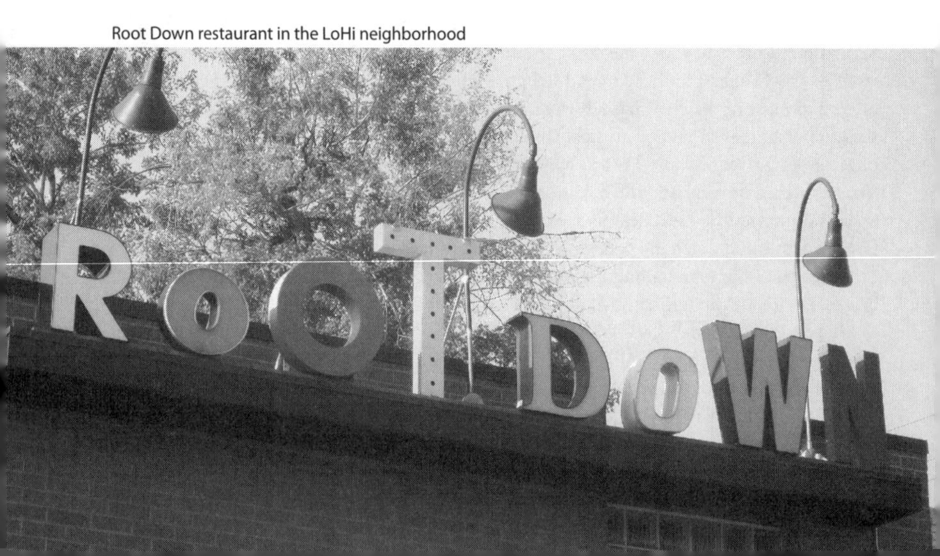

the Truffle Table in LoHi

all delicious. The feta cheese omelet on the brunch menu took me back to a childhood trip to a tiny Greek island, but there are also pancakes and French toast for those in the mood for a more traditional meal in the morning.

French

On a small residential side street in the eastern part of the Highlands neighborhood is the popular French bistro **Z Cuisine** (2245 W. 30th Ave., 303/477-1111, www.zcuisineonline.com, 5pm-10pm Wed.-Sat., $12-24). Each day, a chalkboard displays the authentic French menu chef-owner Patrick DuPays has created using fresh, seasonal ingredients from local growers. The cramped space adds to the ambience, as you can hear people at neighboring tables chatter in French and English. Two doors down, Dupays also has a wine bar that offers a smaller menu selection.

Italian

Parisi (4401 Tennyson St., 303/561-0234, www.parisidenver.com, 11am-9pm Mon.-Thurs., 11am-9pm Fri.-Sat., $10-19) is a modern take on a traditional neighborhood pizzeria and market, with wonderful sandwiches, wood-oven-baked pizzas, and salads for lunch or dinner. Customers line up to place their order, then take their number to a table. While waiting for their food, they can browse the Italian market and deli or get gelato and other pastry desserts for something to take home. Downstairs is **Parisi's Firenze a Tavola** (Florence at Your Table, 303/561-0234, 5:30pm-10pm Wed.-Sat.), a more formal restaurant with a full bar that is perfect for a private party or special date night.

This modern Italian addition to the Highlands dining scene was instantly popular. **Sarto's** (2900 W. 25th Ave., 303/455-1400, www.sartos.com, 5pm-10pm Mon.-Sat., 10am-2pm Sat.-Sun., $11-30) is chic, with enormous windows and a white interior that it makes even a casual night out feel special. Start with the tavola, then enjoy a housemade pasta.

Spuntino (2639 W. 32nd Ave., 303/433-0949, www.spuntinodenver.com, 11am-3pm Mon., 11am-9pm Tues.-Thurs., 11am-10pm Fri.-Sat., 10am-8pm Sun., $8-14) is the go-to lunch spot with neighborhood friends. Order sandwiches and salads with a gelato to share (try the apricot-blueberry tart with cardamom cream, toasted graham cracker, and fior di panna gelato). This is impeccably made food with fresh ingredients in ideal portions.

Latin American

Off the beaten path of Highlands hot spots, **Cafe Brazil** (4408 Lowell Blvd., 303/480-1877, www.cafebrazildenver.com, 5pm-10pm Tues.-Sat., $16-24) remains a perennial favorite for South American fare. With orange walls and blue tablecloths, it has a playful and casual feel. My personal favorites here include *palmito* (hearts of palm in a white wine cream sauce) and the *feijoada completa,* a Brazilian black bean stew with fried bananas, collard greens, sausages, and oranges. Housemade desserts change daily. Reservations are recommended.

El Chingon Mexican Bistro (4326 Tennyson St., 303/248-3641, www.elchingondenver.com, 10:30am-10pm Tues.-Thurs., 10:30am-1am Fri.-Sat., 10:30am-10pm Sun.,$15-20) is the place for simple, rustic food done in the style of Mexico City, prepared with locally butchered, grass-fed pork, free-range chicken, and Colorado wine and beer. You might not have guessed that chef David Lopez studied the classics in France, or that he works alongside his grandmother Gloria Nuñez to make traditional, authentic salsas, chile rellenos, and tacos.

Visit **Lola Mexican Fish House** (1575 Boulder St., 720/570-8686, www.loladenver.com, 4pm-10pm Mon.-Thurs., 4pm-11pm Fri., 10am-2pm and 5pm-11pm Sat., 10am-2pm and 5pm-9pm Sun., $10-27) for Mexican-inspired fare any night of the week. A buzzing (if not raucous) atmosphere made up of young socialites and loyal neighbors gives this restaurant a fun energy. The fundido or Lola guacamole (prepared tableside) are perfect starters, and the ceviche is a refreshing choice on a hot night. Sundays bring live music and family-style paella.

As Denver's Highlands neighborhood has changed, it has lost some of the Mexican restaurants that filled the storefronts for years. But **Patzcuaro's** (2616 W. 32nd Ave., 303/455-4389, www.patzcuaros.com, 11am-9pm daily, $8-17) has held its ground and remains a favorite for locals still craving pork smothered with green chile and platters of enchiladas or burritos. Menudo is served on weekends only. The favorite drink here is a *liquado,* a very sweet fruit juice loved by adults and children.

Thai

Denver has a fair amount of Thai restaurants to choose from, but **Swing Thai** (4370 Tennyson St., 303/477-1994, www.swingthai.com, 11am-9pm Sun.-Thurs., 11am-10pm Fri.-Sat., $10-14) stands out for their dependably good food, appealing decor, and fast service. This location is one of their largest, with a bar, banquette, and tables inside, as well as a patio out back. In an effort to be more health-conscious, Swing Thai offers gluten-free and vegan menu items, as well as all-natural beef and chicken and organic tofu. Takeout and delivery are available.

Dessert

There's just enough room for cupcakes and one or two eager customers in tiny **Happy Cakes** (3434 W. 32nd Ave., 303/477-3556, www.happycakesdenver.com, 10am-6pm Mon.-Sat.) in Highlands Square. This petite place sells itty-bitty gourmet cupcakes in addition to regular and jumbo size. Gluten-free cupcakes are available in limited flavors daily, and there is a vegan flavor on Fridays. The main cupcake flavors rotate daily; make a date to try the French Toast on Wednesday, the Cherry Limeade on Friday, or the Dirt Cake on Saturday. On Tuesdays, the cupcakes are a bargain ($2).

You would think people had never tasted ice cream before **Little Man Ice Cream** (2620 16th St., 303/455-3811, www.littlemanicecream.com, 11am-midnight daily) came along. Built on the site of the Olinger Mortuary in the Lower Highlands neighborhood, Little Man is a giant replica of a silver milk can, and named after its founder's nickname. People gaze at the Denver skyline as they wait in the line that stretches up the block all summer. Little Man Ice Cream runs out of the favorite flavors early every day, but cross your fingers for the salted Oreo because it is the best.

WASHINGTON PARK AND CHERRY CREEK

American

What people like about the **Cherry Cricket** (2641 E. 2nd Ave., 303/322-7666, www.cherrycricket.com, 11am-2am daily, $6-9) is that it hasn't changed much, if at all, with the rest of the neighborhood. Year after year, this is the place to go in Denver for a green chile burger—or any burger. They also serve Mexican food, sandwiches, and salads. There is free parking in the lot behind the building.

A former Super Bowl-winning quarterback for the Denver Broncos, John Elway is one of Denver's biggest celebrities. For years he put his name on car dealerships, but he has now switched to restaurants. **Elway's** (2500 E. 1st Ave., 303/399-5353, www.elways.com, 11am-10pm Mon.-Thurs., 11am-11pm Fri.-Sat., 11am-9pm Sun., $16-78) is a brightly lit, modern steak house with lots of windows and a piano bar that offers seafood, steak, and a few surprises, like tacos for an appetizer and s'mores for dessert. Certainly the restaurant draws a lot of sports fans hoping for a glimpse of Elway himself as well as other celebrities. Other locations are downtown at the Ritz-Carlton Hotel (1881 Curtis St., 303/312-3107), at Denver International Airport (Concourse B, 303/342-7777), and in Vail.

Asian

★ **Sushi Den** (1487 S. Pearl St., 303/777-0826, www.sushiden.net, 11:30am-2:30pm and 4:45pm-10:30pm Mon.-Thurs., 11:30am-2:30pm and 4:45pm-midnight Fri., 4:30pm-midnight Sat., 5pm-10:30pm Sun., $8-17) has a consistently long wait, but no one is complaining—it's see and be seen here among a young, good-looking clientele in the cramped waiting area and bar. Pull up a chair to watch and listen as the sushi chefs make their beautiful creations, or grab a table and start ordering sushi or another of the house specialties. Then sink your teeth into what many consider to be the city's best sushi. Chefs here will also take custom orders.

An offshoot of Sushi Den comes in the form of **Izakaya Den** (1518 S. Pearl St., 303/777-0691, www.izakayaden.net, 5pm-10pm Tues.-Thurs., 5pm-11pm Fri.-Sat., 11:30am-2:30pm Sat., $12-16). Certainly this serene restaurant benefits from the overflow crowd at Sushi Den across the street, but Izakaya Den has been gaining a reputation of its own for its delicate and flavorful small plates. In addition to sushi and sashimi, Izakaya has a Japanese-Mediterranean fusion tapas menu featuring combinations like Kobe beef with edamame and watermelon.

Sushi Tazu (300 Fillmore St., #G, 303/320-1672, www.denver-sushi.net, 11:30am-2:30pm and 4:30pm-10pm Mon.-Thurs., 11:30am-2:30pm and 4:30pm-11pm Fri.-Sat., noon-10pm Sun., $16-34) offers daily specials along with an extensive menu of fresh sushi and cooked entrées. Sushi Tazu is often a "reader's choice" vote for best sushi in Denver in local magazines' annual surveys. They are also recognized for their many vegetarian selections, including veggie sushi. Their daily happy hour (4:30pm-6pm) includes half-price sushi and discounted sake. Because the restaurant is small, it fills up fast on weekend evenings. There is some parking behind the restaurant.

Breakfast and Brunch

It's crepes for breakfast, lunch, and dinner at **Crépes N' Crépes** (2816 E. 3rd Ave., 303/320-4184, www.crepesncrepes.com, 9am-10pm Tues.-Fri., 8:30am-10pm Sat., 8:30am-3pm Sun., $9-15), and still people can't seem to get enough of them. Perhaps it's because this is a true French *crêperie,* with French sweet or savory ingredients filling the thin pancakes cooked on hot French griddles—even the menu is in French (with English translation). Crépes N' Crépes feels like a find even if you've been here before, with tables squeezed up to the walls so there is just enough room to maneuver between the well-stocked bar and each table. Inside, and on the adorable patio out back, it feels like a trip to Europe. It's a great little dessert stop after a movie or dinner elsewhere, too. There is a second location in LoDo's Writer Square (1512 Larimer St., 303/534-1620, Mon.-Tues. 10am-3pm, Wed.-Sun. 10am-10pm).

The **Pajama Baking Company** (1595 S. Pearl St., 303/733-3622, www.pajamabaking-company.com, 7am-9pm Mon.-Sat., 7am-8pm Sun., $7-9) is a modern version of a community hub, with a garage door rolled up to relieve the roomy space where neighborhood families can stroll in for breakfast, a sandwich, or a treat.

Wild West Dining

For a one-of-a-kind dining experience in the West, **The Fort** (19192 Hwy. 8, Morrison, 303/697-4771, www.thefort.com, 5:30pm-9:30pm Mon.-Fri., 5pm-9:30pm Sat.-Sun., $28-59) is the place to go. Inspired by a drawing of a historic fort, Sam Arnold bought the land in the 1960s and hired a crew to build (or re-create) a true 1840s fort. When it wasn't feasible as a private home, Mr. Arnold decided to make it a restaurant and studied cooking so that he could provide only the best ingredients and menu. Today, with Mr. Arnold's daughter Holly Arnold Kinney at the helm, The Fort offers what can only be described as exotic Western, with a large variety of game meats, trout, Rocky Mountain oysters, Southwestern spices, and other unexpected culinary delights. There is a gift shop on-site, and annual Western-themed events, such as a powwow, are held here.

Deli

When it comes to Jewish deli food, **Zaidy's Deli** (121 Adams St., 303/333-5336, www.zaidysdeli.com, 6:30am-7pm Mon.-Fri., 7:30am-7pm Sat.-Sun., $7-12) is the place. This Cherry Creek mainstay has a loyal clientele—including me, especially when I am in need of matzo-ball soup. Every table is given a bowl of pickles to munch on before ordering. There are a variety of sandwiches to choose from, as well as latkes, knishes, corned beef hash, and large slices of cake for dessert.

Cafés

It started out as a place for sweets and just kept growing until **Devil's Food Bakery & Cookery** (1024 S. Gaylord St., 303/733-7448, www.devilsfooddenver.com, 7am-10pm Tues.-Sat., 7am-4pm Sun.-Mon., $10-17) turned into an all-day restaurant for every meal. Whether you're in the mood for a full breakfast, lunch, brunch, or supper, or simply an afternoon tea or just something sinfully sweet, Devil's Food Bakery & Cookery can fill your craving. Try the grapefruit tart, vanilla-bean cream puffs, or double-chocolate "doughnut." There can be a wait for brunch on weekends.

Contemporary

Black Pearl Restaurant (1529 S. Pearl St., 303/777-0500, www.blackpearldenver.com, 11am-2:30pm Fri.-Mon. and 5pm-9pm daily, $17-29) is an intriguing mix of the owners' East Coast roots and the seasonal availability of fresh, organic ingredients in Colorado. Set in a small building in South Pearl Street's dining and shopping district, Black Pearl is sleek and simple in design and menu. Out back, there is a stone communal table surrounding a fire pit. The "contemporary American" dinner menu at this award-winning restaurant includes raw oysters, mussels, crawfish, steaks, duck, and pasta. At weekend brunch, the bottomless mimosas mean a bit of a wait for a table. There are also happy hour and late night menus and hours.

Gaia Bistro (1551 S. Pearl St., 303/777-5699, www.gaiabistro.com, 7am-2pm Tues.-Fri., 8am-2pm Sat.-Sun., 5pm-8:30pm Wed.-Thurs., 5pm-9pm Fri.-Sat., $7-12) uses organic ingredients grown in the backyard of this Victorian house. And while being green is certainly an appeal to many customers, what really keeps them coming back are the crepes and large patio out front. Expect a wait for a table outside if the weather is nice. In addition to their crepes, Gaia offers sandwiches, soups, and salads that have helped it establish a devoted crowd of regulars. Gluten-free crepes are available on request.

Italian

Everyone who works at **Barolo Grill** (3030 E. 6th Ave., 303/393-1040, www.barologrilldenver.com, 5:30pm-10:30pm Tues.-Sat., $20-34) is an expert on northern Italy, since the owner takes the entire staff there each year to experience the inspiration for the restaurant's food and wine. This firsthand knowledge equals first-class service that matches the excellent menu, which changes seasonally with the exception of a single dish: the braised duckling with kalamata olives. Barolo also offers a five-course tasting menu with optional wine pairing. The grill has a warm and inviting atmosphere year-round, but a table next to the fireplace is especially cozy in winter. Reservations are recommended on weekends.

On the corner of a quiet block in Cherry Creek North is one of the neighborhood's best restaurants. **Cucina Colore** (3041 E. 3rd Ave., 303/393-6917, www.cucinacolore.com, 11am-10pm Sun.-Thurs., 11am-11pm Fri.-Sat., $13-34) offers upscale, contemporary Italian food and a pleasant wine list for lunch and dinner. Try the *pollo e orzo* salad or a crisp pizza with the house sangria for lunch. Patio seating at umbrella-sheltered tables is available on both sides of the restaurant, and indoor tables are bathed in natural light from the many windows.

Occupying a busy corner near Washington Park on Old South Gaylord Street, **Homegrown Tap & Dough** (1001 S. Gaylord St., 720/459-8736, www.tapanddough.com, 11am-10pm Sun.-Wed., 11am-11pm Thurs.-Sat., $5-15) is a lively, friendly bar and restaurant with a fun outdoor patio and expansive bar seating. This is primarily a pizza joint, with chewy, charred wood-fired pies of all toppings and sauces. And since Homegrown comes from the owners of legendary Park Burger, they have a killer burger on the menu. It's family-friendly and often crowded, with a reliable draft list of local suds.

A staple in the Cherry Creek neighborhood for more than a decade, **North Italia** (190 Clayton Ln., 720/941-7700, www.northitaliarestaurant.com/locations/cherry-creek, 11am-10pm Mon.-Sat., 11am-9pm Sun., $8-17) is a bright, rustic-chic oasis on a bustling shopping district corner. Families gather around bowls of spaghetti and meatballs, while couples sip glasses of wine at low tables adjacent to floor-to-ceiling windows. Enormous light fixtures and an exposed brick wall draw the eye to the community table and cushy central booths, while plentiful bar seating attracts singles, pairs, and those eager to learn about the latest barrel-aged cocktail behind the bar. Start with grilled artichoke or zucca chips, then savor a margherita pizza or hearty bolognese.

One of Cherry Creek North's best-kept dining secrets is a little find of a café, **Pasta Pasta Pasta** (2800 E. 2nd Ave., 303/377-2782, www.pastapastapasta.us, 10:30am-5:30pm Mon.-Fri., 10:30am-4pm Sat., $8-12) offering simple and always tasty Italian food. Customers walk up to the counter and see what's available that day—such as a slice of salmon, chicken Milanese, ravioli, spaghetti, and salads—and order and pay before seating themselves at one of the small tables. The walls are adorned with ornate Italian ceramic plates and bowls (all for sale).

Transportation and Services

GETTING THERE AND AROUND

Air

Denver International Airport (DIA, 8500 Peña Blvd., 303/342-2000, www.flydenver.com) is the major regional hub for domestic and international flights. This is the fifth-busiest airport in the country and the 15th busiest in the world, with more than 53 million passengers annually. There isn't really a hometown airline anymore, but competition helps ensure sale fares are available both to and from this airport. The airport itself could be a destination, with offshoots of some of the city's best eateries, public art on display, and a new hotel. The airport is about 25 miles from downtown Denver, typically a 30-minute drive. You will exit the airport on Peña Boulevard heading west, then merge with I-70 west and continue west to

I-25 south. Take the Speer Boulevard exit east to get to downtown. The traffic on I-70 can get jammed (especially during rush hour or at sunset with the glare); an alternate route downtown is Quebec Street south to Martin Luther King Drive west, then left on Colorado Boulevard and right on 17th Street.

Denver International Airport is serviced by many international airlines such as British Airways, Lufthansa, AeroMexico, Icelandair, and Air Canada, and of course many domestic airlines including Southwest Airlines, United Airlines, American Airlines, US Airways, and Delta Airlines. Budget carriers like JetBlue, Frontier, and Spirit also fly out of DIA.

AIRPORT TRANSPORTATION

When making your hotel reservations, ask if they have a free shuttle pick-up from the airport. Several hotels that are within 10 miles of the airport have shuttle service.

You'll need to prearrange limo service, but there are plenty of companies to choose from; see the www.denverfly.com website for a full list of limo companies. When you are meeting a limo ride, go to Level 5, Island 2 outside the Jeppesen Terminal, outside doors 505-507 and 511-513 on the east side and doors 504-506 and 510-512 on the west side.

Commuter shuttles can be prearranged or are available on demand from Jeppesen Terminal, Level 5, Island 5, outside doors 505-507 (east side) and doors 510-512 (west side). **Super Shuttle** (800/258-3826, www.supershuttle.com) is one of the many companies that can get you to downtown.

Taxis have flat rates for airport transportation; it costs $55 one-way to go from DIA to downtown Denver. Taxis can be found on Level 5, Island 1 outside doors 505, 507, and 511 on the east side and 506, 510, and 512 on the west side. Call **Denver Yellow Cab** (303/777-7777) or **Metro Taxi** (303/333-3333) to schedule a ride.

Car

I-25 runs north to south along the west side of downtown Denver. I-70 runs east to west and is the highway that leads into Denver from the airport. These two highways intersect just north of downtown.

If you are planning to head up I-70 to visit a mountain town, check traffic online (www.cotrip.org) because there can be significant delays for any number of reasons (snow, ice, rockslides, wildlife). I-25 has a significant amount of commuter traffic, as well as jams near downtown exits when there are sporting events and concerts. I-25 south will get you to Colorado Springs in about one hour; I-25 north will reach Fort Collins in about one hour. To drive to Boulder, you'll need to exit to Highway 36 from I-25; plan the drive to take 30 minutes or less from downtown Denver.

RENTAL CARS

You'll need to take a shuttle from Denver International Airport to one of the more than 10 rental car companies located "on property" (beyond the closest airport parking lots). Rental car shuttles pick up and drop off from Jeppesen Terminal, Level 5, Island 4 outside doors 505-513 on the east side and outside doors 504-512 on the west side. You'll find **Enterprise** (800/261-7331, www.enterprise.com) and **Hertz** (800/654-3131, www.hertz.com) among the car rental agencies that also have locations in the city.

Train

Amtrak (www.amtrak.com) provides train service through Denver on the *California Zephyr* route that goes to Chicago and San Francisco. Tickets can be bought at Union Station (1701 Wynkoop St., 303/592-6712) and trains pull up on the west side of the historic station. There are two trains departing and arriving daily from this station—one leaves for Chicago and the other for San Francisco.

Light Rail

The **RTD light rail system** (303/299-6000, www.rtd-denver.com, $2.25-5) is getting better and making more sense as it grows tracks to more destinations, including Denver International Airport. The C, D, E, F, H, and

W lines are convenient for commuters, as well as for suburbanites coming into the city to bar hop or attend sporting events so they don't have to pay for parking or worry about driving home tipsy. All of these lines pass through downtown, with lines C, E, and W stopping at Union Station. Fares vary depending on the number of zones your trip travels through. Service is available 24 hours a day, 365 days a year. In 2016, four new lines will expand light rail service: A, B, G, and R are part of the FasTracks project with the A line going from the airport to downtown.

Bus

You can travel by **Greyhound** (1055 19th St., 303/293-6555, www.greyhound.com) in and out of downtown Denver. Greyhound travels to Salt Lake City from Denver, with stops along the way on I-70 through the mountains. **Burlington Trailways** (800/992-4618, www.burlingtontrailways.com) provides bus service out of the Greyhound terminal to points east such as Fort Morgan, Brush, and Sterling.

The **Regional Transportation District** (1600 Blake St., 303/299-6000, www.rtd-denver.com, $2.25-5 one-way) has daily bus service across eight counties in the Denver metro area, including service to Boulder. An underground bus concourse is found behind Union Station (17th and Wewatta Sts.). RTD provides local bus service around Denver, regional bus service to Boulder, and light rail service. There are also specialty rides for sporting events, service for people with disabilities, and more. In 2016, the bus between Boulder and Denver will be called the Flatiron Flyer.

Guided and Walking Tours

It's a rare thing to see a Segway rolling along the streets of the Mile-High City, where people prefer to get exercise by simply walking from point A to point B. Nonetheless, **Colorado Adventure Segway Tours** (303/449-6780 or 866/573-6749, www.coloradosegwaytours.com, $75 per person) offers the opportunity to see the city's historic high points without wearing oneself out too much. Instead of walking alongside the South Platte River through Confluence Park, you get to "glide." Tours are guided and helmets are required (and provided) for everyone.

There's a theme for every kind of tour, and a range of ways to tour, with **Denver History Tours** (720/234-7929, www.denverhistorytours.com, $20 adults, $10 children age 12-18, free for children under 12). There are haunted-house tours, a visit to historic Littleton, and a look back at the seamy side of the city when bordellos and saloons thrived. Many of these are guided walking tours that usually last about two hours. There are also bus tours that can take an entire day and go well beyond the downtown environs to everywhere from local infill projects to Victorian towns in the foothills. Prices vary. Call ahead to make reservations; a minimum of two people are needed for a tour.

Lower Downtown has a rich history, from the first encampments along the South Platte River to the first buildings, including all of the colorful characters along the way. **LoDo Historic Walking Tours** (303/628-5428, www.lodo.org, $10-20 adults, $5-15 students and military, free for children under 12) offers three different walking tours, each departing from a different locale with a unique schedule and itinerary. The two-hour tour is a chance to learn about the businesses that first occupied many of the beautiful buildings, or that still do, such as the Oxford Hotel.

Departing from behind REI, just off of 15th and Platte Streets, the **Platte Valley Trolley** (15th and Platte Sts., 303/458-6255, www.denvertrolley.org, 11am-4pm Thurs.-Mon. Memorial Day-Labor Day, $5 adults, $2 children age 4-13, children under 4 free) is a quirky tour of Confluence Park and the businesses along this stretch of the South Platte River, including the Children's Museum. Perhaps more interesting is the history of this open-air car, a "breezer," and the fact that there used to be an entire trolley-car system throughout the city. The trolley serves as a shuttle ride to Broncos games during the football season. The trolley schedule has been cut back each year, so double-check the website for the most current days and times.

SERVICES

The **Denver Convention and Visitors Bureau** (303/892-1112, www.visitdenver.org) is where to begin learning about the Mile-High City. There are also three Denver Tourist Information Centers: one downtown on the 16th Street Mall (1575 California St., 303/892-1505, 9am-6pm Mon.-Fri., 9am-5pm Sat., 10:30am-2:30pm Sun. May-Oct.); at the airport (8500 Pena Blvd., 5th Fl., 303/317-0629); and at the Colorado Convention Center (700 14th St., 303/228-8000).

Denver Public Library has 25 branch library locations in addition to the Central Library (10 W. 14th Ave. Pkwy., 720/865-1111, www.denverlibrary.org, 10am-8pm Mon.-Tues., 10am-6pm Wed.-Fri., 9am-5pm Sat., 1pm-5pm Sun.), which has a robust children's library with story times, an art gallery, a Western History and Genealogy department, and of course lots of books and media. The library also hosts monthly events from musical performances to craft classes. All library locations have free unlimited Wi-Fi available.

Emergency Services

In an emergency, dial 911 for immediate assistance. **Denver Health** (777 Bannock St., 303/436-6000, www.denverhealth.org) and **Presbyterian/St. Luke's Hospital** (PSL, 1719 E. 19th Ave., 303/839-6000, www.pslmc.org) are both close to downtown. **Children's Hospital Uptown** (1830 Franklin St., 720/777-1360, www.childrenscolorado.org) is on the same block as PSL.

Golden

As the western suburbs have sprawled out, the town of Golden now feels like a corner of Denver and not a separate destination—it's only a 15-minute drive from downtown. However, this historic town—briefly the first capital of the Colorado Territory (1862-1867), when it was called Golden City (now it's the City of Golden)—retains a distinct identity. Home to the Colorado School of Mines, Golden has museums, restaurants, creekside paths, and close access to the foothills. A day in Golden can feel like a little vacation from Colorado's capital.

SIGHTS

Astor House Museum

The **Astor House Museum** (822 12th St., 303/278-3557, www.goldenhistory.org, 10am-4:30pm Tues.-Sat., noon-4:30pm Sun. in summer; 11am-4:30pm Tues.-Sat., noon-4:30pm Sun. Nov. 1-Apr. 30, $3 age 6 and over) was a rooming and boardinghouse from the time it was built in 1867 until 1971. Today visitors can walk through the furnished rooms, take in the view, and imagine a time when it was a luxury to take a hot bath in a tub for a mere $0.25. The museum closed in September 2015 for restoration; work was expected to be completed in five to six months.

Bradford Washburn American Mountaineering Museum

The country's only museum devoted to the culture, technology, and history of mountaineering is right in downtown Golden at the **Bradford Washburn American Mountaineering Museum** (710 10th St., 303/996-2755, www.mountaineeringmuseum.org, 10am-4pm Mon.-Tues., 10am-6pm Wed., 10am-4pm Thurs.-Fri., noon-5pm Sat., $5 adults, $1 children under 12). Inside, visitors will see a rare scale model of Mount Everest, experience interactive exhibits on Colorado's highest mountains and what it's like to sleep on a mountain face, and learn more about many famous mountain climbers.

Golden

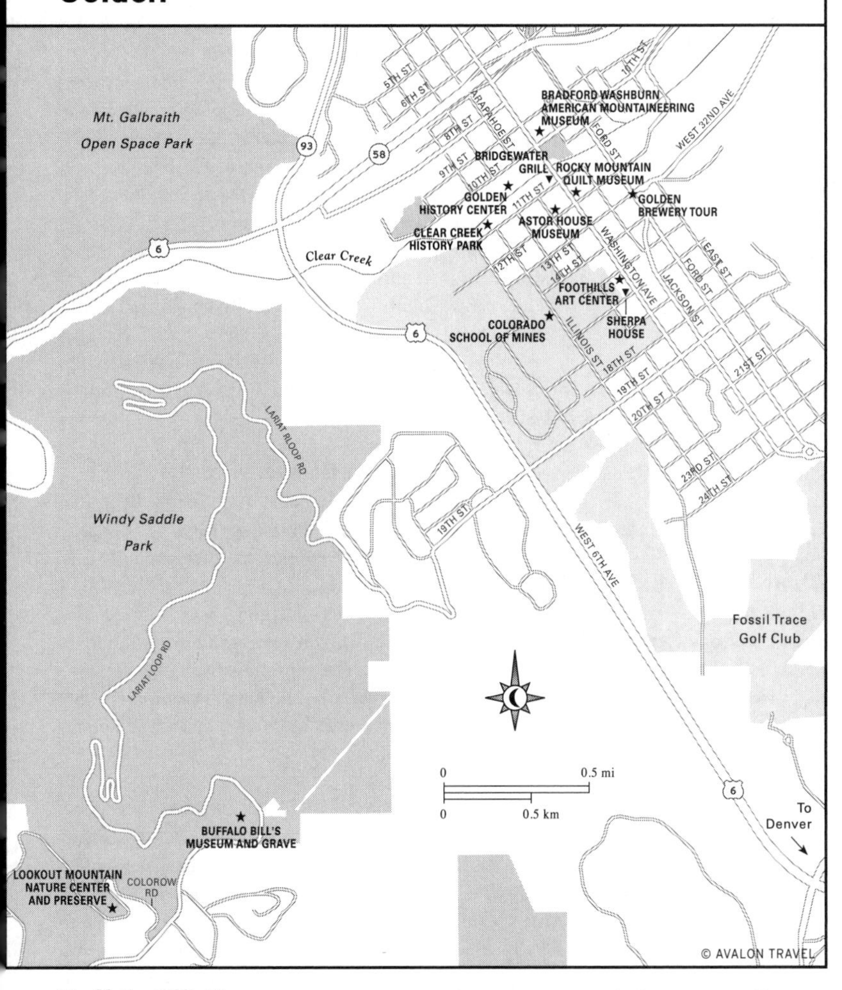

Buffalo Bill Museum and Grave

Above Golden and with a view of both the plains and the mountains is the **Buffalo Bill Museum and Grave** (987 Lookout Mountain Rd., 303/526-0747, www.buffalobill.org, 9am-5pm daily May 1-Oct. 31; 9am-5pm Tues.-Sun. Nov. 1-Apr. 30, $5 adults, $4 seniors, $1 children age 6-15, children 5 and under free). This spot so impressed frontiersman and showman William F. "Buffalo Bill" Cody that he asked to be buried here. More than 20,000 people came to this site on Lookout Mountain in 1917 when Cody was laid to rest.

Close to the grave is a 3,000-square-foot museum where visitors learn about the thrilling life and times of Buffalo Bill Cody. He worked herding cattle and riding for the Pony Express, but earned his nickname from his skills as a buffalo hunter. He truly became a legend as a magnificent performer in his Wild West shows. On display at the museum are the costumes he wore in the shows, silent and talking movies, original posters, and guns from Cody's own collection. While the memorabilia is interesting enough, what many people come here for is the view. A breezy and scenic picnic spot is not far from the grave, and the **Pahaska Teepee Gift Shop** (8:30am-8:30pm daily May 1-Labor Day; 9am-5pm daily Labor Day-Apr. 30, $4-10) between the museum and gravesite serves food such as buffalo burgers, buffalo chili, and ice cream.

The best route from downtown Denver is to go through Golden and follow 19th Street as it goes up into the mountains. You can also take I-70 west; just past the Lookout Mountain exit there is a buffalo herd, most visible in winter and early spring.

Clear Creek History Park

Not all museums are indoors. The **Clear Creek History Park** (11th and Arapahoe Sts., www.goldenhistory.org, sunrise-sunset daily, free), just one block off the main street in downtown, can be visited year-round. The park is made up of a reconstructed ranch that was moved here in the 1990s. It includes a schoolhouse, cabins, a blacksmith shop, and more.

Colorado School of Mines

The **Colorado School of Mines** campus (1500 Illinois St., 303/273-3000, www.mines.edu) is relatively small, but just the right size for Golden. The campus has some attractive historic buildings, such as the Guggenheim Building that was home to the school's first Geology Museum. Today, the **Geology Museum** (1310 Maple St., 303/273-3815, www.mines.edu, 9am-4pm Mon.-Sat., 1pm-4pm Sun.) is two levels filled with rocks, fossils, and gemstones from all over the world—and beyond, since it has a moon rock and meteorites on display. Learn more about the mining history that helped to found this town.

Foothills Art Center

On the perimeter of the School of Mines campus are two historic buildings—a former church and a former home—that house the **Foothills Art Center** (809 15th St., 303/279-3922, www.foothillsartcenter.org, 10am-5pm Tues.-Sat., 1pm-5pm Sun., $8 adults, $5 seniors), which draws surprisingly big names to this small town. The center has hosted exhibits by internationally known artists like glass artist Dale Chihuly and painter Edgar Degas, and it has watercolor shows and sculpture exhibits annually that include work by local artists.

Golden Brewery Tour

Founded in 1873, the **Coors Brewing Company** (13th and Ford Sts., 303/277-2337, www.millercoors.com, 10am-4pm Thurs., Fri., Sat., Mon., noon-4pm Sun., free)—now MillerCoors—has long been making beer and showing off how it's done right here in Golden. The tour ends with sampling some of the beers, so a valid ID is required. Be sure to call ahead for current hours and holiday closures.

Golden History Center

For a small town, Golden has a lot of varied history, and one can learn about it all at the **Golden History Center** (923 10th St., 303/278-3557, www.goldenhistory.org, 10am-4:30pm Wed.-Mon., $3 age 6 and over). Learn about dinosaurs, mining, pioneers, and beer.

Lookout Mountain Nature Center and Preserve

Not exactly in Golden, but worth the drive (or bicycle ride, for the extremely fit) is the **Lookout Mountain Nature Center and Preserve** (910 Colorow Rd., 720/497-7600, http://jeffco.us/open-space/parks/lookout-mountain-nature-center, 10am-4pm Tues.-Fri., 9am-5pm Sat.-Sun in summer;

10am-4pm Tues.-Fri. off-season), with grand views of the Queen City of the Plains far below. The land was once owned by the prominent Boettcher family of Denver, and their summer home remains on the property near the nature center and along one of the hiking trails here.

Rocky Mountain Quilt Museum

Quilts truly are works of art, and the **Rocky Mountain Quilt Museum** (1213 Washington Ave., 303/277-0377, www.rmqm.org, 10am-5pm Mon.-Sat., 11am-5pm Sun., $6 adults, $5 seniors, $4 students, free for children under 5) hosts marvelous exhibits showing off quilters' skills. The museum looks like a storefront, and does have a cute gift shop right inside the front door, so people often walk right by when they are looking for it.

RECREATION

Golden feels like Denver's backyard, and for residents here, it is! Hiking trails are very close to downtown Golden.

Some popular trails for hikers are the **Matthews/Winters Park** trails (1103 County Hwy. 93, 303/271-5925, http://jeffco.us/openspace). A basic understanding of geologic formations is helpful as you explore this foothills area, where the plains meet the hogbacks before the mountains rise up. For a hike with views of Red Rocks Park and the city, take about a 10-minute drive from downtown on I-70 west and get off at exit 259. From the parking lot, begin the 6.5-mile loop up to the top of the hogback for the best views. The hike is moderately difficult and the trail is used by mountain bikers as well. Bring a hat, since this trail does not provide much shade.

The **White Ranch Open Space Park** (25303 Belcher Hill Rd., 303/271-5925, http://jeffco.us/openspace) is just outside the town of Golden and has several trails to choose from. The Rawhide Trail is a 4.8-mile loop that goes through forest and grassy plains. The trail is shared with mountain bikers and sometimes wildlife, including deer, mountain lions, and bears.

For winter fun in the foothills, try snowshoeing or cross-country skiing at **Golden Gate Canyon State Park** (92 Crawford Gulch Rd., 303/582-3707, http://cpw.state.co.us/placestogo/parks). This park is accessible via County Highway 93. All trails in Golden Gate Canyon State Park can be used for snowshoeing and cross-country skiing, and on the website is a list of the best trails and where conditions tend to be consistently good, with less wind or melt-off. The site also provides helpful detailed directions to each trailhead.

Right in downtown Golden is some fun for kayakers at the **Clear Creek Whitewater Park** (1201 10th St., 303/384-8133, www.cityofgolden.net). Built in 1998, the park is designed for canoeing and kayaking. It includes a stretch of flat water, giant boulders to steer around, drop-offs, and fast-moving eddies. There are roughly seven city blocks of whitewater fun. The park is used for many championship events during the year, and can also be rented for private functions. Rent a tube at **Golden River Sports** (806 Washington Ave., 303/215-9386, www.goldenriversports.net, 10am-6pm Mon.-Fri., 9am-6pm Sat., 9am-5pm Sun., $20-30) and give it a go *if* you are a strong swimmer and/or wear a life vest; this is white-water tubing complete with rapids.

For those who just want to cool off, head over to **Splash Aquatics Park** (3151 Illinois St., 303/277-8700, www.splashingolden.com, daily 10am-6:30pm in summer, $3-9 day-use fee). The littlest children will enjoy the spray fountain, sandy beach area, and smaller, slippery slides. Older kids and their grown-ups are sure to have a blast on the two huge curly slides and getting splashed by the giant bucket of water. Splash is about a 10-minute drive from downtown. Go early on the hottest days, as this place gets jammed.

Play a round at the **Fossil Trace Golf Club** (3050 Illinois St., 303/277-8750, www.fossiltrace.com), a stunningly beautiful golf course designed by golf course architect Jim Engh. The 18-hole course is highlighted by rocks with dinosaur fossils still visible. This course has received accolades for being a "top course for women" and having the "most fun holes," and is generally one of Denver's best golf courses by everyone from *Golf Digest* to *5280 Magazine.*

SHOPPING

Every one of the sights listed for Golden has a unique gift shop for finding that special item from Colorado. Along Washington Avenue is a variety of local stores in which to browse. If you're planning a hike, go to **Vital Outdoors** (1224 Washington Ave., 303/215-1644, www.vitaloutdoors.com, 10am-7pm Mon.-Thurs., 10am-8pm Fri.-Sat., 10am-5pm Sun.) to get gear for the whole family. The store's helpful staff might also have some insider tips on hikes. Stop in at **Red Wagon Gift Shop** (1118 Washington Ave., 303/278-3994, www.redwagongiftshop.com, 10am-6pm Mon.-Sat., 11am-6pm Sun.) for that Colorado-themed gift to take home. If you are inspired by what you see at the Rocky Mountain Quilt Museum, shop for supplies at the **Golden Quilt Company** (1108 Washington Ave., 303/277-0717, www.goldenquiltcompany.com, 10am-5:30pm Mon.-Sat., noon-4pm Sun.).

ACCOMMODATIONS

Being so close to Denver, it is completely practical to spend a day in Golden and rest your head back in the Mile-High City. However, Golden does have some lovely hotels for those making a weekend of it here.

The Southwestern architecture of the **Table Mountain Inn** (1310 Washington Ave., 303/277-9898, www.tablemountaininn.com, $179-299) makes it one of the most distinctive buildings in downtown. Many of the rooms have beautiful views of the mesas and foothills from the balconies.

The Golden Hotel (800 11th St., 303/279-0100, www.thegoldenhotel.com, $129-299) is right on both Clear Creek and Washington Avenues, making it possible to walk to nearly every sight and shop mentioned.

FOOD

Certainly you can make a day of it in Golden and dine out for every meal at a different local place. Playing off the town's history is the **Old Capitol Grill** (1122 Washington Ave., 303/279-6390, 11am-8:30pm Sun.-Thurs., 11am-9:30pm Fri.-Sat., $13-25), located in the old capitol building where the first legislature sessions were held. Come in for sandwiches at lunchtime or steak for dinner.

To learn about a completely different history from another part of the world, walk over to the **Sherpa House Restaurant & Cultural Center** (1518 Washington Ave., 303/278-7939, www.ussherpahouse.com, 11am-2:30pm, 5pm-9:30pm Sun.-Thurs., 11am-2:30pm, 5pm-10pm Fri.-Sat., $9-13). Here you can taste authentic Himalayan cuisine while learning about Sherpa culture, Tibet, and Nepal.

The **Table Mountain Inn Grill & Cantina** (1310 Washington Ave., 303/277-9898, www.tablemountaininn.com, 6:30am-3pm and 4:30pm-10pm Mon.-Fri., 7am-2pm and 4:30pm-10pm Sat.-Sun., $12-23) serves Southwestern cuisine inspired by its Santa Fe-like architecture and decor. If the weather is cooperating, go for a creekside patio table at the **Bridgewater Grill** (800 11th St., 303/279-2010, www.bridgewatergrill.com, 7am-10pm Mon.-Fri., weekend breakfast buffet, $9-28), for breakfast, lunch, or dinner.

For dessert (or anytime), **Golden Sweets** (1299 Washington Ave., www.golden-sweets.com, 303/271-1191, 11am-7pm Sun.-Thurs., 11am-9pm Fri.-Sat.) sells ice cream, taffy, chocolates, and a key-lime bar on a stick that is divine. The **Windy Saddle Café** (1110 Washington Ave., 303/279-1905, www.windysaddlecafe.com, 7am-6pm daily) is your go-to coffee shop.

TRANSPORTATION AND SERVICES

To reach downtown Golden from downtown Denver, either take 6th Avenue—which turns into a highway as you drive west—and turn off at 19th Street, or take I-70 west to the exit for Highway 58 and then take the Washington Avenue exit.

For more information, contact the **Golden Visitors Center** (1010 Washington Ave., 303/279-3113, www.goldenvisitorsbureau.com, 8:30am-5pm Mon.-Fri., 10am-4pm Sat.) to learn more about other interesting things to see and do in this charming town. They also have detailed directions for a bike route to town from Denver.

Boulder

Sitting at the base of the purple Rocky Mountains, the breathtaking city of Boulder invites even the most committed couch potato to get outside.

While the city's 45,000 acres of open space and hundreds of miles of hiking, biking, and jogging trails are a big attraction, there is plenty more to see and do in this busy college town. Though Boulder's reputation as a home to eco-minded, rock-climbing vegetarians is not totally inaccurate, there is much more going on here, with impressive regional-fare restaurants, a hip art scene, and nationally significant scientific research organizations.

Amazingly, it was on a visit to the new town of Boulder in 1908 that famed landscape architect Frederick Law Olmsted Jr. adequately summed up what remains true of the place today: "He wrote that the citizens of Boulder should not have to simply endure working in a community in order to move elsewhere for recreation and beauty. Recreation and beauty were already present if the people had the good sense to use them properly," wrote Beverly Halpin Carrigan in a 1992 report about Olmsted. It is this combination of living and working in a beautiful place with easy access to outdoor recreation that makes Boulder the appealing place it is today, with more than 40,000 acres of open space, almost 30 miles of trails, and more than 50 parks.

Despite its reputation as a foodie destination and a mecca of all things outdoors, people still ask, "So what is there to do in Boulder?" The answer to that question is: explore. Visiting Boulder is very different than spending a day in Denver. For all its sophistication and natural appeal, Boulder is refreshingly not a big city. Sights like the Pearl Street Mall allow you to take in the town's authentic flavor through street performers, shops, and a mix of locals. Or wander through the Boulder County Farmers Market in the summer, ride a bike along Boulder Creek and into the foothills, stroll a path at Chautauqua Park or around the University of Colorado campus, and then take in a movie under the stars.

As Denver has been striving—and arguably succeeding—at becoming a world-class city, Boulder has comfortably established itself as a world-class town. This is a place that inspires entrepreneurs, artists, and writers, and

Previous: downtown Boulder; hot-air balloon over Boulder. **Above:** hiking trail into Indian Peaks Wilderness.

Look for ★ to find recommended sights, activities, dining, and lodging.

Highlights

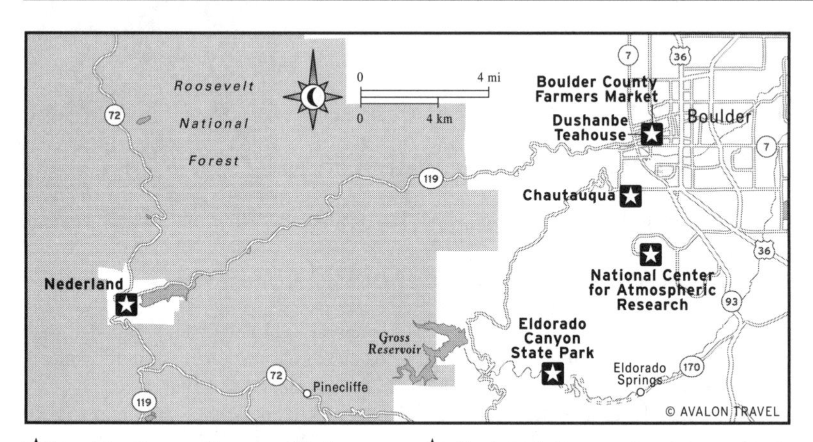

★ **Boulder County Farmers Market:** This weekly farmers market brings in the ranchers and growers producing the best of what Colorado has to eat—Western Slope peaches, corn, chickens, and more (page 143).

★ **Chautauqua:** At this historic educational and cultural summer retreat, there is lodging, dining, hiking, concerts, and movies, or you can just sprawl on the lawn at the base of the Flatirons (page 144).

★ **Dushanbe Teahouse:** Make time to stop here for a cup of tea and appreciate the magnificent details carved by 40 artisans over a three-year period (page 145).

★ **National Center for Atmospheric Research:** The I. M. Pei-designed center is home to the Walter Orr Roberts Weather Trail, the only trail that will educate you about the local weather history and patterns (page 146).

★ **Eldorado Canyon State Park:** This park just outside Boulder is where rock climbers, day hikers, mountain bikers, and anglers head to spend a beautiful day (page 172).

★ **Nederland:** This small mountain town has long embraced a counterculture reputation and offers a different vibe from Boulder (page 174).

Boulder

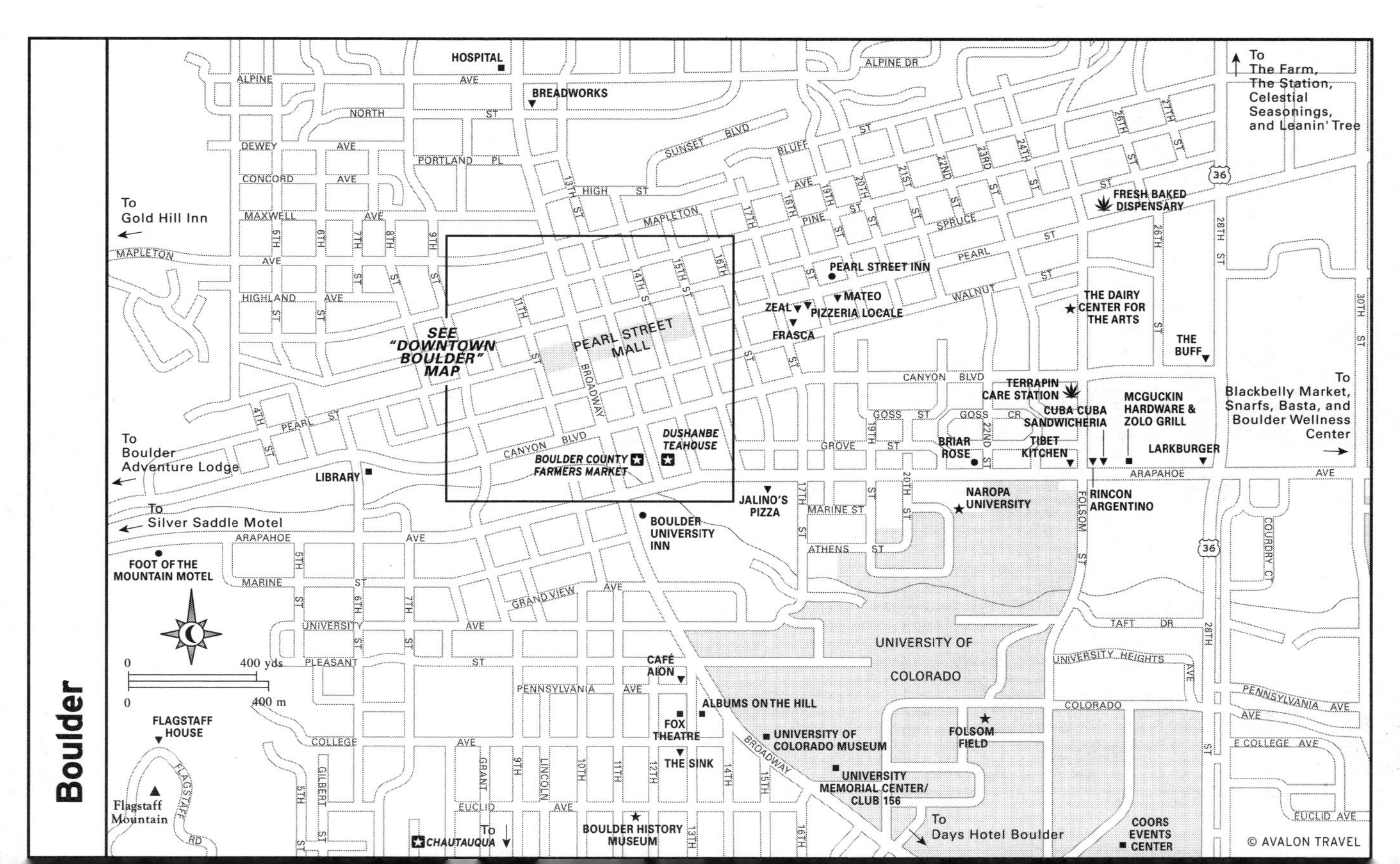

HOSPITAL
BREADWORKS
To The Farm, The Station, Celestial Seasonings, and Leanin' Tree
To Gold Hill Inn
FRESH BAKED DISPENSARY
PEARL STREET INN
MATEO
ZEAL
PIZZERIA LOCALE
FRASCA
THE DAIRY CENTER FOR THE ARTS
THE BUFF
SEE "DOWNTOWN BOULDER" MAP
PEARL STREET MALL
TERRAPIN CARE STATION
CUBA CUBA SANDWICHERIA
MCGUCKIN HARDWARE & ZOLO GRILL
To Blackbelly Market, Snarfs, Basta, and Boulder Wellness Center
To Boulder Adventure Lodge
DUSHANBE TEAHOUSE
BOULDER COUNTY FARMERS MARKET
BRIAR ROSE
TIBET KITCHEN
LARKBURGER
LIBRARY
JALINO'S PIZZA
NAROPA UNIVERSITY
RINCON ARGENTINO
To Silver Saddle Motel
BOULDER UNIVERSITY INN
FOOT OF THE MOUNTAIN MOTEL
UNIVERSITY OF COLORADO
0 400 yds
0 400 m
CAFÉ AION
ALBUMS ON THE HILL
FLAGSTAFF HOUSE
FOX THEATRE
UNIVERSITY OF COLORADO MUSEUM
FOLSOM FIELD
THE SINK
UNIVERSITY MEMORIAL CENTER/ CLUB 156
Flagstaff Mountain
To CHAUTAUQUA
BOULDER HISTORY MUSEUM
To Days Hotel Boulder
COORS EVENTS CENTER
© AVALON TRAVEL

welcomes a crop of freshman students each fall. Swing by and hang out to discover the laid-back lifestyle for yourself.

PLANNING YOUR TIME

As Boulder has gained a reputation for itself in recent years as this hip place, people naturally want to come see what all the buzz is about. While the view coming into Boulder is breathtaking and it can seem obvious why people like it here, it can take a bit of planning and effort to really experience this college town. What do you want to get out of this visit? A great workout? To soak up local arts culture? A meal to write home about? An intellectual high? It's all here, but you have to plan it right.

If you are coming from sea level, factor in the altitude before you take off for any hikes or long bike rides here. You are over a mile above sea level and it can take a day or two to acclimate.

If you come in the summer—whether solo, as a couple, or with family—you can do a little of all these things and get a real flavor for what sets Boulder apart from other destinations. On a Saturday morning, hit the Boulder County Farmers Market for a nibble and a walk. Later you can go up to Chautauqua for a late-afternoon hike, have dinner, or take in a concert. Or maybe you planned ahead and got tickets to the Shakespeare Festival on the University of Colorado campus. If you still have some energy later that night, stop in at one of the bars in the Hotel Boulderado for a drink and a look around the historic lobby.

Boulder is a haven for runners, triathletes, and other fitness buffs, but that doesn't mean you have to be an athlete to have a great time here. The Pearl Street Mall is four long pedestrian-only blocks, with more shops and restaurants on the surrounding blocks. You can spend hours leisurely wandering from shop to shop, with a break for a bite to eat, and never leave this general neighborhood.

The University of Colorado campus includes museums, a planetarium, art exhibits, and again, with some planning ahead, interesting events worth attending. Here too you can pack a lot into one location and easily walk from place to place.

The buffalo is the team mascot for the University of Colorado.

Sights

★ BOULDER COUNTY FARMERS MARKET

The **Boulder County Farmers Market** (www.boulderfarmers.org, Wed. and Sat. Apr.-Nov.) is the best farmers market along the Front Range, if not in the entire state. The biweekly market (Wednesday afternoons and Saturday mornings) begins in April and runs through early November—but my favorite time to come is in summer for fresh, locally grown strawberries (June) and Colorado peaches (August). This is the real deal—a farmer might still have dirt on his or her hands from digging up vegetables to display and sell. At many booths, you may overhear (or become part of) a conversation about what the farmer grows and how productive the season has been.

BOULDER HISTORY MUSEUM

Boulder is a pretty special place. To learn how it became the city it is today, visit the **Boulder History Museum** (1206 Euclid Ave., 303/449-3464, http://boulderhistory.org, 10am-5pm Tues.-Fri., noon-4pm Sat.-Sun., $6 adults, $4 seniors, $3 children and students). First-floor exhibits change several times annually, but tend to focus on a historical Colorado event. On the second floor are artifacts more specific to Boulder history. Programs and events range from the ongoing *Boulder Conversations with Extraordinary People* series, which features local professors, businesspeople, and civic leaders, to crafts and games for kids.

The museum has been housed in a historic home, but there are plans to move to a new building in 2016. Check the website for details.

BOULDER MUSEUM OF CONTEMPORARY ART

The **Boulder Museum of Contemporary Art** (1750 13th St., 303/443-2122, www.bmoca.org, 11am-5pm Tues.-Fri., 11am-4pm Sat.-Sun., $5 adults, $4 seniors or students, children under 12 free) is in a great location next to the Dushanbe Teahouse and Boulder Creek. The museum includes three galleries and a small black-box theater where regional,

the Boulder County Farmers Market

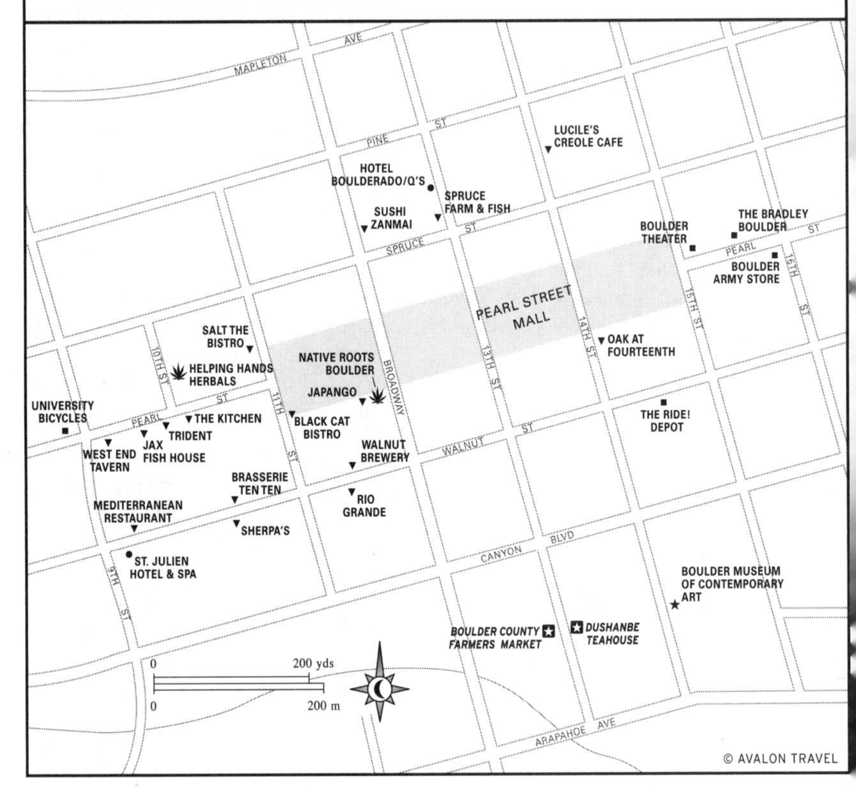

national, and international contemporary visual and performing arts are showcased year-round. This is also a popular venue for special events, so be sure to check the schedule before stopping by, or make it a point to be here during the **Boulder County Farmers Market** (www.boulderfarmers.org) Saturday mornings or Wednesday evenings in the summer.

CELESTIAL SEASONINGS

It's hard to remember a time when herbal tea was a cutting-edge health food concept, but back in the 1960s a group of tea radicals began picking fresh herbs in the nearby Rocky Mountains and bagging them dried for sale in health food stores. Now **Celestial Seasonings** (4600 Sleepytime Dr., 303/530-5300, www.celestialseasonings.com, 9am-6pm Mon.-Sat., 10am-5pm Sun.) is a household name and visitors can take free daily tours to watch the millions of tea bags roll off the assembly line. Tours last 45 minutes and are offered hourly (10am-4pm Mon.-Sat., 11am-3pm Sun., free).

★ CHAUTAUQUA

It's not just that **Chautauqua** (Colorado Chautauqua Assoc., 900 Baseline Rd., 303/442-3282, www.chautauqua.com) is a beautiful gateway to the broad meadow of Bluebell Shelter and other well-worn hiking trails that lead up to the Flatirons; with its historic auditorium, cabins, and dining hall (breakfast, lunch, and dinner year-round), it's also a relaxed setting for wonderful summer events like the Silent Film Festival (June-Aug.) and the Colorado Music Festival (June-Aug.). In addition to its natural attributes, the park includes a large playground and grassy area perfect for playing Frisbee, enjoying a picnic, or sunbathing. Located on 26 acres leased from the city, Chautauqua was part of the nationwide Chautauqua Movement, an effort to provide cultural and educational programs in the summer.

Chautauqua is located west and south of downtown and the University of Colorado campus. There is free parking at the ranger station and near the restaurant, but it can be crowded during the summer; people often park along Baseline Road and walk in. Lodge rooms and cottages are available for nightly rental.

★ DUSHANBE TEAHOUSE

Thanks to a sister-city partnership, Boulder has the unique **Dushanbe Teahouse** (1770 13th St., 303/442-4993, www.boulderteahouse.com, 8am-9pm daily), just a couple blocks from the Pearl Street Mall. It took three years for artisans in Tajikistan to create the hand-carved and hand-painted ceiling, columns, and ceramic tiles of the building before it was sent to the United States in the 1990s. The rose garden out front and the creekside location complement the delicate architecture inside. It's worth stopping by just to gawk, but the teahouse is also a full-service restaurant and offers an extensive tea menu. This place can be busy—especially on weekends when the Boulder County Farmers Market is set up on the street out front—so call for a reservation if you want to eat here and not just see the architecture.

LEANIN' TREE

What started as a small greeting-card business featuring Western scenes on holiday cards evolved into such a successful empire that the founder amassed a large art collection from his favorite Western artists. The **Leanin' Tree Museum and Sculpture Garden of Western Art** (6055 Longbow Dr., 303/530-1442, www.leanintreemuseum.com, 8am-5pm Mon.-Fri., 10am-5pm Sat.-Sun., free) is the private collection of founder Edward P. Trumble's bronze sculptures and paintings of cowboys and Western landscapes.

the historic dining hall at Chautauqua

★ NATIONAL CENTER FOR ATMOSPHERIC RESEARCH

The mountains are the first thing to grab your attention if you drive into Boulder from the east—but then you begin to wonder about the distinctive building just below those magnificent rocks. It's the **National Center for Atmospheric Research** (1850 Table Mesa Dr., 303/497-1000, www.ncar.ucar.edu, 8am-5pm Mon.-Fri., 9am-4pm Sat.-Sun.), a federal research center that studies all aspects of weather. There is a lot of important and fascinating work going on here daily, but the building and its surroundings have a reputation and history all their own. The center was designed by renowned architect I. M. Pei, whose 1960s design was influenced by Native American cliff dwellings in southern Colorado and the dramatic rocks above the site. The building was immortalized in Woody Allen's film *Sleeper*. Free guided tours are offered daily at noon, and there's a gift shop and art gallery inside the building. Outside, you can walk the **Walter Orr Roberts Weather Trail** to learn about local weather and take in the view of the city below. Organized group tours require reservations, but audio tours and self-guided tours are available anytime the center is open.

the Dushanbe Teahouse

UNIVERSITY OF COLORADO

Most of the people at the **University of Colorado** (CU, 914 Broadway, 303/492-1411, www.colorado.edu) are either students or their visiting parents or professors. But this place is also open to the public and it's worth a stop for anyone.

The university was founded in 1876, the same year that Colorado became a state, and there were a mere 44 students. Now the school is like a small town, with over 30,000 students arriving each fall. While the misbehaviors of partying students and a few sports team members have made headlines, it is actually a very well-regarded school academically, with four Nobel laureates on staff and seven MacArthur fellows. Prestigious annual events such as the **Colorado Shakespeare Festival** (www.coloradoshakes.org) and the **Conference on World Affairs** are held on the campus.

To learn more about the history of the campus, start with the **Heritage Center** (Old Main 3rd Fl., 1600 Pleasant St., 303/492-6329, www.cuheritage.org, 10am-4pm Mon.-Fri.), where you can get an overview of the school's early history, learn about "CU in Space," read the roster of distinguished alumni (most of whom have buildings named after them on the campus), and see the trophies in the CU Athletics Gallery. There is also the **University of Colorado Museum of Natural History** (303/492-6892, http://cumuseum.colorado.edu), which is very child-friendly, with permanent dinosaur collections and changing exhibits that feature everything from meteorites to Inuit culture.

The University Memorial Center is the hub of the campus with the **Alferd Packer Grill** and other restaurants, a bowling alley, and a bookstore. The halls of the center have become like a small fair or mall, with tables often set up where you can buy sweaters, T-shirts, or phone cards.

Fiske Planetarium (303/492-5002, http://fiske.colorado.edu, 9am-4pm Mon.-Fri., admission cost varies) has star and laser shows with different themes, such as Perseus and Andromeda or Pink Floyd. You can't miss the white dome of the **Sommers Bausch Observatory** (303/492-6732, http://lyra.colorado.edu/sbo); it's open to the public with free stargazing through the telescopes on Friday night and during other special events.

Entertainment and Events

NIGHTLIFE

In a college town with a reputation for wild parties, there is no shortage of places to go for a drink after dark. The two main parts of town for nightlife are The Pearl Street Mall and The Hill, which is the small business district adjacent to the University of Colorado campus (literally up the hill from downtown).

Bars and Clubs

The West End Tavern (926 Pearl St., 303/444-3535, www.thewestendtavern.com, 11:30am-10pm daily), located on the west end of the Pearl Street Mall, has a very appealing rooftop deck with a view of the mountains that is perfect for happy hour and watching the sunset. There is live music on Tuesday nights.

the Corner Bar in the Hotel Boulderado

The Walnut Brewery (1123 Walnut St., 303/447-1345, www.rockbottomrestaurantsinc.com, 11am-midnight daily) can be a bit loud, especially during happy hour or on weekends, but that's part of the boisterous fun at this bar. The beers have names that reference local places, like Indian Peaks Pale Ale and Devil's Thumb Stout.

The **Absinthe House** (1109 Walnut St., 303/443-8600, www.absinthehouseboulder.com, 4pm-close daily Apr.-Oct., 8pm-close Thurs.-Sat. Nov.-Mar.) claims to have the "largest selection of genuine absinthe of any bar in North America." It also has a rooftop bar with a view of the Flatirons.

The Corner Bar (Hotel Boulderado, 2115 13th St., 303/442-4880, www.cornerbarboulderado.com, 11:30am-11:30pm daily), right on the corner of Spruce and 13th Streets, has been a Boulder favorite for the past 20 years—in large part due to the daily happy hour (3pm-6pm). This bar evokes an Old West saloon feel with tasteful taxidermy and tufted booths inside and a modern, sunny patio outside.

Descend into the basement of the Hotel Boulderado for a taste of liquid history at **License No. 1** (2115 13th St., 303/442-4880, www.boulderado.com/dining-drinks/license, 5pm-midnight daily), which holds the city's first legal liquor license, issued in 1969—60 years after the hotel opened. Enjoy $4 cocktails and casual bites during happy hour

(5pm-7pm daily) and be sure to take a moment to look over the ample whiskey list.

The **Bitter Bar** (9th and Walnut, 303/442-3050, www.thebitterbar.com, 5pm-1am daily, happy hour 5pm-8pm Mon.-Fri.) serves trendy cocktails with hipster names, but at the end of the day these are craft cocktails made with sublime expertise. These aren't your ordinary bartenders—not just anyone can whip up a Blue Velvet (vodka, crème de violette, lemon, and orgeat). Small bites from Blackbelly are also on the menu.

Brewpubs

BRU Handbuilt Ales & Eats (5290 Arapahoe Ave., 720/638-5193, www.bruboulder.com, 11:30am-10pm Mon.-Thurs., 11:30am-11pm Fri.-Sat., 9:30am-10pm Sun.) is one part brewery, one part restaurant, making for double the enjoyment for beer lovers. Owner, head brewer, and executive chef Ian Clark built the business—and the building—from the ground up, showcasing his creative sensibilities in both food and beer form. This makes for some great pairings around lunch and dinnertime. Try a Kölsch with a banh mí sandwich, or the Amarillo IPA with the chile-rubbed hanger steak. Beer styles vary widely at BRU, so you're sure to find something you love to sip.

If beer is your drink, then **FATE Brewing Company** (1600 38th St., 303/449-3283, www.fatebrewingcompany.com, 11am-10pm Mon.-Fri., 10am-10pm Sat.-Sun.) is your fate. And we have to say, it's not a bad way to go. Owner Mike Lawinski worked in Boulder restaurants for years before making his move, and now operates FATE Brewing Company with a palpable dedication to bringing innovative brews to the community. From the Coffee IPA to the Watermelon Kölsch, the beers are varied and drinkable. Come for lunch, brunch, or even a cocktail if beer's not your thing. I especially like the FATE Cuban, with smoked pork shoulder, sliced ham, white cheddar, sliced pickles, tomatoes, stout mustard, and chile aioli on crispy Cuban bread.

Mountain Sun Pub & Brewery (1535 Pearl St., 303/546-0886, www.mountainsunpub.com, 11:30am-1am Mon.-Sat., noon-1am Sun.) is just to the east of the Pearl Street Mall. Mountain Sun has a groovy kind of reggae vibe with tasty burgers and lots of vegetarian options. Stacks of games for kids and adults make this a family-friendly place.

Avery Brewing (4910 Nautilus Ct., 303/440-4324, www.averybrewing.com, 11am-11pm daily) has made a name for itself far beyond Colorado, despite the fact that it

the Bitter Bar

Mountain Sun Pub & Brewery

grew up in a tiny industrial space in Boulder. In 2015 it got a new home, expanding to two levels, about 150 seats, and a full dinner menu featuring Southern soul food like gumbo, pork green chile, fried rabbit and waffles, and blackened catfish. There are daily specials, barbecued dishes from the house smoker, and 30 taps of Avery beer. Loving what you're drinking? Be sure to plan a brewery tour (4pm weekdays, 2pm weekends), then get a growler filled at the bar to take home with you.

Although the Front Range is overflowing with craft beer, **PMG Wine Bar** (2018 10th St., 303/440-4324, www.pmgwine.com, 4pm-11pm Wed.-Sat., 4pm-10pm Sun.-Mon.) is quickly making a name for itself. PMG—named for a French expression meaning "for my mouth"—offers interesting, approachable wines in a cozy, hip space decked out in cherrywood tables backdropped by a yellow accent wall. The simple menu changes daily and features items like burrata with heirloom tomatoes, charred octopus, and grilled whole fish with salsa verde. French and Italian wines are a favorite here, with many options and price points by the glass and bottle. During happy hour (4pm-6pm) the house wine with an order of gougère, prosciutto, and apple butter just might make you say *oui!*

THE ARTS

Boulder has a rich arts scene throughout the year, but perhaps more so in the summer when there are concerts at Chautauqua in the historic auditorium, the Shakespeare Festival on the University of Colorado campus, and other events featuring live dancers and actors. It's a well-rounded life here with exposure to all facets of the arts, though the big traveling theater shows still require a trip to Denver.

Dance

The **Boulder Ballet** (2590 Walnut St., 303/443-0028, www.boulderballet.org) performs at different locations around town—Macky Auditorium on the CU campus, the Boulder Theater, the Dairy Center for the Arts, and more. In June, they offer free performances as part of the annual "Ballet in the Park" (with at least one performance in the Boulder Central Park Bandshell).

Live Music and Radio

Up on "The Hill" (the area near the CU campus up the hill from downtown) is **The Fox Theatre** (1135 13th St., 303/447-0095, http://foxtheatre.com), known for booking bands that appeal to its audience—the college crowd, in other words. Many shows are all ages. Chances are if you are over the age of 25, you've never heard of many of these bands that sell out here: Pigeons Playing Ping Pong, Taylor McFerrin, The Nth Power, and more.

You might have heard **eTown** (1535 Spruce St., 303/443-8696, www.etown.org) on the radio, and this is the place where those shows are recorded in front of a live audience...in a solar-powered studio, no less. This independent radio program features well-known live musicians as well as thought leaders answering a few questions on a variety of topics. Shows often feature the house band, the eTones. Check the website for videos of past events and to get a feel for the type of performances here, as well as to view the calendar for upcoming events and to buy tickets.

Performance Spaces

It took decades to secure funding to turn the old Watts-Hardy Dairy into a cultural facility, but once the transformation was complete in 1992 it became an instant success. The **Dairy Center for the Arts** (2590 Walnut St., 303/440-7826, www.thedairy.org, 9am-5pm Mon.-Tues., 9am-8:30pm Wed.-Fri., 1pm-8:30pm Sat.-Sun.) is home to three art galleries, two theaters, a performance space, and classrooms for ballet. The place is humming with creative energy, as all art forms are practiced or displayed here throughout the year. The box office hours are 1pm-5pm Monday-Friday and many of the events at the Dairy are free.

The **Boulder Theater** (2032 14th St., 303/786-7030, www.bouldertheater.com) is a century-old theater that started out as an opera house and has gone on to host many other types of performances. The art deco-style facade was part of a 1930s expansion to the theater, and the building has had many owners and incarnations over the years. Today there are over 250 events held here such as the Boulder International Film Festival, eTown performances, and the Boulder Adventure Film Festival. A peek at the calendar shows the impressive breadth of acts who play here: Govinda and the Dub Kirtan All Stars, Marc Maron, Graham Nash, Joan Armatrading, Dweezil Zappa, and Bruce Cockburn.

FESTIVALS AND EVENTS

Annual events in Boulder tend to have a connection to sports or at least being outdoors. Throw on jeans, a pair of Nikes or Birkenstocks, and a T-shirt or lightweight fleece, and you'll fit in at almost any festival here.

Spring

Even non-runners have heard of the **BolderBOULDER** (www.bolderboulder.com, May), an annual 10K that takes over the town on Memorial Day and has become one of the largest road races in the world. It's so popular that there are 90 wave starts—it would otherwise be pandemonium for that many people (over 55,000 ran, jogged, or walked during the 2014 event) to start running at the same time.

Over the same weekend as the BolderBOULDER is a three-day event that seems to grow each year: the **Boulder Creek Festival** (www.bceproductions.com, May), which features multiple stages for live music, activity areas for kids, hundreds of vendors, local food, and, best of all, a huge rubber ducky race in the creek.

Each spring the Tulip Fairy parades down the Pearl Street Mall with lots of little fairies and elves trailing during the **Tulip Fairy and Elf Festival** (www.boulderdowntown.com, Apr.). Gossamer wings in a rainbow of colors fill the pedestrian mall as kids run along behind the Tulip Fairy to a main stage where this half-day festival offers face painting, live music, ballet dancers, arts and crafts, cookie decorating, and more.

Composer Gustav Mahler is celebrated during the weeklong Colorado **MahlerFest** (http://www.mahlerfest.org, May). Concerts take place in Macky Auditorium on the University of Colorado campus and films are shown at the Dairy Center for the Arts. There is also a symposium about the Austrian composer and conductor who was once the director of the New York Metropolitan Opera and New York Philharmonic.

The **Conference on World Affairs** (http://www.colorado.edu/cwa, Apr.) is an incredible week of intellectual discussion on the University of Colorado campus. Panelists discuss everything. Yes, everything. Or so it seems. The topics include immigration, economics, human rights, weapons of mass destruction, satire, politics, sex, drugs, sports, health, and much more. The panelists are experts on these many and varied topics, and they come from around the world: Germany, Saudi Arabia, Uganda, Japan, and across the United States, as well as professors from CU. And they are not just professors, but judges, storytellers, musicians, attorneys, authors, and entrepreneurs. Famed film critic and author Roger Ebert hosted Cinema Interruptus at this event for over a decade; the program involves showing a film, then each day after that people can come and basically dissect the film by stopping it frame by frame. Cinema Interruptus continues each year with a new host.

Summer

The annual **Colorado Shakespeare Festival** (www.coloradoshakes.org, June-Aug.) takes place outdoors in the Mary Rippon amphitheater and indoors at the University Theatre, both on the University of Colorado campus (914 Broadway). The tradition of Shakespeare under the stars in the historic Mary Rippon Outdoor Theatre has been going on for about 60 years. In addition to the traditional plays of the bard, there are also plays *about* his most famous works; for example, *I Hate Hamlet* and *Unexpected Shaxpere!* have been performed in previous years.

The **Silent Film Festival** (Chautauqua Auditorium, 900 Baseline Rd., www.chautauqua.com/events/film, June-Aug., $12) is a special treat for film buffs and families. Weekly through the summer you can catch classics like Charlie Chaplin's *The Great Dictator* or Buster Keaton's *Steamboat Bill Jr.* and enjoy the live accompaniment of pianist Hank Troy. The audience participates just like audiences did when these films were originally shown—booing and hissing when the bad guy appears on the screen or cheering for the hero.

The **Colorado Music Festival** (Chautauqua Auditorium, 900 Baseline Rd., www.comusic.org/concerts-events/summer-festival, June-Aug., ticket prices vary) holds Young People's Concerts and Family Fun Concerts during the day, with full orchestra and chamber music at night, as well as a few surprises each year. It's typical for people to settle themselves outside of the theater and enjoy the beauty of both nature and music.

Admittedly not quite as scenic but still plenty of fun, the **Boulder Outdoor Cinema** (http://www.boulderoutdoor-cinema.com, Sat. July-Aug.) is held in the parking lot behind the Boulder Museum of Contemporary Art. Movies shown here are more contemporary than those shown at Chautauqua—you might see *The LEGO Movie* or *The Princess Bride,* or even *This is Spinal Tap.* It's conveniently located in downtown Boulder. Bring your own chair.

Fall

The **Boulder International Fringe Festival** (www.boulderfringe.com, Sept.) is about two weeks' worth of art performed and displayed throughout Boulder. This festival is in the same spirit as fringe festivals around the world, and as such attracts an international lineup of artists, musicians, and performers. Check the calendar for those arts you might not see every day—puppetry, circus arts, and poetry, in addition to dance and theater. There are workshops offered during this event.

The Pearl Street Mall is transformed into the **Downtown Boulder Fall Fest** (www.boulderdowntown.com/events/fall-fest, late Sept.) as art booths, music stages, and food vendors set up to entertain during this three-day event. There is also a children's carnival, and grown-ups have microbrews to sample.

Dudes and dudettes, if you like your movies to get you on the edge of your seat with heart-stopping reality, then plan to go to the **Adventure Film Festival** (www.adventurefilm.org, Sept.). Boulder is one of four locations to host this multiday festival each year—the others are Asheville, Chile, and New York. What you'll see on the big screen at the Boulder Theater are people scaling ice falls, riding bikes over slick rock, and otherwise engaging in sports in breathtakingly beautiful spots in the great outdoors.

Get your "fat pants" out before Thanksgiving and make a reservation for

First Bite: Boulder Restaurant Week (www.firstbiteboulder.com, mid-Nov.). More than 50 local restaurants participate with three-course menus ($27 per person). On the list are some of the most popular dining spots in town: Salt, the Dushanbe Teahouse, The Kitchen, Boulder Cork, and dozens more.

Winter

Switch on the Holidays (www.downtownboulder.org, Dec.) with a lighting ceremony and Santa visit the weekend after Thanksgiving. The Boulder Chorale provides the sounds of the season as the Boulder County Courthouse on the Pearl Street Mall is illuminated.

Just because it's cold out doesn't mean people have given up on crazy outdoor fun in Boulder. Each New Year's Day many hardy souls take the **Polar Bear Plunge** (www.bcap.org, Jan.) into Boulder Reservoir to benefit the Boulder County AIDS Project. As if freezing cold wasn't enough, there are a lot of silly—and soon frozen!—costumes worn for this event too.

Cannabis Dispensaries

Boulder is also home to many cannabis dispensaries—each with its own style so you can choose your buds based on the vibes of the establishment. The dispensaries are not cookie-cutter franchise businesses where you walk in and know exactly what's on the menu at each place: These places have "craft cannabis" and "award-winning strains" to choose from, along with different edibles (food made with marijuana), pipes, and other marijuana accessories.

A popular spot on the east side of town, **Boulder Wellness Center** (5420 Arapahoe Ave. Unit F, 303/442-2565, www.boulderwc.com, 11am-6:45pm Mon.-Sat., 11am-5pm Sun.) channels the sort of Eastern philosophies the community is known for, with ornate lacquered furniture and ceremonial masks on the walls. If that doesn't get you into a Zen-like state, the moderately priced buds, concentrates, and edibles certainly will.

Garnering attention from the likes of *Vogue* and *GQ*, the **Farm** (2801 Iris Ave., 303/440-1323, http://thefarmco.com/, 8am-6:45pm Mon.-Fri., 9am-6:45am Sat., 11am-6:45pm Sun.) fashions itself the Rolls Royce of Colorado cannabis. The north Boulder operation feels like a high-end fashion boutique, with polished wood accents, an endless variety of glassware, and accessories branded with the Farm's logo (a cow sporting a marijuana leaf on its hide). It's all to showcase the Farm's small-batch, pesticide-free (and slightly pricey) "craft cannabis," all of which is grown locally in Boulder. This is marijuana's response to the farm-to-table movement.

Located in a cozy, single-level house on Pearl Street east of the mall, **Fresh Baked Dispensary** (2539 Pearl St., 303/440-9393, www.freshbakedcolorado.com, 10am-6:50pm daily) feels like your neighborhood hangout, complete with old-school arcade games in the waiting area and relaxed, friendly budtenders eager to answer your burning questions. Best of all, this chill-out zone boasts a hefty selection of award-winning strains.

Tucked away behind a nondescript door on a busy stretch of the Pearl Street Mall, **Helping Hands Herbals** (1021 Pearl St., 720/476-6186, www.helpinghandsdispensary.com, 9am-6:45pm Mon.-Fri., 10am-6:45pm Sat.-Sun.) is a cozy second-floor recreational pot shop that offers a huge variety of strains, edibles, and concentrates that belies its small size. Helping Hands is also known for in-house strains you won't find anywhere else, including "Gupta Kush," named in honor of Sanjay Gupta, the CNN medical correspondent who's become a major medical marijuana advocate.

What's 420?

April 20 is known as a day to smoke weed, and it has been since long before it became legal to smoke marijuana in Colorado. The day has its origins in a pot smokers' meeting held at 4:20pm to get high together. It has since evolved into a celebration at various locales around the globe to smoke marijuana on April 20.

The University of Colorado campus has been one such location for these informal gatherings; upwards of 10,000 people converge on the campus on April 20 to publicly smoke marijuana. Campus security has dealt with this in a variety of ways, whether by closing the entire campus for the day or just closing the popular meeting spot on the Norlin Quadrangle. (It seems legalization has helped to spread the number of events surrounding this "pot holiday," therefore reducing the intensity of the crowds on campus.)

Remember, although it is legal to buy marijuana in Colorado, it cannot be smoked in public.

Pop into **Native Roots Boulder** (1146 Pearl St., 720/726-5126, www.nativerootsboulder.com, 9am-7pm daily), a slickly designed basement-level shop in a prime location on the Pearl Street Mall, and you'd be forgiven if you thought you'd wandered into an Apple Store. However, there are no iPads for sale behind these sleek modern counters—just a healthy selection of indicas and sativas.

It's not a coincidence that **The Station**'s (3005 28th St., 303/442-0892, www.thestationboulder.com, 9:30am-6:30pm Mon.-Sat., noon-5pm Sun.) ornate dark-wood display cases make the place resemble a jewelry store; this standalone shop at the corner of Valmont and 28th in north Boulder has earned a reputation for treating its high-quality buds and concentrates like fine diamonds. Best of all, you won't be paying jewelry-store prices; the Station's rates are exceedingly reasonable.

The excellently named **Terrapin Care Station** (1795 Folsom St., 303/954-8402, ext. 2, www.terrapincarestation.com, 9am-6:45pm daily) was the first recreational shop to open in Boulder, and it scored enviable real estate just off the CU campus. The timing and location seems to have paid off. These days, this hippie-inspired joint boasts its own line of

Terrapin Care Station

T-shirts, specially branded "TerraPen" vaporizers, and even online ordering through its own smartphone app. Just be prepared: The place can get busy, so it might not be the best option for those who are looking to browse at their leisure.

Rock climbers are partial to **Headquarters** (537 Canyon Blvd., 720/287-1635, http://hqmmj.com, 10am-6:45pm Mon.-Sat., 11am-5pm Sun.), which describes itself as a "boutique dispensary." This place was recommended in *Climbing Magazine* for its convenient location to stop at to or from rock climbing in Boulder Canyon.

Shopping

The Pearl Street Mall is the heart of locally owned business in Boulder. There are other pockets of independent shops scattered around town, but if you're on foot you can find books, men's, women's and kid's clothes, body care products, toys, and more somewhere along this street.

PEARL STREET MALL

The **Pearl Street Mall** (Pearl St. between 10th and 15th Sts., 303/449-3774, www.boulderdowntown.org) started as a 1970s antidote to the indoor mall craze and has since become more than a shopping destination. Shops and restaurants trickle off Pearl Street for several blocks in every direction. In addition to shops like the Boulder Bookstore and The Peppercorn, there are carts selling hats, sunglasses, and other items. In the summer, entertainers hang out on each block (often in front of the courthouse) to perform magic tricks, eat fire, sing songs, make balloon animals, and deliver other unexpected delights to throngs of people.

Books

A longtime staple and anchor on the west end of the mall is **The Boulder Bookstore** (1107 Pearl St., 303/447-2074, www.boulderbookstore.net, 10am-10pm Mon.-Sat., 10am-8pm Sun.), with many floors of books (children's, travel, cooking, science fiction, and much more) and magazines, as well as a popular coffee shop.

the Boulder Bookstore

The **Beat Book Shop** (1200 Pearl St., 303/444-7111, www.beatbookshop.com, 3pm-8pm Sun.-Tues., 1pm-9:30pm Wed., noon-10pm Thurs.-Sat.) is a rare store. The owner is a fan of Beat Generation authors such as Jack Kerouac (author of *On the Road)* and Allen Ginsberg (poet of *Howl)* and is also locally known as a cofounder of the Jack Kerouac School of Disembodied Poets at Naropa University. You don't just come here to buy a book—you come to talk about the meaning of life, poetry, and writing.

If you are on a spiritual journey (or want to be on one), there's a book for you at **The Lighthouse Bookstore** (1201 Pearl St., 303/939-8355, 10am-8pm Mon.-Fri., 10am-9pm Sat., noon-6pm Sun.). Learn about your chakras, get a psychic reading, pick up some tarot cards, or read up on any number of New Age, religious, metaphysical, and spiritual topics.

Clothing and Shoes

Women who like Prada, Bottega Veneta, Missoni, and other high-end designers are sure to find something special and sophisticated at **Max** (1177 Walnut St., 303/449-9200, www.maxfashion.com, 10am-6pm Mon.-Sat., noon-5pm Sun.).

For more casual clothes (and prices), **Starr's Clothing & Shoe Company** (1630 Pearl St., 303/442-3056, www.starrsclothingco.com, 10am-8pm Mon.-Fri., 10am-7pm Sat., 11am-6pm Sun.) has a huge selection of Levi's and cute tops, dresses, and skirts.

The **Pedestrian Shop** (1425 Pearl St., 303/449-5260, www.comfortableshoes.com, 10am-8pm Mon.-Thurs., 10am-9pm Fri.-Sat., 11am-7pm Sun.) has been keeping men, women, and children shod in practical, durable, and comfortable shoes for more than four decades. Need Birkenstocks or Merrells? They've got them here, as well as Dansko, Ecco, Keen, and other brands.

Weekends (1200 Pearl St., 303/444-4231, http://weekendsboulder.com, 10am-7pm Mon.-Sat., 11am-6pm Sun.) is a one-stop shop for both men and women who like to dress business-casual or just stylishly casual. Choose from a large selection of denim, including brands such as Rag & Bone and Citizens of Humanity.

Gift and Home

As the Pearl Street Mall has grown and changed over the years, **The Peppercorn** (1235 Pearl St., 303/449-5847, www.peppercorn.com, 10am-6pm Mon.-Thurs., 10am-7pm Fri., 10am-6pm Sat., 11am-5pm Sun.) has remained and grown considerably itself. Peppercorn calls itself a "home" store, but it's largely a kitchen store with cookbooks, dishes, and flatware. In the front of the store are featured Colorado products and books.

It's really hard to categorize **Cedar & Hyde** (2015 10th St., 720/287-3900, www.cedarandhyde.com, 10am-7pm Mon.-Sat., noon-5pm Sun.)—it's like a modern boutique meets old-fashioned department store. In other words, those are bath towels next to that gorgeous sweater over by the shoes just to the left of the bowls. Somehow, it all goes together perfectly like a well-styled magazine spread, and it makes sense to be shopping for kitchen, bath, and wardrobe in the same place.

El Loro Jewelry & Clog Co. (1416 Pearl St., 303/449-3162, www.ellorobouider.com, 10am-9pm Mon.-Thurs., 10am-9:30pm Fri.-Sat., 11am-9pm Sun.) is another shop that is difficult to categorize. I just have a soft spot for this Pearl Street Mall institution that has stuck it out for nearly 40 years with the same sensibility for moccasins, clogs, and a large assortment of semiprecious stones and jewelry.

Given Boulder's connection to climbing, there is also Tibetan culture such as **Old Tibet** (948 Pearl St., 303/440-0323, 10am-9pm daily), which carries Buddha statues, incense, singing bowls, Tibetan music, and clothing.

I think of **Poppy** (2098 Broadway, 303/444-0927, www.poppyllc.com, 10am-6pm Mon.-Sat., noon-5pm Sun.) as a baby and children's boutique, but it is much more than that. Look for Petit Bateau, Claesen's, Splendid, and other children's brands as well as cute little gifts and things for Mommy too.

Outdoor Gear

Not quite a gear shop, but with a motto of "The fit shall inherit the earth," it's clear that **Endurance Conspiracy** (1717 Pearl St., 720/542-3137, http://enduranceconspiracy.com, 10am-6pm daily) is by athletes, for athletes. This combination store and work space designs and sells T-shirts, hats, and cycling gear for men and women.

The **Newton Running Lab** (1222 Pearl St., 303/494-0321, www.newtonrunning.com, 10am-6pm Mon.-Fri., 10am-4pm Sat.) has their world headquarters in Boulder because the city is a mecca for runners. Step inside and get a personal fitting—even if you're not a marathoner.

The bicycles at **Vecchio's Bicicletteria** (1833 Pearl St., 303/440-3535, www.vecchios.com, 10am-6pm Mon.-Sat.) are custom built to order, with hand-built wheels and hand-assembled parts. Bike servicing is also done here. If you want to look the part, check out their many colorful bike jerseys.

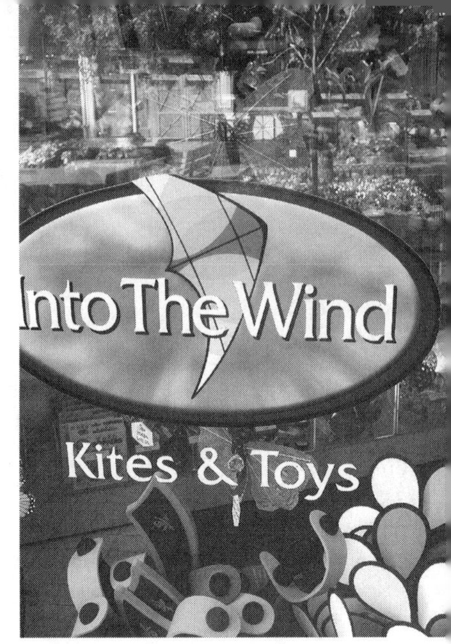

Into the Wind

Toys

Given the high winds along the Front Range, there is often a chance to go fly a kite in Boulder. Take advantage of the skies at **Into the Wind** (1408 Pearl St., 303/449-5356, www.intothewind.com, 10am-9pm Mon.-Sat., 10am-5pm Sun. June-Dec., 10am-5pm daily Jan.-May), a kite store with a large selection of toys for all ages.

Vintage

Candy's Vintage Clothing & Costumes (2512 N. Broadway, 303/442-6186, www.candysboulder.com, 11am-6pm Mon.-Sat.) is a Boulder institution. If you have a costume party, can't decide what to be for Halloween, or just want a retro look for your everyday clothes, you will find it here. I love how it offers not just costumes, but shoes and accessories in great condition to really complete a look.

VILLAGE SHOPPING CENTER

Between Arapahoe Avenue and Canyon Boulevard is **The Village** (2525 Arapahoe Ave., http://www.villageboulder.com), a little jumble of shops and restaurants that are worth a stop.

It's something of a Boulder tradition to shop at **McGuckin Hardware** (2525 Arapahoe Ave., 303/443-1822, www.mcguckin.com, 7:30am-8pm Mon.-Fri., 8am-7pm Sat., 9am-6pm Sun.), and this giant store has much more than the name might lead you to believe. Helpful salespeople will answer all of your questions about picking out seeds for the garden or a new waffle iron, as well as give advice about actual hardware.

Another Boulder staple is **Grandrabbit's Toy Shoppe** (2525 Arapahoe St., 303/443-0780, www.grtoys.com, 9:30am-7pm Mon.-Sat., 10am-5pm Sun.), with a big selection of books, games, and dolls. The store has expanded with other locations, but this is the one that has it all. If you come with your kids, they can put a coin in the old-fashioned pony and go for a ride while you shop. Or take a seat between the bookshelves and read a little. Or chase some toy cars around. It's so fun to shop here—even if you leave the kids at home.

INDEPENDENT SHOPS

Not all retail locations are grouped together with others of their kind in Boulder. It can be worth a drive or checking pop-up market dates to shop at a few places in Boulder.

The **Firefly Handmade Market** (www.fireflyhandmade.com) is a pop-up market that occurs seasonally in different indoor and outdoor locations in Boulder. This is where hipster craftspeople come together to sell their very cool goods. You might find baby onesies, stationery, felted creatures, jewelry, ceramics, and lots of other handmade stuff that you just have to have.

Skirt Sports (6205 Lookout Rd., 877/754-7871, www.skirtsports.com, 10am-5pm Mon.-Fri., 10am-2pm Sat.) was founded by a female triathlete who wanted to look cute while running. Think pink, hot pink, and bright patterns, all in figure-flattering fabrics and styles to help you look feminine while being active.

Founded by a runner, the **Boulder Running Company** (2775 Pearl St., 303/786-9255, www.boulderrunningcompany.com, 10am-7pm Mon.-Fri., 10am-6pm Sat., 10am-5pm Sun.) seems to be staffed primarily by local runners who can help you find the perfect pair of running or walking shoes. In-store treadmills help staff assess your gait, and there is a full selection of orthotics and stylish seasonal shoes (sandals or boots) that will be good for your feet when you're not out for a jog. You can also get outfitted for a run with colorful pants, shorts, and T-shirts.

DSH Perfumes (4593 N. Broadway, 720/563-0344, www.dshperfumes.com, noon-5pm Tues., 11am-5pm Wed.-Fri., noon-4pm Sat.) is off the beaten path, but if you have an interest in one-of-a-kind fragrances you should make time to visit. During the 2012 Yves Saint Laurent exhibit at the Denver Art Museum, the owner of DSH Perfumes, Dawn Spencer Hurwitz, led a guided tour about the history of scent as it related to the fashion. At her shop, she combines this sense of history and knowledge about scents to create a personal perfume just for you.

Sports and Recreation

What makes Boulder so appealing is its easy access to the great outdoors, where you can simply start running, biking, or hiking right out the front door. This city is often voted the fittest in America due to its low obesity rate. While the football games at Folsom Field on the University of Colorado campus are very popular, many of the popular sports such as cycling and bouldering aren't necessarily spectator sports.

Whatever sport you choose—even a casual guided walk—keep the altitude in mind. Boulder is 5,430 feet above sea level and many recreational activities will take you higher than that as you hike or bike into the foothills. Each person has a different experience as the body adjusts to a higher altitude, but difficulty breathing is the most common symptom. If possible, don't go for that 25-mile bike ride or 10-mile hike on your first day in town. Instead, drink plenty of water and acclimate with minimal physical exertion.

PARKS

If you just want to hang out with the little ones and enjoy a playground, the best options are **Chautauqua** (900 Baseline Rd.), where there is a playground and large grassy field; **Scott Carpenter Park** (30th and Arapahoe Sts., 303/441-3427, www.bouldercolorado.gov), which has a large outdoor pool, skatepark, and playground; and **Eben G. Fine** (3rd and Arapahoe Sts., www.bouldercolorado.gov), with a playground, picnic spots, and a chance to wade into the creek.

BALLOONING

Look over the mountains, not just up at them during a hot-air balloon ride with **Adventure Balloon Sports** (303/530-0747, www.adventureballoonsports.com, $265-295 adults, $175-195 children 12 and under). Start the day with a light breakfast and then celebrate with a champagne toast when you are back on terra firma. This unforgettable 1.5-hour experience starts at dawn and allows guests to take in both the mountain peaks to the west and the grassy plains to the east.

Fair Winds Hot Air Balloon Flights (303/939-9323, http://hotairballoonridescolorado.com, $199-229 adults, $149-179 children 12 and under) also offers 1.5-hour flights from Boulder with your pilot/guide explaining points of interest. Go online to get $50 off during spring specials; note that prices are about $30 higher on weekends.

hot-air ballooning over the Rocky Mountains

BIKING

Bike paths along Boulder Creek and designated bike lanes on most city streets make it easy to navigate the town on two wheels. There are about 200 miles of bikeways and trails in Boulder; a popular portion of that is on the **Boulder Creek Bike Path** (https://bouldercolorado.gov), which stretches east of town to Cherryvale Road from its starting point in the foothills at Fourmile Canyon. The trail is very popular and there are speed-limit signs on this seven-mile path.

The popular **Greenbelt Plateau Trail** (0.1 mile east of the intersection of Hwy. 128 and Hwy. 93, https://bouldercolorado.gov/osmp/greenbelt-plateau-trailhead) offers a chance to see a bit of wildlife, some birds, and probably some equestrians. It's an easy ride on the plains below the foothills and connects to other trails.

Yes, you can ride bikes on all kinds of roads and trails around Boulder—or, you can ride at the **Boulder Valley Velodrome** (303/818-5817, www.bouldervalleyvelodrome.com), 15 miles from Boulder in the town of Erie. This track-cycling facility isn't just for athletes—anyone can take the three-hour "Day at the Track" introductory lesson. While the bike is provided, check the website for a list of mandatory items you will need to bring, like a helmet, cycling shorts, socks, and more.

The **Valmont Bike Park** (3160 Airport Rd., 303/413-7200, https://bouldercolorado.gov, 5am-11pm daily, weather permitting, free) has 42 acres of natural-surface cycling terrain. Given the size of the park, there is room for both families with little ones on the balance bikes and cyclocross riders practicing their skills on ramps. There are no dogs allowed on the trails. The park is accessible by bike or car. Call ahead to check trail conditions.

Bike Rentals

There are about 20 bike stores in Boulder. That may seem like a lot for a town of this size, but there is a demand for new, used, rentals, repairs, parts—in short, everything to do with bikes for all ages and abilities.

University Bicycles (839 Pearl St., 303/444-4196, http://ubikes.com, 10am-7pm Mon.-Fri., 10am-6pm Sat., 10am-5pm Sun.) is just west of the Pearl Street Mall and offers rentals of all kinds—kids' bikes, mountain bikes, road bikes, and more—with a really helpful staff that knows the area. **Boulder B-cycle** (https://boulder.bcycle.com) has bike rental kiosks around town, which allows you to rent a bike for a daily, weekly, or annual fee (bring your own helmet). These red bikes come with a handy basket in front so you can run small errands.

BIRD-WATCHING

The **Boulder Bird Club** (www.boulderbirdclub.org) meets the first Sunday of each month at Cottonwood Marsh at **Walden Ponds Wildlife Habitat** (75th St. between Jay Rd. and Valmont St.) at 8am and 11am May-September or 9am and noon October-April. There are additional Wednesday meetups from mid-April through September with different destinations. While these events do not require reservations (bring your own binoculars though!), you can check the club's newsletter for information on guided field trips offered throughout the year. You might see the occasional pelican or egret here, but mostly you will see and hear warblers and ducks.

FISHING

Where you fish in Boulder might depend on your age. So often activities need to be all-inclusive of ages and abilities, but here people might be able to enjoy this sport while only with others of similar ages and ability.

Cattail Ponds at the Boulder County Fairgrounds (9595 Nelson Rd., Longmont, 303/678-6200, www.bouldercounty.org) is open exclusively to kids age 15 and under; they do not need a fishing license. The ponds are stocked with bluegill and channel catfish. On the other end of the spectrum is **Wally Toevs at Walden Ponds** (75th St. and Valmont St., 303/678-6200, www.bouldercounty.org), which has wheelchair-accessible ramps and is for people age 64 or older and people with disabilities. This pond has bluegill, rainbow trout, and largemouth bass. There is fishing allowed for all ages at other locations at Walden Ponds too.

Stream fishing is permitted at **South Boulder Creek on Walker Ranch Open Space** (303/678-6200, www.bouldercounty.org), where the creek is regularly stocked with rainbow trout. To get there, take Baseline

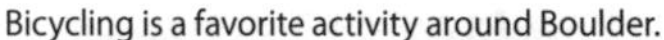

Bicycling is a favorite activity around Boulder.

Rock On

Those ubiquitous **Flatirons** were pushed into place some 40 million years ago; today they serve as an enticement to rock climbers and photographers who want to conquer or capture them. Images of the five slabs of rough sandstone that once made up a seafloor are everywhere in Boulder, as is the name (there are Flatirons car dealerships, churches, malls, and more).

Rock climbers have been scaling the Flatirons since 1906, and much has been written about the technical aspects of climbing each of the formations. Nesting raptors—including peregrine falcons and prairie falcons—are protected here, and therefore climbing is off limits in mating season.

Over the years the Flatirons have not only been climbed on but also roller skated on, skied on, and unfortunately, painted on (though the giant "C" and "U" have since been covered). These gigantic rocks inspire all kinds of zany behavior (full moon hikes, hikes in "the buff," racing) as people come up with new ways to experience the climb.

Unless you have the equipment and/or skill, it's probably best to just enjoy the view though.

Road west out of town to where it becomes Flagstaff Road, and then continue 7.9 miles on Flagstaff.

Front Range Anglers (2344 Pearl St., 303/494-1375, http://frontrangeanglers.com, 9am-6pm Mon.-Sat., 9am-5pm Sat., 10am-4pm Sun.) is probably the best place to check in on fishing conditions in the area, take a fly-fishing lesson, or get your fishing gear. They also give guided fishing trips in the area so you don't have to go it alone your first time.

HIKING

When there are numerous books written with detailed advice on where to hike in and around Boulder, it's a daunting task to select just a few to include here. Just know that this is not a comprehensive list of hikes for this area, but this author's personal favorites that will provide a taste of Boulder hiking. Also note there is wildlife—mountain lions, coyotes, foxes, deer, and more—on many of these trails, as well as other natural hazards to factor in such as lightning. The **Boulder County Open Space and Mountain Parks** (https://bouldercolorado.gov/osmp) website has detailed tips on how to mitigate these dangers and how to handle the situation if you do encounter adverse conditions or situations (there is a whole page devoted to bears and lions, for example). Know the symptoms of altitude sickness and be sure to rest as needed.

CHAUTAUQUA

Chautauqua (900 Baseline Rd., www.bouldercolorado.gov) is a great place to start for hikes of varying length and difficulty. Go to the **Ranger Cottage** near the entrance of the park (9am-4pm Mon.-Fri., 8am-6pm Sat.-Sun.) for maps, brochures, and expert advice from the staff. **Royal Arch,** a natural arch that you reach via an easy and rewarding hike, is less than a mile one-way and offers a great view. This is also a starting point to reach the base of the three Flatirons, which can also be climbed. For a bit steeper climb, **Gregory Canyon** is pretty and thick with trees before opening up to beautiful views.

You can climb up to the rocks on the **Flatirons #1** hike. This 2.9-mile round-trip hike rewards you with views along the way. There are switchbacks and you are gaining elevation, but it's not too steep and is considered a moderate hike.

Boulder Falls is a wonderful hike 11 miles up Boulder Canyon. There is a pullout parking area and you will likely need to cross the road to the trailhead, so use care here. Check the website for the latest conditions, as the trail was closed after 2013 flooding in this area.

FLAGSTAFF MOUNTAIN

Once you've acclimated to the altitude, go for the **Flagstaff Mountain** hike and take in the view of the valley below you from 6,850 feet above sea level. The **Flagstaff Nature Center** (Flagstaff Summit Rd., 303/441-3440, https://bouldercolorado.gov/osmp/flagstaff-nature-center, 10:30am-4pm Sat.-Sun. Memorial Day-Labor Day) is worth a visit, especially with small children who will enjoy some of the interactive exhibits. Flagstaff Trailhead is where Baseline Road turns into Flagstaff Road; the trail is 1.5 miles and increases more than 1,000 feet elevation.

The **Mt. Sanitas Trail** (0.5 mile west of 4th St. on Mapleton Ave., 303/441-3440, https://bouldercolorado.gov/mount-sanitas-trailhead) is very popular for day hikers and trail runners—and their dogs! Part of the appeal is that you don't necessarily need to drive here if you are already in downtown Boulder.

How often do you get science and nature combined in a trail? Well, maybe more often than you realize, but it's especially the case at the **NCAR Trailhead** (1850 Table Mesa Dr., 303/441-3440, https://bouldercolorado.gov). The trail begins at the NCAR's iconic Mesa Lab building. The first stretch is called the Walter Orr Roberts Trail and includes interesting signs about the local weather (fun for kids who might find plain old hiking dull). After this the trail meets up with a handful of popular hiking trails. There is a very good chance of seeing deer around the NCAR building or along the hike.

For something easier and with less altitude gain, try the **Anne U. White Trail** (www.bouldercounty.org), which is 3 miles round-trip. Take Broadway north to Lee Hill Road west. Turn left on Lee Hill Road, then take a left on Wagonwheel Gap Road, and another left on Pinto Drive to reach the trailhead. This area was significantly damaged during 2013 flooding, so check the Boulder County website for the latest conditions.

HORSEBACK RIDING

Many of Boulder's trails are multiuse, so be aware that you might be walking along and have a horse and rider come clomping up or a mountain biker zoom by.

The **Cherryvale Trail** (66 S. Cherryvale Rd., 303/441-3440, https://bouldercolorado.gov) is on the east side of Boulder and is an easy trail. What I like about this trail is that you get to experience a different side of Boulder, and not just literally. There is different wildlife here, and you're enjoying that view of the mountains and Flatirons instead of being *in* the mountains. This can also be less crowded than the foothills.

Resources for horseback riders include the **Boulder County Horse Association** (www.boulderhorse.org) and **Colorado Wilderness Rides and Guides** (720/242-9828, www.coloradowildernessridesandguides.com), which offers guided rides for all abilities.

ROCK CLIMBING

Yep, you can climb them. The **Boulder Flatirons** are climbed regularly, but know that this is not for the inexperienced. Ill-prepared climbers are rescued here what seems like annually as they get stuck for lack of proper equipment or they start too late in the day and cannot find their way out in the dark. Contact the **Colorado Mountain School** (2829 Mapleton Ave., 800/836-4008, ext. 3, $195) to sign up for a full-day guided climb (beginners must also take a prep course for an additional fee the night before the climb) on the 1st or 3rd Flatiron.

Climbing in **Boulder Canyon** is so legendary that there have been books written about the granite rock faces here. If you have the experience and gear, drive west on Canyon Boulevard to where it turns into Highway 119; there you'll see both groups of cars and people along the roadside. There are many different skill levels and interest levels for climbers here, so do a little more detailed research before you head into the hills. A great place to start is **Neptune Mountaineering** (633 S. Broadway, 303/499-8866, www.neptunemountaineering.com), which has all the climbing gear you might need. While you can shop online, visiting the store means you can also get advice from the people who work here—and who happen to be experienced local rock climbers. Rental gear is also available here.

SPAS

The Spa at St. Julien (900 Walnut St., 877/303-0900, www.stjulien.com) is where I would want someone to buy me a gift certificate to enjoy a day of pampering in Boulder. Just imagine, after a strenuous hike in the foothills, getting a "Sole Delight" treatment here, in which reflexology and aromatherapy blend together to rejuvenate those tootsies. Or counteract the effects of the altitude and dry climate with a "Canyon Rain" treatment: soak in a warm bath before being thoroughly scrubbed under a Vichy shower. Bliss! Their spa menu offers dozens of possible treatments sure to bring a smile to your face.

Find your Zen at the **Dragontree Holistic Day Spa** (1521 Pearl St., 303/219-1444, www.thedragontree.com), where you can improve your sense of well-being both inside and out. The spa offers acupuncture, herbal medicine, and nutrition services in addition to the usual spa massages, skin care, and body treatments. Check out the Sangha room here if you like a community atmosphere while getting a hand or foot treatment.

the St. Julien Hotel and Spa

SWIMMING

There are a few options for cooling off in Boulder on a hot summer day. First, the **Boulder Reservoir** (5100 51st St., 303/441-3468, www.bouldercolorado.gov) east of town is Boulder's version of a beach. It's a shadeless, sandy park along the water, and fun in the summer for sailing, swimming, fishing, or just floating. Boulder Creek is used for kayaking and tubing, but be aware of the rough conditions before trying either activity. The creek is very choppy in spots and dotted with large rocks. **Scott Carpenter Park** (30th and Arapahoe Sts., 303/441-3427, www.bouldercolorado.gov) also has a large outdoor pool.

Accommodations

Always keep in mind that Boulder is a college town; when booking a hotel, do so in advance for those times when the families of the thousands of students come to visit such as graduation in May or when school starts in late summer. There are lodging options within walking distance of the campus for those who are here to say, "Farewell!" to their freshman or "Congratulations!" to their graduate.

While Boulder isn't necessarily the place for budget lodgings, chances are you will find a place that embraces that quintessential Boulder quality you desire. Meditation room? Check. Hiking trails right outside? Check. Luxurious spa? Check. Historic character? Check. Whether you are in town to visit the campus or just as a tourist, you can walk or ride a bike to many fine restaurants or trailheads, or go shopping near many of these hotels.

There are not any designated "420 marijuana-friendly" hotels in Boulder at this time, but there are private residences on sites like AirBnB that are available for those who want a place to partake of their cannabis.

$50-100

The ★ **Boulder Adventure Lodge** (91 Four Mile Canyon Dr., 303/444-0882, www.a-lodge.com, $40-107) is popular with the rock climbers who come to the area with big dreams and little cash. It's in a very pretty setting and rooms were updated in 2015.

The **Days Hotel Boulder** (5397 S. Boulder Rd., 303/499-4422, www.dayshotelboulder.com, $89-199) offers a convenient location at a reasonable rate. It's not close to downtown, but if you're in town to visit the university campus, then this location makes sense.

Technically in Boulder, but closer to the suburb of Gunbarrel, is the **Boulder Twin Lakes Inn** (6485 Twin Lakes Rd., 303/530-2939 or 800/322-2939, www.twinlakesinnboulder.com, $89-165). Accommodations resemble short-term, corporate apartments with some level of kitchen supplies in each room. Guests have use of a communal kitchen and guest laundry, and there are running trails nearby with a view of the Flatirons. Weekly and monthly rates are available.

Cabins at the **Silver Saddle Motel** (90 W. Arapahoe Ave., 303/442-8022, www.silversaddlemotel.net, $95-145) are just under $100 per night in high season. There is no hiding the fact that the Silver Saddle is dated, but the location in the foothills means easy access to trails and it's a reasonable walk to downtown and the many amenities found there.

$100-250

The **Boulder University Inn** (1632 Broadway, 303/417-1700, www.boulderuniversityinn.com, $109-189) has a very convenient location a block from Boulder Creek, just at the base of The Hill adjacent to campus, and a short stroll from the Pearl Street Mall. There's even an outdoor pool to use in the summer months. Rates are generally under $200 per night in high season. While this isn't the most modern or stylish accommodation in town, it makes up for that with its central location and clean rooms.

Get away from downtown just a bit at the **Foot of the Mountain Motel** (200 W. Arapahoe Ave., 303/442-5688 or 866/773-5489, www.footofthemountainmotel.com, $150 rooms, $200-300 suites) where it's 1930s rustic on the outside and modern and tidy on the inside. While this place is dog-friendly, they do not allow dogs in all of the rooms so be sure to ask when making your reservation if you intend to bring your pooch. You're still easy walking and cycling distance from all downtown amenities.

To stay someplace truly unique and just-so-Boulder, book a cottage at ★ **Chautauqua** (900 Baseline Rd., 303/442-3282, www.chautauqua.com). Cottages ($185-285 per night) range from studios to three-bedrooms with kitchens; lodge rates range $1,155-1,275 per night for the entire eight-bedroom facility. From mid-June to mid-August, nightly rentals ($75-126) are available at the Columbine Lodge. There is no air-conditioning in some of the cabins and daily housekeeping is not offered.

A short drive from downtown, the **Lookout Inn Guesthouse & Suites** (6901 Lookout Rd., 303/530-1513, www.lookoutinnguesthouse.com, $99-184) caters to business travelers who need weekly or monthly stays. Each clean and comfortable room is named after a Colorado town—Golden, Boulder, etc.—and has a private balcony, kitchenette, and fireplace. The prices are incredible considering the size of the room or suite, and a yummy complimentary breakfast is included with your stay.

The **Briar Rose Bed and Breakfast Inn** (2151 Arapahoe St., 303/442-3007, www.briarrosebb.com, $139-219) is a very cute property with eight rooms available between the main house and carriage house. Tea and organic breakfast are served daily and can be enjoyed outside in the sweet garden. This is one of the closest lodging options to Naropa University. The inn has a meditation room for those who need to find their Zen.

The ★ **Bradley Boulder Inn** (2040 16th St., 303/545-5200, www.thebradleyboulder.com, $225-300) is like a home away from home, if home is just steps away from the city's shops, restaurants, and nightlife. Mingle with your fellow guests in the inn's great room, which has a fireplace and comfy sofas and chairs. Note that children under age 14 are not allowed and there are only stairs to the second floor. This is a nonsmoking facility.

OVER $250

The Victorian architecture and decor make the ★ **Hotel Boulderado** (2115 13th St., 303/442-4344, www.boulderado.com, $270-400) timeless and always appealing for a comfortable night's stay. It's one block off the Pearl Street Mall and walking distance to many recommended restaurants and shops. Meet friends for a drink and a nibble at **The Corner Bar** (303/442-4880, www.cornerbar-boulderado.com, 11:30am-11:30pm daily) or **License No. 1** (303/442-4880, www.boulderado.com/dining-drinks/license, 5pm-midnight daily) on the ground floor of the Boulderado. The Boulderado not only has a wonderful history since its opening in 1909, but much of it *is* history by now—the distinctive red sandstone came from Fort Collins, the mosaic tile in the lobby and elsewhere is original, and you can use the white marble drinking fountain, which once piped water directly from a glacier. Go to the hotel's third floor for what they call a "living history museum" to learn more about who has stayed here and other local lore.

One of Boulder's newest hotels is the swanky ★ **St. Julien Hotel and Spa** (900 Walnut St., 720/406-9696, www.stjulien.com, $329-489), a AAA 4-diamond hotel with more than 200 rooms and suites. This place evokes the mountains that can be seen from several key vantage points on the property, with liberal use of pink-red sandstone throughout the design. But it's not just designed to make you think of rocks like those stunning Flatirons you look out at, but the entire natural world you may well be here to enjoy: The St. Julien has its own "Green Committee" that continually reviews how the hotel can minimize its ecological footprint. Add in the 10,000-square-foot spa and indoor pool, and the result is true modern luxury in which you can feel good about your stay.

the historic Hotel Boulderado

While the St. Julien has become a favorite happy hour spot for locals, one of the charming new traditions here is afternoon tea (2pm Sat.), which takes place in the lobby. I usually think of historic hotels when I think of a formal tea, but the St. Julien has pulled this off to make it a favorite new occasion for many locals.

Food

Boulder has become a foodie town, with menus at various restaurants that feature the bounty of local produce and meats from nearby farms and ranches. The chefs and owners here have been featured on TV shows and in food and wine magazines. Some local chefs own their own farms and participate in farm-to-table dinners—you might even meet one while shopping at the Boulder County Farmers Market. The selection of Boulder restaurants includes everything from casual vegetarian options to upscale, once-in-a-lifetime meals served amid wonderful views. If you live here or are visiting in the fall, see if you can get a reservation during First Bite: Boulder Restaurant Week (mid.-Nov.) to sample prix fixe menus at dozens of restaurants.

COFFEE AND TEA

The **Dushanbe Teahouse** (1770 13th St., 303/442-4993, www.boulderteahouse.com, 8am-9pm daily, $12-18) is worth a visit on its own, but is also a great place for a meal and a cup of tea. Breakfast, lunch, and dinner menus are fairly simple, but with a mix of cultures—Tajikistani *plov* (a traditional beef rice dish), Indian tikka masala, and pizza are all offered.

My go-to coffee and tea shop in Boulder is ★ **Trident Booksellers and Café** (940 Pearl St. 303/443-3133, http://tridentcafe.com, 6:30am-11pm Mon.-Sat., 7am-11pm Sun.), just west of the Pearl Street Mall. A doorway connects the separate café and bookshop spaces. On the bookstore side are new and used books on art, religion, and poetry, many of which are rare or hard-to-find titles. On the café side there is selection of coffees, teas, and pastries to choose from and a lovely back patio to visit with friends over an iced beverage in summer.

So suitable for the University Hill neighborhood is the **Innisfree Poetry & Bookstore Café** (1203 13th St., 303/495-3303, www.innisfreepoetry.com, 7am-5pm Mon., 7am-9pm Tues.-Fri., 8am-5pm Sat.-Sun.). Stop for a cup of coffee or espresso, then attend a poetry reading or one of the other events held here regularly.

The **Laughing Goat Coffeehouse** (1709 Pearl St., 303/440-4628, www.thelaughinggoat.com, 6am-11pm Mon.-Fri., 7am-11pm Sat.-Sun.) has three locations around Boulder. This downtown branch serves Kaladi Brothers coffee (based out of Denver), but it's more than just a place for a morning pick-me-up. They host regular events, serving as an evening out for poetry, jazz, and other performances when they also serve beer and wine.

BREAKFAST AND LUNCH

Tangerine's (2777 Iris Ave., 303/443-2333, www.tangerineboulder.com, 7am-2:30pm daily, $10) playful, bright orange-accented interior will certainly wake you up. If not, order a velvety latte and brioche French toast to ease into the day. Owner/chef Alec Schuler is mindful of maintaining a healthy, balanced lifestyle. His creative breakfast dishes like polenta and romesco with poached eggs sure make a statement, as do the caprese frittata and trout and apple benedict.

★ **Lucile's Creole Café** (2124 14th St., 303/442-4743, www.luciles.com, 7am-2pm Mon.-Fri., 8am-2pm Sat.-Sun., $10) started here. The original Lucile's—the iconic yellow Victorian on 14th Street—is a culinary landmark in Boulder, especially for the brunch-minded. Even if you show up early, expect to wait a while for a spot in this popular breakfast and brunch restaurant, where the chicory coffee and beignets are as good as they are in the Deep South. Don't miss the shrimp and grits or pain perdu, and beware—the famous home-style buttermilk biscuits are larger than life. There are five locations of Lucile's, including in Denver and Fort Collins.

What would Boulder be without its mascot? Roll into **The Buff** (2600 Canyon Blvd., 303/442-9150, www.buffrestaurant.com, 6:30am-2pm Mon.-Fri., 7am-2pm Sat.-Sun., $10) on a weekend morning, and you'll find a hungry breakfast crowd, slow-moving college kids, and tourists looking for a hearty mountain meal. You'll also find lots of local products like Ozo Coffee, Teatulia organic teas, Avery beer, and Boulder granola—plus fancy mimosas, giant bloody marys (ask for the Tatanka), and a chai they call The Dirty Hippie. They also serve breakfast staples like omelets and griddle cakes, as well as a few Southwestern dishes like huevos rancheros and *buffaquiles*.

One of the best burger restaurants in Colorado has a place in Boulder: ★ **Larkburger** (2525 Arapahoe St., 303/444-1487, www.larkburger.com, 11am-9pm Sun.-Thurs., 11am-10pm Fri.-Sat., $2-8) has yummy burgers and to-die-for truffle Parmesan fries. And right next door is another favorite, **Cuba Cuba Sandwicheria** (2525 Arapahoe St., 303/442-1143, www.cubacubasandwicheria.com, 11am-8pm daily, $4-8), with a lunch version of what's on the menu at their original restaurant in Denver, Cuba Cuba Café & Bar.

Sandwiches are big business, and **Snarf's** (5340 Arapahoe Ave., 303/444-3404, www.eatsnarfs.com, 11am-10pm, Mon.-Sat., 11am-9pm Sun., $10) is proof of that. Snarf's opened in 1996 as a humble, family-owned sandwich shop. The chain now has nearly 20 locations in Colorado, St. Louis, Austin, and Chicago. What makes it so good? The homemade, oven-toasted bread, the house giardiniera peppers, and the scratch-made dressings add a little something special to your made-to-order 5-, 7-, or 12-inch sandwich. There are even "Snarflettes"—mini-sandwiches with kid-friendly ingredients—for the young'uns.

Exposed brick, cozy window seats, and a rustic central fireplace are doused in sunlight at **Cafe Aion** (1235 Pennsylvania Ave., 303/993-8131, www.cafeaion.com, 11am-10pm Tues.-Fri., 9am-10pm Sat., 9am-2pm Sun., $10-40), a convivial Spanish tapas restaurant done the Boulder way. Join a relaxed, social crowd sampling small plates of locally farmed and ranched ingredients like Moroccan-spiced pork sliders and fried cauliflower with saffron yogurt. Breakfast is practically legendary here, so come in the morning and enjoy egg dishes and breakfast tapas, even better with Ozo espresso. By night, try the house-cured salt cod croquettes and Colorado lamb merguez sausage over flatbread, washed down with a glass of cava.

Rincon Argentino (2525 Arapahoe Ave., 303/442-4133, www.rinconargentinoboulder.com, 11am-8pm Mon.-Thurs., 11am-9pm Fri.-Sat., $5-10) has a menu of empanadas—South American sandwich pies, if you will, mostly savory and served with a variety of dipping sauces. This makes for a quick, affordable, and filling lunch with a little spice or a great simple meal before a movie night.

The ★ **Mediterranean Restaurant** (1002 Walnut St., 303/444-5335, www.themedboulder.com, 11am-10pm Mon.-Thurs., 11am-11pm Fri.-Sat., 11am-9pm Sun., $10-25)—affectionately known as The Med here—has been a fixture in the Boulder restaurant scene since 1993. Its warm ambience, fresh flower arrangements, and friendly team make it a solid choice for a romantic night out, a dinner with the kids, or a group celebration. The place is lively and bustling, with a decided Greek island theme and tapas plates that span the Mediterranean, from margherita pizza to paella valenciana. There's even an on-site bakery producing artisan breads for The Med and sister restaurant Brasserie Ten Ten—as well as retail locations like Alfalfa's Market.

Zeal is a locavore's dream.

AMERICAN

My lunch favorite (though it's also open for dinner) is ★ **The Kitchen** (1039 Pearl St., 303/544-5973, http://thekitchen.com, 11am-3pm and 5:30pm-9pm Mon., 11am-3pm and 5:30pm-10pm Tues.-Fri., 5:30pm-10pm Sat., 5:30pm-9pm Sun., $12-30). The Kitchen made a name for itself by being "green" in a variety of ways—using wind power, recycling grease—and because of its delicious food. Check out the giant blackboard to see the list of local purveyors who grow the food you eat.

Located on "The Hill" in Boulder, **The Sink** (1165 13th St., 303/444-7465, www.thesink.com, 11am-2am daily, $15) boasts more than 90 years of serving casual sandwiches, pizza, burgers, and more to the hungry public. Still a family-owned eatery, The Sink caters especially to locals and University of Colorado students and alumni, whom you'll find in abundance on any given day. But celebrities know the spot, too: Guy Fieri made a stop in 2011, and President Barack Obama paid a visit in 2012. The interior is decorated with wall murals and eclectic marker art, giving you something to contemplate over your Cowboy Reuben or SinkBurger.

SALT the Bistro (1047 Pearl St., 303/444-7258, www.saltthebistro.com, 11am-9pm Mon.-Thurs., 11am-10pm Fri., 10am-10pm Sat.-Sun., $15-30) comes from chef/owner Bradford Heap, the man behind the countryside-chic Colterra in nearby Niwot. Walk in and marvel at the interior design, constructed completely from recycled materials by local artists. Heap is big on local farmers and non-GMOs, which you'll notice on the tempting menu featuring produce from his own farm and countless others. For dinner, select from pastas, entrées, and small plates, as well as a lineup of seasonal, creative cocktails and several local craft beers.

Black Cat Bistro (1964 Pearl St., 303/440-5500, www.blackcatboulder.com, 5:30pm-close Mon.-Sat., $16-24) doesn't have quite the same buzz as The Kitchen or Frasca, but it's popular with locals who appreciate the simple, organic fare made into unexpected dishes like "Juxtaposition of Duck" with lavender honey or "Blue Crab, Hot and Cold." Black Cat offers a few tasting menus (including vegetarian or vegan) paired with wines.

OAK at fourteenth (1400 Pearl St., 303/444-3622, www.oakatfourteenth.com, 11:30am-10pm Mon.-Wed., 11:30am-2am Thurs.-Sat., 5:30pm-10pm Sun., $15-30) is where Boulder's modern style blends with Colorado's rustic environs. The food is driven by seasonal ingredients and unmatched service, and OAK centers around the restaurant's oak-fired oven and grill, the primary inspiration for chef/owner Steve Redzikowski's take on contemporary New American food. Locally sourced meats and produce, as well as sustainable seafood, top house-made pastas and crisp greens, all seasoned with that signature oak flavor.

Opened in 2014, **Zeal—Food for Enthusiasts** (1710 Pearl St., 720/708-6309, www.zealfood.com, 8am-9pm Mon.-Thurs., 8am-10pm Fri., 9am-10pm Sat., 9am-9pm Sun., $10-20) is committed to locally sourced, mostly organic, and regional ingredients that celebrate a true zest for life. Walk in and you'll see the list of local farms and purveyors on a chalkboard on the wall. Zeal finds most of their ingredients in and around Boulder County, serving breakfast, lunch, and dinner made from the purest food they can get their hands on. Try their fresh, cold-pressed juices (and juice cocktails), veggie bowls, and a range of fermented goodies like kimchi and house pickles.

★ **Blackbelly Market** (1606 Conestoga St., 303/247-1000, www.blackbelly.com, 4pm-10pm Wed.-Sat., 4pm-11pm Sun.-Tues., $15-40) opened in 2014 in Boulder to much anticipation. Award-winning chef/owner Hosea Rosenberg (winner of Bravo TV's season 5 of *Top Chef*) serves fresh and expertly butchered charcuterie, burgers, steaks, and hand-cut Kennebec fries in this sleek and social environment, where the philosophy hinges on the hyperlocal. Rosenberg raises his own lambs and pigs, supplies organic produce from his greenhouse, and even operates a catering service out of a food truck. Parking at the restaurant is plentiful, and seating includes dining room tables, the chef's counter, an intimate bar, and two outdoor patios.

The ultimate in fine dining has long been the ★ **Flagstaff House** (1138 Flagstaff Dr., 303/442-4640, www.flagstaffhouse.com, 6pm-10pm Mon.-Fri. and Sun., 5pm-10pm Sat., $32-76). Everything will make you swoon—the view, the food, the wine. This family-owned gem is one of the country's premier dining experiences, and well worth the drive up the twisting mountain road.

FRENCH

Seeking approachable French fare? Say *bonjour* to **Brasserie Ten Ten** (1011 Walnut St., 303/998-1010, www.brasserietenten.com, 11am-10pm Mon.-Thurs., 11am-11pm Fri., 9am-11pm Sat., 9am-9pm Sun., $15-25). Opened in 2003 by the same owners behind The Med, this cozy, colorful bistro draws guests with its open-air terrace and bustling European vibe. Try the savory steak frites or classic bouillabaisse to get a taste of their signature items, and if you're with a group, *Le Grand* platter—a three-tier tower piled with raw oysters, steamed shrimp, mussels, and fresh lobster salad—will certainly entertain. If you want the best of Boulder and Paris, choose the roasted rack of Colorado lamb served with vegetable ratatouille and crumbled chèvre.

ITALIAN

It's a special night out to dine at ★ **Frasca** (1738 Pearl St., 303/442-6966, www.frascafoodandwine.com, 5:30pm-close Mon.-Sat., $28-36), where the menu is based on the cuisine of the Fruili region of Italy. Frasca also emphasizes using local sources for its Italian dishes. Dining here is a total experience—therefore reservations are recommended—which makes sense when you consider the owner has done a TEDx Talk and the restaurant has won the James Beard Foundation Award for its wine program, among many other accolades. Come with friends and linger over the wine and food to make it a really special night.

Local food lovers can't get enough of **Basta** (3601 Arapahoe Ave., 303/997-8775, www.bastaboulder.com, 5pm-10pm daily, Friday lunch 11:30am-2:30pm, $15-20), Boulder's hip and casual Italian concept. Chef Kelly Whitaker cooks everything over a wood-fired oven—taking the techniques he learned in Italy, sprinkling on his own innovation, and achieving a mouthwatering char on pizzas and entrées. Guests enjoy the locally grown ingredients, seasonal menus, and a creative beverage list. If you have time for a long lunch on Friday, order the wood-fired half chicken with *farro* and *agrodolce*.

From the owners of Frasca—Boulder's top spot for northern Italian fine dining, located right next door—**Pizzeria Locale** (1730 Pearl St., 303/442-3003, www.localeboulder.com, 11:30am-2:30pm and 4:30pm-10pm Mon.-Thurs., 11am-10:30pm Fri.-Sat., 11:30am-9pm Sun., $15) offers a comfortable place to

Déjà Vu

A guy walks into a Boulder restaurant. He thinks, "Have I been here before?" But this can't be, because it's his first trip in Boulder. Yet it's possible he has been to the **Lucile's** in Fort Collins or the **Snarf's** in Denver or…any number of other restaurants that got their start here and have since expanded to cities on the Front Range (and beyond, in some cases). Many of the restaurants recommended in Boulder have other locations or iterations in other Colorado cities.

Mountain Sun Pub & Brewery (1535 Pearl St., Boulder, 303/546-0886, www.mountainsunpub.com, 11:30am-1am Mon.-Sat., noon-1am Sun.) first opened on Pearl Street in 1993. Now there are two more locations in Boulder: Southern Sun Pub & Brewery (627 S. Broadway, 303/543-0886) and Under the Sun Eatery & Taphouse (627A S. Broadway, 303/927-6921), as well as one in Denver (1700 Vine St., 303/388-2337) and another in Longmont (600 Longs Peak Ave., 303/651-7885).

Lucile's Creole Café (2124 14th St., 303/442-4743, www.luciles.com, 7am-2pm Mon.-Fri., 8am-2pm Sat.-Sun.) began in Boulder, and now has five locations where those giant hot biscuits with strawberry jam are just as delicious.

The Kitchen (1039 Pearl St., 303/544-5973, www.thekitchencafe.com, lunch 11am-3pm Mon.-Fri., community hour 3pm-5:30pm, dinner 5:30pm-9pm Sun.-Mon., 5:30pm-10pm Tues.-Sat., $12-30) opened on Pearl Street in 2004 and quickly became a staple of dining out in Boulder. They have since expanded to Denver's LoDo neighborhood where the place is just as popular, if not more so.

In 1996, the first **Snarf's** (5340 Arapahoe Ave., 303/444-3404, www.eatsnarfs.com, 11am-10pm Mon.-Sat., 11am-9am Sun.) opened here. There are now about a dozen locations between Denver, Boulder, Golden, and Longmont, and they have expanded into other states as well. Just use "snarf" to describe anything here: snarf-alicious, Snarflettes (kid-size sandwiches), and so on.

experience Neapolitan-style pizza in Boulder. Pizzas are fired in a 10,000-pound, Italian-made pizza oven, which cooks pies to chewy, charred perfection in less than two minutes. High-quality ingredients and warm service make it great for a casual date or a family dinner—especially with a pair of *aperitivos* and a shared side of meatballs.

Contemporary and health-conscious Italian food is done at **Arugula Bar e Ristorante** (2785 Iris Ave., 303/443-5100, www.arugularistorante.com, 11:30am-2:30pm Wed.-Fri., 5pm-9pm Sun.-Thurs., 5pm-10pm, Fri.-Sat. $20-25). Simple, elegant Mediterranean dishes are served in a modern and welcoming environment. The menus change twice weekly, showcasing naturally raised meats, seasonal local produce, and sustainable seafood. Have a seat and check out the intriguing antique corkscrew art adorning the walls before poring over the extensive wine list.

JAPANESE

Japango (1136 Pearl St., 303/938-0330, www.boulderjapango.com, 11am-midnight Fri.-Sat., 11am-10pm Sun.) has graced bustling Pearl Street for years, but a recent remodel has brought out the best in this Boulder mainstay. Japango springs into the current era with an expanded, illuminated bar, a bustling open-air patio, and (still) the largest sake collection in Boulder. A seat at the sushi counter will give you a good view into the artistry behind your maki. And if you stick around for the late-night, DJ-driven happy hour, you're bound to make a few new friends over a round of sake bombs.

★ **Sushi Zanmai** (1221 Spruce St., 303/440-0733, 11:30am-2pm and 5pm-10pm Mon.-Fri., 5pm-midnight Sat., 5pm-10pm Sun.) has long been Boulder's favorite sushi restaurant. Thirty years is an impressive run in the restaurant industry! There are great deals here during happy hours (5pm-6:30pm daily, 10pm on Sat., evenings Sun.). If you don't eat sushi, their menu has a lot of tasty entrées featuring chicken, beef, or cooked fish.

MEXICAN

After a hike in the foothills, nothing hits the spot like some spicy Mexican food washed down with a margarita. **Zolo Grill** (2525 Arapahoe Ave., 303/449-0444, www.zologrill.com, 11am-3:30pm and 4pm-close daily, happy hour 3pm-6pm, Sat.-Sun. brunch 10am-2:30pm) has all of the usual yummy Mexican dishes—tacos, enchiladas, tamales—as well as with special items like duck tacos and trout tostadas. A kids' menu makes this a good option for families too.

If you like your Mexican food basic but delicious, then stop by **Sancho's Authentic Mexican Restaurant** (2850 Iris Ave., #H, 303/440-0228, www.sanchosmexican.com, 10am-9pm Mon.-Sat., 10am-6pm Sun.) for a smothered burrito or some spicy tamales. Prices are reasonable for the amount of food and it's incredibly filling too.

Taco (1175 Walnut St., 303/443-9468, http://tacocolorado.com) has street tacos at street food prices, plus larger entrees like Mexican pizza for bigger appetites.

NEPALESE

With rock and mountain climbers comes climbing food, and that means traditional Himalayan and Nepalsese fare. **Sherpa's** (825 Walnut St., 303/440-7151, www.sherpasrestaurant.com, 11am-3pm and 5pm-9:30pm Sun.-Wed., 11am-3pm and 5pm-10pm Thurs.-Sat., $15) is more than an opportunity to sample the tastes of the Mount Everest region. This is also a cultural center with a gallery of mountain-trek photos and a library of mountaineering books—you can even sign up for a trek! But first, order some warm naan and... yak stew. You only live once, right? The menu is a combination of Indian, Himalayan, and Nepalese foods.

The sound of it rolling off your tongue is almost as good as the flavor: momo. These Tibetan dumplings served at **Tibet Kitchen** (2359 Arapahoe St., 303/440-0882, www.tibetkitchen.com, 11am-10pm Mon.-Sat., noon-10pm Sun., $10) make for an affordable, delicious, and filling meal. At these prices, you can experiment to find the flavors you prefer in sauces, rice, soups, and more.

Get your seafood fix at Jax.

SEAFOOD

Jax Fish House (928 Pearl St., 303/444-1811, www.jaxfishhouse.com/boulder, 4pm-10pm Sun.-Thurs., 4pm-11pm Fri.-Sat., $15-20) has served the fruits of the briny sea to Boulder (and locations in Fort Collins, Denver, and Glendale) for more than 20 years. Grab a seat at the raw bar for a round of freshly shucked oysters before diving into their sustainably sourced seafood menu, guaranteed to make you feel a little less landlocked.

Spruce Farm & Fish (2115 13th St., 303/442-4880, www.spruceboulderado.com, 6am-10pm Mon.-Sat., 7am-10pm Sun., $15-30) is the recently renovated, smartly outfitted eatery in the classy, historic Hotel Boulderado. Spruce holds on to its early 1900s heritage (think stained glass and black-and-white floor tiles) while entertaining contemporary guests with cozy booths, handsome wooden tables, and crowd-pleasing dishes like the smoked trout dip, stuffed *piquillo* peppers, and the show-stopping crispy whole snapper. Don't forget dessert; the rustic apple pie is worthy of a visit all on its own.

Transportation and Services

CAR

Boulder is an easy, 30-mile drive west from Denver. The most common route is to take Highway 36 north from I-25 in Denver; a handful of exits point out how to get to the University of Colorado campus or other locales. Another route is to take I-70 west for 15 miles to Highway 6 in Golden, then head north for about 30 miles on Highway 93 to Boulder, where the highway turns into Broadway. While this is a more scenic drive closer to the foothills—there is not much development this close to the old Rocky Flats Nuclear Weapons Facility—the road is not safe during high winds.

PUBLIC TRANSIT

The **RTD** (Regional Transportation District, www.rtd-denver.com, $6.75 day pass) offers regional bus service several times daily from Union Station in downtown Denver to the Boulder Transit Center. In-town buses then originate from the **Boulder Transit Center** (14th and Walnut Sts., 303/229-6000, $2.25). Look for the affordable, around-town buses with their silly names like Hop (downtown, CU campus), Skip (Broadway), and Dash (South Boulder Rd.).

Greyhound and Amtrak do not service Boulder.

TOURS

If you like history with low-impact exercise, don't miss the **Boulder Walking Tours** (720/243-1376, http://boulderwalkingtours.com, $20 adults, $15 youth age 13-17, children under 12 free). Reservations are required for groups of 8-12 people. Tours last about two hours and include summer tours of the Pearl Street Mall (10am Mon., Wed., Fri.-Sat.) and Chautauqua's Living History (10am Sun.).

For a unique biking/touring/dining experience, check out **Awe-Struck Outdoors** (303/807-6634, www.awestruckoutdoors.com, rates vary) and do a bike-to-farm tour: On a Thursday night in the summer, visitors ride bikes from downtown Boulder to a local family-owned farm where dinner is served alongside the garden plots. Or try the "Cadence and Decadence" bike tour where you visit a few Boulder-area farms who will be serving appetizers at each stop.

Boulder Bike Tours (303/747-6191 or 303/570-9177, http://boulderbiketours.com, rates vary) offers mountain or road biking tours in the foothills of Boulder that last a half day or a full day. There are also two-hour rides around Boulder. Each tour includes a guide, snacks or lunch, water, a bike, and a helmet. You don't have to be an expert—these guides can go at a leisurely pace and roll along or get your heart racing with something more intense.

SERVICES

For more information, visit the **Boulder Convention and Visitors Bureau** (2440 Pearl St., 303/442-2911, www.bouldercoloradousa.com). The city's major daily newspaper is the *Boulder Daily Camera* (www.dailycamera.com). There's also the *Colorado Daily* (www.coloradodaily.com), a free tabloid-style paper found all over town. The town's "alternative" newspaper is the *Boulder Weekly* (www.boulderweekly.com), with long feature stories and weekly events. The glossy *Boulder Magazine* (www.getboulder.com) offers lots of suggestions for fun activities in the area.

Vicinity of Boulder

ELDORADO SPRINGS

The town of Eldorado Springs, south of Boulder, provides access to wonderful outdoor recreation. You can rock climb, hike, go to a yoga class, trail run, and cool off in a natural springs pool. The road into Eldorado Springs usually has a few cyclists on it too, so consider that as an alternative mode of transportation for getting here from Boulder. While it is possible to ride a bike from Boulder to Eldorado Springs (it's under 10 miles one-way), keep in mind the high altitude and the fact that you might be hiking or biking on a trail later. It's a short drive to Eldorado Springs, but totally worth it for a real mountain experience.

★ Eldorado Canyon State Park

Eldorado Canyon State Park (9 Kneale Rd., 303/494-3943, http://cpw.state.co.us/places-togo/parks/EldoradoCanyon, sunrise-sunset daily year-round, $3-8) is at the end of the road into Eldorado Springs. The park is popular with rock climbers—there are more than 500 technical climbing routes—but you can also hike in the summer or snowshoe in the winter on trails ranging from easy to difficult. Fishing is allowed for brown and rainbow trout (a valid Colorado fishing license is required). Golden eagles also nest here, so there may be trail closures at times to protect wildlife.

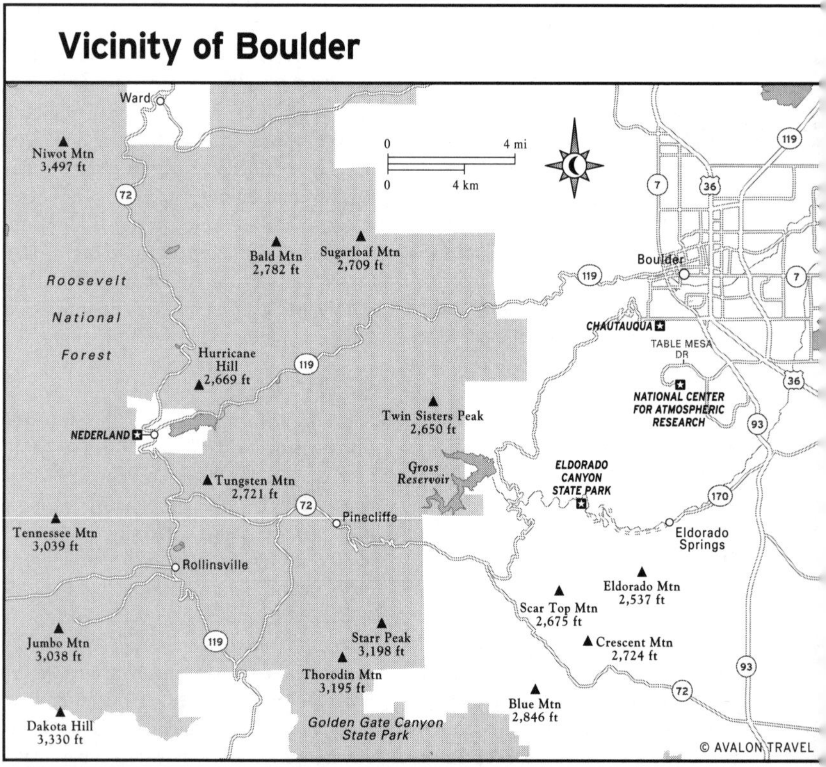

Vicinity of Boulder

Tackle the rapids at Eldorado Springs.

There are fees for park use that vary depending upon whether you drive in or not. If you are driving into the park, try to go on a weekday when it is less crowded with rock climbers and fellow day hikers—this is a popular place.

Hikes include easy-to-moderate options suitable for families with young children and those who want a bit of a workout. The **Streamside Trail** (0.5 mile) will stimulate your senses with the roar of South Boulder Creek, the cool creek air and the shade of nearby canyon walls, and the beautiful scenery. The **Fowler Trail** (0.7 mile) is just a bit longer, but is still an easy walk with benches for sitting and gazing up at the rock climbers scaling the steep canyon walls.

The **Rattlesnake Gulch Trail** (1.4 miles) qualifies as a moderately difficult hike, but your reward is the site of the former Crags Hotel. Once you've arrived at the viewpoint, take in the broad views from this elevation. The trail is also open to mountain biking, but this is a steep and bumpy ride with an 800-foot elevation gain and switchbacks. (Portions of this trail may close to protect wildlife; check the park website.)

The **Eldorado Canyon Trail** (3.5 miles one-way) is the park's most challenging, but you have excellent views to look forward to. The Eldorado Canyon Trail is also a good one for horseback riders, but it's wise to opt for weekdays when there are fewer people—horse trailers may not be allowed in the parking lot on a busy weekend.

Biking

Doudy Draw (https://bouldercolorado.gov/osmp/doudy-draw-trailhead, fee for parking) is a 1.7-mile multiuse trail that is popular with mountain bikers. The trail passes over creeks (or creekbeds, depending on the time of year) and connects with other bike-friendly trails in the area. While it's lovely to hear the songbirds in the fields as you ride along, be mindful that bears and mountain lions live here too. (I've also been here when the University of Colorado cross-country team practically leapt off a bus for practice and barreled past me like a herd of gazelles.) The trailhead is located 1.8 miles west of Highway 93 on Eldorado Springs Drive (Hwy. 170).

Hiking

Along the drive to Eldorado Canyon State Park is the **South Mesa Trail** (https://bouldercolorado.gov/osmp/south-mesa-trailhead), which starts out as a gentle hike in grasslands and shrubs, then gets more interesting as you begin stepping "stairs" and increasing elevation. The trail is wheelchair-accessible and has picnic tables, restrooms, and a fee-based parking lot. Leashed dogs are permitted, but cyclists are not. Be aware that mountain lions, bears, and other wildlife inhabit this area. The trailhead is located 1.7 miles west of Highway 93 on Eldorado Springs Drive (Hwy. 170).

Swimming

The **Eldorado Springs Pool** (294 Artesian Dr., 303/499-9640, www.eldoradosprings.com, 10am-6pm daily Memorial Day-Labor

Day, $10 adults, $7 children and seniors) is a classic Boulder experience in the summer. (Notice these are *not* "hot springs.") The pool opened in 1905 and has remained true to its origins—the water is not heated. If you ride a bike here from Boulder on a hot summer day, it will feel absolutely perfect to cool off! There is a small snack shop on site, or you can picnic at the pool. Be warned: It's a bit of a dare to use the old-fashioned slide here.

Yoga

With all the hiking, biking, and climbing, one might get the impression that the only way to enjoy Colorado is to be a semiprofessional athlete. The **Eldorado Yoga Mountain Ashram** (2875 County Rd. 67, 303/249-1671, http://eldoradoyoga.org) is a gentle reminder that you can just be one with nature here. This special place offers drop-in yoga, meditation, and other classes. There is a family yoga class every Sunday and other family offerings on a seasonal basis as well.

Getting There

Eldorado Springs is located about nine miles southwest of Boulder. To get here from Boulder, follow Broadway (Hwy. 93) south for about six miles to Highway 170. Turn west on Highway 170 and drive three miles to Eldorado Springs.

★ NEDERLAND

Funky is a word that sums up Nederland, a mountain town less than 20 miles west of Boulder. Nederland initially came to be due to mining in the area; it has continued thanks to its location on the Peak to Peak Highway, a scenic byway that winds from Estes Park down to a suburb west of Denver. It's a prime spot for many outdoor adventures.

Just outside of Nederland is the Eldora ski resort and the Brainard Lake Recreation Area, which offers many wonderful hiking or snowshoeing trails, depending on the season.

Sights

Nederland isn't exactly full of sights, but there is one place that's worth the drive up the canyon. The **Carousel of Happiness** (20 Lakeview Dr., 303/258-3457, www.carouselofhappiness.org, 10am-6pm Mon.-Thurs., 10am-8pm Sat.-Sun., $1) is made from so many dreams. In 2010, Nederland resident Scott Harrison bought a used carousel, minus the animals, and taught himself how to carve wooden creatures. He spent 25 years making 56 carousel animals; kids now squeal with delight as they ride them today. But he couldn't have pulled this off without the town's support; together they raised the funds to build a home for the carousel. Even if you don't have young kids, it's worth a visit to check out the one-of-a-kind carousel animals such as an alpaca, a dolphin, and a dragon boat.

Festivals and Events

Ned (as locals call Nederland) has become known for its annual **Frozen Dead Guy Days** (http://frozendeadguydays.org, early Mar.), held while the weather at 8,236 feet is still wintry and cold. The annual event includes a parade through town, people dressed as though cryogenically frozen, coffin races, and other questionably appropriate activities.

It's a long story, but yes—there is a real frozen dead guy. Known simply as "Grandpa," Bredo Morstoel was cryogenically frozen (in a very amateur way) by his grandson, a Ned resident. Grandpa's body lies stored in a Tuff Shed (the kind used to store a lawn mower) on private property in town. (Local filmmakers made a movie, *Grandpa's in the Tuff Shed,* that tells the whole story.)

NedFest (Jeff Guercio Memorial Baseball Field, www.nedfest.org, late Aug., $32-128) is a summer music festival that seems to get bigger each year. Over three days, a mix of bluegrass, rock-n-roll, and jazz music gets the crowds dancing, with art vendors and activities for kids. If you bring a tent, you can camp in nearby Chipeta Park (Lakeview Dr.) and make a weekend of it.

Sports and Recreation

Pack your hiking or skiing gear when you go

to Ned because there are some beautiful places to explore.

HIKING

In summer, you can choose a fairly short hike or really challenge yourself with something longer at the **Brainard Lake Recreation Area** (Boulder Ranger District, 303/541-2500, www.fs.usda.gov, June-Oct., $10 per vehicle). Hikes to various lakes range 1-2 miles (one-way) and reach elevations of more than 10,000 feet. There are picnic tables near the parking area and the lakes, so bring a lunch and relax after your hike. To get here, take Highway 72 north, then take a left on County Road 102.

In the greater Indian Peaks Wilderness Area surrounding Nederland are the **Hessie Trail** (2.7 miles round-trip) and the **Fourth of July Trail.** You can hike to Lost Lake from the Hessie Trail, reaching 9,800 feet elevation in about 1.5 miles. Along the way you'll see and hear waterfalls crashing down the mountain. It's a longer hike of 2.6 miles (one-way) to Diamond Lake on the Fourth of July Trail, which blooms with wildflowers in July and August. All of these trails are popular, so come early to avoid parking hassles.

To reach the Hessie Trail, take Highway 119 through Nederland and turn right at County Road 130. Stay right when the road forks for Eldora. To reach the Fourth of July Trailhead, drive four miles past the Hessie Trailhead on a dirt road.

SKIING

A mere 21 miles west from Boulder, the **Eldora Mountain Resort** (2861 Eldora Ski Rd., 303/440-8700, www.eldora.com) is where the University of Colorado ski team practices. Though these aren't the highest peaks or runs in the state, it's still a great place for a day on the slopes. Group and private lessons are available for downhill and cross-country skiing; their bunny hill for beginners is always popular. There is also a Nordic Center for cross-country skiers and snowshoers.

There is a casual restaurant on-site (pizza, burgers, chili, etc.) and beer is served in the Corona Bowl Bar. You can rent skis and boots for both alpine and cross-country skiing, and there are two shops that sell anything you forgot—snow pants, goggles, mittens. Here's a tip for a little free trail use: Look for signs for the Jenny Creek Trail, just to the east of the bunny slope, and start hiking up. (I'm a snowshoer, but I've seen telemark skiers on this trail too.) This U.S. Forest Service trail is free, though you must stay on the trail and cannot access the ski slopes from here.

Cross-country skiers and snowshoers flock to **Brainard Lake Recreation Area** (303/541-2500, www.fs.usda.gov) in the winter. There is a large parking lot (also bathrooms here) where the gate closes the road in the off-season. Depending on conditions, you can snowshoe up this snow-covered road or go through the trees, while skiers can trek up the road. There is no trail use fee in the winter. To get there, take Highway 72 north, then take a left on County Road 102.

Food

Nederland represents a different time for dining out in Colorado, and far different than Boulder. Here it's about tradition, locals, and familiarity, and not so much about farm-to-table ingredients and award-winning wines.

The **New Moon Bakery & Café** (1 W. 1st St., 303/258-3569, www.newmoonbakery.com, 6:30am-5pm Mon.-Fri., 7am-5pm Sat.-Sun., $10) is where locals go for a cup of "Ned-roast coffee" and a pastry before starting their day on the slopes or trails. Plan ahead and get a picnic lunch to take with you.

Salto Coffee Works (112 E. 2nd Ave., 303/258-3537, www.saltocoffeeworks.com, 7am-6pm Sun.-Thurs., 7am-8pm Fri.-Sat., $5-10) is more than the name might lead you to believe. The simple menu harbors delicious breakfast, lunch, and dinner items such as house-made granola, a fried egg with house-made pesto, or even duck tamales. There is also beer on tap. Check their online events calendar for live music, pizza nights, and other fun goings-on.

Talk about traditional: the ★ **Black**

Forest Restaurant (24 Big Springs Dr., 303/279-2333 or 303/258-4248, 11am-9pm daily, $11-30) has been serving German fare to locals since 1959. (The restaurant originated in the nearby town of Black Hawk and relocated to Nederland in 2000). Goulash and schnitzel, with a wild game or fowl twist, make for a hearty meal, topped off with strudel for dessert—make sure to hike, ski, or snowshoe the next day to shed those calories! The mountain chalet decor and views through the expansive windows make a visit here appealing.

Getting There

Nederland is located 21 miles west of Boulder. To get here from Boulder, take Highway 119 (Canyon Blvd.) west for 16 miles into the mountains. Highway 119 travels west through Nederland to reach Eldora in five more miles.

Fort Collins

Look for ★ to find recommended sights, activities, dining, and lodging.

Highlights

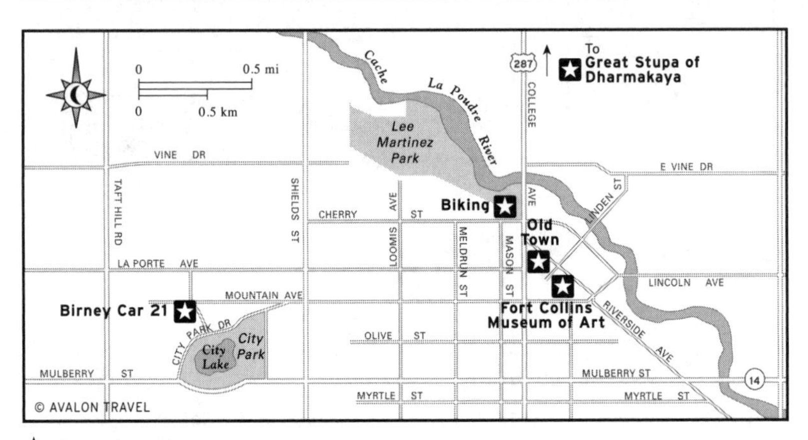

★ **Birney Car 21:** This historic trolley travels from Old Town to City Park, past historic neighborhoods and well-tended homes (page 181).

★ **Fort Collins Museum of Art:** This little museum shows off the best of local and regional artists, as well as big names such as Dale Chihuly and Andy Warhol (page 182).

★ **Old Town:** Charming, practical, and inviting Old Town offers shops, eateries, and bars, all in an appealing pedestrian-friendly area (page 182).

★ **Biking:** Explore town from a two-wheeled perspective and discover why Fort Collins is one of Colorado's best cycling cities (page 191).

★ **Great Stupa of Dharmakaya:** The Great Stupa of Dharmakaya shrine at the Shambhala Mountain Center is worth the hike to get there (page 202).

Fort Collins has its own unique personality, with a reputation for craft breweries, excellent cycling, and a historic charm mixed with college energy.

Located about 60 miles north of Denver, Fort Collins is the fourth-largest city in Colorado. The town has consistently been named as one of the best places to live in the United States by *Money* magazine and the population is expanding steadily. As of 2014, it was estimated to be home to more than 156,000 lucky people.

Beer aficionados will find a robust craft beer scene here that is considered one of the best—if not *the* best—in the state. Yet even with one of Colorado's greatest concentrations of microbreweries, Fort Collins maintains a physically fit populace. The city was designed so that residents could easily cycle along a creekside bike path, enjoy a meal outdoors, or take a leisurely walk from one point to the next. Visitors can stroll in the courtyards along College Avenue to shop, eat, or sip coffee or a cocktail in the city's Old Town neighborhood.

The town's biggest draw, Colorado State University (CSU) was originally founded as an agricultural college; today it is known for its veterinary and forestry schools, and its campus offers gardens, art galleries, and a museum to explore.

What I love about Fort Collins is its connection to Disneyland. Fort Collins native Harper Goff did set design in Hollywood and ended up working with Walt Disney. Goff showed Disney pictures of his hometown and Fort Collins, along with Disney's own childhood home in Missouri, served as the inspiration for Disneyland's Main Street, U.S.A.

PLANNING YOUR TIME

You can really explore at your own pace in Fort Collins, a small city with an ideal balance of culture and physical activity. Plan at least **one day,** with an **overnight** option.

Start with a hike in Lory State Park, less than 30 minutes from downtown. Return to Old Town for lunch at a craft brewery where you can sample the wares. To explore the town, hop on the Birney Car 21, a historic trolley car that goes past historic homes on a tree-lined street, all the way to City Park and

Previous: Birney 21 in Old Town Fort Collins; Odell Brewing Company. **Above:** The Fort Collins Museum of Discovery.

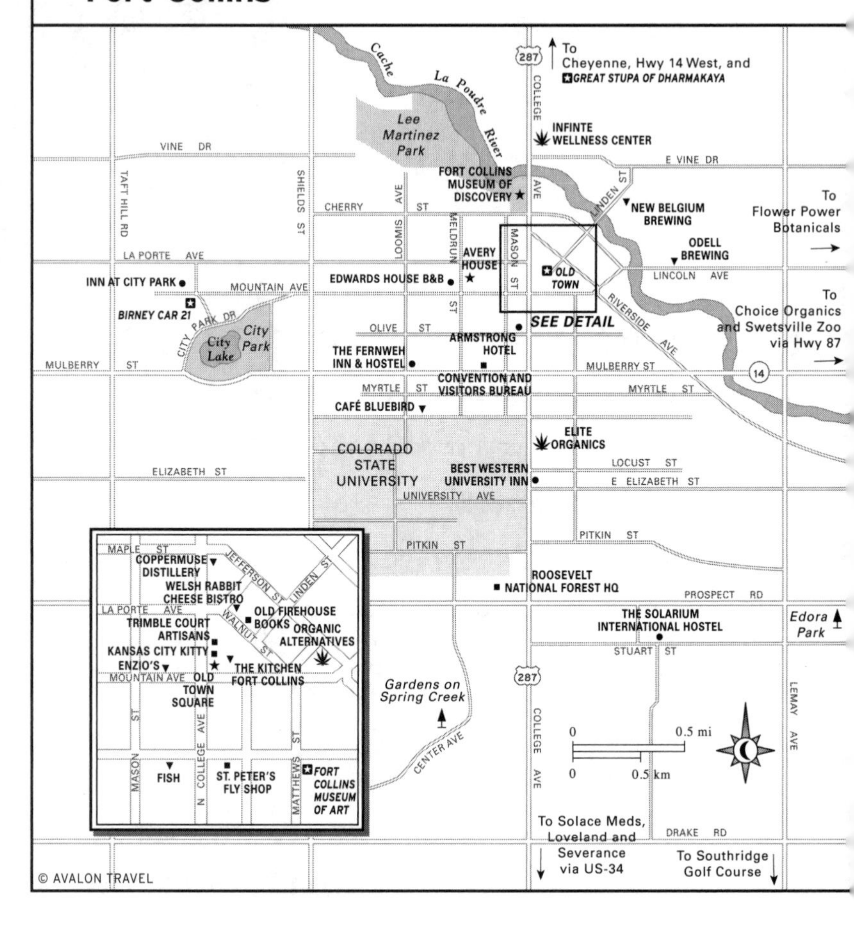

back. Back in Old Town, visit the Fort Collins Museum of Art and then do a little shopping.

Spend the night at the Armstrong Hotel, Fort Collins's only historic hotel. Head down to the hotel's subterranean bar, Ace Gillett's, for cocktails and live music.

The next day, extend your visit by renting a bicycle and riding along the creekside paths around the Colorado State University campus. Enjoy a foamy lunchtime beverage at one of this college town's many craft breweries or go on a brew tour before heading home.

Sights

You can see quite a bit of Fort Collins in one day, depending on your pace. Just walking around Old Town puts you in proximity to some of the city's worthwhile sights, including one of the best sights—Old Town itself. The Colorado State University campus is a worthwhile stop, or opt for the Poudre Landmarks Foundation's **self-guided walking tour** (108 N. Meldrum St., 970/221-0533, http://poudrelandmarks.org), where you can learn about the original uses of many of the town's still-standing historic buildings. Tour highlights include Trimble Court in Old Town, the Hattie McDaniel house (an actress in the classic movie *Gone with the Wind*), the old post office now art museum, the Armstrong Hotel, a Carnegie library and much more.

AVERY HOUSE

An early resident of Fort Collins, Frank Avery is credited with creating the city's wide streets when he surveyed the town in 1873. Avery also founded the First National Bank and had a hand in the development of Fort Collins's agricultural enterprises. In 1879, Avery and his wife, Sarah, built a home for their family from locally quarried stone. Today the **Avery House** (328 W. Mountain Ave., 970/221-0533, http://poudrelandmarks.org, 1pm-4pm Sat.-Sun., free) is in the National Register of Historic Places and is open to the public for guided tours.

★ BIRNEY CAR 21

At one time there was a rail line between Fort Collins, Denver, and Boulder, but it came to a halt in 1918 when transport began to favor cars. In the 1980s, after many years of restoration, the Birney Car 21 came back to life. Today, locals and visitors alike can enjoy this 1.5-mile trip through history. Riding on this little streetcar through Fort Collins's historic neighborhood reminded me of taking the streetcar in New Orleans.

The **Fort Collins Municipal Railway Society** (http://fortnet.org/trolley, noon-4pm Sat.-Sun., $2 adults, $1 children and seniors, children under 3 free) is an all-volunteer organization that runs the Birney Car 21. Boarding locations are located at Howes Street and Mountain Avenue; Loomis Street and Mountain Avenue; Shields Street and Mountain Avenue; and City Park (at the tennis courts).

COLORADO STATE UNIVERSITY

Opened in 1879 as the Colorado Agricultural College, **Colorado State University** (970/491-6444, www.colostate.edu) is the flagship of the state university system. The school may be best known today for its veterinary medicine program, though it offers doctoral degrees in 40 fields of study. If you can time your visit right, you will be able to see the campus's **Trial Gardens** (www.flowertrials.colostate.edu) in full bloom. Between May and October, this display shows off the college's horticultural research.

The **Oval** is a large green space in the center of the campus, surrounded by American elm trees and the historic buildings of the school. It's more than just a favorite gathering place for students—President Barack Obama gave a 2008 campaign speech here.

The **Curfman Gallery** (Lory Student Center, www.curfman.colostate.edu, 9am-9pm Mon.-Thurs., 9am-9:30pm Fri., noon-4pm Sat.) shows off local artists' work, as well as that of national and international artists. **The University Center for the Arts** (1400 Remington St., www.colostate.edu) in the old high school houses performance spaces and two museums, the **University Art Museum** (970/491-1989, www.artmuseum.colostate.edu, 11am-7pm Tues.-Sat.) and the **Avenir Museum of Design and Merchandising** (970/491-6648, www.dm.cahs.colostate.edu, 11am-6pm Mon.-Wed., 11am-8pm Thurs., 11am-6pm Fri.).

★ FORT COLLINS MUSEUM OF ART

In a historic post office building in the city's charming Old Town area is the **Fort Collins Museum of Art** (201 S. College Ave., 970/482-2787, http://ftmca.org, 10am-5pm Wed.-Fri., noon-5pm Sat.-Sun., $3-6), which hosts an interesting variety of shows throughout the year. Past exhibits have included works by Marc Chagall, Ansel Adams, local artists, and themed group shows. Just outside of the building on the Oak Street Plaza is a public art sculpture, *Confluence*, by artist Lawrence Argent, who also created the *I See What You Mean* (aka The Big Blue Bear) sculpture in Denver.

the Fort Collins Museum of Art

FORT COLLINS MUSEUM OF DISCOVERY

The **Fort Collins Museum of Discovery** (408 Mason Ct., 970/221-6738, www.fcmod.org, 10am-5pm Tues.-Sun., 10am-8pm Thurs., $9.50 adults, $7 seniors and students, $6 children age 3-12, children under age 2 free) has a few exhibits that you won't find at the Denver Museum of Nature and Science. Exhibits on local wildlife include black-footed ferrets, while the histories of people and land are presented in a variety of formats (photos, books, videos, etc.). But what makes this museum different is the **Music Garage**—where you can not only learn about music, but play music and even register for a recording session—and the **Otterbox Digital Dome Theater,** which shows a regular lineup of family-friendly movies that aren't your usual multiplex offers.

GARDENS ON SPRING CREEK

One of the city's lesser-known sights, the **Gardens on Spring Creek** (2145 Centre Ave., 970/416-2486, www.fcgov.com/gardens, 9am-5pm Mon.-Fri., 9am-4pm Sat., noon-5pm Sun. May 1-Sept. 30; 9am-5pm Mon.-Fri., 9am-4pm Sat. Oct. 1-Apr. 30; free) lets visitors stroll through a variety of gardens filled with primarily native plants. A real highlight here is the children's garden, with colorful and interactive sculptures. Check the website for upcoming events and programs like yoga in the garden, summer tours, and farm-to-table garden dinners.

★ OLD TOWN

If you like Disneyland's Main Street, U.S.A., then you are going to love Fort Collins—the theme park attraction was modeled on its downtown. The **Old Town** (www.downtownfortcollins.com) district contains 23 historic

Public Art

The Fort Collins **Art in Public Places Program** (417 Magnolia Ave., 970/221-6735, www.fcgov.com/artspublic) turns ordinary objects into art. Through innovative programs like "pedestrian pavers" and "transformer cabinet murals," local artists are creating works of art throughout town. These public art sculptures are on display at the Colorado State University campus and around Old Town. Visit the website for a map of the artwork so you can take a self-guided tour—or just take your chances and hope to spy some while you are out and about.

buildings, and it's bisected by broad and well-landscaped College Avenue, with public art and fountains arrayed alongside restaurant patios. Shops, galleries, a hotel, a museum, and brewpubs can all be found here. Wait, what was that about restaurants? Yes, there are more than 80 restaurants in this historic district. Old Town was listed in the National Register of Historic Places in 1978 and named a Preserve America city in 2005.

SWETSVILLE ZOO

Swetsville Zoo (4801 E. Harmony Rd., 970/484-9509, free) is not really a zoo; it's more like a collection of rusted folk art or a whimsical sculpture park. It's the culmination of one man's dream: Bill Swets built more than 150 "animals" out of old metal parts, including dinosaurs, bugs, and other things that defy categorization. Kids will be enchanted by this place.

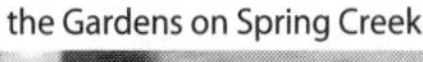
the Gardens on Spring Creek

More than a Brew Tour

Fort Collins is proud to be Colorado's largest producer of beer. The city has come a long way since 1969, when it repealed prohibition. Every brewery has its own claim to fame—the first microbrewery, the biggest, the most sustainable and eco-friendly, and other bragging rights. If you stop by for a pint, choose from this short list of creative possibilities.

Anheuser-Busch Tour Center (2351 Busch Dr., 970/490-4691, www.budweisertours.com, 11am-6pm Mon.-Sat., 11am-4pm Sun. Oct.-Feb.; 10am-6pm Mon.-Sat., 11am-4pm Sun. Mar-Sept.). Take a tour of this Budweiser plant when the Clydesdale horses are on the premises.

Beer & Bike Tours (2451 Stanley Ct., 970/201-1085, www.beerandbiketours.com, from $50). Drinking and riding can be a thing when you choose from several tours that stop at various breweries around town.

Magic Bus Tours (701 Aztec, 970/420-0662, www.themagicbustours.com, reservations required, $39-55). Hop on a Magic Bus and be driven from one brewery to the next where you will get a tour of behind-the-scenes alecraft.

Foam on the Range Tour (Fort Collins Convention and Visitors Bureau, www.visitftcollins.com). Go it alone with this self-guided tour, a combination of driving (early on in the tour) and walking around Old Town.

Fort Collins Brewery (1020 E. Lincoln Ave., 970/472-1499, http://fortcollinsbrewery.com, Thurs.-Sun. noon-5pm). Earn that drink by participating in a power yoga class before you throw back a cold one. Or just come for a traditional tour of the beermaking facilities.

New Belgium Brewery (www.newbelgium.com, 11am-8pm Tues.-Sat., reservations recommended). This massive facility is massively popular; their Fat Tire Amber Ale is just the foam on the top of a full mug of offerings. Tours run every half hour, from 11:30am until 4:30pm, and include storytelling, souvenirs, and sipping samples.

Entertainment and Events

Fort Collins has a college town vibe, evident at many of the downtown bars and at annual local festivals that emphasize beer. However, there is also a celebration of local music at both festivals and clubs. With a symphony orchestra, a professional dance company, and an opera, this town has a cultivated arts scene that appeals to many different audiences.

NIGHTLIFE

If you're staying in Old Town—and better yet, at the Armstrong Hotel—check out **Ace Gillett's Lounge** (239 S. College Ave., 970/449-4797, www.acegilletts.com, 4pm-2am Mon.-Sat., 4pm-midnight Sun.). Located under the Armstrong, there is music four nights a week, as well as fine dining and cocktails every night.

Elliot's Martini Bar (234 Linden St., 970/472-9802, http://www.elliotsmartini.com, 4:30pm-2am Mon.-Sat., 8pm-2am Sun.) offers a seasonally changing menu of classic and original martinis, including "dessertinis." Order a Mikhail's Cousin is in Town, one of the bar's creative martinis, or opt for a Naked in the Woods dessertini.

You've got to love the name of this place: **The Mayor of Old Town** (632 S. Mason St., 970/682-2410, http://themayorofoldtown.com, 11am-midnight daily) is where you can enjoy a pint, a bite to eat, and some live music any night of the week. Come on a Friday for stuffed pretzels and a flight of beer.

For those of you saying "Enough with the beer already!" there is an alternative—craft ciders. **Compass Cider Lounge** (216 N. College Ave., 970/372-1350, www.compasscider.com, 4pm-10pm Tues.-Thurs., noon-10pm Fri.-Sat., noon-7pm Sun.) began with the planting of an orchard on Colorado's Western Slope; it then took five years for the trees to mature and grow the fruit necessary for making cider. Today, you can enjoy this cider version of a craft brewery, which offers unique and seasonal flavors, tastings, and food pairings.

Social (1 Old Town Sq., 970/449-5606, www.socialfortcollins.com, 4pm-midnight Sun.-Wed., 4pm-1am Thurs.-Sat.) is the place for properly crafted cocktails, sommelier-selected wines, and charcuterie. Located underneath a shop at the entrance to Old Town Square, Social is designed with a soft yet modern industrial decor that keeps the focus on what they do best—quality food and drinks. Though there isn't a dress code, it tends toward a business-casual or cocktail attire kind of vibe.

The **Forge Publick House** (232 Walnut St., 970/682-2578, 4pm-midnight Mon.-Sat., 2pm-10pm Sun.) is the antithesis of some of the well-known craft mega-breweries in town. Off the beaten path, with an entrance in an alley, this one-room pub feels like a cozy den that is more like a typical bar. The dark wood, artwork, and lighting give it an Old World feel. Live music adds to the appeal, along with quality beer from all over (not just local breweries).

For something different from the bar and music scene, the **Lyric Cinema Café** (300 E. Mountain Ave., 970/493-0893, http://lyriccinemacafe.com, check showtimes) offers an alternative to the multiplex. This twin theater shows independent or foreign movies during the afternoon and evening, then shows free classic cartoons on Saturdays in summer. They serve beer, wine, and snacks, including a cereal bar during the cartoons.

Blue Skies Winery (251 Jefferson St., 970/407-9463, www.blueskieswinery.com, 1pm-6pm Mon., noon-8pm Wed.-Thurs., 1pm-9pm Fri.-Sat., noon-6pm Sun.) is part of the craft scene, but serves wine made on-site. They specialize in tastings.

For comedy, there is **Comedy Brewers** at Bas Bleu Theatre Company (401 Pine St., 970/498-8949, www.basbleau.org, one Sun. per month, check showtimes). There's often a beer theme ("comedy six-pack" and "improv group is at the top of their craft"), but it's still all about the laughs.

THE ARTS

The **Aggie Theatre** (204 S. College Ave., 970/482-8300, www.aggietheatre.com) is

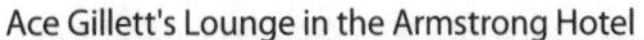

Ace Gillett's Lounge in the Armstrong Hotel

a tiny venue with big-name acts, such as Reverend Horton Heat and Blues Traveler. It's a college town crowd here.

The **Lincoln Center** (417 W. Magnolia St., 970/221-6730, http://lctix.com) is home to a 1,180-seat performance hall and a 220-seat theater, as well as three galleries and an outdoor performance space/sculpture garden. This is where you will see **Opera Fort Collins Guild** (www.operafortcollins.org) performances, including an annual Summer Soiree in the garden and some of the **Fort Collins Symphony Orchestra** (www.fcsymphony.org) concerts. (The symphony also performs a series of concerts called "Outside the Box," in which they perform at a variety of locales away from the center.) This is also where you will see performances by **Canyon Concert Ballet** (www.ccballet.org), which puts on *The Nutcracker* each December and another classic ballet each spring. **Open Stage Theatre & Company** (www.openstage.com) is an award-winning theater group that produces about six shows a year—everything from Shakespeare to *The Rocky Horror Picture Show*—that can be seen at the center. There are also performances by touring theater companies and dance, music, and comedy groups.

Just when you think it's all happening at Lincoln Center, you discover **The Midtown Arts Center** (3750 S. Mason St., 970/225-2555, https://midtownartscenter.com) and its three separate performance spaces, including a Broadway-style dinner theater. In addition to the dinner theater shows like *Oklahoma!* and *Sweeney Todd,* they also have an award-winning Young Audiences series with shows such as *The Cat in the Hat.*

Avogadro's Number (605 S. Mason St., 970/493-5555, www.avogadros.com) is a combination music venue, bar, and restaurant that is best known for bluegrass bands, but also hosts burlesque, folk rock, and other genres. A night at "Avo's" is considered by many to be a quintessential Fort Collins experience.

You'll need a car—or plan to take the shuttle bus—to get to **The Mishawaka Amphitheatre** (13714 Poudre Canyon, Bellevue, 970/482-4420, www.themishawaka.com), but it's worth the drive to sit under the stars and dance the night away while a band plays on the riverfront stage. The on-site restaurant serves Odell's beer along with burgers and other bites.

FESTIVAL AND EVENTS

First Friday Gallery Walk (http://downtownfortcollins.com, 6pm-9pm Fri.

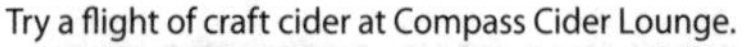
Try a flight of craft cider at Compass Cider Lounge.

year-round) is held on the first Friday of each month. Galleries serve drinks and snacks and are open later hours. Head downtown and start wandering from place to place, taking in the town's paintings, photographs, and sculptures.

Foodie Walk Fort Collins (http://downtownfortcollins.com, 5pm-8pm Fri.) offers an opportunity to nibble, walk, then nibble some more through specialty food shops such as Nuance Chocolate and the Welsh Rabbit Cheese Shop. Every third Friday of the month there is a different theme, along with presentations and of course, samples.

Spring

FoCoMX (http://focomx.focoma.org, Apr.) is about numbers: one weekend, more than 20 venues, and more than 200 bands. At the Fort Collins Music Experiment (FoCoMX, get it?), many local bands get a chance to win over new audiences as they rock out at places like the Aggie Theatre, Compass Cider, and the Fort Collins Museum of Discovery.

Each spring **Kites in the Park** (Spring Canyon Park, www.fcgov.com/recreation/kites.php, May) draws kite fliers and builders from around the world. Not only is it spectacular to watch so many kites flying in the breeze, but you can also make kites and compete in kite flying.

Lace up for the **Colorado Marathon** (www.thecoloradomarathon.com, early May) and enjoy the scenery. What's different about this run is that it is downhill. Begin the day early by shuttling up to the race start in Poudre Canyon. As the sun rises, descend more than 1,000 feet in elevation to end in Old Town in 26.2 miles. This is a Boston Marathon qualifying run and includes a 10K and 5K.

The **Larimer County Farmers Market** (200 S. Oak St., http://larimercountyfarmersmarket.colostate.edu, 8am-noon Sat. May-mid-Oct.) starts in late spring each year and includes only Colorado- and Wyoming-grown, raised, and made products. (Now that you're this far north, the Wyoming state line is pretty close.)

The **French Nest Open-Air Market** (Civic Center Park, www.thefrenchnestmarket.com, May-mid-Oct.) occurs every third Saturday from late May to mid-October. This is a great place for college students to pick up one-of-a-kind trinkets to furnish their new dorm room—from vintage and handmade housewares to other unique items.

the Aggie Theatre

Summer

If there isn't enough time to sample all the beers made in Fort Collins, you just might be able to squeeze it in during the **Colorado Brewers' Festival** (Laporte Ave. and Mason St., http://downtownfortcollins.com/events/colorado-brewers-festival, June, free). You can attend "Beer School" for tastings and demonstrations, listen to live music, eat great food, and of course, drink more beer.

The **Larimer County Fair & Rodeo** (www.larimercountryfair.org, July-Aug.) harkens back to the town's roots as an agricultural boomtown. The rodeo features roping, barrel racing, a horse show, and a lot of animals for the little ones to see (and smell, and hear too!), as well as carnival rides, food vendors, music, and an outdoor cinema night.

The **Bohemian Nights at NewWestFest** (www.boheminanights.org, Aug.) is a three-day free music festival held in Old Town. The emphasis is on the Colorado bands and musicians who play sets in between national headline acts like the Flobots.

Chances are that you can join a Tour de Fat celebration in a city near you, but this is where it started. **Tour de Fat** (Civic Center Park, www.newbelgium.com/events/tour-de-fat, Sept.) was created by the New Belgium Brewing Company to celebrate bike riding and to raise money through beer sales for nonprofit cycling clubs. This one-day event includes a parade of thousands of costumed people riding bikes through town.

Fall

At the **Fort Collins Fall Fest** (720/272-7467, http://coloradoevents.net, Oct.), local artists set up shop in the pedestrian-friendly outdoor area of Old Town to sell their wares. You can meet with them and ask about their handmade goods. Live music, food vendors, and beautiful fall weather make it a perfect way to spend a weekend.

Every season is beer season. Check out the **Fall Harvest Brewfest** (http://www.fallharvestbrewfest.com, Sept., $38-55) at the Lincoln Center on the first Friday in September. The event not only includes live music and the chance to sample hundreds of brews, but proceeds benefit a local animal rescue.

Winter

Come December you can celebrate with the **Downtown Festival of Lights** (www.visitfortcollins.com, Dec.) or the **Garden of Lights** (www.fcgov.com/gardens, Dec.). The Festival of Lights is spread out around the plazas and streets of Old Town and offers traditional Christmas displays. The Garden of Lights is held at the Gardens on Spring Creek (2145 Centre Ave.), with lights draped on plants and funny sculptures.

Cannabis Dispensaries

Marijuana dispensaries have popped up like weeds since it became legal to buy marijuana in Colorado. As a college town, Fort Collins has its fair share of dispensaries to choose from.

Choice Organics (813 Smithfield Dr., Unit B, 970/472-6337, www.choiceorganicsinc.com, 10am-8pm Mon.-Fri., 10am-6pm Sat., 10am-5pm Sun.) prides itself on being first—the first Colorado dispensary to be licensed by the state in 2011 and the first retail cannabis store to open in Larimer County. The operation's longevity is evident thanks to its experienced budtenders and impressive selection of strains. Located just off the highway a few miles from downtown, Choice Organics is perfectly situated for a pre-road trip pit stop, especially since there's ample parking for RVs, trucks, and trailers.

Across the street from the Colorado State University campus is **Elite Organics** (804 S. College Ave., 970/214-9889, 9am-6:50pm

Trimble Court Artisans

Mon.-Sat., 10am-6pm Sun.), a hole-in-the-wall spot on the back side of Rock N' Robin's Smoke Shop (which doubles as Elite Organics' waiting room). Though it can be hard to find, it's worth the effort. Fans rave about the personal, homey vibe and all-natural flower.

Flower Power Botanicals (1310 Duff Dr., 970/672-8165, www.flowerpowerbotanicals.com, 8:15am-6:45pm daily) hints to its success in the name. Located in a strip mall east of downtown, Flower Power won't be winning any aesthetic points for its sparse, industrial ambience, but those in the know swear it boasts some of the most powerful buds available anywhere.

Spacious and welcoming, **Infinite Wellness Center** (900 N. College Ave., 970/484-8380, www.iwc8.com, 10am-6:50pm Mon.-Sat., 10am-6pm Sun.) is located north of downtown and is known for its ample selection, competitive prices, and fun games like Trivia Friday (answer a pot-related quiz question correctly and you score a free joint).

Centrally located in Old Town Fort Collins, **Organic Alternatives** (346 E. Mountain Ave., 970/482-7100, www.organicalternatives.com, 10am-7pm Mon.-Sat., 11am-6pm Sun.) is about ambience and quality. The hardwood bar and ornate display shelves, salvaged from a former area music hall, make this swanky shop resemble a historic pharmacy. But the goods for sale are all cutting edge: top-shelf bud, edibles, concentrates, and everything in between.

South Fort Collins's lone retail pot shop, **Solace Meds** (301 Smokey St., 970/225-6337, www.solacemeds.com, 9am-6:55pm Mon.-Fri., 10am-6pm Sat.-Sun.) prides itself on a huge selection of edibles, including its signature drinks: Canna Cappuccinos and Chai High Teas ("Colorado's Strongest Tea").

Shopping

The shops in Old Town are a fun mix of outdoor gear, hipster favorites, and local crafts. A handful of shops also have locations in Denver.

ART GALLERIES

The **Center for Fine Art Photography** (400 N. College Ave., 970/224-1010, www.c4fap.org, 10am-6pm Tues.-Fri., 11am-5pm Sat.) is a real gem in the local arts scene, focused entirely on the art of photography. In addition to the changing exhibitions, there are photography workshops and portfolio reviews, and they participate in the regular First Friday Art Walk. Exhibits here might include local artists as well as international photographers.

Yes, it appears there are a lot of tchotchkes at **Trimble Court Artisans** (118 Trimble Ct., 970/221-0051, www.trimblecourt.com, 10am-8pm Mon.-Sat., noon-6pm, Sun.), but they are the wares of local artists and craftspeople. The shop is filled to the brim with pottery, photography, paintings, and all kinds of knickknacks for the home.

The **Downtown Artery** (252 Linden St., 970/682-2668, www.downtownartery.com, 10am-6pm daily) is a combination gallery, music performance space, and cafe. With an attached living space for visiting artists, you just might meet a band member or visual artist while touring the space.

BOOKSTORES

Old Firehouse Books (232 Walnut St., 970/484-7898, www.oldfirehousebooks.com, 9am-8pm Mon.-Thurs., 9am-9pm Fri.-Sat., 9am-6pm Sun.) is a classic independent local bookstore with a rich selection of books for adults and kids with events to match. Come for story time on Tuesday morning, or plan to attend an author book signing and reading.

Bizarre Bazaar Books & Music (1014 S. College Ave., 970/484-1699, www.fortcollinsbazaar.com, 10am-8pm Sun.-Wed., 10am-9pm Thurs.-Sat.) is not just a bookstore; you can buy used hardbacks, paperbacks, and comic books, and even sheet music, posters, and magazines. If it's old school (VHS tapes, vinyl albums), you might find it or be able to sell it here. See if they're interested, and look for that hard-to-find item you've been searching for.

CLOTHING

Fashion lovers should stop by **Kansas City Kitty** (136 N. College Ave, 970/482-5845, www.kckitty.com, 11am-6pm Mon.-Fri., 11am-7pm Sat., noon-5pm Sun.). They carry everything from Japanese denim brand One Green Elephant to local designers and Kansas City Kitty's own line. **Cira Ltd.** (21 Old Town Square, 970/494-0410, 10am-8pm Mon.-Thurs., 10am-9pm Fri.-Sat., 11am-7pm Sun.) sells fashions that appeal to college-age women who like to dress up on weekends in something sheer and slinky. **Solemates** (172 N. College Ave., 970/472-1460, http://solematesinc.com, 10am-7pm Mon.-Sat., noon-5pm Sun.) has shoe lovers covered. Come here for the latest in heels, wedges, sandals, and boots from designers such as Kate Spade, Michael Kors, Frye, Diane von Furstenberg, and more. Of course, the perfect shoes need a matching handbag; fortunately Solemates also sells accessories.

CHILDREN'S TOYS AND CLOTHING

Even if you don't have kids, it's tempting to wander through **Clothes Pony and Dandelion Toys** (111 N. College Ave., 970/224-2866, www.clothespony.com, 9:30am-8pm Mon.-Thurs., 9:30am-9pm Fri.-Sat., 11am-5pm Sun.). The store is filled with the most adorable onesies, jammies, diaper bags, and stuffed animals plus so very much more. Familiar brands include Tea Collection, Brio, Petunia Pickle Bottom, and Toms.

Science Toy Magic (11 Old Town Sq., 970/484-2377, 10am-6pm Wed.-Sat.) is a teeny space with big ideas. The owner practically puts on a show as he demonstrates how these toys spin, fly, juggle, and delight young children.

OUTDOOR GEAR

Yes, there is an REI and the usual outdoor gear retailers at which to get your tent, sleeping bag, fishing rod, and more, but locals know to go to **Jax Mercantile** (1200 N. College Ave., 970/221-0544, www.jaxmercantile.com, 8am-9pm Mon.-Fri., 8am-8pm Sat., 9am-6pm Sun.), which also has gear for ranching and hunting, not just camping and recreating. The store is locally owned and has multiple locations in the greater Fort Collins and Boulder areas.

Gearage Outdoor Sports (119 E. Mountain Ave., 970/416-6803, http://gearageoutdoorsports.com, 11am-6pm Mon., 1pm-6:30pm Tues.-Fri., 10am-7pm Sat., 11am-5pm Sun.) is your affordable place for new and used outdoor gear, bike repairs, and bike rentals. The knowledgeable and friendly staff make it even more appealing.

Khumbu Adventure Gear (109 S.

Nuance Chocolate

College Ave., 970/530-3321, http://khumbuadventuregear.com, 10am-6pm Mon.-Thurs., 10am-7pm Fri.-Sat., 11am-6pm Sun.) sells men's, women's, and kids' sportswear designed in Colorado and Nepal; many items are hand-knit in Nepal.

SPECIALTY FOODS

The Cupboard (152 S. College Ave., 970/493-8585, http://thecupboard.net, 9:30am-8pm Mon.-Fri., 9:30am-6pm Sat., noon-5pm Sun.) is a large kitchen supply shop where you can sign up for cooking lessons with local chefs.

Nuance Chocolate (214 Pine St., 970/484-2330, www.nuancechocolate.com, 11am-7pm Mon.-Thurs., 11am-8pm Fri., 10am-8pm Sat., noon-4pm Sun.) is the chocoholic's answer to craft food. During pairing events you can learn what goes into making one delectable little truffle, eat chocolate, or sip a mug of hot chocolate. Everything is made from scratch in-house.

The **Welsh Rabbit Cheese Shop** (216 Pine St., 970/443-4027, www.thewelshrabbit.com, 10am-6pm Mon-Thurs., 10am-8pm Fri.-Sat.) is a cheese lover's paradise—locally made, flown in from Europe, just so long as it's cheese. Other kitchen staples sold here include mustard, preserves, butter, and more. Order a gift of cheese or walk around the corner and settle in for a meal at the Welsh Rabbit Cheese Bistro.

Sports and Recreation

You can enjoy Fort Collins by going for a bike ride or walk, or opt for a short drive into the foothills or to a local reservoir for wildflower hikes or boating. Horsetooth Reservoir, just outside of Fort Collins, provides boating activities, while the Cache La Poudre River makes this area a destination for whitewater rafting.

BALLOONING

Float high above the Poudre Canyon and Fort Collins in a hot-air balloon with **Flights of Fancy** (970/581-5042, www.flightsoffancyllc.com, $230 per person, year-round weather depending). Each balloon ride is appropriate for groups up to four, but a second balloon is available if there are more in your party. Reservations are required.

★ BIKING

Fort Collins proudly took the silver in a *USA Today* 2014 poll of the best cycling cities. The city has a 310-mile network of paths and bike lanes and a bike share program; in the nearby foothills of the Rocky Mountains are more miles of biking trails, or cyclists can head east for trails on the plains. Whether you are a mountain biker or a road cyclist, there is a path that will appeal to you.

Spring Creek Trail (www.fcgov.com/

parks/trails.php) offers seven miles of paved trail on relatively flat terrain that traverses the city from east to west. Start at the Poudre River Trail (near East Prospect Rd.) and ride west to Spring Canyon Park (2626 W. Horsetooth Rd.). This popular trail goes through the city, so you can lock up your bike and stop for lunch before you turn around. In spring, be mindful of runoff on this trail.

The **Poudre Trail** (www.fcgov.com/parks/trails/php) is currently 10 miles long, but there are plans to extend it. The trail follows the Cache La Poudre River, with one end at Lyons Park and the other at the Environmental Learning Center on the CSU campus. The trail travels from wooded areas to industrial areas. In spring, this path can become flooded and there might be detours.

Fossil Creek Trail (5381 South Shields St. and Luther Ln., www.fcgov.com/parks/trails/php), southwest of town, offers a paved riding experience for five miles between the Cathy Fromme Prairie Natural Area and Spring Canyon Park (2626 W. Horsetooth Rd.).

Mountain Biking

Mountain bikers will surely prefer to get off the paved trails and over to **Lory State Park** (708 Lodgepole Dr., Bellevue, 970/493-1623, http://cpw.state.co.us, $3-7 daily). The **Corral Center Mountain Bike Park** (http://cpw.state.co.us) is a rare dirt jump/pump track within the state park; this former horse corral has miles of trails in a 70,000-square-foot bike park suitable for both beginner and advanced riders. The **Mill Creek Link Trail** is a mixed-use dirt trail in Lory State Park; though it is less than one mile long, it is considered difficult. It links to a similar trail called Mill Creek in the **Horsetooth Mountain Open Space** (County Rd. 38E, http://www.co.larimer.co.us, open year-round), four miles west of Fort Collins.

To reach Lory State Park from Fort Collins, take Highway 287/College Avenue north to Road 54G. Make a left on Rist Canyon Road and turn left again on N. County Road 23.

the Welsh Rabbit Cheese Shop

After making a right on County Road 25G/Lodgepole Drive, look ahead for parking.

Soapstone Prairie Natural Area (Rawhide Flats Rd., http://www.fcgov.com/naturalareas/finder/soapstone, dawn-dusk Mar.-Nov.) is worth the trip thanks to its 28 square miles of prairie to explore. The Cheyenne Rim Trail, a shared-use single track, is the longest of the trails at nearly 12 miles. It's pretty, with views of the wide horizon and the sounds of native birds.

Soapstone Prairie Natural Area is 25 miles north of Fort Collins. Take I-25 north to Buckeye Road (exit 288) and turn left (west) to follow County Road 15. Drive north on County Road 15 and then onto Rawhide Flats Road to the entrance station.

Bike Rentals and Tours

If you need a bike to ride around town, start with the **Fort Collins Bike Library** (250 N. Mason St., 970/419-1050, www.fcbikelibrary.org, hours vary seasonally, $10). Better yet, have a local give you a tour with **Front Range**

Oh, the Things You Can Do...on Bikes

Just riding bikes isn't enough in this town. There is also the ongoing celebration of all things bike.

Bike-In Cinema is held every summer on the front lawn at New Belgium Brewing (500 Linden St.), with bikes, brews, and films shown outdoors. At **Bikes-n-Ales** (http://bikefortcollins.org, July, $20), you can ride around and drink beer at participating brewpubs on a beautiful summer weekend.

Many of these events serve as fundraisers for **Bike Fort Collins** (http://bikefortcollins.org), a nonprofit that supports bicycle education and safety. They also advocate making Fort Collins a place that welcomes cycles on paths and roads.

Guides (Canby Way, 720/208-0152, www.frontrangerideguides.com, $159-219), where you can choose between half- or full-day tours that include bike rental, helmet, snacks or lunch, expert guide, and transportation to and from the trailhead.

Leisurely Pedaling (374 Cajetan St., 970/420-5603, http://leisurelypedaling.com, $77) offers full-day and multiday tour options (bicycle, helmet, and other gear included) in and around Fort Collins and beyond.

Recycled Cycles (4031-A S. Mason St., 970/223-1969, www.recycled-cycles.com, 9am-6pm Mon.-Sat., 10am-6pm Sun., $20-25 per day) rents bikes and sells reconditioned bikes (at discounted prices); they can service your bike here, too. A second location in the Lory Student Center (451 Isotope Dr., 970/491-9555, 9am-5pm Mon.-Fri.) on the CSU campus has different hours and inventory, but the same concept.

BIRD-WATCHING

With more than 44 protected natural areas covering at least 41,000 acres around Fort Collins, the region offers some hot spots for birders. **Soapstone Prairie Natural Area** (Rawhide Flats Rd., http://www.fcgov.com/naturalareas/finder/soapstone, dawn-dusk Mar.-Nov.) is one of the best areas. At this site 25 miles outside Fort Collins, more than 130 bird species have been spotted including Northern goshawks, white-tailed ptarmigans, mountain bluebirds, Western tanagers, sandhill cranes,

Soapstone Prairie Natural Area

and burrowing owls. Take I-25 north from Fort Collins to Buckeye Road (exit 288) and turn left (west) to follow County Road 15. Drive north on County Road 15 and then onto Rawhide Flats Road to the entrance station.

The **Fort Collins Audubon Society** (http://www.fortcollinsaudubon.org) offers free birding field trips throughout the year. The Nature Conservancy's 1,700-acre **Phantom Canyon Preserve** (www.nature.org), located 30 miles northwest of Fort Collins, is home to more than 100 species. The preserve is open to the public through Nature Conservancy guided hikes and volunteer outings, which include birding hikes.

The **Environmental Learning Center** (2400 S. County Rd. 9, 970/491-1661, www.csuelc.org) on the CSU campus is an ideal setting for owls, hawks, and a variety of waterfowl and songbirds.

BOATING

It's been said that the only thing missing from Colorado is a beach (or an ocean); the local solution to this problem is **Horsetooth Reservoir** (County Rd. 38E, www.co.larimer.co.us/parks/horsetooth.cfm, $7) west of Fort Collins. This 6.5-mile-long body of water is open to all kinds of water sports activities—water-skiing is very popular, Jet Skis are permitted, and there is a swimming beach. The reservoir is surrounded by public lands offering hiking opportunities.

Horsetooth Reservoir is less than 10 miles from Fort Collins (about a 15-minute drive). From the intersection of Harmony and Taft Hill Roads, drive west onto County Road 38 to the entrance.

CLIMBING

Rock climbing and its close cousin, bouldering, are available in the Fort Collins area. The best source for information is **Northern Colorado Climbers Coalition** (http://nococlimbing.com), a local nonprofit that sells books exclusively about rock climbing in the area and organizes rock climbing meet-ups and events.

Lory State Park (708 Lodgepole Dr., Bellevue, 970/493-1623, http://cpw.state.co.us, $3-7 daily) is your best bet for rock climbing, particularly on and near Arthur's Rock. There are bolted routes, so this does require some gear and technical knowledge. Park fees apply when inside the state park.

FISHING

There are plenty of fishing holes in and near Fort Collins, for all skill levels. Anglers can fish in designated natural areas in ponds, rivers, reservoirs, and creeks. Start by visiting the **City of Fort Collins** (www.fcgov.com/naturalareas/fishing.php) website for a list of areas, the fish stocked in each, and details on access. Depending on where you go, you might catch largemouth bass, yellow perch, common carp, or bluegill.

Horsetooth Reservoir (County Rd. 38E, www.co.larimer.co.us/parks/horsetooth.cfm, $7), managed by Larimer County Parks Department, posts the latest fishing conditions on their website. Shoreline fishing and boat fishing are allowed. There are daily limits on the number of different types of fish that can be taken. The reservoir is stocked with rainbow and brown trout, walleye, smallmouth and largemouth bass, and a variety of panfish such as bluegill.

If you need to buy bait, get some friendly local advice, take a class, or hire a guide, visit **St. Peter's Fly Shop** (202 Remington St., 970/498-8968, 9am-6pm Mon.-Sat. Apr.-Sept., 10am-6pm Mon.-Sat. Oct.-Mar.; 2008 E. Harmony Rd., 970/377-3785, 9am-6pm Mon.-Sat., 10am-4pm Sun. Apr.-Sept., 10am-6pm Tues.-Sat., 10am-4pm Sun. Oct.-Mar.; www.stpetes.com), with two locations in Fort Collins. You'll find all the fishing gear you need and can opt for a half day or full day of guided angling.

GOLF

Fort Collins doesn't have quite the attraction for golfers that Colorado Springs does, but there are some beautiful and challenging courses with good mountain views. The

City of Fort Collins operates three public golf courses: City Park Nine, Collindale, and Southridge. There are also public golf courses not operated by the city.

City Park Nine (411 S. Bryan Ave., 970/221-6650, www.fcgov.com/golf, $15-35) is a nine-hole par 36 course that has been here since 1940. The earliest tee times are 6:30am (mid-Apr.-mid-Sept.) and 9am (fall-winter).

Situated on 160 acres, **Collindale Golf Course** (1441 E. Horsetooth Rd., 970/221-6651, www.fcgov.com/golf/collindale.php, $15-37) is an 18-hole par 71 championship-length golf course that hosts the local U.S. Open qualifying every year.

Southridge Golf Course (5750 S. Lemay Ave., 970/416-2828, www.fcgov.com/golf/southridge, $15-37) is an 18-hole course on 128 acres. It has scenic views, is suitable for all skill levels, and is considered a great value for the quality of course.

HIKING

There are many opportunities for head-clearing nature walks in the foothills near Fort Collins. A favorite local hiking trail is **Greyrock Mountain Trail** (http://www.fs.usda.gov, 7 miles round-trip, moderate-strenuous), which is about a 20-mile drive outside of town in the Poudre Canyon. Get there early because this popular trail's parking lot fills up fast. To reach the trailhead, drive 11 miles northwest on Highway 287 then turn left on Highway 14. Continue 9 more miles to the parking lot.

Horsetooth Mountain Open Space (http://www.co.larimer.co.us) is not far from town, with popular hikes of moderate intensity and beautiful views.

There are a dozen hiking trails (some mixed use, others pedestrian only) in **Lory State Park** (http://cpw.state.co.us). My favorite is the hiker-only **Arthur's Rock Trail** (1.7 miles), which includes wildflowers in spring, a small waterfall, and a gurgling creek along part of the path. Oh, and there is a great view of Horsetooth Reservoir when you reach the summit.

The **Soapstone Prairie Natural Area** (http://www.fcgov.com) is a relatively new recreation option. Part archeological site, bison were recently reintroduced here. The **Lindenmeier Overlook** (0.25 mile) is a very short paved trail with benches and interpretive signs, making this a good introductory hike for young children.

HORSEBACK RIDING

With so many mixed-use trails on the prairie, in the foothills, or creekside, all you need is a horse and you can gallop away. **Beaver Meadow Stables** (100 Marmot Dr., Red Feather Lakes, 970/232-8326 or 970/231-1955, http://beavermeadowstables.com, Memorial Day through early fall, $39-99) has everything from one-hour rides for the young'uns to full-day rides or even overnight trips. Rides are in the Roosevelt National Forest, about 30 minutes from Fort Collins.

Red Feather Lakes is less than one-hour from Fort Collins. Take Highway 287 north for 21 miles to Livermore then left onto County Road 74E/Red Feather Lakes Road. Drive 24 miles until reaching Red Feather Lakes. Follow the road as it bends north and becomes Creedmore Lakes Road/County Road 73C; the road becomes a dirt road after one mile. Drive 3.3 miles to the Beaver Meadows Ranch entryway.

Shiloh Guest Ranch (2720 Stove Prairie Rd., Bellevue, 970/295-4557, http://shiloh-guestranch.com), near Horsetooth Reservoir, offers hourly trail rides that go up into the mountains or out into rolling foothills amid wide-open vistas and beautiful scenery.

RIVER RAFTING

White-water river rafting is a blast, and the Cache La Poudre (the only waterway in the state that is a federally designated Wild and Scenic River) has everything from Class I to Class IV rapids. It's served by plenty of experienced commercial outfitters who can take you on a wild ride.

Mountain Whitewater Descents (1329 N. Hwy. 287, 970/419-0917, www.raftmwd.

com, hours vary seasonally) has a variety of options, including renting your own kayaks and canoes ($30-50 per day). Select your raft trip based on how fun (or scary) you want it to be. Raft trips ($55-295 per person) include a variety of rapids classes with enticing names like "Splash" and "Plunge" that give you an idea of what to expect.

A Wanderlust Adventure (4120 W. County Rd. 54G, LaPorte, 800/745-7238 or 970/482-1995, www.awanderlustadventure.com, spring and summer, $55-69 per person) offers two options for raft trips: "Taste of Whitewater" (beginner) and "Blast of Whitewater" (advanced). Either way, you're getting soaked.

Accommodations

There are plenty of chain hotels in Fort Collins, many of which are located close to I-25. For non-chain lodging, the most appealing options are found in and around Old Town; these have some historic characteristics and are in walkable communities.

In addition to the accommodations listed that allow smoking marijuana on the premises, you can find more **marijuana-friendly rental properties** (www.coloradopotguide.com/marijuana-friendly-hotels) in the Fort Collins area.

UNDER $100

Step into the ★ **Solarium International Hostel** (706 Stuart St., 970/599-3817, www.hostelfortcollins.com, $29-69) and you will no longer feel like you are in Fort Collins. The bright colors in the rooms and the abundant greenery outside resemble south Florida or a Caribbean island. The budget-friendly options include traditional hostel shared rooms, private rooms, and a communal (bright green!) kitchen. You can rent bikes and there is access to Spring Creek Trail right out the back door. All six rooms wrap around a courtyard filled with perhaps the only fig trees and rubber trees in Colorado.

The **Fernweh Inn & Hostel** (616 W. Mulberry St., 970/219-9493, www.fortcollinshostel.com, $29-59) is a cheery old house that has been converted into very affordable accommodations. Choose from a ladies-only shared bunk room, a coed bunk room, or two private rooms, or simply rent the whole house ($299 per night). Guests have 24-hour access to a communal kitchen, receive free parking, and are welcome to borrow a bike.

$100-250

Once the tallest building in Fort Collins, the ★ **Armstrong Hotel** (259 S. College Ave., 970/484-3883, www.thearmstronghotel.com, $129-220) has been renovated into a hip and historic lodging option in Old Town. The hotel's 43 rooms and suites have an eclectic mix of vintage and modern furnishings, set off by bright colors on the walls and in other accents. The central location makes it easy to walk to shops, restaurants, and the campus. Don't miss **Gillett's Lounge,** the underground bar at the hotel, where you can sip cocktails and listen to a little jazz music in the evening.

The **Edwards House Bed & Breakfast** (402 W. Mountain Ave., 970/493-9191, http://edwardshouse.com, $99-175) has eight rooms named after people who were significant to the history of Fort Collins. The updated decor reflects a more contemporary feel than the home's 1904 origins, but it's very comfortable, clean, and welcoming. The location—an easy walk to Old Town's amenities—can't be beat.

The **Best Western University Inn** (914 S. College Ave., 970/484-2984, www.bestwestern.com, $120-240) is in a prime place for those in town to attend a function on the CSU campus. Guests have access to an indoor pool and fitness center and receive complimentary daily breakfast.

The **Hilton Fort Collins** (425 W. Prospect

Rd., 970/482-2626, www.hilton.com, $189-285) has more than 200 rooms and suites, many of which have a terrific view of the Rocky Mountains. There is a pool, fitness center, and restaurant on-site for guests. This hotel can be fun for families, but it also serves business travelers who need conference rooms, AV equipment, and printing services.

IN THE VICINITY

The ★ **Inn at Whiskey Belle Ranch** (2030 Cherokee Park Rd., Livermore, 970/482-0248, http://whiskeybelleranch.com, $150-195) is a working cattle ranch located 22 miles northwest of Fort Collins. Guests can experience a "true Western experience" by joining a cattle drive, fly fishing, or going on a trail ride. It's part dude ranch, part bed-and-breakfast, and all appropriately elegant in a cattle ranch sort of way.

The Western feel can also be found 30 miles south at the **Sylvan Dale Guest Ranch** (2939 N. County Rd. 31D, Loveland, 877/667-3999 or 970/667-3915, www.sylvandale.com, $138-468). These comfy cabins are suitable for a romantic weekend or a family gathering. Guests also can use the outdoor heated pool (summer only), tennis courts, and game room. Check their calendar for activities like the annual Native American week, cattle drive, cowgirl week, and more.

420 Hotels

The guest cottage at **The Shangri-la Inn at Gaia's Farm and Gardens** (4328 W County Road 54G, Laporte, 970/817-2186, www.gaiascsa.com, $130-150) is on a three-acre sustainable permaculture farm about six miles northwest of Fort Collins. Enjoy meeting the farm animals and exploring nature trails. Their celebrated breakfast features farm-fresh eggs and other locally produced delicacies. The cottage is marijuana-friendly, as is the accompanying hot tub room and private garden area.

About 30 miles south of Fort Collins is the **Stoney River Lodge** (80 Idlewild Ln., Loveland, 970/663-5532, www.stoneyriverlodgecolorado.com, $89-160). Stoney River's rustic cabins are located along the Big Thompson River midway between Loveland and Estes Park. A stay here will make you feel like you're back at summer camp, complete with barbecues, campfire sing-alongs, and outdoor lawn games. Marijuana use is permitted in designated outdoor areas.

Food

Many of the town's craft breweries double as restaurants serving both beer and food, and most restaurants will have a local brew on tap. Many Front Range eateries have expanded here, so you might find yourself at the Fort Collins version of a Boulder or Denver establishment.

COFFEE AND TEA

In a town where many successful business owners have made their name with craft beer, it seems only natural for someone to fill the niche of craft coffee. Dedicated to that experience, **Harbinger Coffee** (505 S. Mason St., 847/274-2253, www.harbingercoffee.com, 7am-7pm Mon. and Wed.-Sat., 8am-6pm Sun.) showcases some of the finest coffees from around the world and from fantastic roasters across the United States. They also serve tea, hot cocoa, and other beverages.

The owners at **Mugs Coffee Lounge** (261 S. College Ave., 970/472-6847, www.mugscoffeelounge.com, 6am-9pm daily) want you to have an experience, not just a cup of joe to start your day. The concept is "community through coffee," and that happens in a few ways: sourcing and growing local ingredients and providing a free community space for meetings and gatherings. A full menu makes this your complete stop for breakfast or a hearty snack later in the day. There is another location, **Mugs @ the Oval** (306 W. Laurel St., 970/449-2265, 6am-10pm Mon.-Thurs., 6am-6pm Fri., 7am-6pm Sat., 7am-10pm Sun.) by the CSU campus.

The **Bean Cycle** (144 N. College Ave., 970/221-2964, www.beancycleroasters.com, 7am-9pm Mon.-Thurs., 7am-10pm Fri.-Sat., 7am-8pm Sun.) is a local favorite for lattes, espresso, and, of course, coffee. They emphasize locally sourced ingredients whenever possible. The coffee shop is part of **Wolverine Farm Bookstore** (970/472-4284, www.wolverinefarm.org, 9am-9pm Mon.-Thurs., 9am-10pm Fri.-Sat., 9am-8pm Sun.), a volunteer-run nonprofit that invites local authors to consign their books for sale.

The Bean Cycle is both coffee shop and bookstore.

BREAKFAST

The **Silver Grill Café** (218 Walnut St., 970/484-4656, www.silvergrill.com, 6:30am-2pm daily, $4-9) is a local favorite for hearty and affordable breakfasts that start with giant cinnamon rolls. Also on the menu are omelets, breakfast burritos, steak and eggs, biscuits and gravy, and more.

★ **Café Bluebird** (524 W. Laurel St., 970/484-7755, www.cafebluebird.com, 6:30am-2pm Mon.-Fri., 7am-2pm Sat.-Sun., $10-12) might have a line out front for a weekend brunch, but it's worth the wait if you're hungry for one of their signature skillets. Kids will like the Mickey Mouse pancakes, even if most of the "kids" here are college students. Located close to the CSU campus, this place is popular with those who attend, work, and live at the school.

AMERICAN

★ **The Kitchen Fort Collins** (100 N. College Ave., 970/568-8869, http://thekitchen.com/the-kitchen-fort-collins, 11am-9pm Mon.-Thurs., 11am-9pm Fri., 9am-2pm and 5pm-10pm Sat., 9am-2pm and 5pm-9pm Sun., $6-38), located in Old Town, highlights ingredients sourced from local farms and ranches. As at The Kitchen's other locations in Denver or Boulder, the atmosphere and service reflect the philosophy of community through food.

Big Al's Burgers and Dogs (140 W. Mountain Ave., 970/232-9815, http://bigalsburgersanddogs.com, 7:30am-9pm Sun.-Thurs., 7:30am-11pm Fri.-Sat., $5-10) is a locally owned and operated business specializing in Chicago-style hamburgers and hot dogs. They have mouthwateringly good burgers, hot dogs, fries, and milkshakes. Enjoy their original 60/40 burger, made with 60 percent beef and 40 percent bacon, with a side of truffle fries.

Much like John Elway in Denver, former Colorado State University Rams football coach Sonny Lubick is a local legend, celebrity, and namesake restaurant owner. **Sonny Lubick Steakhouse** (115 S. College Ave., 970/484-9200, www.sonnylubicksteakhouse.com, 4pm-10pm Mon.-Thurs., 11am-midnight Fri.-Sat., 4pm-9pm Sun., $12-46) draws people in the mood for an upscale steak dinner—or those interested in the local football team.

This is only slightly confusing: **The**

Pateros Creek Brewing

Welsh Rabbit Cheese Bistro (200 Walnut St., 970/232-9521, www.thewelshrabbit.com, noon-9pm Mon.-Wed., noon-10pm Thurs.-Fri., 11am-10pm Sat., $6-10) is where you can sit down and order various cheese plates with a glass of wine or a mug of beer. This should not be confused with the Welsh Rabbit Cheese Shop, which simply sells the cheese and other high-quality, locally sourced groceries. Either one is delicious for cheese lovers!

The Fox and the Crow (2601 S. Lemay Ave., 970/999-2229, www.thefoxandthecrow.net, 9am-7pm Tues.-Wed., 9am-9pm Thurs.-Sat., 10am-5pm Sun., $7-10) is the perfect place to stop for a snack or a small meal. The emphasis is on cheese: cheese plate, grilled cheese, mac n' cheese, plus great local beers. There is also a tasty selection of charcuterie. Stop here for your picnic supplies.

Comfort food with a modern twist is found at **Restaurant 415** (415 S. Mason Ave., 970/407-0415, http://thefourfifteen.com, 11am-2pm and 5pm-10pm Tues.-Sat., 11am-2pm and 5pm-9pm Sun., $4-15) where much of the menu is based on price: Order $6.30 plates or $8.10 plates, each with a variety of options such as meatballs or Brussels sprouts. Or opt for "When Pigs Fly," a category with only one option: chicken and waffles. There are separate gluten-free and vegan menus available.

BREWERIES AND DISTILLERIES

Odell Brewing Company (800 Lincoln St., 970/498-9070, www.odellbrewing.com, taproom 11am-6pm Mon.-Thurs., 11am-7pm Fri.-Sat., tours 1pm, 2pm, and 3pm Mon.-Sat.) has award-winning beers available for sampling. With a variety of food trucks to keep you snacking, it's easy for a summer afternoon to turn into evening on their large backyard patio. Check their events page for live music nights.

Coopersmith's Pub & Brewing (5 Old Town Square, 970/498-0483, http://coopersmithspub.com, 11am-11pm Sun.-Thurs., 11am-midnight Fri.-Sat., $8-20) has a full pub menu, billiards, and brewery tours by appointment.

Fort Collins Brewery (1020 E. Lincoln Ave., 970/472-1499, www.fortcollinsbrewery.com, 11am-9pm Mon.-Thurs., 11am-10pm Fri., 10am-10pm Sat., 10am-6pm Sun., tours noon-5pm Thurs.-Sun., $10-20) offers a pairing menu with its brews or food prepared with beer. Chocolate stout appears as an ingredient in some unusual places like onion soup or tamales. It's fun to keep trying the different dishes to see how strong the beer taste is.

Pateros Creek Brewing (242 N College Ave., 970/484-7222, www.pateroscreekbrewing.com, 2pm-9pm Mon.-Wed., noon-10pm Thurs.-Fri., 11am-10pm Sat., noon-7pm Sun.) is a small, family-owned brewery that started in 2011. Their focus is on using local history and ideals to bring forth new styles that speak to the community. Try one of their five standard beers or one of the constantly rotating seasonals.

★ **Coppermuse Distillery** (244 N. College Ave., 970/999-6016, www.coppermuse.com, 4pm-9pm Wed.-Thurs., 2pm-10pm

Fri., noon-10pm Sat., noon-7pm Sun.) has a mission—to build upon Fort Collins's excellent craft brewing heritage and apply the same standards of quality to their distilling works. Coppermuse produces premium handcrafted spirits such as vodka, gin, rum, whiskey, and bourbon. Enjoy great bites and a comfy environment in the lively tasting room.

New Belgium Brewing Company (500 Linden St., 970/221-0524, www.newbelgium.com, 11am-8pm daily) is most likely the brewery you've heard of without having ever been to Fort Collins. The makers of Fat Tire and the creators of the Tour de Fat, New Belgium has set the bar high for other brewers. Come for live music, tours, tastings, and lots more beer-related fun.

ITALIAN

Family owned since 1979, **Bisetti's Ristorante** (120 S. College Ave., 970/493-0086, www.bisettis.com, 11am-9pm Sun.-Thurs., 11am-10pm Fri.-Sat., $12-18) serves traditional Italian entrees with excellent service.

Café Vino (1200 S. College Ave., 970/212-3399, www.cafevino.com, 7am-midnight daily, $6-18) is that rare Italian restaurant serving breakfast, lunch, and dinner. Stop in for a morning pick-me-up or enjoy an after-dinner caffeine boost and you'll get to taste Silver Canyon Coffee, a Colorado roaster. If beer isn't your thing, then you might appreciate the impressive wine list (they also offer wine tastings and wine menus). Entrees here are scrumptious, but what keeps people coming back are the tapas (bacon-wrapped dates) or desserts (toffee date cake).

If you crave thin-crust Neapolitan pizza, look no further than ★ **Enzio's Italian Kitchen** (126 Mountain Ave., 970/484-8466, http://enzios.com, 11am-9pm Sun.-Thurs., 11am-10pm Fri.-Sat., $13-25). After one visit, you'll be craving their polenta Asiago tots (tater tots, but better) and goat cheese fondue. They have a full gluten-friendly menu that even includes pizza.

Coppermuse Distillery

VEGETARIAN AND VEGAN

Rainbow Restaurant and Catering (212 Laurel Ave., 970/221-2664, www.rainbow-fortcollins.com, 6:30am-2pm Mon.-Thurs., 6:30am-3pm Fri., 7am-3pm Sat., breakfast only 7am-2pm Sun., $9-12) serves breakfast and lunch with a twist that includes non-vegetarian options like bacon and turkey. The large portions—such as the tofu scramble with toast or the sweet potato burrito—make this a favorite for breakfast and lunch.

Tasty Harmony (130 S. Mason St., 970/689-3234, www.tastyharmony.com, 11am-9pm Tues.-Thurs., 11am-10pm Fri.-Sat., 11am-8pm Sun., $12-15) makes eating vegan fun and delicious. Menu items include silly names like Kentucky Fried Freedom, Heart of Provence, and the Ricky Bobby Wrap. It's a world of flavors with Thai, Mexican, and barbecue all on the menu in "mock" dishes.

our de Fat

u saw this coming, right? Beer *and* bikes. The **Tour de Fat** (www.newbelgium.com, Sept.) rted as a local event held by New Belgium Brewing in order to increase bicycle use in Fort llins. It has since exploded into a national "rolling carnival of creativity." This costumed bicycle rade is free to participate in and attend. There is music, beer, dance contests, and general wacky velry; funds raised through beer and merchandise sales benefit local charities. The hometown ent celebrated 15 years in 2014 with 25,000 people in attendance, and it raised more than 00,000 for three local cycling clubs. Tour de Fat events extend to 10 U.S. cities, where funds sed benefit nonprofits in each city.

Transportation and Services

TOURIST INFORMATION

The **Fort Collins Convention & Visitors Bureau** (19 Old Town Square, 970/232-3840 or 800/274-3678, www.visitftcollins.com, 8:30am-5pm Mon.-Fri., 11am-5pm Sat.-Sun.) has an online events calendar. You can request a free guide to the area as well.

The *Fort Collins Coloradoan* (www.coloradoan.com), the city's daily newspaper, is available online and in print. The *Rocky Mountain Collegian* (www.collegian.com) is a student-run daily or weekly newspaper. *Fort Collins Magazine* (www.ftcollinsmag.com) is a monthly glossy magazine that covers Northern Colorado happenings.

GETTING THERE AND AROUND

Car

From Denver, take I-25 north for 60 miles, then head west on Highway 14 for about 5 miles to Fort Collins; the Prospect Road exit leads downtown. From Boulder, it's possible to take Highway 52 east to join I-25 north for 30 miles to Highway 14; I-287 also leads north from Highway 52. Either drive can take about one hour.

Airport Transportation

From Denver International Airport, **Super Shuttle** (970/482-0505, www.supershuttle.com) offers service to Fort Collins, specifically the Colorado State University campus and a few hotels in the area. Shuttle service is also available from **Shamrock Airport Express** (970/482-0505, www.rideshamrock.com, advance reservations are required).

Public Transit

Greyhound (www.greyhound.com, $17-30) buses stop at the Valero gas station (1660 N. College Dr.) in Fort Collins en route to and from Denver daily. Within Fort Collins, the **Transfort Bus Service** (970/221-6620, www.ridetransfort.com, $1.25) offers multiple routes around town. Route 2 (Mon.-Sat.) visits the CSU campus, while Route 5 (Mon.-Sat.) services downtown.

More tourist attraction than actual transportation, the antique Fort Collins Municipal Railway **trolley car** (1801 W. Mountain Ave., 970/224-5372, www.fortnet.org/trolley, noon-5pm Sat.-Sun. May-Sept.) runs a three-mile round-trip between downtown and City Park on weekends in the summer months.

Amtrak does not service Fort Collins.

Bike

The **Fort Collins Bike Library** (13 Old Town Sq., 970/419-1050; 222 La Porte Ave.,

970/221-2453; www.fcbikelibrary.org, 10am-3pm Thurs., 10am-5pm Fri.-Sun., seasonal hours vary) provides bike rentals around town for a reasonable fee. The library also provides maps for self-guided, themed tours around Fort Collins.

Vicinity of Fort Collins

SHAMBHALA MOUNTAIN CENTER

The **Shambhala Mountain Center** (Red Feather Lakes, 4921 County Rd., Ste. 68-C, 970/881-2184, www.shambhalamountain.org, 9am-6pm daily, $8-10 donation) is not just for Buddhists or admirers of the Dalai Lama—anyone with an interest in religious architecture will enjoy a visit here.

The 600-acre Shambhala Mountain Center is mostly wilderness, with eight miles of hiking trails, a garden, and access to the activities at nearby Red Feather Lakes. The center offers a number of programs for children and those interested in yoga, meditation, massage, and Buddhism.

★ Great Stupa of Dharmakaya

Consecrated in a 10-day ceremony in 2001, the Great Stupa of Dharmakaya is one of the largest examples of sacred Buddhist architecture in North America. The word "stupa" refers to the 108-foot-tall building, which is painted white and other bright colors to symbolize the body of the Buddha. All around the building are other statues and "mandalas," or patterns that represent the universe. The interior of the Buddhist shrine houses a very large gold statue of the Buddha. Unlike typical stupas that are sealed shut, this one allows public visitation on the first floor, where pillows and chairs are available for peaceful meditation. The stupa holds the ashes of Chogyam Trungpa Rinpoche, a Tibetan exile who founded the Naropa University in Boulder and the Rocky Mountain Shambhala Center where the shrine now sits.

Public tours are available on weekends at 2pm, and group tours can be arranged in advance. The Great Stupa of Dharmakaya is sometimes closed for special events. After parking, head to the visitors center to register and get a map. It's a 20-minute hike up a gravel path to the stupa, which sits at more than 8,000 feet above sea level. Bring water and wear comfortable shoes and sun protection.

Accommodations

Lodging at the Shambhala Mountain Center (reservations 888/788-7221) ranges from tents to luxurious suites. From June through September, **platform tents** ($79 double, $109 single) are available throughout the property; some are situated close to the dining halls and gift shop, while others are scattered higher in the trees and require a bit of a walk. Guests use shared public restrooms while staying in the tent sites.

Red Feather Lodge ($109) is a group of four cabins with a shared bathhouse that is removed from the core of the community, but still within walking distance of the dining and meeting facilities. One cabin, Earth ($79), is set up like a dormitory; others have five double rooms each.

The rooms at **Ridgen Lodge** ($109) and **Shambhala Lodge** ($147-263) are more like traditional hotel rooms, with private baths in some (but not all) rooms, along with desks, public phones, and Internet access.

Food

The Shambhala Mountain Center is used for many large conferences and the dining facilities are set up to accommodate hundreds of people at one sitting. There are two indoor dining halls, an outdoor dining tent, and picnic tables outside. Three meals per day are included with lodging. If you're just visiting for the day, lunch (12:30pm-1:30pm, $10 per person) and dinner (5:30pm-6:30pm, hours and rates vary) are served.

Getting There

The center is an hour's drive west from Fort Collins, and a 2.5-hour drive from Denver. From Fort Collins, take College Avenue/U.S. 287 north for 3.4 miles. Turn right on N. Shields Street to stay on U.S. 287 for another 16.6 miles until you reach County Road 74E/ Red Feather Lakes Road. Turn left and after 16 miles, take another left on County Road 68C/ Boy Scout Road (look for a blue and white sign for the center). Drive 5 miles (not all of the road is paved), then turn left at the entrance, where there is a large parking lot.

SHAMBHALA SHUTTLE

The **Shambhala Shuttle** (970/881-2184, ext. 235, travel@shambhalamountain.org, $88 round-trip) offers transportation between Fort Collins and the center. Pickup is from the Fort Collins Hilton at 2pm the day of scheduled programs. Reservations are required three weeks in advance and require careful timing for arrival and departure.

Colorado Springs

As the state's second-largest city, Colorado Springs has come into its own, with appealing sights, outdoor activities, restaurants, and nightlife.

Situated at 6,035 feet above sea level (that's more than a mile high for those who are keeping score), Colorado Springs reaches into the foothills of the Rocky Mountains and boasts 300 days of sunshine per year. The scenic beauty of these mountains is what initially put Colorado Springs on the map, and some of the city's best attractions—such as Seven Falls and the Cheyenne Mountain Zoo with the Will Rogers Shrine—lie in these foothills.

The smaller metro population gives the city a more laid-back feel than Denver, but don't let that fool you that there isn't much going on. Within the town are many subcultures: the military, cowboys and cowgirls, athletes in training, college students, and fundamentalist Christians. The military is the largest employer in Colorado Springs, as the Fort Carson United States Army base, the United States Air Force Academy, and the North American Aerospace Defense Command (NORAD) are all represented here. Tourism and the high-tech industry also bring an estimated 5-6 million people to the area each year.

PLANNING YOUR TIME

It's not possible to see all of the sights in both Colorado Springs and Manitou Springs in one day, so it's best to plan a whole **weekend** to explore the area.

Spend the first day in Colorado Springs. Grab coffee and a bite at Ivywild, a former school turned farm-to-table collective of restaurants. Visit the Colorado Springs Fine Arts Center and peruse the current exhibits, or see a performance in their theater. If you are traveling with young children, the Cheyenne Mountain Zoo will be a hit—there is a large giraffe herd that visitors can feed. Families may prefer to spend their vacation at The Broadmoor, where they can take in a movie, bowl, swim, golf, play tennis, do a little boating, and dine out (or in)—all without leaving the premises.

The next day, head to Manitou Springs,

Previous: Pikes Peak from Colorado Springs; Garden of the Gods. **Above:** rock climbing in the Garden of the Gods.

Look for ★ to find recommended sights, activities, dining, and lodging.

Highlights

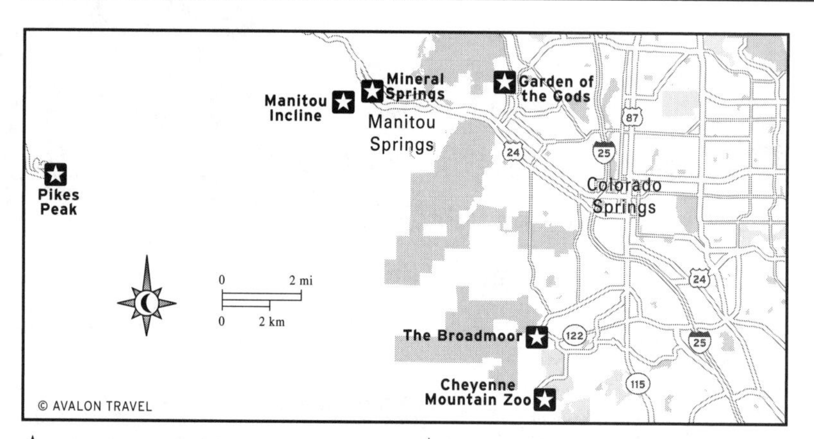

★ **The Broadmoor:** This family-friendly resort is home to many of the city's best restaurants, and its incomparable service makes every guest feel like a celebrity (page 208).

★ **Cheyenne Mountain Zoo:** Hand-feed a giraffe herd at this unique zoo perched on a hillside overlooking Colorado Springs (page 209).

★ **Garden of the Gods:** By foot or by horseback, in a car or on a mountain bike, the natural beauty of these red rocks will awe you (page 209).

★ **Manitou Springs Mineral Springs:** Drink these potentially healing waters as they trickle from decorative spigots and fountains around the historic town (page 231).

★ **Pikes Peak:** You can hike, drive, or ride a cog railway for epic views from the top of this famed 14,115-foot mountain (page 232).

★ **Manitou Incline:** Hikers climb leftover railroad ties to the top of the old Manitou Springs Incline—only one mile long, but with a 40 percent grade (page 234).

Colorado Springs

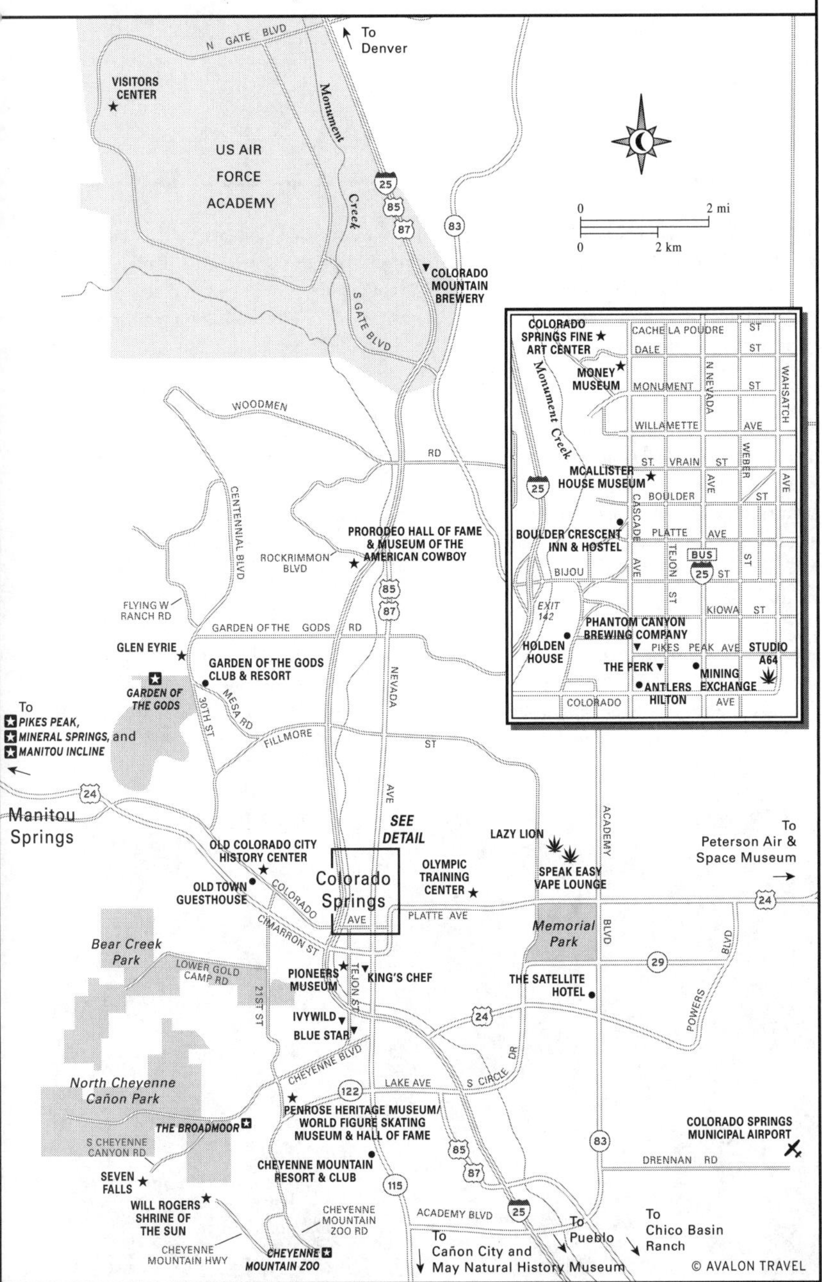
To Denver
N GATE BLVD
VISITORS CENTER
US AIR FORCE ACADEMY
Monument Creek
COLORADO MOUNTAIN BREWERY
S GATE BLVD
2 mi
2 km
WOODMEN RD
CENTENNIAL BLVD
ROCKRIMMON BLVD
PRORODEO HALL OF FAME & MUSEUM OF THE AMERICAN COWBOY
FLYING W RANCH RD
GARDEN OF THE GODS RD
GLEN EYRIE
GARDEN OF THE GODS CLUB & RESORT
GARDEN OF THE GODS
To PIKES PEAK, MINERAL SPRINGS, and MANITOU INCLINE
MESA RD
30TH ST
FILLMORE ST
NEVADA AVE
Manitou Springs
OLD COLORADO CITY HISTORY CENTER
SEE DETAIL
LAZY LION
SPEAK EASY VAPE LOUNGE
ACADEMY BLVD
To Peterson Air & Space Museum
OLD TOWN GUESTHOUSE
COLORADO
Colorado Springs
OLYMPIC TRAINING CENTER
PLATTE AVE
CIMARRON ST
Memorial Park
Bear Creek Park
LOWER GOLD CAMP RD
21ST ST
PIONEERS MUSEUM
KING'S CHEF
TEJON ST
THE SATELLITE HOTEL
POWERS BLVD
IVYWILD
BLUE STAR
CHEYENNE BLVD
LAKE AVE
S CIRCLE DR
North Cheyenne Cañon Park
PENROSE HERITAGE MUSEUM/ WORLD FIGURE SKATING MUSEUM & HALL OF FAME
THE BROADMOOR
S CHEYENNE CANYON RD
CHEYENNE MOUNTAIN RESORT & CLUB
COLORADO SPRINGS MUNICIPAL AIRPORT
DRENNAN RD
SEVEN FALLS
WILL ROGERS SHRINE OF THE SUN
CHEYENNE MOUNTAIN ZOO RD
ACADEMY BLVD
CHEYENNE MOUNTAIN HWY
CHEYENNE MOUNTAIN ZOO
To Cañon City and May Natural History Museum
To Pueblo
To Chico Basin Ranch
© AVALON TRAVEL
COLORADO SPRINGS FINE ART CENTER
CACHE LA POUDRE ST
DALE ST
MONEY MUSEUM
MONUMENT ST
N NEVADA AVE
WAHSATCH AVE
WILLAMETTE AVE
ST. VRAIN ST
WEBER ST
MCALLISTER HOUSE MUSEUM
BOULDER ST
CASCADE AVE
BOULDER CRESCENT INN & HOSTEL
PLATTE AVE
TEJON ST
BUS 25
BIJOU ST
EXIT 142
KIOWA ST
PHANTOM CANYON BREWING COMPANY
HOLDEN HOUSE
PIKES PEAK AVE
STUDIO A64
THE PERK
MINING EXCHANGE
ANTLERS HILTON
COLORADO AVE

enjoying a scenic drive through the Garden of the Gods en route. Once in Manitou Springs, walk around town sampling the mineral springs while window shopping. If it's summer, take the shuttle to the Pikes Peak Cog Railway so you can claim to have scaled a fourteener. At night, tuck into a historic guesthouse like the Rockledge Country Inn, or return to Colorado Springs for the evening.

Sights

★ THE BROADMOOR

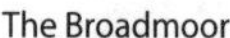

The Broadmoor (1 Lake Ave., 719/577-5775 or 855/634-7711, www.broadmoor.com, May 1-Oct. 31) is a five-star resort that is a destination in itself—not just a place to stay for the night. Set at the base of Cheyenne Mountain, the large, pink, Mediterranean-style hotel opened in 1918 and was meant to capture the luxury of Asian and European designs seen by owners Spencer Penrose and Julie Penrose in their travels. The numbers tell the story here: There are more than 700 rooms and suites, 18 restaurants, 3,000 acres of meticulously landscaped grounds, six tennis courts (The Broadmoor is rated one of the top 10 tennis resorts in the country), three golf courses, three swimming pools, and a spa.

The Broadmoor also has an incredible collection of Western art. Sign up for a tour or, if the art inspires you, take a class or attend an art retreat with resident artist Patience Heyl. There are historical tours and arts with reservations (even for non-guests of the resort) available year-round.

COLORADO SPRINGS FINE ARTS CENTER

The **Colorado Springs Fine Arts Center** (30 W. Dale St., 719/634-5583, www.csfineartscenter.org, 10am-5pm Tues.-Sun., $8.50-10) is a wonderful little museum that has an impressive permanent collection (with art from John Singer Sargent, Fritz Scholder, and many other familiar names) and intriguing temporary exhibits. In the Lane Family Gallery, the hand-blown glass creations of artist Dale Chihuly are shown alongside Native American artworks—blankets and

The Broadmoor

baskets—that influenced his work. Also look for Chihuly chandeliers elsewhere in the center.

The art deco building with Southwestern flair was designed in 1936 by Santa Fe architect John Gaw Meem. On the west end of the building is **Taste by Garden of the Gods Gourmet** (719/634-5583, 11am-2pm Thurs.-Tues.). The outdoor patio is a terrific place for a lunch with a view of Pikes Peak.

Group tours of the museum are available; advance reservations are required. Free weekend tours start at 2pm with no reservations required.

★ CHEYENNE MOUNTAIN ZOO

What sets the **Cheyenne Mountain Zoo** (4250 Cheyenne Mountain Zoo Rd., 719/633-9925, www.cmzoo.org, 9am-5pm daily year-round) apart from other zoos is its elevation of 6,800 feet and the large giraffe herd that lives and breeds here. The zoo's setting in the foothills beyond The Broadmoor gives the area a natural feel. There's the usual assortment of creatures—lions, elephants, meerkats, and a lot more—but the giraffes are very popular, and the zoo sells special treats ($3-5) that can be fed directly to them by guests. There is also a **carousel** (9am-5pm daily May-Labor Day, Sat.-Sun. Labor Day-May, $2) and an open-air chairlift **Sky Ride** (9am-5pm daily May-Labor Day, 10am-4pm Sat.-Sun. Labor Day-May, $5) that tours the entire zoo.

Ticket prices vary seasonally. May through Labor Day is considered **peak season** ($17.25 adults, $12.25 children 3-11, $15.25 seniors over 65, $9.25-14.25 military families, children under 2 free). After Labor Day, **off-season** ($14.25 adults, $10.25 children 3-11, $12.25 seniors over 65, $7.25-11.25 military families, children under 2 free) lasts until April.

Will Rogers Shrine of the Sun

Spencer Penrose, developer of The Broadmoor and the Pikes Peak Highway, was close friends with actor and humorist Will Rogers. In 1935, Penrose had begun construction of a tower overlooking the Cheyenne Mountain Zoo when he learned that Rogers had died in a plane crash. Penrose dedicated the tower as the **Will Rogers Shrine of the Sun** (9am-4pm daily) to honor the memory of his friend.

The shrine is constructed from granite and bound by steel and cement—no wood or nails were used—and its unique design resembles a castle turret or stone fortress. On the lower level are the ashes of Spencer and Julie Penrose, housed in a chapel decorated with artwork that honors the couple's efforts to bring culture to Colorado Springs. The real draw, however, is the spectacular view from the top deck of the five-story shrine at 8,136 feet. (Acrophobics, just enjoy the zoo instead.)

Visitors must pay admission to the Cheyenne Mountain Zoo (4240 Cheyenne Mountain Zoo Rd., 719/578-5367, http://www.cmzoo.org) in order to visit the tower. The shrine is located 1.4 miles up a road within the zoo. Entrance fees to the zoo include access to the shrine.

COLORADO SPRINGS PIONEERS MUSEUM

Before even stepping inside the **Colorado Springs Pioneers Museum** (215 S. Tejon St., 719/385-5990, www.cspm.org, 10am-5pm Tues.-Sat., free), visitors are treated to a bit of local history: The museum is located in the restored El Paso County courthouse in the middle of Alamo Square Park in the heart of downtown. The museum is home to permanent collections that are uniquely local, such as a display of Van Briggle pottery and the former home (furnished, no less) of author Helen Hunt Jackson. Other exhibits tell the story of the city's prominent early creators such as Spencer Penrose, and how early city leaders marketed the health benefits of this area to people suffering from tuberculosis.

★ GARDEN OF THE GODS

Before white settlers named it the Garden of the Gods, Native American tribes made annual pilgrimages to these beautiful red rocks that stand so distinctly against the green mountain slopes just west of town. The **Garden of the Gods** (1805 N. 30th St., 719/634-6666, www.gardenofgods.com, 5am-11pm May-Oct., 5am-9pm Nov.-Apr., free) remains the top tourist attraction around, with an estimated two million visitors each year.

Like many other sensational natural wonders in the area, Garden of the Gods has been tinkered with too much and has a heavy theme-park atmosphere that can be a big turnoff. There are bus tours, not one but three gift shops, and Native American dances for lunchtime entertainment. That said, you can take a number of easy hiking trails to escape the crowds (some trails also allow mountain biking and horseback riding) and appreciate the 1,350-acre park.

Stop in at the **Visitor and Nature Center** (8am-8pm daily Memorial Day-Labor Day, 9am-5pm daily Labor Day-Memorial Day) to learn more about the geology of the rocks and the plants and critters that dwell here. Visiting the park is free year-round, but there are fees for guided tours and special programs.

GLEN EYRIE

Glen Eyrie (3820 N. 30th St., 719/634-0808 or 719/265-7050 for reservations, www.gleneyrie.org) is an English-style stone castle featuring 17 guest rooms, 24 fireplaces, two dining rooms, and four meeting rooms. The castle was built by General William Jackson Palmer, the founder of Colorado Springs, and is now owned by The Navigators, a Christian organization headquartered here. Tours (1pm daily June-Sept., 1pm Thurs.-Mon. Oct.-May, $8) of the Christian conference and retreat center, as well as high tea (2:30pm Mon.-Fri., $20) and overnight stays ($85-199) are available.

MAY NATURAL HISTORY MUSEUM

The **May Natural History Museum** (710 Rock Creek Canyon, 719/576-0450, http://coloradospringsbugmuseum.com, 9am-6pm daily May 1-Sept. 30, open to groups of 10 or more by appt. only, Oct. 1-Apr. 30; $6 adults, $5 seniors, $3 children ages 6-12, children 5 and under free) has a lovely history all its own, as well as a stunning collection of preserved butterflies, moths, beetles, and other small creatures. The May Natural History Museum boasts that they have the "World's Largest Private Insect Collection," and who am I to doubt them? The bug collection is so spectacular here, it's rumored that Walt Disney wanted it but was turned down. Look

the May Natural History Museum

for the giant steel beetle replica in front of the museum, founded by James May in the 1940s as he put down roots for his traveling exhibition of insects collected from around the world. A big appeal of this place is how low-tech it is—simply the wow factor of freakishly large bugs.

MCALLISTER HOUSE MUSEUM

Given that there are castles to visit in this area, a small historic home may not seem worth the stop. However, the **McAllister House Museum** (423 N. Cascade Ave., 719/635-7925, http://mcallisterhouse.org, 10am-4pm Tues.-Sat. May 15-Aug. 30, 10am-4pm Thurs.-Sat. Sept. 1-May 14, closed Jan.; $5 adults, $4 seniors, $3 children 6-12, children under 5 free) is an impressively preserved example of a family home built here when the town was known as "Fountain Colony," before being named Colorado Springs. Remember the three little pigs? This house of bricks was built in 1873 and was once surrounded by neighbors who built theirs with wood—now it's the only one of its vintage left standing. Plan 45 minutes for a docent-led tour to learn about Henry McAllister Jr., who served under General William Jackson Palmer, founder of Colorado Springs, and later moved west from Pennsylvania to work for General Palmer.

MONEY MUSEUM

At the American Numismatic Association **Money Museum** (818 N. Cascade Ave., 800/367-9723, www.money.org, 10:30am-5pm Tues.-Sat., $5 adults, $4 seniors and military with ID, children under 12 free) on the Colorado College campus, there is a monthly **Mini-Mint** (noon-4pm every third Sat.) demonstration in addition to several fascinating and family-friendly exhibits about money. The Kids Zone is an interactive space for children to learn about money (shh! maybe a little math too).

OLD COLORADO CITY HISTORY CENTER

Initially named El Dorado, Colorado City became the first permanent town in the Pikes Peak region. The story of the distinctive town that was later annexed by Colorado Springs is told at the **Old Colorado City History Center** (1 South 24th St., 719/636-1225, www.occhs.org, 11am-4pm Tues.-Sat. May-Sept., 11am-4pm Thurs.-Sat. Oct.-mid-Dec., 11am-2pm Thurs.-Sat. mid-Dec.-early Apr., free). The remaining buildings of

the Money Museum

Colorado City are mainly home to tourist shops, restaurants, and bars, so it is worthwhile to learn more about the early life that went on here.

OLYMPIC TRAINING CENTER

Headquartered in Colorado Springs, the United States **Olympic Training Center** (1 Olympic Plaza, 719/866-4618, www.teamusa.org, 9am-4:30pm Mon.-Sat. June 1-Aug. 15, 9am-4pm Mon.-Sat. Aug. 15-May 31, $5 adults, $3 seniors, $2 children 5-12, children under 5 free) is open for tours year-round. These guided one-hour tours include a video presentation and a glimpse of the facilities, which are home to swimming and shooting, as well as gymnastics, fencing, weightlifting, taekwondo, wrestling, modern pentathlon, and judo. Call ahead if you want to be there when you can actually see athletes training. Either way, save time for the gift shop so you can support Team USA.

PENROSE HERITAGE MUSEUM

Given that tourists and locals are still enjoying the places that Spencer Penrose created in Colorado Springs, it's not surprising that there is a place devoted just to learning about this visionary. The **Penrose Heritage Museum** (11 Lake Circle, 719/577-7065, www.elpomar.org, 9am-5pm Mon.-Sat., 1pm-5pm Sun., free) showcases the auto collection of the Penrose family. Exhibits tell the story of how Mr. Penrose founded the Pikes Peak Hill Climb and the Pikes Peak Automobile Company as a way to give scenic tours of the area.

PETERSON AIR & SPACE MUSEUM

Colorado Springs is home to a few military bases, including Peterson Air Force Base in the southeast of the city. The **Peterson Air & Space Museum** (150 E. Ent Ave., Peterson AFB, 719/556-4915, http://petemuseum.org, 9am-4pm Tues.-Sat., free, non-military ID card holders must call base 24 hours in advance to request a pass) is on the base, which is the home of the 21st Space Wing, Air Force Space Command, United States Space Command, and the North American Aerospace Defense Command (NORAD). Billing itself as the state's oldest aviation museum, Peterson Air & Space Museum has free tours (or allows visitors to wander independently) both inside and outside.

the Carol Grotnes Belk Sculpture Garden outside the Olympic Training Center

PRORODEO HALL OF FAME AND MUSEUM OF THE AMERICAN COWBOY

A reminder of Colorado's Western cowboy culture, the **ProRodeo Hall of Fame and Museum of the American Cowboy** (101 Pro Rodeo Dr., 719/528-4764, www.prorodeohalloffame.com, 9am-5pm daily May-Aug., 9am-5pm Wed.-Sun. Sept.-Apr., $8 adults, $7 seniors, $6 military, $5 children 6-12, children under 5 free) is a unique place to learn about historic and modern rodeo cowboy (and cowgirl) culture, gear, and artwork. Tours begin with a 15-minute film about rodeo history. You can see dozens of saddles, costumes, and tributes to past rodeo champions and possibly a team roping event in their arena (check the event schedule).

SEVEN FALLS

A natural wonder, **Seven Falls** (2850 S. Cheyenne Canyon Rd., 855/923-7272, www.sevenfalls.com, 9am-7pm daily Mar.-Apr., 9am-9pm daily May-Sept., 9am-7pm daily Oct.-Nov., 9am-5pm daily Dec.-Feb., $14 adults, $8 children 2-12, children under 2 free) is a tourist destination that contains seven cascading waterfalls. Purchased by a local businessman in the late 1800s to preserve its scenic beauty, the sight has had different owners over the past 100 years; each has put their own touch on this rocky box canyon. In 1885 owner James Hull created the road to the cascading falls and a stairway to the top—and a toll booth to charge visitors who came up on burros and in wagons. In the 1940s, owner Albert Gatalyn Hill installed lights so that the falls could be viewed at night; he also built the Eagle's Nest platform and added an elevator in 1992. Do your own research into the story behind the name of each of the falls: Ramona, Feather, Bridal Veil, Shorty, Hull, Weimer, and Hill.

UNITED STATES AIR FORCE ACADEMY

Depending on the current U.S. security color code, visitors are generally welcome at the **United States Air Force Academy** campus (2346 Academy Dr., 719/333-2025, www.usafa.af.mil). One of the highlights is the **Cadet Chapel** (9am-5pm Mon.-Sat., 1pm-5pm Sun.), known for its unique architecture and all-faiths worship model. Visitors are welcome to learn about the "cadet experience" during self-guided tours of the campus and at the **Barry Goldwater Visitor Center** (9am-5pm daily).

the Cadet Chapel at the United States Air Force Academy

WORLD FIGURE SKATING MUSEUM AND HALL OF FAME

During those years without a winter Olympics to watch, there is still a place to revel in the glory of one of the most popular winter sporting events—figure skating. The **World Figure Skating Museum and Hall of Fame** (20 First St., 719/635-5200, www.worldskatingmuseum.org, 10am-4pm Tues.-Fri., $5 adults, $3 children ages 6-12) showcases not just the big names of the sport, but also the outfits they wore. Displays explain the physics of making those seemingly impossible spins. Don't miss the gift shop for your skating enthusiast back home.

Entertainment and Events

Colorado Springs is not the place one thinks of for a night of wild revelry, but make no mistake: There is plenty to do after dark here. The city's social calendar is filled with live music, annual events worth the trip, and plenty of bars and lounges. Since retail marijuana sales are prohibited in El Paso County, cannabis entrepreneurs have created social clubs, places for people to smoke the weed they bought outside of the county (quite possibly in nearby Manitou Springs) inside the city.

NIGHTLIFE

Tejon Street is the center of Colorado Springs nightlife, with multiple venues spanning a few blocks. **The Mezzanine** (20 N. Tejon St., 719/428-6974, www.themezzcos.com, 4:30pm-close Thurs.-Fri., one hour before showtime Sat.-Tues., happy hour 4pm-6pm) is unique in terms of space and performance. Shows run the gamut—from classical music to burlesque and jazz to musical theater—and creative cocktails complement a small-bites menu of savory delicacies. Attending events here supports the Colorado Springs Conservatory, a performing arts school.

There's definitely a country-and-western scene in Colorado Springs. A good place to kick up your heels is **Cowboys** (25 N. Tejon St., 719/596-1212, www.cowboyscs.com, 5pm-2am Wed., 4pm-2am Fri., 6pm-2am Sat., 4pm-2am Sun., no cover), which has live music and dancing (lessons on Sun.).

Just the entrance of **The Rabbit Hole** (101 N. Tejon St., 719/203-5072, www.rabbitholedinner.com, 4pm-1:30am daily) lends an evening out a subversive feel as you descend stairs to enter this bar and restaurant. Once you put your lips to a flaming martini, you'll know this is no ordinary night on the town. The menu is just as full of surprises, with clever spins on comfort food like bacon-wrapped rabbit meatloaf and truffle tricolor cauliflower mac-n-cheese.

Jack Quinn Irish Alehouse & Pub (21 S. Tejon St., 719/385-0766, www.jackquinnspub.com, 11am-close daily, Sun. 11am-3pm) has a loyal clientele who come back for tried-and-true Irish and Scottish whiskeys and ales. The menu never disappoints with fried soda bread, Irish breakfast, fish-and-chips, and more. Come for live music or the Geeks Who Drink Pub Quiz (8pm Mon.).

In the historic Cheyenne building is the **Phantom Canyon Brewing Company** (2 E. Pikes Peak Ave., 719/635-2800, www.phantomcanyon.com, 11am-10pm Sun.-Thurs., 11am-11pm Fri.-Sat.), which offers a full floor of billiards in addition to the locally brewed beers. The menu sometimes even incorporates beer into the dinner offerings—think blonde lager and smoked gouda soup.

On the west side of town is **Motif** (2432 Cucharras St., 719/635-5635, http://motifwest.com, 5pm-11pm Thurs., 5pm-midnight Fri.-Sat.) with live jazz music featuring local musicians. Look for the bamboo fence, as signage is lacking for Motif.

Head over to Old Colorado City to sip brews on tap at **Alchemy** (2625 W. Colorado

Ave., 719/471-0887, www.alchemypubcolorado.com, 11am-2am daily) and enjoy the classic pub atmosphere. On Friday and Saturday nights at 11pm, a DJ gets things going for those who want to dance. Come for happy hour (4pm-7pm daily) when all draft beers are $1 off and well drinks start at $3. Make a meal out of shared starters like untwisted pretzels or Scotch quail eggs, but save room for traditional pub fare like Irish breakfast.

The largest gay and lesbian nightclub in Colorado Springs is **The Underground Pub** (110 N. Nevada Ave., 719/578-7771, 4pm-2am daily), which offers game nights, karaoke, and a huge dance floor. Food and drink is a curious mix of Mexican and pub-style fare.

CANNABIS SOCIAL CLUBS

Colorado Springs prohibits the sale of recreational marijuana, which means you'll have to head to nearby Manitou Springs to find pot shops. But Colorado Springs offers something Denver doesn't: private marijuana social clubs, which operate as civic organizations. Anyone age 21 and older who pays a membership fee can consume marijuana on the premises. Some take "donations" in exchange for products offered on-site, while others require you to BYOW (bring your own weed).

Don your fedora or your flapper dress and head over to the roaring '20s-style **420 Speakeasy** (1532 N. Circle Dr., 719/471-3398, 3pm-3am daily, $50 monthly membership fee, $10 daily membership fee for men, $5 daily membership fee for women), which revels in the outlaw vibe of its offerings. At this cannabis club, you get activities similar to a regular old-fashioned bar: throw some darts, play some pool, and hit the dance floor. Hopefully the coppers won't come knocking!

At the **Lazy Lion** (2502 E. Bijou St., 719/634-8337, www.thelazylion420.com, 10am-10pm Mon.-Thurs., 10am-midnight Fri.-Sat., 11am-7pm Sun., $5 daily membership fee), you'll get access to a dab bar, loads of video games, and a munchies-filled concession stand. It's just like sampling buds with your buds back in college, albeit slightly more legal.

Speak Easy Vape Lounge (2508 E. Bijou St., 719/445-9083, www.speakeasycannabisclub.com, noon-midnight Mon.-Sat., noon-9pm Sun., $5 daily membership fee) sports a funky, hip-hop vibe and prides itself on its well-stocked dab bar, where folks can sample a variety of high-THC concentrates using the in-house selection of dabbing pipes. Speak Easy also offers live music, not to mention stand-up comedy. Cannabis and live comedy—what could be better than that?

Studio A64 (332 E. Colorado Ave., 719/930-9846, www.studioa64.com, 6pm-midnight Tues.-Sat., $5 daily membership fee) is the granddaddy of Colorado Springs marijuana social clubs. Studio A64 fought the civic battles that paved the way for the city's unique private smoking establishments. Unlike most of its competitors, the upscale operation requires that you bring your own product, but that also means it's operating on the safest legal grounds. Looking to throw a party? Studio A64 rents out its upper floor for private events.

PERFORMING ARTS

The **Fine Arts Theatre School** (30 W. Dale St., 719/634-5581, www.csfineartscenter.org) performs a handful of comedies, musicals, and dramas each year. Some offerings, such as *Mary Poppins,* are for families. More experimental is the Rough Writers: A New Play Fest, a two-week-long festival held twice a year whereby people from around the world submit their work for readings. This is also one of the local venues where the **Veronika String Quartet** (veronikastringquartet.com) performs; the award-winning foursome is known worldwide, but this is their home.

The **Pikes Peak Center for the Performing Arts** (190 S. Cascade Ave., 719/576-2626, www.pikespeakcenter.com) is the place for the biggest acts in town. Previous shows include the blockbuster *Mythbusters*, Lyle Lovett & His Large Band,

Todd Rundgren, and comedian Bill Maher. Centrally located, it is easy to access when staying downtown.

From fall to spring, the **Colorado Springs Philharmonic** (http://csphilharmonic.org) performs everything from Brahms to Disney's *Fantasia* at the Pikes Peak Center for the Performing Arts (190 S. Cascade Ave., 719/576-2626, www.pikespeakcenter.com). They also offer concerts featuring music from well-known movies such as Star Wars or from rock legends like Pink Floyd.

Improv and kids seems to go together like peanut butter and jelly, so the geniuses behind the **Millibo Art Theatre** (1626 S. Tejon St., 719/465-6321, www.themat.org) combined the two. Performances include RIP Improv nights, Kids First performances (puppet shows, plays, or a circus), and a variety of touring shows for grown-ups.

Built in the 1960s as a United Artist Cinema 150 Cinerama Theater, the dome-roofed **Stargazers Theatre** (10 S. Parkside Dr., 719/476-2200, www.stargazerstheatre.com) is a 560-seat venue that showcases local music and film talents. Here you can catch the Flying W Wranglers, a classic cowboy band, and the Jake Loggins Band, a local blues group.

Theatreworks (3995 Regent Circle, 719/255-3232, www.theatreworks.org) is a regional theater company that has its home in the 200-seat Dusty Loo Bon Vivant Theater on the University of Colorado at Colorado Springs campus. The company turns out seven plays a year with fresh takes on Shakespeare and Beckett alongside original works.

FESTIVALS AND EVENTS

Colorado Springs has quite a few fun events each year that are embraced by locals, but also welcome out-of-towners to join in the frivolity. The theme of these festivals is typically tied into the local history or something that is distinctly Colorado, like bighorn sheep or Pikes Peak.

Spring

Territory Days (http://shopoldcoloradocity.com, May) is held every Memorial Day—just as it has been for 40 years—in Old Colorado City. This popular event features performances by Native American dancers in their traditional costumes and Wild West-style gunfight reenactments. There are more than 100 food and craft booths, live music, and kid-friendly areas for the whole family.

Grab those binoculars and lace up your hiking boots in the hopes of seeing a flitting hummingbird during the **Cheyenne Cañon Hummingbird Experience** (http://cheyennecanon.org, May). Guided hikes with a leader from the Audubon Society, nature photography workshops, and bird banding are part of this weekend of fun for a whole family of birders. Check out hummingbird-themed activities at the **Starsmore Visitor and Nature Center** (2120 S. Cheyenne Cañon Rd., 719/385-6086, www.coloradosprings.gov). This festival is held in conjunction with the **Pikes Peak Birding and Nature Festival** (http://pikespeakbirdingandnaturefestival.org, May).

Summer

The **Pikes Peak International Hill Climb** (www.ppihc.com, June) is unlike any other auto race you will ever witness. Way back in 1901 two men drove up to the summit of Pikes Peak—in nine hours. Spencer Penrose, Colorado Springs' benefactor and champion, turned this carriage road into a highway and started the annual road race. The road to the top is now paved and the race is open to motorcycles and automobiles who vie to make it to the peak first—in minutes, not hours—and collect the prize. Check the website for a full schedule of events.

Not into auto racing? The **Pikes Peak Marathon** (www.pikespeakmarathon.org, Aug.) is for those who prefer to make it to the top on foot. Held since 1955, the marathon is for serious runners: to qualify you must have previously completed the Pikes Peak Ascent (occurs the same weekend) of 13 miles and 7,815 elevation gain or finish another marathon in under 5:45 in the past three years. Or...you can just take a shuttle bus to the top and cheer on those people!

Git yer buckaroos and buckarinas all saddled up for the **Pikes Peak or Bust Rodeo** (www.pikespeakorbust.org, July, $16-44), which has been going strong since 1940. The event kicks off with a parade through town. Daily events show off the best of the best rodeo athletes in roping, steer wrestling, and bull riding. Yeehaw!

The **Broadmoor Recital Series** (http://broadmoormusic.com, May-Oct.) is a lovely Friday afternoon concert series that takes place at the historic Pauline Memorial Chapel located just outside the grounds of the resort. The Broadmoor Brass Quintet is the most popular act to perform here, but others include the Veronika String Quartet and Mango fan Django. Arrive by 3pm to get a seat.

Fall

The **Rocky Mountain Women's Film Festival** (http://rmwfilminstitute.org/festival, Nov.) features films—documentaries, narrative shorts, animated films—about women and by women in a special weekend of cinema celebration. Don't miss the opening night gala held at the Colorado Springs Fine Arts Center (30 W. Dale St., 719/634-5583, www.csfineartscenter.org). Centrally located screening rooms on the Colorado College campus (14 E. Cache La Poudre St.) make for a chance to explore downtown on foot.

Winter

Bighorn Sheep Day (www.visitcos.com/bighorn, Feb.) takes place in the Garden of the Gods (1805 N. 30th St., 719/634-6666, www.gardenofgods.com, free) and there's a good chance you'll spy some bighorns through a high-powered telescope or your own binoculars. There are guided nature walks and shuttles to viewing areas.

Shopping

Colorado Springs is home to many independent shops that specialize in toys, women's fashions, books, souvenirs, and arts and crafts. You don't have to be staying at The Broadmoor to shop there and it's worth the trip, whether you are looking for shoes or fossils.

You'll have to trek over to Manitou Springs to score at the dispensaries, which curiously also strive to have a "boutique vibe" and bragging rights to locally made (or grown, in this case) products.

Shopping Districts

OLD COLORADO CITY

Just northwest of downtown is historic **Old Colorado City** (24th through 27th Sts. along West Colorado Ave., 719/636-1225, www.shopoldcoloradocity.com), which was a town during the early gold rush days before Colorado Springs was developed. Now it's a few blocks of specialty shops, art galleries, and antique stores mixed in with some restaurants and bars. Highlights include **Thunder Mountain Trading Company** (2508 W. Colorado Ave., 719/632-7331, www.thundermountaintrading.com, 10am-5pm daily), which boasts not only "the largest selection of antler chandeliers in the state of Colorado," but other home decor items made in part from the antlers of elk and deer.

The **Michael Garman Museum & Gallery** (2418 W. Colorado Ave., 719/471-9391, www.michaelgarman.com, 10am-5:30pm daily) features the sculptures of Garman, as well as his Magic Town—a highly detailed miniature replica of a town. If there is such a thing as nostalgia art, then this is it.

Arati Artists Gallery (2425 W. Colorado Ave., 719/636-1901, www.aratiartists.com, 11am-5pm Mon.-Sat., noon-4pm Sun.) is an artists' cooperative. The 20 member-artists not only create paintings, drawings, and sculptures, but work as sales clerks in the gallery. Take home jewelry, pottery, or a painting that evokes your trip to Colorado Springs.

THE BROADMOOR

The shops at **The Broadmoor** (1 Lake Ave., 855/634-7711, www.broadmoor.com, hours vary at each shop) are not what you expect—or at least not what I expected on my first visit. Yes, they have the requisite souvenir shop with postcards, T-shirts, and hats that have "The Broadmoor" stitched on them. Beyond that are boutiques with a solid inventory of books, shoes, men's and women's fashions, sports apparel, and jewelry that is in keeping with everything at this luxury resort—only the finest.

A personal fave is **Yarid's Shoes,** which squeezes shoes for men, women, and kids into a tiny space, but still provides a good selection of casual and dressy from known designers like Stuart Weitzman and Tory Burch.

The Great Republic has a wonderful selection of U.S. flags, maps, and other "Americana" merchandise that you don't see in many mainstream shops. **Gibson's Gallery** is a lovely space filled with fossils, exotic stones, and artwork. (I loved the stories about stones found around the area.) The **Broadmoor Gallery** offers a small taste of the impressive art collection on display at the resort. In these shops, you can see paintings and sculpture evocative of the West by well-known artists.

Books and Toys

Regularly voted "Best of" by locals, **Poor Richard's Toystore** (10am-7pm Mon.-Sat., 11am-5pm Sun.) and **Poor Richard's Books & Gifts** (320 N. Tejon St., 719/578-0012, www.poorrichardsdowntown.com, 9am-9pm Mon.-Wed., 9am-10pm Thurs.-Sat., 10am-9pm Sun.) are designed for kids and readers who like to linger while they shop. The toy store sells plushy toys for infants and will continue to delight the kiddos right into their teen years with games, puzzles, science kits, dolls, and much more. The bookstore sells good-condition used books that are well organized into many categories for all interests.

Clothing

Downtown Colorado Springs has a few charming boutiques, primarily for women

Old Colorado City

shops at The Broadmoor

looking for the latest in a great-fitting pair of jeans or a sexy top, or seeking to discover local designers. The **Colorado Co-op** (315 N. Tejon St., 719/389-0696, www.coloradoco-oponline.com, 10am-6pm Mon.-Sat., noon-5pm Sun.) sells lesser-known designers alongside those you would find at your local Nordstrom, including dresses, jeans, stationery, and jewelry. **Eve's Revolution** (1312 W. Colorado Ave., 719/633-1357, www.evesrevolution.com, 10am-5pm Mon.-Sat., noon-4pm Sun.) carries "emerging designers" (similar to those on Modcloth.com) with a few consignment items sprinkled in. If you're looking for a special flirty top or girlfriend gift, try **Terra Verde** (208 N. Tejon St., 719/444-8621, http://terraverdestyle.com, 10am-5pm Mon.-Sat., noon-5pm Sun.). The prices for everything from soap to jewelry and jeans to dresses are quite reasonable.

Sports and Recreation

Colorado Springs is as close to the mountains as people *think* Denver is; therefore it is possible to hike, run, and ride a bike right into the foothills from downtown. It is all closer here—the dramatic red rock formations of Garden of the Gods, the 14,000-foot Pikes Peak, the mountain creeks—and you're welcome to explore it. In a few places you have to earn your view, but you're always glad you made it to the top.

Although winters are fairly mild, the best seasons to get outside are fall, spring, and summer. Whenever pursuing any solo recreational activities, always tell someone else where you are headed and when you plan to return. It is possible to become lost or ill as a result of altitude sickness, even on a popular trail on a beautiful day.

Wildfires and floods may impact trail conditions. Contact the U.S. Forest Service (www.fs.fed.us) prior to your visit in order to ensure all trails and areas are open and accessible.

BALLOONING

Soar over Pikes Peak and Colorado Springs in a hot-air balloon ride with **Adventures Out West** (1680 S. 21st St., 888/501-5586, www.advoutwest.com, sunrise daily). Choose the basic 54-minute flight ($189 per person) or opt for the longer five-star flight ($250 per person, 3-4 hours).

BIKING

In town, you might want to try riding the **Santa Fe County Trail,** which crosses through Air Force Academy grounds and connects with the 16-mile **Pikes Peak Greenway** (https://coloradosprings.gov), part of the city's 118 miles of urban bicycle trails. Northwest of Colorado Springs is **Ute Valley Park** (1705 Vindicator Dr., 719/385-5940, http://friendsofutevalleypark.com), a hidden gem of sandstone mesas with hiking and biking trails winding through prairie grasses.

An easy way to see Pikes Peak is to bike down the mountain—that's right, down *only*. **Challenge Unlimited** (204 S. 24th Ave., 800/798-5954 or 719/633-6399, www.bikithikit.com, May 1-Oct. 20, weather permitting, $90-120) will meet you for breakfast and then drive you up Pikes Peak in their van before unloading the bikes and setting you free to roll down. They also offer a package in which you take the Cog Railway up the mountain, after which they meet you at the top with bikes so you can ride down.

Pikes Peak Mountain Bike Tours (302 S. 25th St., 719/337-5311, www.bikepikespeak.com, $55-120) offers several options both on and off the peak. Your van ride up to the peak includes breakfast, the bike down, and lunch at the end. Their self-guided Bike Gold Camp tour follows a 1800s-era locomotive railway (not on the peak), which can also be combined with a horseback ride at The Broadmoor Stables.

To explore **Garden of the Gods Park** (1805 N. 30th St., 719/634-6666, www.gardenofgods.com) you will need to BYOB—bring your own bike. The visitors center has trail maps and tips for mountain biking through the park, which involves sharing the road and/or trail with cars or hikers.

Bike Rentals

Bikes can be rented at **Criterium Bikes** (6150 Corporate Dr., 719/599-0149, www.criterium.com, 8am-8pm Mon.-Sat., 10am-6pm Sun., $30-50).

If you're staying at **The Broadmoor** (855/634-7711, www.broadmoor.com/broadmoor-outfitters, $45-85 for 2-4 hour rentals, $159 per person for guided rides), there are mountain bike rentals and guided mountain bike rides available. Call ahead for reservations for guided rides.

BIRD-WATCHING

The **Aiken Audubon Society** (http://aikenaudubon.com) is the Audubon chapter for the Pikes Peak Region; contact them for the latest information about local birding and guided hikes. **Pinello Ranch** (4940 S. U.S. Hwy. 85/87, www.ppcf.org/pinello-ranch, $9) has several ponds that attract nearly 300 bird species; the Aiken Audubon Society offers guided tours.

Chico Basin Ranch (22500 Peyton Hwy. S., Peyton, 719/683-7960, www.chicobasinranch.com), also called "The Chico," is a working cattle ranch that is also home to hundreds of bird species. In partnership with the Rocky Mountain Bird Observatory (http://www.rmbo.org), there is bird banding here in the fall and spring. The ranch maintains a birding trail, but asks that visitors check in first or that groups call ahead. Western meadowlarks, red-winged blackbirds, several kinds of sparrows, different species of waterfowl, and many more birds have been spotted here.

HIKING

It sounds counterintuitive to tell you to go east—away from the mountains—for a hike, but it's so worth it. One hour east of Colorado Springs (but still within El Paso County) is the **Paint Mines Interpretive Park** (29950 Paint Mines Rd., Calhan, 719/520-7529, http://adm.elpasoco.com, 5am-11pm daily), a 750-acre park with dramatic white-and-yellow hoodoo rock formations, as well as both Native American and ranching history. Come in the spring to see the wildflowers blooming in the prairie.

Pikes Peak

If you don't want to take the cog railway up to the top of Pikes Peak, you can get there on your own two feet via the **Barr Trail** (www.barrtrail.net). This is no casual day hike—you are climbing 12 miles and gaining almost 8,000 feet in elevation. While this is not a technical climb, be prepared with the proper gear for the elements at 14,115 feet. Given that there also is a highway (used for an auto race) and a cog railway bringing people up to the summit, it's a pretty busy spot and not a solitary jaunt in the wilderness. The view, though, is breathtaking—as is the elevation!—and it's something to brag about to "bag" a fourteener.

Garden of the Gods

Garden of the Gods (1805 N. 30th St., 719/634-6666, www.gardenofgods.com) has 15 miles of hiking trails. Stop in at the visitors and nature center (8am-7pm daily May-Sept., 9am-5pm Sept.-May) for maps of designated hiking, biking, and horseback riding areas. The center is also the meeting point for free, guided nature walks (10am and 2pm daily). The easy **Garden of the Gods Loop** (4 miles) is family-friendly and allows leashed dogs; keep an eye out for cars where the trail crosses the road. For a short stroll, try the **Ridge Trail** loop (0.5 mile) or the **Perkins Central Garden Trail** (1.5 mile), which is wheelchair accessible.

North Cheyenne Cañon Park

North Cheyenne Cañon Park (719/633-5701, http://cheyennecanon.org, 5am-11pm May-Oct., 5am-9pm Nov.-Apr.) is a 1,600-acre park with natural waterfalls and wildlife (especially hummingbirds). The on-site **Starsmore Visitor and Nature Center** (2120 S. Cheyenne Cañon Rd., 719/385-6086, 9am-5pm daily June-Aug., 9am-3pm Tues.-Sat. Apr.-May and Sept.-Oct.) informs kids and adults with hands-on nature exhibits, a climbing wall, and a gift shop. This is a good place to pick up trail maps and find out more about the park. Nearby is the trailhead for the **Columbine Trail**, which climbs up the canyon for four miles (one-way) to Helen Hunt Falls.

An easy hike with my favorite reward—a waterfall—starts at the **Helen Hunt Falls Visitor Center** (3440 N. Cheyenne Canyon Rd., 719/385-5701, www.coloradosprings.gov, 9am-5pm June-Aug.). The trail to the falls is less than one mile long with minimal elevation gain, making it both family- and dog-friendly. The falls are named after Helen Hunt Jackson, an author, poet and Native American activist who came to Colorado Springs in 1873.

The **Seven Bridges Trail** (6 miles round-trip) includes a walk across seven wooden bridges and a 1,500-foot elevation gain. Dogs are permitted on the trail. To get here from Colorado Springs, go south on Nevada from I-25, then west on Cheyenne Boulevard. Drive 3 miles before taking a right on Cheyenne Canon Road, where you will go 3.2 miles to the trailhead parking lot.

HORSEBACK RIDING

It's a truly Colorado experience to see this area on horseback. For a fun way to explore Garden of the Gods, contact **Academy Riding Stables** (719/633-5667, www.academyridingstables.com, 8:30am-4:30pm daily in summer, $50-75) to make a reservation for a one- to two-hour ride in the summer. In the fall, winter, and spring check on availability and conditions for the 2.5-hour perimeter ride that skirts the 1,400 acres of the park. A whole family can enjoy this mode of travel and sightseeing—sometimes it's easier than bike riding with younger children.

The Stables at The Broadmoor (1 Lake Ave., 866/837-9482, www.broadmoor.com/colorado) have one- to two-hour guided horseback rides and horse-drawn rides by reservation only. Guides lead riders through the mountains where you learn about a bit of the mining history and wildlife in the area—with hopes of seeing a little of both. As with everything The Broadmoor does, you can count on impeccable service and attention to detail.

GOLF

Some of area resorts have remarkable golf courses. **The Broadmoor** (1 Lake Ave., 855/634-7711, www.broadmoor.com/golf-courses, $85-275) has three courses: West Course, Mountain Course, and East Course. The 18-hole West Course (open year-round, weather permitting) is described as "challenging and rewarding." Jack Nicklaus won the U.S. Amateur championship on the links at The Broadmoor in 1959; more than 50 years later, Nicklaus Design was here to redesign the 18-hole Mountain Course. When the East Course opened in 1918, it was the highest golf course in the United States at 6,400 feet elevation (the newer West Course is 6,800 feet elevation). Today its expansive greens and tree-lined fairways make it one of the best in the country, if no longer the highest.

Cheyenne Mountain Resort & Club (3225 Broadmoor Valley Rd., 719/538-4095, www.cheyennemountain.com, $15-125) has an 18-hole Pete Dye-designed course along its 35-acre lake. Look into junior golf discounts and afternoon price specials.

Valley Hi Golf Course (610 S. Chelton, 719/385-6917, https://parks.coloradosprings.gov), owned by the city of Colorado Springs, is considered one of the best courses in the region. It's an 18-hole par 72 course with views of Pikes Peak and Cheyenne Mountain. The **Patty Jewett Course** (900 E. Espanola St., 719/385-6934, https://parks.coloradosprings.gov) was built in the late 1800s and has both an 18-hole course and a 9-hole course to play.

JEEP TOURS

Guess what? You can go up Pikes Peak or tour Garden of the Gods by Jeep! I know, it is amazing the number of ways to visit just these two places so close to one another. **Adventures Out West** (888/501-5586, www.advoutwest.com) offers a variety of options, including pairing a top-down Jeep tour with other adventures, like horseback riding.

For something different, try **The Broadmoor**'s (www.broadmoor.com/colorado-springs-tour, $60-119) High Country Jeep Tour that goes to 11,000 feet near Pikes Peak.

ROCK CLIMBING

It doesn't seem like it should be possible, given the fragile nature of the red sandstone formations in Garden of the Gods, but rock climbing is indeed allowed here. **Front Range Climbing Company** (719/632-5822 or 866-404-3721, www.frontrangeclimbing.com,

Mountain Course is one of three golf courses at The Broadmoor.

$100-200) offers guided climbs and classes in Colorado Springs and other locations in the area.

The Broadmoor (855/634-7711, www.broadmoor.com, $157 per person) has three climbing packages that take place in either Garden of the Gods or Cheyenne Canyon.

First Ascent Mountain School (719/304-6677, www.firstascentmountainschool.com, $97-277) has half-day and full-day rock climbing trips in Garden of the Gods and other locales. You can save money by joining a group. Reservations are required.

SPAS

With so many resorts in Colorado Springs, there is a good chance your accommodations include a spa not far from your room.

Cheyenne Mountain Resort (3225 Broadmoor Valley Rd., 719/538-4095, www.cheyennemountain.com) added a spa in 2015. They already have one of my very favorite qualities—local Colorado products—in addition to the usual massage, manicure, and pedicure pampering treatments.

You won't be surprised to learn that **The Broadmoor** (1 Lake Ave., 719/577-5770 or 866/686-3965, www.broadmoor.com/spa-treatments) has a decadent spa with a whole menu of treatments including facials (yes, even for the "gentlemen"), hydrotherapy (the climate and altitude can be very drying), body massages, and polishes. Plan to arrive well before your appointment so you can take advantage of the waiting room with beverages, light snacks, and a view of the East Golf Course.

Mateos Salon & Day Spa (5919 Delmonico Dr., 719/266-9295, http://mateos-dayspa.com) has been voted the best in town by readers of the *Colorado Springs Gazette* for seven years in a row. While they have your standard deep tissue massage, I am always intrigued by places that take it to the next level with unexpected ingredients. For example, Mateos has a Peruvian chocolate massage ("chocotherapy") and a Tuscan Wine Antioxidant Massage, which apparently offer unique health benefits. When traveling, I suggest doing that which can only be done here to have that authentic local experience.

Accommodations

When it comes to accommodations in Colorado Springs, The Broadmoor is the ultimate destination. Yet there are many lodging options for different styles and budgets between downtown Colorado Springs and throughout Manitou Springs. And, like The Broadmoor, it seems every hotel or inn here has an interesting history behind it—or at least an enviable view to take in.

For those looking for marijuana-friendly rental properties in the Colorado Springs area, check out www.coloradopotguide.com/marijuana-friendly-hotel as well as the listings below.

UNDER $100

The centrally located ★ **Boulder Crescent Inn and Hostel** (312 N. Cascade Ave., 303/912-3538, www.bouldercrescenthostel.com, $50-90) has welcomed lodgers for more than a century. Now the Victorian inn has stepped proudly into the future with a "Cannabis Cove" smoking lounge on its top floor. Don't worry about being a bad influence on the younger set; this is an adults-only establishment.

Historical in a different way, **The Satellite Hotel** (411 Lakewood Circle, 719/596-6800 or 800/423-8409, http://satellitehotel.net, $67-115) is a hybrid hotel that has been half converted into apartments/condominiums. Many of the rooms in this 14-story hotel feature sliding glass doors with views of the mountains. There is an outdoor pool for use in the summer.

The **Two Sisters Inn** (10 Otoe Pl.,

719/685-9684, www.twosisinn.com, $79-155) is a little pink house with bedrooms in the main house (with private or shared bathrooms) and a private guesthouse out back in the garden. The rates are reasonable and the service attentive.

$100-250

For that prime downtown location, stay at ★ **The Mining Exchange** (8 S. Nevada Ave., 719/323-2000, www.wyndham.com, $200-300), a Wyndham Grand Hotel. This building was constructed in 1902 as the stock exchange for the area's 20th-century mining companies. Guests will see the original bank vault in the lobby. Upstairs rooms resemble cool downtown lofts with high ceilings, exposed brick walls, and modern amenities such as flat-screen TVs and bathrooms with dual showerheads. Remodeled in 2012, this 117-room hotel also has a wonderful restaurant, Springs Orleans, and the Stratton Lobby Bar offers pub-style food to go with cocktails.

Before there was AirBnB there were places like the **Holden House Bed & Breakfast Inn** (1102 W. Pikes Peak Ave., 719/471-3980 or 888/565-3980, www.holdenhouse.com, $175) that make guests feel like they are staying over at a friend of a friend's place. Isabel Holden is credited with building this home in 1902, and it was restored in 1985. Today the six guest rooms of Holden House include the Victorian home next door, which was purchased by the inn's owners and renovated in 1994.

In downtown Colorado Springs, the **Antlers Hilton Colorado Springs** (4 S. Cascade Ave., 719/955-5600, www.antlers.com, $179-369) is popular with business travelers, but it is also a convenient location for seeing the sights. The original Antlers Hotel was built within a few years of General Palmer founding the city of Colorado Springs; the hotel's name was derived from the general's large collection of deer and elk antlers that was housed here. After the original hotel burned down, the Antlers was rebuilt in 1901 and then again in 1967 (that is the hotel where guests stay today). West-side rooms have views of Pikes Peak and guests can dine at the Antlers Grille for breakfast or Judge Baldwin's for lunch or dinner, both on site.

The **Old Town Guesthouse** (115 S. 26th St., 719/632-9194 or 888/375-4210, www.old-town-guesthouse.com, $185-265) is located in Old Colorado City. Despite the name, this is a new building (1997 meets 1859) and their most popular room is one that "exceeds ADA requirements." Nearly every room here has a view of Pikes Peak, a fireplace, and a personal hot tub...and a waterbed. Yes, a throwback to yet another era. Your total comfort is the goal—between a good soak while taking in the view, you can drift off to dreamland.

OVER $250

★ **The Broadmoor** (1 Lake Ave., 719/577-5775 or 855/634-7711, www.broadmoor.com, $270-635, year-round) is a five-star resort that has been expanding its accommodations. Guests can choose from rooms and suites ($750-1,000) in the hotel spread out along Cheyenne Lake, cottages ($750-1,000), and the all-inclusive The Ranch at Emerald Valley or Cloud Camp.

Open for seasonal stays in summer only, the **The Ranch at Emerald Valley** is a recent addition to The Broadmoor. It includes 10 perfectly appointed cabins surrounded by Pike National Forest and sitting at over 8,000 feet elevation. Meals are served in the Grand Lodge and days are spent hiking, riding bikes, fishing, and just soaking up the scenery. It's not quite "glamping" (glamorous camping that gets people outdoors with nary an inconvenience), but it's close—modern luxury meets the great outdoors.

On the historic site of founder Spencer Penrose's Cheyenne Lodge is the new **Cloud Camp.** Perched at 9,200 feet elevation, it contains a mix of lodge accommodations and cabins for couples or groups. Just getting here from The Broadmoor is an adventure—Jeep or mule? Neither? OK, then you can hike in with a guide...in three hours. Cloud Camp is only available seasonally.

The most rustic of The Broadmoor's outlying "Wilderness Experience" accommodations is also the newest. **Broadmoor Fishing Camp** debuted in 2015 on the Tarryall River. Guests of The Broadmoor will have day-use access to this private camp, where fly fishing, horseback riding, and hiking are all available. Seven cottages can accommodate overnight stays with a communal lodge nearby for meals.

★ **Cheyenne Mountain Resort & Club** (3225 Broadmoor Valley Rd., 719/538-4000, www.cheyennemountain.com, $199-350) might be the closest competition to The Broadmoor. In fact, the four-diamond resort has many of the same amenities found at The Broadmoor: Spread out across 217 acres, the grounds include a private 35-acre lake that has its own beach, as well as tennis courts, a golf course, three restaurants, and indoor and outdoor pools. Yet it's a different vibe altogether and the decor is more contemporary. Still, it's all about the amenities, even if it's not possible to take advantage of them all in one stay. Once here it's hard to take yourself away from just sitting on a deck and gazing at Cheyenne Mountain while the sun goes down. Go kayaking, sailing, or paddleboating on the beautiful lake or take lessons on the Pete Dye-designed golf course.

Garden of the Gods Club & Resort (3320 Mesa Rd., 719/632-5541, www.gardenofthegodsclub.com, $300-900) was once a playground for Hollywood luminaries such as John Wayne and Walt Disney. Rooms feature spectacular views of the park's jutting red rocks. In addition to an infinity pool and recreation pool, there is a seasonal splash park for families, tennis courts, and adult and junior golf programs at the 27-hole golf course. Since new ownership took over, millions have been invested in sprucing up the entire resort.

Chico Basin Ranch (22500 Peyton Hwy. South, 719/683-7960, www.chicobasinranch.com, $1,995 per person for six nights, all-inclusive) is a working cattle ranch 30 miles southeast of the city, but still part of Colorado Springs. While this is a family-run ranch, it is owned by the Colorado State Land Board and managed by Ranchlands, and what it offers is unique. Lakes and creeks on the property attract wildlife and there is hunting and fishing allowed on the property. The all-inclusive deal includes meals and activities. Rooms are in a historic adobe building with double beds or bunks.

a suite at The Broadmoor

Food

Given that Colorado Springs is a large city, it is easy to forget the ranching and agriculture communities that surround it. But these close connections mean that many menus feature locally sourced ingredients. From The Broadmoor to a pay-what-you-can-café, there are local farmers to thank for the fresh produce and other food served. This means that diners will be eating what's seasonally available—from lamb to herbs.

COFFEE AND TEA

Coffee shops aren't just for hitting on your way into the office in the morning. The **Coffee Exchange** (526 S. Tejon St., 719/635-0277, www.thecoffeeexchangecolorado.com, 7am-8pm Mon.-Thurs., 7am-10pm Fri., 8am-5pm Sat., 8am-3pm Sun.) is ready with live music on Friday nights, when it becomes more of a bar. The food is geared toward breakfast, but incudes gluten-free pastries too.

There's a theme at The Perk: local. Come to listen to the local music while sipping locally roasted coffee and noshing on locally baked breads and pastries. **The Perk** (14 S. Tejon St., 719/635-1600, www.theperkdowntown.com, 6am-8pm Mon.-Thurs., 6am-11pm Fri., 7am-11pm Sat., 7am-8pm Sun.) is locally owned and loved by those in need of a hot cup of coffee or tea and some free Wi-Fi.

Colorado Springs is home to dozens of evangelical Christian organizations. If this speaks to your interests, you can explore some Christianity with your coffee at **Café 225** (225 N. Weber St., 719/884-6225, www.cafe-225.com), a venue for films, discussions, and other Christian events.

BREAKFAST AND LUNCH

Whenever we travel, we support local economies and that's a good thing. But there are places that locals and visitors can do business with that have been created to do good for others. **Seeds Community Café** (109 E. Pikes Peak Ave., 719/473-8206, http://seedscommunitycafe.org, 10am-2:30pm Mon.-Fri.) is a nonprofit "pay what you can afford" restaurant that serves weekday coffee, pastries, and lunch. Not only that, the menu is vegan and gluten-free and features produce and other ingredients sourced from local farmers and ranchers. Get a boxed lunch to go if you're heading out on a hike.

With two locations in town, **Over Easy** (28A S. Tejon St., 719/471-2311 or 5262 N. Nevada Ave. #100, 719/598-2969, www.overeasycolorado.com, 7am-2pm Mon.-Fri., 7am-2:30pm Sat.-Sun.) is the city's go-to breakfast spot. Balance your day with a fresh-squeezed juice made with Colorado honey before you dig into the stack of bananas Foster pancakes. Gluten-free options are also available, along with—of course—many egg dishes.

Do you trust Guy Fieri, host of *Diners, Drive-ins, and Dives?* I kinda do, though I don't quite have his appetite for extra-spicy food. Fieri featured the ★ **King's Chef Diner** (110 E. Costilla Ave., 719/634-9135, www.cosdiner.com, 8am-2pm Mon.-Fri., $5-11) on his show and he was right on. Voted a local favorite for years, this is the place for a green chile-smothered breakfast burrito. In fact, their Colorado Green Chili is sold in jars at markets throughout the state. Other menu items include sandwiches and eggs, and incorporate ingredients from local ranches and farms.

Once in your life you should treat yourself to Sunday brunch at the **Lake Terrace at The Broadmoor** (1 Lake Ave., 866/381-8432 or 719/577-5771, www.broadmoor.com, 7am-11am Mon.-Sat., 9am-1:30pm Sun., Sun. brunch $17-52, children 3 and under free). Crepes, biscuits and gravy, eggs Benedict, omelets, pastries, fresh fruit, bacon, sausage… okay, I won't list the more than 150 food items on offer at this indulgent brunch feast, but it is

Ivywild

A beautiful old elementary school has been turned into a "community marketplace" in Colorado Springs. **Ivywild School** (1604 S. Cascade Ave., 719/368-6100, www.ivywildschool.com) is where the cool kids hang out as they flaunt their local roots. Under one roof you will find: the **Old School Bakery** (7:30am-7pm daily), **Bristol Brewery & Pub** (11am-10pm Mon.-Thurs., 11am-11pm Fri.-Sat., 11am-8pm Sun.), **The Principal's Office** coffee shop, (7:30am-10pm Mon.-Thurs., 7:30am-11pm Fri.-Sat., 7:30am-8pm Sun.), **Hunt or Gather** (noon-7pm Tues.-Sat.), a farmers market (3pm-7pm Wed.), and **The Meat Locker** charcuterie (11am-9pm Mon.-Thurs., 11am-10pm Fri.-Sat., 9am-8pm Sun.). Also on-site are a community garden, a live music venue, and artwork by children and local artists on display. Start the morning with a coffee and pastry or end the day with a brew and a bite.

a marvelous meal. Reservations are required and attire is resort casual.

AMERICAN

Start with the crème de la crème. ★ **The Penrose Room** (The Broadmoor, 1 Lake Ave., 855/634-7711, www.broadmoor.com, 6pm-9pm Tues.-Sat., tasting menu $84-135 pp) is Colorado's only five-star, five-diamond restaurant. Whether it's beets or beef, chances are good that your meal is fresh and local—maybe even sourced from The Broadmoor's own farm. Each dish has its own take, even if it's a classic like duck à l'Orange, chateaubriand, or lamb loin. The tasting menu offers selections from the sommelier, and there is selection of signature cocktails and wines by the glass. Note that there is a dress code—no denim allowed.

At the opposite end of the spectrum is **Play at The Broadmoor** (1 Lake Ave., 855/634-7711, www.broadmoor.com, hours vary seasonally, $6-28), which is as close as the resort gets to a sports bar. The idea is in the name: There's a restaurant on one side and a bowling alley on the other. Whether you order the popcorn appetizer, tacos, or pizza, it's playful food and a fun night out for families. Reserve a lane so you can enjoy a game with dessert.

A sister brewpub to the iconic LoDo Wynkoop Brewery, the **Phantom Canyon Brewing Company** (2 E. Pikes Peak Ave., 719/635-2800, www.phantomcanyon.com, 11am-close daily, $12-25) is located in a historic building downtown with a second floor devoted to billiards. They serve standard but dependably good pub food for lunch or dinner, with fresh beer on tap.

The **Ritz Grill** (15 S. Tejon St., 719/635-8484, www.ritzgrill.com, 11:30am-2am Mon.-Fri., noon-close Sat., 11am-close Sun., $13-27) offers a sophisticated art deco look and a late-night menu that makes it a local favorite. Check the website for live music nights.

If there was a category for Colorado food, the ★ **Colorado Mountain Brewery** (1110 Interquest Pkwy., 719/434-5750, www.cmbrew.com, 11am-9pm Sun.-Thurs., 11am-10pm Fri.-Sat., $7-18) would be in it. Bison poppers, venison egg rolls, steak burgers named after Colorado peaks, and brisket soaked in their Ole 59er Amber Ale set this menu apart from other brewpubs. There are three locations in the area and all offer military and college student discounts.

The **Blue Star** (1645 S. Tejon St., 719/632-1086, www.thebluestar.net, 11am-10pm Mon.-Fri., 3pm-10pm Sat.-Sun., $23-34) is Colorado Springs' answer to Boulder and Denver's The Kitchen, with a community vibe, an emphasis on "environmental harmony" using local suppliers, and a seasonal menu (including the cocktails). It's open for lunch and dinner and includes many vegetarian options.

BRITISH

Located just outside the main building of The Broadmoor is a classic English-style pub, the **Golden Bee** (1 Lake Ave., 719/577-5776, www.broadmoor.com, 11:30am-midnight Sun.-Thurs., 11:30am-1:30am Fri.-Sat., $11-21). Bangers and mash, Scottish salmon, and lamb burger are all featured on a menu enhanced by English and Irish drafts. Fans collect the restaurant's golden bee patches—tiny little decals that are locally stitched with a variety of themes. Join the nightly sing-along that starts at 9:30pm.

FUSION

It's not every day you see a fusion of Hawaiian and Mexican food, and it's even more surprising to find it in Colorado Springs. **La'au's Taco Shop** (830 N. Tejon St. #110, 719/578-5228, http://laaustacoshop.com, 11am-9pm daily, $7-10) masterfully blends these flavors in tacos, burritos, and salads. What makes it Hawaiian is the addition of pineapple, mango, and green papaya spiced up with jalapeños. Don't miss the Huli Huli chicken, marinated in peanut butter and miso.

ITALIAN

For truly authentic Italian food, **Ristorante de Lago** (1 Lake Ave., 855/634-7711, www.broadmoor.com, 5:30pm-9pm Mon. and Thurs.-Fri., 7am-11am Sat., 7am-11:30am Sun., hours vary seasonally, $16-36) is the place—they have some of their ingredients flown in from the home country. Not only do you get to know the story behind your mozzarella, but you also learn about the cows and trees of Italy, where generations of families have made the same delicious cheeses and oils.

There is such a nostalgic charm to **Fargo's Pizza** (2910 E. Platte Ave., 719/473-5540, www.fargospizza.com, 11am-9pm Sun.-Thurs., 11am-11pm Fri.-Sat., $4-22)—housed in a historic two-story, 500-seat building—that eating almost seems beside the point. This Wild West Italian version of Denver's Casa Bonita restaurant includes a full arcade for family entertainment. The thin-crust pizza is pretty tasty and there is a large salad bar.

VEGETARIAN

At The Broadmoor's ★ **Natural Epicurean** (1 Lake Ave., 855/634-7711, www.broadmoor.com, 6am-5pm Thurs.-Tues., 6am-11:30am Wed., hours vary seasonally, $7-25), the food is almost too pretty to eat. Get a green smoothie, delectable soup, or any vegetarian, vegan, or gluten-free seasonal salad, soup, or entrée for lunch or dinner (dinner is offered in summer only). The restaurant's "living wall"

the Natural Epicurean

of plants and a patio garden are reminders that you are eating what grows here.

Does 50 percent vegetarian appeal to vegetarians? **TAPAteria** (2607 W. Colorado Ave., 719/471-8272, www.tapateria.com, 11:30am-close Tues.-Sat., $3-9) must be on to something because their menu is 100 percent gluten free, 50 percent vegetarian, and 25 percent vegan small plates, including meat and seafood. There is a full wine list to accompany these Spanish goodies too.

Transportation and Services

AIR

The **Colorado Springs Airport** (COS, 7770 Milton E. Proby Pkwy., 719/550-1900, https://flycos.coloradosprings.gov) offers daily flights on Alaska Airlines, Allegiant, American Airlines, Delta, and United to 11 nonstop destinations. There is transportation to rental car agencies as well as check-in counters for those agencies at baggage claim. Some hotels offer shuttle service to and from the airport; check the airport website. The airport is located about 10 miles east of Colorado Springs, accessible via I-25.

Airport Transportation

Ground transportation options from the Colorado Springs Airport include limos, taxis, shuttles, and buses. **Colorado Springs Shuttle** (719/687-3456, www.coloradoshuttle.com) offers shuttle service to and from Colorado Springs airport, as well as a shuttle to the Denver airport. For taxi service, contact **Springs Cab** (719/444-8989) or **Yellow Cab** (719/777-7777).

CAR

Unless you are going straight to a resort or plan to stay in Manitou Springs, you might want a car so that you can visit local attractions from downtown Colorado Springs. Colorado Springs is just over a one-hour drive from Denver and many people make a day trip from the Mile-High City.

To reach Colorado Springs from Denver, take I-25 south for about 60 miles and look for signs to the various sights or downtown. **The Front Range Shuttle** (719/237-2646, http://frontrangeshuttle.com) is a commuter shuttle and executive car service between Denver and Colorado Springs with multiple ride options daily.

Car Rental

Car rental agencies are available at the **Colorado Springs Airport** (7770 Milton E. Proby Pkwy., 719/550-1900, https://flycos.coloradosprings.gov) and include most of the major companies, including Budget (719/597-1271) and Enterprise (719/591-6644).

PUBLIC TRANSIT

Greyhound (120 S. Weber St., 719/635-1505, www.greyhound.com, 8am-9pm daily, $10-15) buses service Colorado Springs from Denver daily. **Mountain Metropolitan Transit** (https://transit.coloradosprings.gov, $1.75) is a citywide bus service that serves as Colorado Springs' public transportation option. Route 3 provides service to Manitou Springs, while Route 2 gets you to Garden of the Gods.

Amtrak does not service Colorado Springs.

SERVICES

Stop by the **Experience Colorado Springs at Pikes Peak Visitor Center** (515 S. Cascade Ave., 719/635-7506, www.visitcos.com, Mon.-Fri. 8:30am-4:30pm) for maps and brochures of the area. The *Colorado Springs Gazette* (www.gazette.com) is the city's main newspaper, with listings of the latest local happenings. There is also the alternative weekly the *Independent* (www.csindy.com).

In an emergency, dial 911 for immediate assistance. **Memorial Hospital Central** (1400 E. Boulder St., 719/365-5000, www.uchealth.

org) offers many services including emergency, trauma, and pediatrics. Penrose-St. Francis Health Services includes **Penrose Hospital** (2222 N. Nevada Ave., 719/776-5000, www.penrosestfrancis.org) and **St. Francis Medical Center** (6001 E. Woodmen Rd., 719/571-1000, www.penrosestfrancis.org) and include an urgent care facility.

Vicinity of Colorado Springs

MANITOU SPRINGS

Manitou Springs is a charming town with its own identity, but it's so close to Colorado Springs that one could walk between the two—if you had the time for a six-mile one-way jaunt. But where downtown Colorado Springs feels very much like a city with office buildings, large hotels, and a campus, Manitou Springs is a walkable town of quaint shops, restaurants, inns, and a creek running through it.

It's been called a "Hippie Mayberry," and the town is certainly an appealing blend of historic allure and New Age trappings. Manitou Springs is also the gateway to Pikes Peak, as well as the Garden of the Gods. On

Manitou Springs

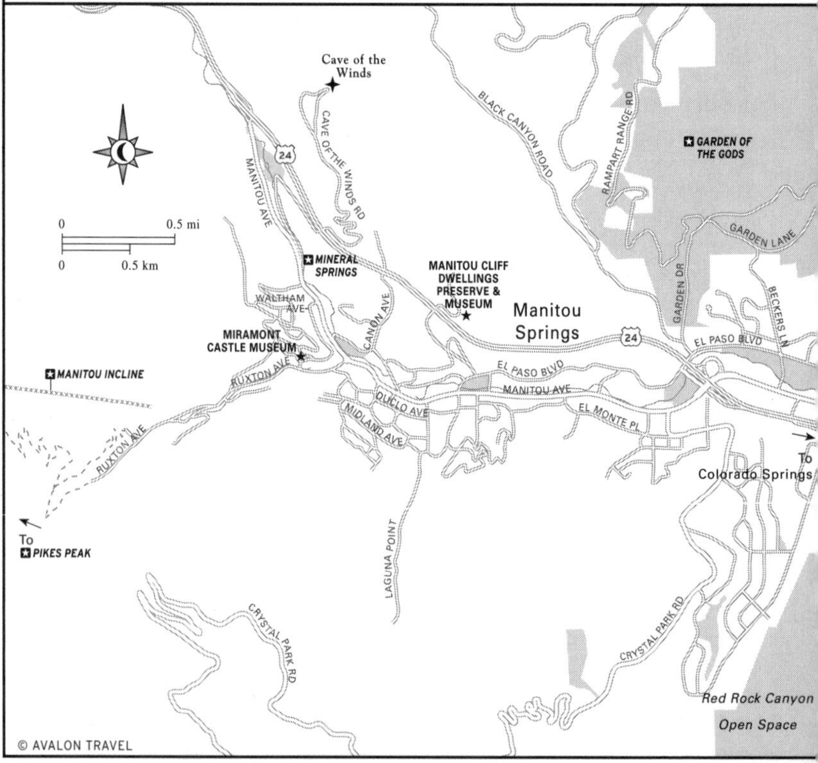

a clear day, the view from Pikes' 14,110-foot peak is incredible—and even inspired the lyrics for *America the Beautiful.*

Cave of the Winds

If you have ever been curious about caves, but too timid to crawl around in the dark, then maybe **Cave of the Winds** (Hwy. 24, 719/685-5444, http://caveofthewinds.com, 9am-9pm daily in summer, 10am-5pm daily in winter, $9-30, children under 5 free, though prices vary depending on the tour and age) is just right. Guided tours of the cave are well lit with wide walkways and handrails, and visitors can clearly see stalagmites, stalactites, and limestone caverns. The Discovery Tour takes 45 minutes and is offered daily every 30 minutes. The Lantern Tour is for the slightly more adventurous spelunker and it takes twice as long, with some stooping and less light. Overall, it can be a fun experience for school-age children.

Cave of the Winds was "discovered" by two brothers in the late 1800s. Today, it is a tourist trap—an enormous gift shop cleverly conceals the cave entrance. There is a pretty incredible view of the canyons below from the gift shop deck, which is equipped with binoculars. Cave of the Winds is about a five-minute drive from Manitou Springs.

Manitou Cliff Dwellings Preserve and Museums

Right off the bat, you should know that the **Manitou Cliff Dwellings** (Hwy. 24, 719/685-5242, www.cliffdwellingsmuseum.com, 9am-6pm daily June-Aug., $9.50 adults, $7.50 children, free for children 6 and under, $8.50 seniors) were relocated from somewhere else, and some of the buildings here are reproductions. The good news is that this lack of authenticity means more access to the entire site, unlike truly preserved cliff dwellings in southwestern Colorado. There are self-guided tours of the site and a lack of "do not touch" signs, as the effort here is to educate people about Native American cultures. Hours change seasonally; call ahead for current times.

★ Mineral Springs

Some of the best attractions in Manitou Springs are the springs themselves, conveniently available in decorative fountains located around the historic downtown. The water that fills the springs begins its journey as snowmelt from Pikes Peak. It then filters

the Manitou Cliff Dwellings Preserve

into the ground and becomes mineralized before resurfacing via cavernous limestone where it develops its effervescence—all over hundreds of years. The Native Americans who lived in this area drank from these unique mineral springs in order to heal themselves; they considered them medicinal as well as spiritual. As this area became settled in the late 1800s, the water was marketed as having healing properties in order to attract visitors.

Today unique, artistic fountains are installed around town so that visitors can sample the waters while learning a bit of their history. Stop in at the **Manitou Springs Chamber of Commerce and Visitors Bureau** (354 Manitou Ave., 719/685-5089 or 800/642-2567, www.manitousprings.org, 8:30am-5pm Mon.-Fri., 9am-4pm Sat.-Sun., free), where you will be given a small plastic souvenir cup for sampling the springwaters, a map of the various springs, and a detailed list of the health benefits of the mineral springwater. I'm not sure why or how, but the water at each of the springs has a completely different taste, some far less palatable than others. Guided tours are available (reservations required in summer), but you can sample the waters throughout the year.

the mineral springs in Manitou Springs

★ Pikes Peak

Pikes Peak (www.springsgov.com) is not only the state's most famous "fourteener" (a mountain peak that stands over 14,000 feet high); it is the second-most visited peak in the world. Over the years, people seem to have come up with every conceivable way to experience or ascend this mountain (all for a fee, unless you are fit enough to hike up). The 360-degree panorama from the top is simply spectacular.

Just up a narrow road from downtown Manitou Springs, the **Pikes Peak Cog Railway** (515 Ruxton Rd., 719/685-5401, www.cograilway.com, $19-35) slowly chugs train cars up the side of the mountain through forests and out to the barren mountaintop—and a gift and donut shop. The trip is a little over three hours, and there are health warnings and restrictions because of the altitude and heights. Several trips are held daily year-round. In the summer, you can catch a free **shuttle** (www.springsgov.com) in Manitou Springs that will take you to the Pikes Peak Cog Railway.

Pikes Peak also has its own toll road. It's 19 miles of curvy mountain driving that is paved for only about half the distance; the last nine miles are gravel.

Every summer, the **Pikes Peak International Hill Climb** (719/685-4400, www.ppihc.com, June) takes place on this seemingly dangerous road.

Barr Trail is the route for hikers to get to the 14,110-foot peak, and this, too, inspires an annual event with the Pikes Peak Marathon in August.

Miramont Castle Museum

Tucked into the town's historic district is a large castle that was constructed as a private home for a French priest and his mother in 1895. **Miramont Castle Museum** (9 Capitol Hill Ave., 719/685-1011, www.miramontcastle.

Saratoga of the West

The first settlement in these parts was Colorado City (now part of Colorado Springs), founded in 1859. Not only was the scenery an attraction, but the high altitude and dry climate were believed to have healing effects for people with tuberculosis. In 1871, the city of Colorado Springs was founded by General William Jackson Palmer. Palmer and Dr. William A. Bell came to the area after reading explorers' accounts of the healing waters found at the base of Pikes Peak. Together the two men founded the town of Manitou Springs, envisioning a spa resort here. Palmer had already founded the Denver & Rio Grande Railroad; in 1881, a railroad spur brought people to the new town.

Many of the hotels in Manitou Springs that still stand today hosted guests in the 1890s when it was dubbed "Saratoga of the West" after Saratoga, New York, also known for its mineral springs.

org, call for seasonal hours, $8 adults, $5 children, free for children 5 and under, $7 seniors) is an amalgam of architectural styles with 46 odd-shaped rooms. The castle has had many uses over the years—sanitarium, apartments—and is now filled with furniture and curiosities of the Victorian era.

Entertainment and Events

Old-fashioned theater fun is found at the Iron Springs **Chateau Historic Melodrama Theatre** (444 Ruxton Ave., 719/685-5104, http://ironspringschateau.com). While the concept of vaudeville ("Cheer the hero, boo the villain!") is not new, the plays are unique with titles such as *Panic on Pikes Peak*. This is dinner theater, so no need to dine out first.

If you haven't already noticed, they do things differently in Manitou Springs. The self-named "Manitoids" like to get in the Halloween spirit of late October with...coffin races in memory of poor Emma Crawford, an early resident who came to the area to cure her tuberculosis. Crawford was buried on Red Mountain, as she requested, but when a rainstorm flooded the area her empty coffin washed down the slopes. It's believed she haunts the mountain. The **Emma Crawford Coffin Races** (http://manitousprings.org/

Miramont Castle Museum

calendar/emma-crawford-coffin-race) take place the Saturday before Halloween.

It's the classic love/hate relationship with fruitcake during the **Manitou Springs Great Fruitcake Toss** (http://www.visitcos.com/fruitcake-toss) in January. First, contestants toss or fling or sling their own fruitcakes or one "rented" for this purpose; there is then a judging that factors in important details like distance. Kids, families, teams, and individuals are all invited to give it a go in this competition. Next, there is a local baking competition for the best fruitcake. People get very creative with both their tossing implements and their fruitcake recipes.

Shopping

Shopping in Manitou Springs means the usual tourist candy stores, T-shirt shops, and art galleries. But then things get more interesting with themed stores. There is the **Hemp Store** (2 Ruxton Ave., 719/685-1189, www.toddshempstore.com, 11am-6pm Mon.-Tues., 2pm-6pm Wed., 11am-6pm Thurs.-Sun.), with a variety of items made from the fiber, and **Nature of Things Chainsaw Art** (347 Manitou Ave., 719/685-0171, www.natureofthingschainsawart.com, 9am-5pm daily), with lots of wooden sculptures and demonstrations available.

Not a store, but worth a look, is **Rockey's Storybook Art Studio** (10-12 Cañon Ave., 719/685-9076, hours vary), where artist and local legend C. H. Rockey displays his sculptures and works on an intricately illustrated storybook.

CANNABIS SUPPLIES

Manitou Springs (or elsewhere outside of El Paso County) is the only place to go for local marijuana dispensaries. **Maggie's Farm** (141 Manitou Ave., 719/685-1655, www.maggiesfarmmarijuana.com, 8am-7pm daily) has won several Best of Colorado Springs awards for its offerings—possibly in part because it was the only game in town for a while. That doesn't mean its offerings aren't top notch, if a bit pricey. True to its name, Maggie's Farm sells only all-natural marijuana grown in the great outdoors on high-altitude farms.

An offshoot of an operation that launched in the Denver area several years ago, **Emerald Fields** (27 Manitou Ave., 719/375-0554, www.emeraldfields.com, 8am-7pm daily) opened to challenge Maggie's Farm's longtime Manitou Springs monopoly. The 3,000-square-foot space has an upscale boutique vibe, with attendants on hand to answer any questions.

Sports and Recreation

Manitou Springs is really in the foothills. No matter where you are in town, you can stroll and see the sights or enjoy a bit of nature on a trail, by foot, or on two wheels.

You can start—and stop—a hike on the **Ring the Peak Trail** (Crags and Horsethief Park Trails, 615 Teller County Rd. 62, www.fotp.com/8-trails/ring-the-peak-trail) that partially encircles Pikes Peak, though it is not a full ring yet. Added together, the Ring offers 63 miles of trails (so it makes sense to just do a section and double back). No matter how much of the ring you choose to hike, you'll see a less-traveled part of famed Pikes Peak.

Those interested in riding around town on two wheels should consider renting a bike for the day. Rental bikes can be found at **Rockhound Rentals** (8825 U.S. Hwy. 24, Cascade, 719/684-2408, www.rockhoundrentals.com, $35-50). They also offer mountain bike tours down Pikes Peak (after a van ride up).

★ MANITOU INCLINE

Where a cable car once crept up the side of the mountain, today people creep up the old rail ties on the **Manitou Incline** (7 Hydro St., www.manitouincline.com). This is a serious hike! In one mile, you will climb 2,000 vertical feet (from 6,500 feet to more than 8,500 feet), and there is a very steep 68 percent grade in some spots. Depending upon your fitness level it can take one to three hours to get to the top—unless you're a professional athlete like Olympic champion speed skater Apolo Ohno, and then apparently you can just run up there in less than 20 minutes. The views are amazing from the top.

Accommodations

$50-100

Pikes Peak Inn (626 Manitou Ave., 719/685-5616 or 800/664-2704, www.pikespeakinn.com, $65-130) is a real bargain, but it feels like a much pricier lodging with its clean, updated rooms decorated to evoke the West. You can walk to many of the sights in downtown Manitou Springs, including the Pikes Peak Cog Railway.

El Colorado Lodge (23 Manitou Ave., 719/685-5485 or 800/782-2246, www.el-colorado-lodge.com, $65-150) isn't a lodge at all, but a group of historic adobe cabins that are both family-friendly (pool, hot tub, and on-site playground) and pet-friendly. The cabins range in size and amenities—some have kitchens or fireplaces—and can sleep up to eight people or only two.

$100-250

It's as much about what's outdoors as indoors at the ★ **Rockledge Country Inn** (328 El Paso Blvd., 719/685-4515, www.rockledgeinn.com, $100-250). Situated on four acres, the inn is partially constructed from Manitou greenstone and surrounded by stunning views with easy access to hikes and downtown Manitou. This is a true getaway for those who want a break from city life. Rooms are more like apartments; at more than 700 square feet, the Spindletop Room has 17 windows, a view of Pikes Peak, and a marble jetted tub for two. Breakfast is included, with wine and hors d'oeuvres at check-in.

Sometimes a bed-and-breakfast crosses the line from quaint to kitsch. This is the case at the **Blue Skies Inn** (402 Manitou Ave., 719/685-3899 or 800/398-7949, www.blueskiesinn.com, $145-240). The theme is fun (there is a Blue Skies room with images of blue skies painted on the walls) and there is a variety of whimsical rooms here—one room is Indian Rock Art, another room is Morning Glory. Beyond the canopied beds and coordinating tile, each room has a gas or electric fireplace and some have jetted tubs large enough for two. The inn is next to a creek and the owners spend time gardening so there are lots of flowers in bloom in spring and summer.

OVER $250

For a small town, Manitou Springs has a lot of lodgings. The best in town has to be ★ **The Cliff House at Pikes Peak** (306 Canon Ave., 719/785-1000, www.thecliffhouse.com, $150-429), right in the heart of the action. The Cliff House began as a stop for miners, but then became popular with those who came for Manitou Springs' famous "healing waters." Such notable guests as Clark Gable and Theodore Roosevelt have laid their heads here. The in-house restaurants, the award-winning Dining Room and Red Mountain Bar and Grill, offer sophisticated contemporary cuisine.

Food

Adam's Mountain Café (934 Manitou Ave., 719/685-1430 or 719/685-4370, www.adamsmountain.com, 8am-3pm daily, 5pm-9pm Tues.-Sat., closed Mon. Oct.-Apr., $8-22) is a homey-feeling restaurant with lots of vegetarian options. They are kid-friendly and have a nice creekside patio where diners can watch other tourists sample the waters of Cheyenne Spring.

The **Cliff House** (306 Cañon Ave., 719/685-3000 or 888/212-7000, www.thecliffhouse.com, 6:30am-10:30am, 11:30am-2:30pm, 5:30pm-9pm daily, $20-35) is open for breakfast, lunch, and dinner with a separate (cheaper) Veranda menu available in the summer months for dining outside. The huge wine list is impressive, and one of the four staff sommeliers can help you make the right choice to accompany the Colorado bass or grilled venison.

A fine-dining option is the **Briarhurst Manor Estate** (404 Manitou Ave., 719/685-1864 or 877/685-1448, www.briarhurst.com, 5pm-8:30pm daily, $20-45), which was the home of Manitou Springs' founder, Dr. William Bell. The pink sandstone Tudor-style house is open for dinner nightly; entrees feature Colorado lamb and deer. Call ahead to verify Monday and Tuesday hours in the fall and winter.

Transportation and Services

To get to Manitou Springs from Denver, take I-25 south just past the exit for downtown Colorado Springs and exit on Cimarron Street (which becomes Highway 24) or Colorado Avenue. The drive takes about one hour and 15 minutes from downtown Denver, but try to time your trip to avoid rush-hour gridlock in Colorado Springs.

To get to Manitou Springs from Boulder, take Highway 36 east to Denver, then drive south on I-25 through Denver and to Colorado Springs. Once in Colorado Springs, take the exit for Manitou Springs.

In the summer, you can catch a free **shuttle** (www.springsgov.com) in Manitou Springs that will take you to the Pikes Peak Cog Railway, the Manitou Incline, and along Manitou Avenue.

The **Manitou Springs Chamber of Commerce and Visitors Bureau** (354 Manitou Ave., 719/685-5089 or 800/642-2567, www.manitousprings.org, 8:30am-5pm Mon.-Fri., 9am-4pm Sat.-Sun.) has more brochures than you will ever need and a helpful staff to answer questions and make suggestions. Take Highway 24 to Manitou Avenue and the visitors center will be on your right before entering town.

Background

The Landscape

Colorado is divided by the Rocky Mountains, with the largest concentration of cities and people lying to the east in what is called the Front Range. The 14,000-foot peaks of the Rockies frame the Front Range cities of Denver, Boulder, Fort Collins, and Colorado Springs. The largest of these cities, Denver, is located on the high plains about 12 miles east of the foothills. Despite an elevation of one mile above sea level, this is the flatter part of the state. Denver is a little bit of both mountains and plains, and the topography of the core neighborhoods varies greatly from floodplains to hills overlooking the city and everything in between.

Shaped by the location and beauty that lie to the west in the Rocky Mountains, Denver, Boulder, Colorado Springs, and Fort Collins each have a natural appeal of their own. All of these elements combine to make Colorado an attractive place to visit and explore, and you can have the best of both worlds—urban cities and the great outdoors.

GEOGRAPHY AND CLIMATE

While plains suggests flatland or lowland, in reality the land is more dynamic than, with the plains east of Denver at an even higher elevation than that of the city. This actually causes the waters of Cherry Creek to flow northwest, unlike rivers that run south and east from the mountains. From a different perspective, Denver is at the western edge of the plains, not the eastern side of the mountains. Boulder, Fort Collins, and Colorado Springs lie closer to the foothills; in some places, folks can just walk out the door and start hiking.

Lush isn't a word used to describe any of these cities on the Front Range. Rivers and creeks run through each city, with numerous reservoirs on the outskirts, but still this is an arid place. This is a high desert climate, with minimal precipitation: The average annual rainfall in Denver is 15.47 inches, and the average annual snowfall is 59.6 inches. Summers are dry and can be quite hot—though statistics put the average high at 88.1°F in July, it frequently climbs into the 100s. Denver has more annual days of sunshine than coastal places like San Diego; typically, a couple inches of snowfall will melt off within a few days.

Winters can be quite chilly, with average January lows at 16.9°F, but snowfall varies significantly. Some years, there's little snow all season, but every few years, it seems like the city is paralyzed by a blizzard. Because those blizzards garner a lot of national headlines, people mistakenly believe that Denver has severe storms every winter. It's a paradox for officials: Because such snowstorms are unusual, they are not adequately prepared with enough plows and staff, yet such emergencies do happen. It can be bad publicity for the city, but is usually good news for the ski resorts.

ENVIRONMENTAL ISSUES

Growth is a double-edged sword for the Front Range cities, and always has been for Denver, resulting in two prominent environmental issues: air pollution and water use.

Since Denver's earliest days, there have been struggles to divert enough clean water to supply the city—and now the greater metro area, which consists of seven counties. There needs to first be a certain amount of precipitation at the highest points in the mountains,

Previous: Colorado State Capitol; Academy Riding Stables.

Floods and Fire

For all the talk of Denver being so arid, water has dramatically shaped the city.

As the first settlements at the confluence of Cherry Creek and the Platte River were being built, Native Americans warned the white men that flooding was a risk. But before they could be proved right, a fire broke out in 1863 when drunken revelers knocked over a lamp. The simple wood-frame structures were engulfed in flames and most of the city's business district was lost. Though precious supplies were gone, the buildings were quickly rebuilt—this time with brick.

Brick, however, was no help a year later, when Cherry Creek became a raging torrent of water after heavy spring rains. Lives, buildings, livestock, and much more were lost, but people kept rebuilding, even in the floodplain. There were many more floods until the 1950s, when the Army Corps of Engineers built the Cherry Creek Dam.

In 1965, the relatively tame South Platte River became swollen with rainwater and crashed through bridges and property, causing $300 million in damage. The floodwaters were full of the refuse that residents freely dumped in the river, including items as big as refrigerators. This disaster led to the Platte Redevelopment Committee, which over the next decade turned the waterways into a greenbelt and a growing source of civic pride.

where rivers and streams are fed by rain and snow each year. Most of the rivers actually head west from the Continental Divide, and what is flowing east doesn't simply end in Denver, but keeps heading south through other parched states to the distant ocean. One source of water is brought "uphill" over the Continental Divide to provide water to Denver and its suburbs. Water laws and rights are complicated issues that have become more prominent during drought years. There are mandatory water-use rules and water "police" who fine people for watering their grass at the wrong time. The strict, hit-them-in-the-wallet restrictions have decreased water use by billions of gallons, but as growth continues amid the naturally arid conditions, conservation efforts are an ongoing part of life in Denver and elsewhere on the Front Range.

While taking fewer showers or living with a yellow lawn turned out to be acceptable conservation measures for residents, helping to

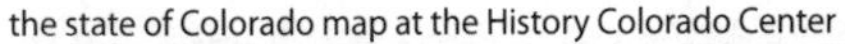
the state of Colorado map at the History Colorado Center

reduce air pollution and the city's notorious "brown cloud" is another challenge.

Once upon a time, Denver had a streetcar system that was done away with to make way for the almighty automobile. As the population boomed between 1960 and 1980, the number of cars on the freshly built highways and roads also exploded. It wasn't until the 1980s that auto emission tests became mandatory here. Cars weren't the only source contributing to the smog (or "smaze," as some called it), and trash burning was prohibited. Coal-burning power plants have had to cut their emissions and wood-burning fireplaces are nearly obsolete, with restrictions on days that they can be used. The fact that Denver lies in a river basin between the plains and the mountains means that the fine particles of pollution—whether from road sand or carbon monoxide emissions or smoke—are going to settle in the air in this low spot.

The brown cloud is not gone, and it can obscure views from the city or of the city itself when approaching it, but there is more and more emphasis on alternative transportation in Denver and beyond to possibly reduce the haze and pollution. Residents and visitors alike are encouraged to ride bikes, take the light rail trains or buses, or simply walk instead of driving. The city often struggles to stay in compliance with Environmental Protection Agency standards and has to keep finding ways to reduce air pollution.

History

It is speculated that Europeans first came through what is now Colorado in the 1500s, and that the search for riches of silver and gold began in the 1700s. The Louisiana Purchase of 1803 meant that the land east of the Continental Divide and north of the Arkansas River was transferred to the United States. Exploratory parties were sent out and by the 1850s prospectors were making their way west into the Colorado Territory. Supply towns were built, along with railroads, and the growth paved the way for Colorado to become a state in 1876.

DENVER

Denver is that rare city that was not built up along a road, railroad, or navigable body of water. There is evidence that people had used the area as a hunting ground as many as 11,000 years ago. The Laramie Treaty of 1851 had conceded this land to the Arapaho and Cheyenne tribes, but that agreement was pretty much ignored when prospectors found flecks of gold in the Platte River in 1858. (Other whites had come through this stretch prior to the gold discovery, only to categorize it as a "desolate wasteland" and keep on going.) Though there wasn't really a fortune to be found in the waters near the confluence of Cherry Creek and the Platte River, prospectors set up their town on the banks of the two waterways. General William Larimer of Kansas put some sticks on a nearby hill to make his claim, which later became Denver.

There were initially three towns, but in 1859, a shared barrel of whiskey was all it took for the two smaller towns to be convinced to become part of Denver. Even the naming of the city was a bit of a bumble: Local leaders strove to impress territorial governor James Denver, who lived in Kansas, by naming the city after him, but he had already retired and never came to Denver.

As the first Denver City was established with cabins and tents set up at what is now Confluence Park, Native Americans were edged out—often in violent and bloody confrontations. The new settlers and members of the Cheyenne and Arapaho tribes clashed, and a new treaty was drawn up in 1861 that gave Denver to the United States.

In those early years, Denver was the "Wild

LITTLE RAVEN
Mayor's South Platte River Commission, Wellington E. Webb, Mayor
Peace Chief of the Southern Arapaho
The Arapaho Indians were one of the last indigenous people to call the South Platte River Valley home. The story of Arapaho Chief Little Raven spotlights the losses of freedom, land and life endured by Plains Indians in the late 19th Century.
A Hell Of A Deal

Learn the history of Native Americans who lived here before Denver was founded.

West," with saloons, brothels, and lawlessness. The city established itself as a supply center for the thousands flocking to the newest gold discoveries in the nearby mountains, and the mountains' harsh winters sometimes drove people back to the more hospitable Denver weather; people also came to Colorado, and specifically Denver as well as other cities like Manitou Springs to the south, seeking a cure for tuberculosis. The town weathered devastating fires and floods, but there were always those optimists who saw the potential for Denver to be more than a dusty frontier town.

The population in Denver was only 3,500 in 1866, when it was among the Front Range cities competing to be the territory's capital. For a brief time the city of Golden held the honor, but in 1867 Denver finagled its way into becoming the territorial capital, and it retained the title when Colorado achieved statehood in 1876. Denver officially became Colorado's capital in 1881.

Railroads are what truly cemented Denver's place on the map. Hundreds of trains a day were passing through here in the late 19th century, many loaded with supplies for mining towns. The Beaux Arts-style Union Station was erected in 1914 and is the city's only remaining train depot, but there are train museums here that show off old locomotives and fancy passenger cars and give a more in-depth telling of how railroads shaped Denver and many cities in the West.

Denver's citizens learned about building a city the hard way. Fire destroyed most of the town's early wood-frame buildings, while floods wiped out structures and took lives. Cyclical economic downturns also affected the city. But the miners making their fortunes in the mountains continued to invest in Denver, and by the turn of the century the population was over 100,000 and grand theaters and hotels were built to meet the needs of the city. When the silver boom crashed, Denver slumped in a depression along with the rest of the country; agriculture and food processing kept the economy going. When the Dust Bowl years came along about 1930 and the Great Depression hit, Denver was brought to its knees. That frontier "can-do" spirit prevailed and the New Deal meant improvements in parks, trails, and roads that brought tourists to the area.

World War II also changed economic fortunes for Denver. Because the city was considered an unlikely place to be bombed, Buckley Air Force Base, the Rocky Mountain Arsenal, and other military installations were built here and created more jobs. Over time, federal scientific, research, and technological facilities also established themselves in the greater Denver area.

After World War II, oil and gas businesses took interest in Denver for its location near energy fields and thus began the upward growth of the city's downtown skyscrapers. As boom-and-bust cycles continued, the city grew and shrank again, but now it is clear how those booms have led to Denver's current moment as a darling city to live in and visit. Mayor Federico Peña, Denver's first Latino mayor, is credited with getting Denver International

Airport funded (that's why you drive on Peña Blvd. coming and going from DIA), getting a tax approved to fund the building of Coors Field (home of the Colorado Rockies baseball team), and getting the Scientific and Cultural Facilities District tax approved by voters. Next up in 1991 was Wellington Webb, the city's first black mayor, and he too had a long-term vision for his hometown as he oversaw development of many of today's urban playgrounds like Commons Park.

Today Denver's population is close to 650,000, and the greater metro area (that includes seven counties) is at nearly three million. The boom may just be beginning.

BOULDER

The Southern Arapaho tribe were the first to live in the Boulder area. Utes, Cheyenne, and other tribes would visit and were also drawn to the region for its natural beauty. In the 1850s European settlers arrived seeking gold, and by 1859 the town of Boulder was created (though it wasn't incorporated until 1871) as supply center for miners headed into the nearby mountains to dig out their fortunes. As the town established itself with a school, railroad service, and other basic necessities, the University of Colorado was able to get its start here in 1876.

As Boulder developed a local economy, it began a lifelong cycle of seasonal population fluxes. In its first few years, the University of Colorado had a tiny enrollment of less than 100 students; today, around 30,000 students pour into Boulder at the beginning of each school year. After Chautauqua Park was built in 1898, Boulder developed a reputation as a summer retreat drawing a few thousand visitors each year. With the influx of students and vacationers, and easy access via the railroad, Boulder began to develop a tourism industry.

Yet Boulder did not rely solely on tourists to keep the economy going. In the 1950s the town became the home of the National Bureau of Standards' Radio Propagation Laboratory—and that got the ball rolling on federal government and scientific organizations basing themselves here. Rocky Flats, a nuclear weapons manufacturing facility, was built south of Boulder; Ball Aerospace was founded here; and Boulder became the headquarters for the National Center for Atmospheric Research. Since then, IBM and many other tech businesses have set up shop here.

As business and organizations attracted new residents, city leaders maintained an emphasis on preserving the natural beauty of Boulder as it grew. Restrictions on building heights were put in place, sanitation lines were brought into the mountains, and green space was preserved.

Today, Boulder sits in a nest flanked by the dramatic rising mountains on one side and open space on the other. This combination of intellectualism, physical fitness, and business savvy surrounded by gorgeous scenery is what makes Boulder so appealing.

COLORADO SPRINGS

There are a few funny misunderstandings in the story of how the city of Colorado Springs came to be. Take the name of Pikes Peak, the 14,000-foot peak to the west of the city. Explorer Zebulon M. Pike did make it to the area in November 1806 and attempted to hike the mountain, but snow and hunger turned him and his party back; the peak and national forest here are thus named after him for his "discovery" of the peak, not for his summiting of it. Of course, the high mountain peak—along with the sculptural red rocks, cascading waterfalls, and mineral springs that attract tourists to Colorado Springs today—drew Native American tribes to the region hundreds of years before Pike and his party set eyes on the area.

After the California Gold Rush was exhausted in 1859, miners (called "Fifty-niners") turned their attention to Colorado. They aimed for Pikes Peak—some even going so far as to paint the mountain's name on their covered wagons—but gold was actually discovered 85 miles north of the mountain, close to what is now Denver. A significant gold mine was discovered on the western slope of

Preserving Historic Buildings

the Molly Brown House Museum

By the 1960s, there was growing concern among preservationists about the demolition of many historic homes, buildings, and neighborhoods within Colorado's towns. These protests were led in large part by Dana Crawford and other like-minded women, such as future congresswoman Patricia Schroeder, who took on developers' plans to tear down all of Denver's Larimer Square. The Daniels and Fisher Tower on 16th Street was saved, but many other buildings were lost to the wrecking ball. The original town of Auraria, founded at the same time as Denver and eventually incorporated into the city, was demolished even though it was a historic Latino enclave. The land—about 20 city blocks—was used to make way for the Auraria college campus.

In 1970, the organization **Historic Denver** (www.historicdenver.org) was formed and the Molly Brown House was successfully saved and restored. This was just the first of many important preservation projects in Denver, and the stories of many of those salvaged edifices are found in Historic Denver's series of small paperback books. The books serve as neighborhood guides or thematic tours of landmarks such as churches. Places like the Molly Brown House Museum and the Colorado History Museum sell the books.

Another preservationist managed to save that most valuable asset: the mountain view. Helen Millet Arndt, founder of the Denver Landmark Preservation Committee, conducted a survey that revealed that locals thought the mountain backdrop was what made their city special. In 1968, city council passed the Mountain View Preservation ordinance, thanks to Arndt and her supporters. This has prevented building that might obstruct the mountain view from the state capitol and numerous city parks.

Pikes Peak in 1891 and the Cripple Creek Gold Camp was created.

The discovery of gold created a population explosion in Colorado Springs, as the area became known, resulting in a "city of millionaires." Much of that money was poured into making the area more attractive to tourists. After Spencer Penrose earned his first million in the Cripple Creek mine (as well as in mines in Utah), he established The Broadmoor, the Cheyenne Mountain Zoo, and the Pikes Peak Highway.

During World War II, military bases were established in Colorado Springs. This industry became an important cog in the local economy. Today, Colorado Springs is home to six major military installations: United States Army base Fort Carson, the United States Air

Force Academy, Peterson Air Force Base, the United States Space Command, Schriever Air Force Base, and NORAD (North American Aerospace Defense Command).

In 2015, the population of Colorado Springs was more than 400,000 and the greater metropolitan population was more than 600,000 (compare that to the metro area population of Denver at 2.7 million). Yet in many ways, Colorado Springs still feels like an up-and-coming metropolis when compared to the more bustling Denver, and that's a good thing for vacationers.

FORT COLLINS

Like many Western towns and cities, Fort Collins's history has to do with water. In 1862, Camp Collins started as a military outpost built on the Overland Trail and situated along the Cache La Poudre River (so named because French-Canadian fur traders hid their gunpowder here). In 1864, it was relocated after a flood to the current location of Old Town Fort Collins.

Soon, settlers began to arrive and Camp Collins ceased being a fort. By the time the railroad arrived in 1877, the former camp had become a town with a hotel, general store, post office, and school. Colorado Agricultural & Mining College built its first classroom here in 1879; in 1957, the institution became Colorado State University.

Water remained an important aspect of the town's economy, as a combination of farming and ranching began to put Fort Collins on the map. Farmers grew sugar beets, which then were fed to sheep, which were then slaughtered. (At one point, Fort Collins was referred to as "the lamb-feeding capital of the world.") Economic times changed, and by the 1960s the university became the primary economic engine of the city.

Even as Fort Collins grew and expanded, preservationists worked to maintain the original buildings and character in the city. Thanks to the combination of outdoor life and good jobs, the town has been named one of the best places to live and one of the best places to retire in the United States. Unfortunately, flooding has continued to be a part of life in Fort Collins, with both Spring Creek and the Cache La Poudre sometimes overflowing their banks.

Government and Economy

Colorado's economic history is one of struggle and reinvention, as the state has weathered dramatic ups and downs through the years. Fortune seekers, entrepreneurs, thinkers, leaders, and visionaries have long come to Colorado to better themselves or make this place better for others.

The economic sectors that shaped Colorado remain important even as new industries add to the bottom line. In mid-2015, the University of Colorado Leeds School of Business found that the state economy was outpacing the United States economy—and tourism is a huge part of that. Investing in the arts is also paying off in Colorado. The Colorado Business Committee for the Arts found that the arts generated $1.85 billion of total economic activity in the Denver metro area (seven counties, including Boulder).

Tourism has been breaking records, and again, outpacing national averages. In 2014, more than 71.3 million visitors spent $18.6 billion in Colorado. Some of those tourism dollars can be attributed to the legalization of recreational marijuana. The Colorado Department of Revenue reported $700 million in marijuana sales in 2014, and that doesn't factor in money spent on lodging, dining, and more.

Essentials

Transportation

GETTING THERE AND AROUND

Air

Denver International Airport (DIA, 303/342-2000, www.flydenver.com) is the fifth-busiest airport in the country, with more than 53 million passengers traveling through it each year. The airport's distinctive white-peaked roof has become a symbol of the city—and copied in smaller versions. The airport is 25 miles from downtown Denver, and like most airports these days, it's a mall of sorts, too (look for local favorites Tamales by La Casita and Dazbog Coffee). In addition to the shops and restaurants, the airport offers free Wi-Fi (call 800/986-2703 for technical support) and has a U.S. Post Office (Level 6, Jeppesen Terminal, closed Sun.), a USO Center (303/342-6876), a Jewish and Christian Interfaith Chapel, and an Islamic Masjid, all open 24 hours. Security wait lines can be miserable; try the line leading to Concourse A, then take the elevator to the trains to reach other concourses. Be sure to note your baggage claim number and location, as there are baggage claim carousels on both sides of the terminal, east and west.

DIA is served by most major domestic airlines. Frontier Airlines (801/401-9000, www.frontierairlines.com), which maintains a hub in Denver, is a low-cost carrier. Southwest Airlines (800/435-9792, www.southwest.com) has provided some good low-airfare competition, and legacy carriers United Airlines (800/864-8331, www.united.com) and American Airlines (800/433-7300, www.aa.com) have many flights daily to and from DIA. International airlines that serve DIA include Aeromexico, Air Canada, British Airways, Icelandair, and Lufthansa.

The **Colorado Springs Airport** (COS, 7770 Milton E. Proby Pkwy., Colorado Springs, 719/550-1900, https://flycos.coloradosprings.gov) offers daily nonstop flights to 11 destinations on Alaska Airlines, Allegiant, American Airlines, Delta, and United.

AIRPORT TRANSPORTATION

It's typically a $55 flat rate to take a cab between DIA and downtown Denver. Bus service (RTD, 303/299-6000, www.rtd-denver.com, $9 one-way or less for seniors, children, and advance purchases) is the cheapest transportation. Shuttle vans are available at the airport to take passengers directly to destinations like Vail, Estes Park, and Boulder, and directly to downtown Denver hotels. **Colorado Mountain Express** (970/754-7433 or 800/525-6363, www.coloradomountainexpress.com) goes to Vail, Aspen, Keystone, and other ski towns; **Estes Park Shuttle** (970/586-5151, www.estesparkshuttle.com) costs $85 round-trip between the airport and Estes Park; and **Super Shuttle** (303/370-1300 or 800/258-3826, www.supershuttle.com) offers door-to-door service with discounts for ride shares. Contact the airport's **Ground Transportation Information Office** (Level 5, Jeppesen Terminal, 303/342-4059, 6:30am-11:30pm daily) for additional information about services.

There are 10 rental car companies based at DIA and each provides free shuttle service to its rental lot. The rental car agencies also have service counters in the Jeppesen Terminal, Level 5.

There is short- and long-term parking at DIA, and even valet parking for $33 per day. The closest garage parking is $24 per day or $3 per hour, and uncovered parking lots that are

Previous: Denver International Airport; Cog Railway.

still within walking distance of the terminal cost $13 per day or $3 per hour. The west-side parking lots seem to fill up faster than the east side. There are cheaper parking lots that require shuttle bus service to reach, and those cost $8 per day or $2 per hour.

Train

Amtrak's *California Zephyr* (800/872-7245, www.amtrak.com) has arrivals and departures at Denver's Union Station (1701 Wynkoop St., 303/592-6712, http://unionstationindenver.com), but there is no further service to Boulder, Fort Collins, or Colorado Springs.

RTD light rail trains (303/299-6000, www.rtd-denver.com) travel from the Denver suburbs to downtown and are packed at rush hour. Regional routes provide service from Denver to Golden, Boulder, and Nederland.

Bus

Denver's **Greyhound Bus Station** (1055 19th St., 303/293-6555, www.greyhound.com) is conveniently located downtown, within walking distance from hotels, car rental agencies, municipal bus depots, and Union Station. Greyhound also provides service to Colorado Springs from Denver ($33 one-way).

To get around Denver, its suburbs, and other Front Range cities, use **RTD** (1600 Blake St., 303/299-6000, www.rtd-denver.com). The main bus terminal is in the LoDo neighborhood of Denver, behind Union Station; you can pick up schedules for just about every route. RTD provides bus service to and from the airport, Boulder, and many other towns in the greater metro area. City and regional buses are almost always equipped with bike racks in front.

Front Range Shuttle (719/237-2646, www.frontrangeshuttle.com, from $49 per person one-way) provides bus service to and from Colorado Springs, Castle Rock, and Monument south of Denver.

Car

No matter where you are coming from by car, you'll end up on I-70 (east-west across the state) or I-25 (north-south across the state) to get to Denver, Colorado Springs, Fort Collins, and even Boulder. The most unpredictable part of the drive can be I-70 in the mountains, where icy roads, traffic accidents, and rock- and snowslides have all closed the road at one time or another.

Like most midsize to large cities, Denver is plagued by gridlock on the highways that

Denver's Union Station

circle much of the city. Light rail trains do not do much to alleviate the rush hour congestion, even though the trains are standing-room-only during those times. Rush hour congestion makes driving from Denver to Fort Collins and Colorado Springs a real challenge. Highway 36 into Boulder added an express lane for those carpooling or willing to pay a fee to travel faster; otherwise it's clogged with traffic too. Fortunately, it is possible to get around Denver on foot, bicycle, bus, or light rail, with limited expense and hassle.

Check **road conditions** (dial 511, 303/639-1111, www.cotrip.org or www.cdot.gov), especially when driving in winter in the mountains.

CAR RENTALS

There are major car rental agencies at the Denver airport (DIA, 303/342-2000, www.flydenver.com) and in downtown Denver, including **Avis** (1900 Broadway, 303/839-1280, www.avis.com, 7am-6:30pm Mon.-Fri., 7am-5pm Sat.-Sun.), **Enterprise Rent-A-Car** (650 15th St., 303/623-1281, www.enterprise.com, 8am-6pm Mon.-Fri., 9am-noon Sat.-Sun.), and **Budget Rent-A-Car** (1980 Broadway, 303/292-9341, www.budget.com, 7am-6pm Mon.-Fri., 7am-4pm Sat.-Sun.).

Car rental agencies are also available at the Colorado Springs Airport (7770 Milton E. Proby Pkwy., 719/550-1900, https://flycos.coloradosprings.gov) and include **Budget** (719/597-1271) and **Enterprise** (719/591-6644).

Taxis

In the Denver metro area and the Front Range cities, it's almost impossible to walk out to the street and hail a cab. Most hotel entrances will be home to a small fleet of cabs waiting for a fare. Otherwise, it's better to call and wait for the taxi to show up.

The most interesting thing to happen with taxis is the transition to hybrid vehicles. **Metro Taxi** (303/333-3333, www.metrotaxidenver.com), Denver's largest taxi company, has converted some of its fleet to hybrid-electric Toyota Prius cars, and **Yellow Cab** (303/777-7777 in Denver, 719/777-7777 in Colorado Springs, www.yellowtrans.com) also added some hybrid vehicles. There is also **Freedom Cab** (303/444-4444, www.freedomcabs.com), which services Denver and Boulder; just look for the purple cars.

Biking

Colorado, and especially Denver, is increasingly accommodating to bicyclists, as two-wheeled transportation gets more support as an environmentally friendly alternative to cars. **Denver B-cycle** (http://denver.bcycle.com) allows anyone to rent a bike and ride around the city for a small fee. Many city streets have bicycle lanes, biking paths are common, and city and regional buses (say, those going to Boulder) have bike racks on the front so people can pedal to the bus stop, ride, and then pedal on home or to the office.

Learn about bicycle ordinances, find bike maps, and get riding tips at www.denvergov.org/bikeprogram, or check out www.bikedenver.org, a bicycling advocacy group's blog. The **Denver Bicycle Touring Club** (www.dbtc.org) organizes group rides for members throughout Denver.

Conduct and Customs

GENERAL ETIQUETTE

Don't be surprised at how friendly people are in Colorado, with total strangers smiling and saying hello as they pass on the street. This is also common when out walking or hiking in the mountains, where it's considered normal behavior for people to greet each other with a simple, "Hi, how's it going?" as they pass one another on a trail. It's a great icebreaker for the next question, "How much farther to the top?"

On busy urban pedestrian and bike paths, it is customary for faster bicyclists to shout, "On your left!" (or something similar) as they approach slower cyclists or pedestrians from behind. Some paths are designated for only cyclists or pedestrians, and others are shared use.

Throughout many popular sights in downtown Denver, such as Civic Center Park and along the 16th Street Mall, there are often homeless people panhandling. In an effort to decrease this presence and help break the cycle of homelessness, the city has established places for donating money to be used by programs for those in need. Dozens of meters have been installed around downtown into which spare change can be deposited for such programs. The meters are distinguished by their red posts (as opposed to the silver posts of traditional meters) and bring in thousands of dollars annually that help provide services for the homeless. People are encouraged to donate their money there rather than give directly to panhandlers. For more information about Denver's plan to end homelessness, visit www.denversroadhome.org.

BUSINESS HOURS

Most shops open at 10am on weekdays and Saturday, but not until noon on Sunday; closing time is usually anywhere from 5pm to 7pm. Local art galleries tend to close on Sunday and Monday, and the Denver Art Museum is always closed on Monday.

Many restaurants also take Monday off, but hours frequently change. Typical kitchen closing time in Denver restaurants is about 10pm, and bars close up by 2am or earlier. If a restaurant has a bar, there is often a late-night menu. Some bars prefer not to specify their closing times so that they can close early on a slow night or extend hours on a busier night.

Cannabis dispensaries in Colorado may operate 8am-midnight most days; however, city ordinances often impose more restrictive hours. In Denver, cannabis dispensaries must close by 7pm. Dispensaries in neighboring Edgewater extend their hours to midnight.

SMOKING

The Colorado Clean Indoor Air Act passed in 2006 and took effect the same year, banning smoking indoors in public places throughout the state. The Denver City Council has passed more specific ordinances, such as banning smoking outside of hospitals. It is not uncommon to see signs outside of some buildings asking smokers to stand a certain distance from a building entrance or exit. More common is the sight of restaurant and bar patios—or simply sidewalks in front of these establishments—filled with smokers in any kind of weather. The lone exception is cigar bars, such as the Churchill Bar in the Brown Palace Hotel, where cigar smoking is permitted. There are also designated smoking areas inside the Denver International Airport.

TIPS FOR CANNABIS CONSUMERS

While Colorado might have been first to regulate and sell recreational marijuana, the state is far from a cannabis free-for-all. Following are some tips to keep you safe and on the right side of the law.

Purchasing

Colorado visitors age 21 or older are allowed

to *purchase* up to one-quarter ounce at a time from a retail marijuana shop; you may *possess* up to one ounce of cannabis in total. What this means is that you cannot purchase the one-ounce allotment in one place. (Colorado residents may purchase their total one-ounce allotment in a single store visit.)

The cannabis sold in stores has been cultivated into varying degrees of potency. At the high end are "dabs," chemically extracted marijuana concentrates that can boast three to four times the psychoactive punch of raw cannabis. On the low end are marijuana edibles, which may seem like a consumer-friendly way to try cannabis, but can take up to several quantities to produce any effect. For expert advice, seek out a knowledgeable "budtender" at the retail dispensary of your choice and ask them to guide you through your first purchase.

Safety

Colorado has set the legal limit of THC (tetrahydrocannabinol) for drivers at five nanograms per milliliter of blood. Marijuana impairment can vary widely depending upon a person's metabolism; some users may retain high THC levels in their blood, yet not feel impaired, while others may have very low levels and be unsafe to drive. The best advice is to let someone else do the driving. Fortunately, there are many cannabis tour companies available that can offer this service, such as **Colorado Cannabis Tours** (303/420-8687, www.coloradocannabistours.com) and **My 420 Tours** (855/694-2086, www.my420tours.com). Both are located in the Denver area.

Colorado law forbids driving with open containers of marijuana in your vehicle. Since it's up to law enforcement to determine what exactly entails an "open container," it's best to transport any marijuana in its original, childproof container inside the trunk of your vehicle.

Use and Consumption

Colorado may have legalized adult possession of marijuana, but *public consumption* is still illegal. That means you may partake in Colorado residences and hotel rooms when and where permitted, and in a handful of communities that host private marijuana clubs. Public consumption by any means—including marijuana vape pens and edibles—is illegal in public spaces such as bars, clubs, theaters, restaurants, and most venues. Fines for public consumption can run $999, and tickets for public consumption increased 471 percent in Denver in the first three quarters of 2014.

Legal Concerns

The purchase and possession of marijuana may be legal within Colorado, but the laws change when traveling beyond the state line. Airline travel is federally regulated, which means your legally obtained cannabis becomes a federal crime as soon as you board the plane home. (Colorado airports have installed marijuana disposal bins; it's best to use them.) So while it may be tempting to bring home a souvenir of your adventures, it's not worth the risk.

A Glossary of Cannabis Terms

marijuana-infused brownie and buds

- **Buds:** A slang term for marijuana, and why people who work at retail marijuana shops and medical dispensaries are known as "budtenders." A marijuana plant's dried buds are the parts that are consumed medically or recreationally. Other common names for cannabis include herb, flower, and, of course, pot and weed.
- **Concentrates:** An extremely potent form of marijuana produced by chemically extracting the psychoactive components of the marijuana plant. Dabs, as concentrates are also known, can come in several different forms: shatter (flat, clear, and solid), budder (opaque and creamy), and oil (a sticky liquid). Concentrates can be consumed in a variety of ways, most prominently via specially designed "oil rigs."
- **Edibles:** Marijuana-infused food products. According to Colorado law, edibles can pack a maximum of 100 milligrams of THC per package and must be broken up into 10-milligram sections. Edible marijuana metabolizes much slower than smoked or vaporized kinds; it might take several hours to take effect.
- **Indica:** One of the two main species of marijuana. Known for a relaxing and calming body high (aka "couch lock"), indica is best used at night before going to bed.
- **Sativa:** The second main species of marijuana. Associated with a more energetic and cerebral high, many prefer sativa for use during the day.
- **Topicals:** Cannabis-infused lotions and creams. These products are believed to help relieve muscle pain, but aren't associated with the typical marijuana "high." Some companies produce transdermal skin patches and sublingual tinctures placed under the tongue that are purported to have both psychoactive and medicinal effects.
- **Vaporizers:** Products that vaporize, rather than combust, cannabis, allowing users to consume marijuana without smoking it. Most large and expensive at-home vaporizer machines have given way to portable vaporizers or "vape pens," small, indiscreet devices that, depending on the product, can be used with marijuana concentrates and/or flowers.

Travel Tips

WHAT TO PACK

Colorado dresses casual, so don't worry about bringing formal wear unless you are coming for a black-tie event. Even the Brown Palace's stately Palace Arms Restaurant in Denver has given up its jacket-and-tie policy, though an evening gown and tuxedo would not look out of place. Jeans, slacks, T-shirts, and sandals are all worn to church or a four-star restaurant.

Finally, a place to acceptably wear that bolo tie! Denver and a couple other Western cities are about the only places I've seen officials—governors, mayors, and the like—donning cowboy boots, hats, and decorative bolo ties for work. If you've got one, throw it in the suitcase and drive up to The Fort for a Western dinner like no other.

You can easily buy the basics—hat, sunscreen, sunglasses, good walking or hiking shoes, thermal underwear—needed for any season in every neighborhood. A small backpack or other tote bag is handy to have for carrying extra water, sunscreen, and snacks on sightseeing walks or if you choose to hike in the nearby foothills.

TOURIST INFORMATION

The official State of Colorado government website (www.colorado.gov) has a lot of helpful information, a place to ask questions, and resources for tourism, government, education, and more. The **Colorado Tourism Office** (www.colorado.com) has Colorado Welcome Centers located at a number of roadside spots around the state. The closest to Denver is in Morrison at Red Rocks Amphitheatre. You can also order a free vacation guide from the website.

VISIT DENVER, The Convention & Visitors Bureau (1555 California St., Suite 300, Denver, 800/233-6837, http://www.denver.org) has a public visitors center where you can pick up bags full of brochures and maps and ask lots of questions. They also have a visitors center at DIA.

Area Codes and Time Zones

There are two area codes used throughout the greater metro area: 303 (Denver) and 720 (Boulder). The area code in Colorado Springs is 719 and the area code in Fort Collins is 970. Always dial the entire 10-digit phone number, including the area code, even for local calls.

Colorado does follow daylight saving time, so it is either on Mountain Standard Time or Mountain Daylight Time.

Newspapers and Periodicals

The ***Denver Post*** (www.denverpost.com) continues to print a daily newspaper, but there are regular layoffs and it has become steadily thinner.

Even though the physical size of the alternative weekly, ***Westword*** (www.westword.com), also keeps shrinking, the voice is still big and strong, thanks largely to longtime editor Patricia Calhoun, who knows Denver inside out. *Westword* magazine is free and can be picked up at businesses all over town. The weekly event listings can be really helpful when looking for something fun to do.

5280 Magazine (pronounced fifty-two eighty, www.5280.com) is a glossy monthly magazine that has a mix of serious news, restaurant reviews, and very popular "Best Of" issues on topics from food to doctors.

Maps

There are maps of downtown available for free at the shuttle bus stops on each block of the 16th Street Mall. **VISIT DENVER, The Convention & Visitors Bureau** (www.denver.org) has maps of area attractions and accommodations available for download from its website. You can also find maps, atlases, and gazetteers at any **Tattered Cover Book**

Store location (www.tatteredcover.com), or at office supply stores.

VISAS AND OFFICIALDOM

Visitors from other countries must have a valid passport and a visa. Visitors with current passports from one of the following countries qualify for the visa waivers: Andorra, Australia, Austria, Belgium, Brunei, Chile, Czech Republic, Denmark, Estonia, Finland, France, Germany, Greece, Hungary, Iceland, Ireland, Italy, Japan, Latvia, Liechtenstein, Lithuania, Luxembourg, Malta, Monaco, the Netherlands, New Zealand, Norway, Portugal, San Marino, Singapore, Slovakia, Slovenia, South Korea, Spain, Sweden, Switzerland, Taiwan, and the United Kingdom. They must apply online with the Electronic System for Travel Authorization at www.cbp.gov and hold a return plane ticket to their home country less than 90 days from their time of entry. Holders of Canadian passports don't need visas or waivers. In most countries, the local U.S. embassy can provide a tourist visa. Plan for at least two weeks for visa processing, longer during the busy summer season (June-Aug.). More information is available online at http://travel.state.gov.

HEALTH AND SAFETY

Whether staying in Denver, Boulder, Fort Collins, or Colorado Springs or venturing up into the mountains, prevention is the key to warding off a few common local illnesses.

The altitude affects everyone differently and increases can be subtle, especially when driving or even hiking. Mild symptoms of fatigue, dizziness, headache, nausea, and nosebleeds can develop into a more serious illness. It's best to drink extra water and rest frequently. The body eventually acclimates to the decreased oxygen.

You're simply closer to the sun at high altitudes, so sunscreen (for lips, too) is a must, and hats and sunglasses are generally a good idea for adults and kids. Even on overcast days or on snowy slopes, you can get sunburned.

Bring your own water or water purification tablets with you while hiking, because you risk getting giardia from drinking infected river or lake water. This intestinal illness causes nausea, cramps, and diarrhea.

For medical or fire emergencies, or to reach the police in an emergency, dial **911.** For issues that are not life threatening, contact the **Denver Police/Fire/Paramedics Communication Center** (720/913-2000), the **Rocky Mountain Poison and Drug Center** (303/739-1123 or 800/222-1222), or **Metro Denver Crimestoppers** (720/913-7867).

Leave No Trace

The city of Denver has a **Keep Denver Beautiful** (311 hotline, 311@ci.denver.co.us, www.denvergov.org) plan that promotes the message to not litter, period—this includes anything from cigarette butts to food wrappers and drink containers. Littering is illegal and fines can add up to $1,000.

While Denver's laws apply to city streets as well as parks and bike paths, there are additional rules and customs to follow once you set off to explore the mountains.

For starters, always stay on designated trails or pathways to minimize your impact on the natural areas that make the area so appealing in the first place. You may even see signs that read, Closed for Restoration in areas that have been trampled by heavy use. These designated trails—whether they are mere dirt footpaths or paved with concrete or asphalt—will also prevent you from getting lost. As people try to explore true wilderness more and more, either by going out of bounds on a ski mountain or breaking their own trail on a summer hike, officials are becoming less patient and understanding because of the high cost of search and rescue. For this same reason, it's a good idea to always let someone know where you are headed when you go out for a run, bike ride, or hike.

Even if you are just going on a short day hike in the foothills, remember to "pack out what you pack in" and don't leave *any* waste.

In some places, even city parks in the foothills of Boulder, you will find special garbage cans that are designed to keep animals (particularly bears) out, but otherwise you need to be prepared to carry out all garbage.

Because of the dry conditions, especially along the Front Range, be extremely cautious about making campfires. During intense drought seasons, fires of any kind are banned, so it's best to check with park rangers on the latest conditions and warnings in the specific park you are visiting. If fires are not banned, still use caution and only build a fire in an established campfire ring, and be sure to put out the fire completely before leaving.

Wildlife and people interact more and more in the foothill communities where mountain lions, bears, deer, and elk will just show up in backyards and even on busy town streets. This is just a reminder that you should never feed wildlife—whether in the confines of a national park or in someone's backyard. State and national park visitors centers always have helpful information about how to react when you encounter wildlife, which is species-specific and depends on mating seasons. Use special care if you are with small children or dogs when hiking, as they are easier prey for hungry wildlife.

Wildlife and pets, especially dogs, are not a good mix. Be sure to verify if dogs are even allowed at the park you are visiting and what the leash laws are.

For more information, visit the **Leave No Trace Center** (www.lnt.org or call 303/442-8222).

ACCESS FOR TRAVELERS WITH DISABILITIES

Many trails and facilities in **Colorado State Parks** (303/866-3437, http://parks.co.state.us) are designed for and open to people in wheelchairs. Nature lovers in Denver can enjoy most of the **Denver Botanic Gardens** (1005 York St., 720/865-3500, www.botanicgardens.org) on the facility's wide, smooth concrete pathways. The gardens also have complimentary wheelchairs available.

There is a theater group in Denver called the **Physically Handicapped Actors and Musical Artists League** (PHAMALY, 303/575-0005, www.phamaly.org) that performs a few times a year in the Denver area and at the Denver Center for the Performing Arts. The group was formed in 1989, when physically disabled acting students became frustrated with the lack of parts available to them.

The Denver Botanic Gardens have smooth paths wide enough for wheelchairs.

There are five companies that offer wheelchair transportation service from DIA and elsewhere around Denver. RTD's **Access-a-Ride** (303/292-6560, www.rtd-denver.com) is for people who cannot board a wheelchair-equipped bus. Metro and regional RTD buses—including the free shuttles on the 16th Street Mall—are wheelchair accessible. Both **Metro Taxi** (303/333-3333, www.metrotaxidenver.com) and **Yellow Cab** (303/777-7777, www.yellowtrans.com) have wheelchair-accessible vehicles available for passengers.

TRAVELING WITH CHILDREN

There are many fun attractions and things to do with young kids in Colorado, but it's a good idea to ask about age limits at local museums and hotels. For example, Denver's Kirkland Museum does not allow any children under the age of 13 with or without an adult, and children ages 13-17 must be accompanied by an adult. While the Molly Brown House Museum in Denver states that children are welcome, they are asked not to touch *anything*, and it's hardly fun for a toddler. (Grown-ups have to follow the same rules.)

Of course, the Children's Museum is a perfect place to play with kids newborn through age eight, and the Platte Valley Trolley that makes a stop outside the museum is fun for adults and children. The Denver Art Museum has built in a variety of child-friendly activities in its permanent exhibits, as well as a small make-your-own-art area. At the Denver Museum of Nature and Science, kids can watch an IMAX movie on the enormous screen, see the stars and planets at the Gates Planetarium, watch volunteers clean off dinosaur bones, step inside replicas of original Native American homes, or pretend to be astronauts. The Denver Zoo appeals to children of any age who like animals. Check ahead to see what's on the schedule for families and kids at the History Colorado Center and the Denver Public Library, where there are different themes monthly.

Some of the best parks with playgrounds for kids include Washington Park, Stapleton Central Park, Cheesman Park, and City Park, and there is a playground at the Children's Museum. City Park also has paddleboats in the summer. In the winter, there is sledding at Commons Park, as well as Stapleton Central Park.

Sometimes kids just like to be outside where they can run free. My daughter loves going to the Denver Botanic Gardens and Commons Park, where there aren't any playgrounds.

Visit **Denver's Family Guide** (www.denverkids.com) to find coupons for various classes and attractions or pick up ***Colorado Parent Magazine*** (www.coloradoparent.com) to get information on local classes and events.

GAY AND LESBIAN TRAVELERS

Denver is a fairly supportive place for the gay, lesbian, bisexual, and transgender community, with many organizations, events, and businesses geared toward this population. In 2008, antidiscrimination laws were expanded to protect against discrimination based on sexual orientation in the workplace and beyond.

For more information on the local LGBT scene, check out the **Denver Gay and Lesbian Chamber of Commerce** (www.denverglc.org) or the **Gay, Lesbian, Bisexual and Transgender Community Center of Colorado** (www.glbtcolorado.org), which puts on the annual two-day Pridefest event. ***Out Front Colorado*** (www.outfrontonline.com) is a free weekly paper available all over the city.

TRAVELING WITH PETS

While Denver is quite pet-friendly, there is less love in the public sector. In most public places, dogs are required to be on a leash and there are fines for not complying with this rule. For a list of off-leash dog parks in Denver and other Colorado cities, visit **Dog Parks**

in Denver (www.dogparksindenver.com), which includes detailed directions, hours, and rules. Owners are required to clean up after their dogs; Dogipots are conveniently located near popular parks and walkways for disposing of those little plastic baggies.

There is a small, enclosed area for pet exercise at Denver International Airport (www.flydenver.com), but keep in mind it is off of the main terminal and travelers must go through security again to get back to their concourse.

Resources

Suggested Reading

HISTORY

Abbott, Carl, Stephen J. Leonard, and Thomas J. Noel. *Colorado: A History of the Centennial State,* 4th ed. Denver, CO: University Press of Colorado, 2005. Tom Noel, a history professor at the University of Colorado at Denver, is nicknamed Dr. Colorado for his bottomless well of knowledge of all things Denver and Colorado.

Brosnan, Kathleen A. *Uniting Mountain and Plain: Urbanization, Law and Environmental Change Along the Front Range.* Albuquerque, NM: University of New Mexico Press, 2002. This was the first book by University of Houston professor Kathleen Brosnan, who specializes in environmental and Western history.

Goodstein, Phil. *Denver in Our Time: A People's History of the Mile High City.* Denver, CO: New Social Publications, 1999. Goodstein has written several books about Denver, most with a specific neighborhood or topic focus, but this one gives a more general overview.

Leonard, Stephen J., and Thomas J. Noel. *Denver: Mining Camp to Metropolis.* Denver, CO: University Press of Colorado, 1989. A precursor to the larger *Colorado: A History of the Centennial State* by the same authors, and just as packed with facts.

Sprague, Marshall. *Colorado: A Bicentennial History.* New York: W. W. Norton & Company, 1976. A brief history of the state of Colorado.

Stephens, Ronald J., and La Wanna M. Larson. *African Americans of Denver (Images of America: Colorado).* Mount Pleasant, SC: Arcadia Publishing, 2008. Learn more about the African Americans who came to Denver and Colorado and their impact on the city and state through the years. Author La Wanna M. Larson is the curator of Denver's Black American West Museum.

Wyckoff, William. *Creating Colorado: The Making of a Western American Landscape, 1860–1940.* New Haven, CT: Yale University Press, 1999. Montana State University geography professor Wyckoff includes maps and historical photographs to illustrate his unique environmental telling of Colorado history.

TRAVEL GUIDES

Berman, Joshua. *Moon Colorado Camping,* 4th ed. Berkeley, CA: Avalon Travel, 2016. Go beyond the skyscrapers of downtown Denver and get out under the stars for a few nights in a tent with the handy maps and insightful descriptions found in this book.

Fielder, John. *John Fielder's Best of Colorado.* Boulder, CO: Westcliffe Publishers, 2002. John Fielder is a local photographer whose images make this hefty guidebook as interesting to look at as it is to read.

Irwin, Pamela, with David Irwin. *Colorado's Best Wildflower Hikes, Volume I: The Front Range*. Boulder, CO: Westcliffe Publishers, 1998. These wildflower hikes invite people of any fitness level to hike with a purpose.

Internet Resources

COLORADO

Bicycle Colorado
www.bicyclecolorado.org
This website offers free online cycling maps and also sells printed copies.

bikepaths.com
www.bikepaths.com
This site has a great selection of less-traveled trails, a calories-burned calculator, and a list of regional cycling events. There are links to nearly every bike shop in the metro area, too.

Colorado Tourism Office
www.colorado.com
Whether you are a resident in search of a "day-cation" or you are coming for a longer stay, be sure to check out this website for vacation ideas and travel values.

The Passport Program
www.thepassportprogram.com
For a fee of about $20, this passport gets you 2-for-1 drinks at participating bars and restaurants during the summer months. Passports are available for Denver, Boulder, Fort Collins, and Colorado Springs.

Pikes Peak Country Attractions
www.pikes-peak.com/blog
Want to explore the outdoors around Colorado Springs but aren't sure where to go? Check this blog for ideas.

State of Colorado
www.colorado.gov
What isn't on this website? You can get a hunting or fishing license, find out current weather, view maps, buy a state park pass, and much more.

DENVER

Bike Denver
www.bikedenver.org
www.denvergov.org/bikeprogram
These websites portray bicycling not just as a sport, but a movement and a way of life. Each includes general information about advocacy for bicycling in Denver, ordinances, and maps.

City of Denver
www.denvergov.org
The city's website is fairly easy to navigate and includes helpful options like "311" and signing up for street-sweeping-day parking alerts. Look for the "Bike Maps" link to plan a two-wheeled excursion or route.

Eater Denver
www.denver.eater.com
Keeping up with the hottest restaurants in Denver and Boulder is a monthly sport. Stay tuned to this site for the places that are coming, going, and still worth it.

Denver Infill
www.denverinfill.com
Find out how Denver is growing *in* with infill projects where there were once industrial sites or parking lots.

Eat Drink Denver
http://eatdrinkdenver.com
Visit Denver's guide to the latest in eating and drinking in the Mile-High City.

5280
www.5280.com
The monthly *5280 Magazine* has in-depth articles, plus regular "Top of the Town" issues

with lists of favorite restaurants and more in Denver.

Gabby Gourmet
www.gabbygourmet.com
A radio show food critic now has a website with reviews, photos, and "find of the month" restaurant listings.

Greenprint Denver
www.denvergov.org/sustainability
An interesting look at the whole concept of a "sustainable city" and what plans are in the works to make Denver more "green."

Metro Denver Economic Development Corporation
www.metrodenver.org
An affiliate of the Denver Metro Chamber of Commerce, the Metro Denver EDC has a lot of statistical data for the greater seven-county area. Request a Relocation Package and Guide if you are a newcomer or are considering relocating to the Denver area.

Regional Transportation District
www.rtd-denver.com
Not only can you find bus and light rail schedules and fare information, but the Regional Transportation District (RTD) website also has a trip-planning feature to help you figure out your mass-transit route.

VISIT DENVER
The Convention & Visitors Bureau
www.denver.org
This website is designed for tourists, locals, and yes, conventioneers. The site is loaded with facts, and it can help with finding hotels, restaurants, and upcoming events.

Westword
www.westword.com
Find out about the latest events around town and check out the annual "Best Of" lists, as well as restaurant reviews.

BOULDER

Downtown Boulder
www.boulderdowntown.com/blog
Handy and insightful content for both locals and tourists on what to do if you're in town for an Ironman competition or looking for deals on a sidewalk sale.

COLORADO SPRINGS

City of Colorado Springs
https://coloradosprings.gov
The official website of the city of Colorado Springs, with maps, business listings, and transportation information.

FORT COLLINS

The Scoop Blog Network
www.thescoopblogs.com
Bicycling, dining, and "budding" are all topics covered by these Fort Collins-area bloggers.

CANNABIS TOURISM

City of Denver marijuana information
www.colorado.gov/pacific/marijuanainfodenver
It's legal, but you need to know the laws about buying and using marijuana within the city of Denver.

Colorado Pot Guide
www.coloradopotguide.com
Touted as a practical guide for the marijuana enthusiast visiting Colorado.

Leafly
www.leafly.com
Information on strains of marijuana and the ability to search where to buy locally.

Weedmaps
www.weedmaps.com
Just look for the little green leaf to find a dispensary near you.

Index

D

E

IJK

L

M

N

O

P

QR

S

T

U

VWXYZ

List of Maps

Front Map

Discover Denver, Boulder and Colorado Springs

Denver

Boulder

Fort Collins

Colorado Springs

Photo Credits

Title page: Millenium Bridge in downtown Denver © arinahabich/123RF

page 4 © VisitCOS.com; page 5 © Visit Denver; page 6 (top left) © VisitCOS.com, (top right) © visitCOS.com, (bottom) © Visit Denver; page 7 (bottom left) © Visit Denver, (bottom right) © Bob Pearce/City of Golden; page 8 © Ellen Jaskol/Visit Denver; page 9 (top) © Rich Grant/Boulder CVB, (bottom left) © visitCOS.com, (bottom right) © VisitCOS.com; page 11 © Jeff Wells/Visit Denver; page 12 © Boulder CVB; page 13 © Stan Obert/Visit Denver; page 14 (top left) © Mindy Sink, (top right) © Chris Parker/Boulder CVB; page 15 © Visit Denver; page 16 © VisitCOS.com; page 17 © VisitCOS.com; page 19 © Mindy Sink, page 20 © VisitCOS.com; page 21 (top) © Stan Obert/Visit Denver, (bottom) © Bryce Boyer/Visit Denver; page 23 © Visit Denver; page 26 © Steve Creclius/Visit Denver; page 27 © Mindy Sink; page 28 © courtesy of Brown Palace Media; page 30 © Ted Stedman/Visit Denver; page 44 © Scott Dressel-Martin/Visit Denver; page 45 © Evan Semón/Visit Denver; page 50 © 123RF.com; page 57 © Mindy Sink; page 58 © Mindy Sink; page 63 © Mindy Sink; page 68 © Mindy Sink; page 72 © Stan Obert/Visit Denver; page 74 © Steve Crecelius/Visit Denver; page 79 © Steve Crecelius/Visit Denver; page 80 © Samuel Schimek; page 82 © Steve Crecelius/Visit Denver; page 85 © Mindy Sink; page 91 © Steve Crecelius/Visit Denver; page 95 © Mindy Sink; page 96 © Mindy Sink; page 101 © Courtesy of the ART Hotel; page 102 © Mindy Sink; page 103 © Mindy Sink; page 112 © Mindy Sink; page 118 © Mindy Sink; page 124 © Mindy Sink; page 125 © Mindy Sink; page 138 (top) © Boulder Convention and Visitors Bureau, (bottom) © Rich Grant/Visit Denver; page 139 © Ronda Kimbrow/123RF.com; page 142 © Mindy Sink; page 143 © Chris Parker; page 145 © Boulder Convention and Visitors Bureau; page 146 © Mindy Sink; page 147 © Mindy Sink; page 148 © Mindy Sink; page 149 © Mindy Sink; page 153 © Mindy Sink; page 154 © Mindy Sink; page 156 © Mindy Sink; page 158 © Scott Murrish | Dreamstime.com; page 159 © GO Boulder/Boulder Convention and Visitors Bureau; page 162 © Mindy Sink; page 164 © Mindy Sink; page 167 © Mindy Sink; page 170 © Mindy Sink; page 173 © Vist Denver; page 177 (top) © Ryan Burke/Visit Fort Collins, (bottom) © Ryan Burke/Visit Fort Collins; page 179 © Visit Fort Collins; page 182 © Mindy Sink; page 183 © Visit Fort Collins; page 185 © Mindy Sink; page 186 © Mindy Sink; page 187 © Mindy Sink; page 189 © Mindy Sink; page 191 © Mindy Sink; page 192 © Mindy Sink; page 193 © Marek Uliasz/123RF.com; page 198 © Mindy Sink; page 199 © Mindy Sink; page 200 © Mindy Sink; page 204 (top) © visitCOS.com, (bottom) © visitCOS.com; page 205 © visitCOS.com; page 208 © visitCOS.com; page 210 © visitCOS.com; page 211 © visitCOS.com; page 212 © visitCOS.com; page 213 © visitCOS.com; page 218 © visitCOS.com; page 219 © Courtesy of the Broadmoor; page 222 © Courtesy of the Broadmoor; page 225 © visitCOS.com; page 228 © Kevin Syms/Courtesy of the Broadmoor; page 231 © visitCOS.com; page 232 © visitCOS.com; page 233 © visitCOS.com; page 237 (top) © Brenda Kean/123RF.com, (bottom) © visitCOS.com; page 239 © Visit Denver; page 241 © Mindy Sink; page 243 © Mindy Sink; page 245 (top) © Visit Denver, (bottom) © visitCOS.com; page 247 © Vlisit Denver/RTD; page 251 © Adam Bailleaux/123RF.com; page 254 © Scott Dressel-Martin/Visit Denver

Acknowledgments

Writing a guidebook is a team sport. This is my third edition, but my first time working on a guidebook with fellow experts.

My sincere thanks to Joel Warner for his contributions on where to buy and smoke marijuana and to Monica Stockbridge for her insights on so many fabulous restaurants, breweries, and bars in Denver and Boulder. I know the book is better because of the knowledge each of you shared.

I also could not have written the Colorado Springs chapter without Chelsy Offutt of *Visit Colorado Springs.* As much as I enjoy visiting, it was invaluable to have her insights as a local. My thanks also to Katy Schneider of Visit Fort Collins who filled in the blanks in that city, and thanks also to Erin Byrne of the Boulder Convention and Visitors Bureau.

A big thank-you to my family, especially my husband Mike Seymour and our daughter Sophie, who sometimes tagged along during my research. They showed loving patience while I met deadlines.

I have so much gratitude for my team at Avalon: Elizabeth Hansen, Sabrina Young, Kat Bennett, and Lucie Ericksen. I know I should have followed directions sooner! Thank you for your patience and smarts.

Finally, thanks to Denver, Boulder, Colorado Springs, and Fort Collins for being awesome cities that are worth visiting!

Also Available

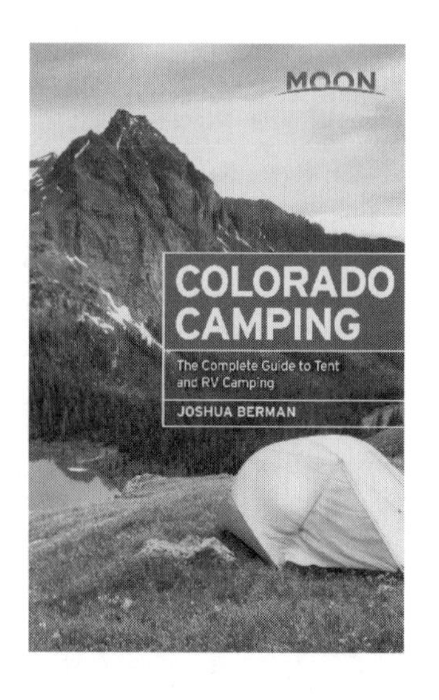

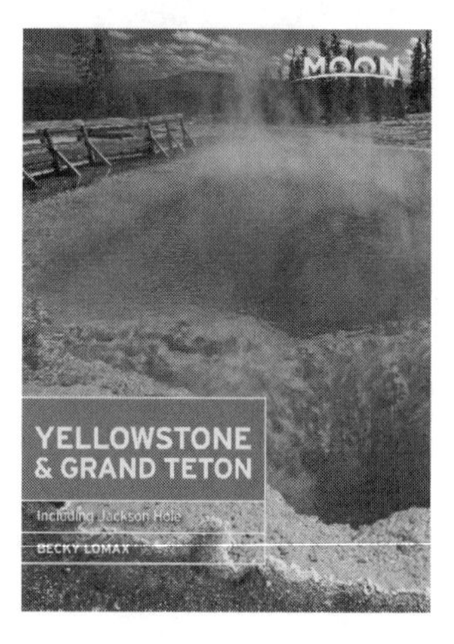

MAP SYMBOLS

- Expressway
- Primary Road
- Secondary Road
- Unpaved Road
- Trail
- Ferry
- Railroad
- Pedestrian Walkway
- Stairs
- Highlight
- City/Town
- State Capital
- National Capital
- Point of Interest
- Accommodation
- Restaurant/Bar
- Other Location
- Campground
- Airfield
- Airport
- Mountain
- Unique Natural Feature
- Waterfall
- Park
- Trailhead
- Skiing Area
- Golf Course
- Parking Area
- Archaeological Site
- Church
- Gas Station
- Glacier
- Mangrove
- Reef
- Swamp

CONVERSION TABLES

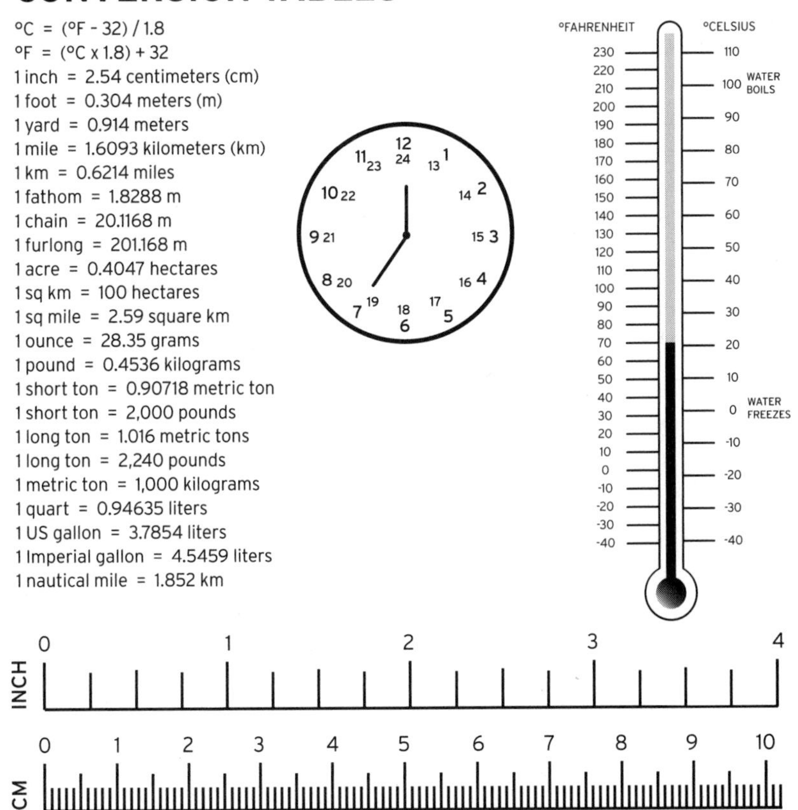

MOON DENVER, BOULDER & COLORADO SPRINGS

Avalon Travel
a member of the Perseus Books Group
1700 Fourth Street
Berkeley, CA 94710, USA
www.moon.com

Editor: Sabrina Young
Series Manager: Kathryn Ettinger
Copy Editor: Brett Keener
Production and Graphics Coordinator: Lucie Ericksen
Cover Design: Faceout Studios, Charles Brock
Moon Logo: Tim McGrath
Map Editor: Kat Bennett
Cartographers: Brian Shotwell, Karin Dahl
Proofreader: Alissa Cyphers
Indexer: Greg Jewett

ISBN-13: 978-1-63121-291-8
ISSN: 1944-544X

Printing History
1st Edition — May 2016
5 4 3 2 1

Front cover photo: Garden of the Gods, Colorado Springs © Blaine Harrington III / Alamy Stock Photo
Back cover photo: Cherry Creek Bike Path in Denver © Stevie Crecelius/Visit Denver

Printed in Canada by Friesens

All recommendations, including those for sights, activities, hotels, restaurants, and shops, are based on each author's individual judgment. We do not accept payment for inclusion in our travel guides, and our authors don't accept free goods or services in exchange for positive coverage.